CATHOLIC EDUCATION IN THE WAKE OF VATICAN II

Catholic Education in the Wake of Vatican II

EDITED BY ROSA BRUNO-JOFRÉ
AND JON IGELMO ZALDÍVAR

UNIVERSITY OF TORONTO PRESS
Toronto Buffalo London

Toronto Buffalo London
www.utppublishing.com

ISBN 978-1-4875-0206-5

Library and Archives Canada Cataloguing in Publication

Catholic education in the wake of Vatican II / edited by Rosa Bruno-Jofré and Jon Igelmo Zaldívar.

Includes bibliographical references and index.
ISBN 978-1-4875-0206-5 (cloth)

1. Catholic Church – Education. 2. Catholic Church – Doctrines. 3. Vatican Council (2nd : 1962–1965 : Basilica di San Pietro in Vaticano). I. Bruno-Jofré, Rosa del Carmen, 1946–, editor II. Igelmo Zaldívar, Jon, 1982–, editor

BX895.C38 2017 371.071'2 C2017-902712-3

This book has been published with the help of a grant from the Federation for the Humanities and Social Sciences, through the Awards to Scholarly Publications Program, using funds provided by the Social Sciences and Humanities Research Council of Canada.

University of Toronto Press acknowledges the financial assistance to its publishing program of the Canada Council for the Arts and the Ontario Arts Council, an agency of the Government of Ontario.

Canada Council for the Arts Conseil des Arts du Canada

Funded by the Government of Canada Financé par le gouvernement du Canada

Contents

List of Images, Figure, and Tables

Images

Figure

Tables

CATHOLIC EDUCATION IN THE WAKE OF VATICAN II

"Casa Abierta / Etxe Irekia / Open House." Sculpture by Joaquín Gogorza. From *Experiencing the Catholic Faith*, an exhibition of art inspired by Catholic spirituality curated by Dr Ana Jofré.

Introduction
Emerging Issues and Approaches in the Analysis of Catholicism and Education: Fifty Years after Vatican II

ROSA BRUNO-JOFRÉ AND JON IGELMO ZALDÍVAR

This collection introduces the reader to the results of the symposium "Catholicism and Education: Fifty Years after Vatican II (1962–1965) – A Transnational Interdisciplinary Encounter," held at the University of the Basque Country, San Sebastían-Donostia, Spain, 2–5 June 2015. The symposium was funded by a Connection Grant from the Social Sciences and Humanities Research Council of Canada[1] and also received organizational and financial support from the Group of Historical and Comparative Studies in Education (Garaian Group), located within the Faculty of Philosophy and Educational Sciences at the University of the Basque Country, Spain.[2] The symposium involved the Theory and History of Education International Research Group (THEIRG), located within the Faculty of Education at Queen's University,[3] and the Garaian Group. Senior and junior specialists from multiple disciplines were invited to the symposium. Scholars from Canada, Chile, France, and Spain exchanged ideas on, and provided input from, their various disciplines. An exhibition of art inspired by Catholic spirituality, "Experiencing the Catholic Faith," curated by Dr Ana Jofré, was presented in conjunction with the symposium, 2 to 5 June, at the University of the Basque Country; images of some of the art displayed at the exhibition are included throughout this book.[4]

Although other prominent symposia and conferences on the occasion of the fiftieth anniversary of Vatican II have been held in various relevant Catholic centres,[5] the impact of the Council's dogmatic constitutions, decrees, and declarations on education has not been thoroughly discussed. Indeed, the *Declaration on Christian Education* (*Gravissimum Educationis*) (1966), its implications for Catholic education, and its reception in various localities deserve particular attention. This volume addresses some of these absences, albeit in a limited way, by means of specific case studies.

Vatican II reignited a concern for the poor in the context of a new encounter with the world. The preoccupation with educating poor boys and girls goes back to the Council of Trent (1545–63) and subsequent related synods and constitutions. At the time, the Church[6] had become aware of the power of "education" to secure faith and avoid deviations from Catholic orthodoxy.[7] Meanwhile the Jesuits were already active and working in the missionary field (their order had been approved by Pope Paul III in 1540). As Francesco Cesareo has pointed out, "during the era of the Catholic Reformation, a new impulse was added to education – the desire to provide basic religious instruction in order to reform morals and save souls. It was this religious dimension that gave identity to the schools of the Society of Jesus" (Cesareo 1993, 28).

Two important emphases of the Jesuits' activity were education of young men, particularly at higher educational levels, and scholarly work. The Jesuits aimed at forming male leaders;[8] they also developed various missions, for example, among Indigenous populations in Latin America. John O'Malley describes the historical context nicely: "By the time the Council of Trent met, the conviction was widespread that 'all the well-being of Christianity and of the whole world depends on the proper education of youth,' that is, education in the Humanistic mode. Pedro de Ribadeneira, a Jesuit, wrote those words, just at the time his order, the Society of Jesus, began establishing its network of Humanistic schools throughout the Catholic World" (O'Malley 2013, 45). The Renaissance culture had entered the Catholic realms of education.

Despite the new direction towards education of the poor in an active apostolate, in 1563 the Council of Trent (and subsequent papal decrees) defined women religious as enclosed, thereby denying them access to apostolic work.[9] Nonetheless, women persisted in enacting their religious vocations; examples include Angela Merici's Italian Ursulines, who had obtained approval from the Pope in 1544,[10] and Mary Ward (1585–1645), whose "English Ladies" institute was modelled after the Society of Jesus and was disbanded by the Vatican.[11] The spirituality of the French School of the seventeenth century, with its debates about Gallicanism, which tried to limit the authority of the Pope, the political and theological presence of Jansenism, which wanted a restatement of the fourth-century Augustinian position on grace – an overall movement seen as a threat to both Rome and Versailles – and voices like Vincent de Paul and Pierre Bérulle, among many others, led to new ways of valuing active apostolates and broadening women's involvement.[12] However, while the social conditions and political context had changed, the definitions of women religious's life had not. Thus, in 1662, Minim Fray Nicholas Barré founded an Institute of Charitable Teachers, allowing women teachers living in a religious community to work with poor girls without the requirement of vows or cloister. The teachers were thereby able to avoid some rules and decrees. (See Rosa Bruno-Jofré's chapter in this volume, "The Sisters of the Infant Jesus in Bembibre, León, Spain, during the Second Stage of Francoism [1957–1975]: The School with No Doors.") In 1684, Barré's spiritual advisee, Jean-Baptiste de La Salle, founded the Institute of Christian Brothers to provide free elementary teaching and religious instruction to poor boys. The institute founded by Barré would later develop into two different female congregations: the Sisters of the Infant Jesus, Saint Maur, discussed in this book,[13] and the Sisters of the Infant Jesus, Providence of Rouen.[14]

We specify these two international congregations as examples of developments in the seventeenth century, because they are addressed in this book in relation to the process of returning to the original inspiration of the founder as mandated by *Perfectae Caritatis* (Vatican II). In the above-mentioned chapter on the Sisters of the Infant Jesus in Bembibre, Rosa Bruno-Jofré examines how the reading of the Vatican II documents by the Sisters was mediated by Nicholas Barré's original intentionality, his work with the poor, and even his understanding of the relationship between the clergy and the people. The chapter suggests that the trans-temporal return to his original inspiration – which was mediated by the historical context and, of course, by the Vatican II documents – provided an element of radicality and freedom.[15] In chapter 4, "Turning Need into a Virtue: The Adjustment to the Educational Demands of the Religious Congregations: The Case of De La Salle in the Basque Country, Spain," Paulí Dávila and Luis M. Naya explore how the De La Salle Brothers' educational apostolate in the Basque Country of Spain went through a process of renewal and adaptation to new conditions (including the development of a renewed semantic field). Those new conditions comprised the need to expand secondary education – a level of education deemed of "little value" by de La Salle, given its middle- and upper-middle-class connotations – while at the same time returning to the founder's principles and consequently to his commitment to the poor.

In the last decades of the seventeenth and the first half of the eighteenth centuries, Europe saw a movement towards political democracy and away from autocracy. The religious wars had generated a weariness with dogmatic theology, a new spirit of philanthropy, and a growing acceptance of realism. (All of this was happening against the backdrop of John Locke's empiricist philosophy.) Following the political turmoil of the eighteenth century in Europe, within the context given by the transition from Church- to state-controlled education (i.e., the building of educational states), the nineteenth century witnessed an explosion of active congregations, in particular of women religious, who were now leading a "mixed life" (i.e., a semi-cloistered one). In the nineteenth century the Church considered it imperative that women religious teach, catechize, and nurse, and saw a need to facilitate the full incorporation of women religious into an active apostolate. The latter process was accompanied by constantly multiplying rules that produced an institutionalization grounded in gendered ideals and subordination. However, to properly understand the expansion of female congregations, it is also important to keep in mind, in Helen Ebaugh's words, that "throughout the 19th and early 20th centuries, religious orders provided an avenue of social mobility for Catholic girls who, like most women in our society, had little or no opportunity for advanced education and careers" (Ebaugh 1993, 69).

Education became for the Church a means to, depending on the setting, consolidate or carve out spaces in the power structures of the modern educational state that was taking shape. The intention was to keep alive a Catholic social order, build a Catholic spirituality, and make the faithful familiar with the social teachings of the Church. The extensive involvement in formal education of female and male teaching congregations took various characteristics contingent on the missionary settings and the original spiritual intuitions of the congregations' founders. Often the congregations moved away from their previous focus on the poor in order to solidify their positions with the upper classes. They had varying intentionalities, ranging from the desire to secure a place in the power structure of particular societies to the attempt to generate an elite sensitive to social issues.

The nineteenth century also brought about both an increasing influence of philosophy on theology, particularly from René Descartes (1596–1650) and Immanuel Kant (1724–1804), and subsequent efforts to reconcile faith with reason, as examined by Michael Attridge in chapter 1 of this volume, "From Objectivity to Subjectivity: Changes in the Nineteenth and Twentieth Centuries and Their Impact on Post-Vatican II Theological Education." However, these efforts were condemned, and the magisterium strongly proposed a form of neo-Scholasticism that would be under the umbrella of neo-Thomism. By the nineteenth century, Gallicanism, which sought to restrict papal power in the French Catholic Church, had lost its influence. Ultramontanism, which emphasized papal authority and the centralization of power, became the dominant ideology in the Church.

Catholic education of the time was, out of necessity, influenced in one way or another by the anti-liberalism and anti-modernism of the popes of the nineteenth and twentieth centuries. The undercurrents of the twentieth century, including the pluralization of neo-Thomism, and the emergence of new, historicized theological approaches in the 1930s and 1940s, did not reach many congregations until later. Instead, one of the documents of most influence on congregations, often cited by Catholic educators, *Divini Illius Magistri*, the 1929 encyclical of Pope Pius XI on Christian Education, had anti-modernist tones, condemned naturalism and co-education, and advocated an integrated approach to the education of youth within the framework of neo-Thomism.[16] Article 23 reads: "Again it is the inalienable right as well as the indispensable duty of the Church, to watch over the entire education of her children, in all institutions, public or private, not merely in regard to the religious instruction there given, but in regard to every other branch of learning and every regulation in so far as religion and morality are concerned." Furthermore, an excerpt from Article 24 reads: "Nor should the exercise of this right be considered undue interference, but rather maternal care on the part of the Church in protecting her children from the grave danger of all kinds of doctrinal and moral evil." Beyond the dictates from the Vatican, the naturalization of the educational work in entire countries as well as in specific regions, and the interplay of Catholic views with local "social imaginaries" (a term coined by Taylor [2004] in reference to how particular groups of people imagine their social existence), generated a kaleidoscope of experiences and ways of being Catholic.

The neo-Thomist principles were abandoned after Vatican II in favour of a theology that embraced the modern world. The difficult encounter with the "long 1960s" (1958–74)[17] and its upheavals gave way to the "age of fracture" and the post–Cold War era (Rodgers 2011). The processes of renewal of the congregations became suffused with overlapping configurations of ideas and events that were related to a rapid process of secularization, including women's repositioning in the world, drastic social changes, and the congregations' own new positionings motivated by Vatican II. The concurrent drastic decline in vocations signalled a new era, characterized in the West by a social imaginary in which contingency and choice were dominant. This process of readjustment was not without difficulty. Religious life had to change both its mission and vision.[18]

The important matter that calls for our examination is not only the history of the process of reception of Vatican II, but how Catholics, and in particular teaching congregations, related to the world – because this time they confronted the world they had been advised to distrust, not as purveyors of truth but in dialogue and solidarity with it (Berger 2014). Furthermore, as Robert Gascoigne (2009) puts it, "the work of the Council (in Vatican II) hastened the process by which Catholics were 'disembedded' from this previous identity, formed in post-Reformation and postrevolutionary conflicts. It empowered them both to return to the biblical and patristic sources of tradition – John XXIII's *approfondimento* – and to commit themselves to a universal human solidarity in the contemporary world – his *aggiornamento*" (150).

Chapter 8, "Women Religious, Vatican II, Education, and the State in Atlantic Canada," by Heidi MacDonald, offers three case studies on teaching congregations in three provinces of Atlantic Canada. Her chapter describes how these congregations recalibrated their goals in terms of their own understandings of reality, charism, and priorities within a gendered situational context. It also makes evident the congregations' inequality in relation to priests and the lack of recognition of their work by St Dunstan's University, the Archdiocesan board of St Mary's University, and the Newfoundland government.

Changes in the curricula of Catholic schools, particularly in the case of religious education, were the natural outcome of the transformations emerging from the Vatican II documents, and not only from the *Declaration on Christian Education.* As Joseph Stafford writes in chapter 10, "The Conditions of Reception for the *Declaration on Christian Education*: Secularization and the Educational State of Ontario," the purpose of the Declaration's educational approach to the modern world was not entirely clear. This made it difficult to enact its principles – a task already complicated by the conditions of each educational setting. Stafford analyses the case of the province of Ontario, Canada, where the conditions of reception were framed both by the dramatic cultural changes of the late 1950s and 1960s – including the secularization of society at large, which invariably affected Catholic schools – and by the lack of political power of the bishops, in virtue of the secularized school boards responsible for curriculum development and school organizations.

The particular context would determine the teaching congregations' agenda and its complexity, as in the case of Chile. In chapter 11, "Catholic Elite Education in Chile: Worlds Apart," Cristián Cox and Patricia Imbarack examine how elite Catholic schools navigated the tension between the doctrinal basis of the faith based on a communion of brothers and sisters, on the one hand, and existing socio-economic structures, on the other, given that the Church – in Vatican II documents, and in particular in documents produced by Latin American bishops such as at Medellín (1968) and at Aparecida (2007) – had condemned poverty and injustice as social sins. Using a sociological methodology, the authors examine how religious orders running Catholic schools that served the elite dealt with this tension, how these schools treated the social dimension of their moral purpose in their mission statement, and how they referred to Vatican II and subsequent statements made by the Latin American episcopate. Cox and Imbarack, who relate the differing approaches to the educational preferences of the Chilean elites, uncover two approaches to social justice: "magisterium ignoring" and "magisterium affirming." These two categories correspond to, respectively, mission statements that paid little attention to social justice, thus ignoring the teachings of the Church, and those that demonstrated commitment.

In this collection, "global/transnational" is used as more than a meta-analytical category; it is substantive to the Church itself and to the historical processes in which she was involved. Thus, most of the contributors to this collection use a global/transnational *longue durée* approach for studying the aims of Catholic education and the impact of Vatican II, and to explain the multivariant process of change that in fact began "outside the walls of the Vatican" (an expression from Parra 2012, 105). These changes included the emergence and circulation of new concepts and semantic fields – a language of renewal – as well as a multiplicity of "translations" of the Vatican II ideas conveyed in documents. The theological shifts that converged in Vatican II opened the doors to an encounter with modernity (even as the Western world was moving towards postmodernity), as Michael Attridge explains in the first chapter of this volume:

> The ecumenical moment of the early twentieth century precipitated a change whereby it is almost unthinkable today to do theology responsibly without the involvement of others in the wider Christian context. The role of philosophy in relation to theology has changed from one of instrumentality and subservience to one of dialogue and mutual interrelationality. Modern philosophies such as existentialism, personalism, and phenomenology have greatly shaped and informed the discipline of theology today. The separation of the Church from the state and the corresponding diminishment of power experienced by the former have meant that the Church no longer has formal control over political and social change. Both types of change are now beyond the reach of magisterial authority. As a consequence, broader cultural and political forces have affected theological education over the past century more profoundly than ever before.

The congregations began to master a psychological language that was new to them, a language that talked of the self, of desires, of individual ministries, of inclinations, and of historical consciousness. They faced the world on new terms and in actual locations – in the field, in local churches, and in missions. This interplay of localism and globalism (in the sense of macro-politics) – the latter involving the politics of the Holy See – has relevance for several chapters in this collection that deal with missions. To be more specific, several of the authors place their analyses of new ways of seeing that the congregations developed in the missionary field in the context of macro-political forces at play at the international level, as well as the context of local desires, interests, political agendas, resistance to internal/external alliances, and ways of living the faith.

This is most evident in chapter 7 by Elizabeth M. Smyth, "From Serving in the Missions at Home to Serving in Latin America: The Post-Vatican II Experience of Canadian Women Religious." The missionary work of the Canadian Sisters in Guatemala cannot be fully explained without an understanding of the Cuban Revolution, the US politics towards Latin America, and the shift of US involvement from the developmentalist Alliance for Progress that began in 1961 to the financial and military support of repressive regimes in the 1970s and 1980s in the "struggle against communism." The agendas of the North American Catholic hierarchy and the Holy See became intertwined, while in Central and South America the people and the progressive Church moved towards a new theology that started from praxis – "liberation theology" – and that was nourished by new visions arising from the grassroots. The encounter with Latin America also changed important sectors of the Church in North America. In her chapter, Smyth contends that "neither the Sisters who served nor the larger community that supported them, financially and with prayers, would ever be the same. No Guatemalan woman ever joined the community, but its former mission sites would remain central in their psyche."

Chapter 9 by Rosa Bruno-Jofré, "The Sisters of Our Lady of the Missions in Canada, the Long 1960s, and Vatican II: From Carving Spaces in the Educational State to Living the Radicality of the Gospel," gives a glimpse of the impact of locality not only on the missionaries from Religieuses de Notre Dame des Missions (RNDM)/Sisters of Our Lady of the Missions in Peru but also on the congregation at large. As written in that chapter: "In the complex interplay of locality and lived experience, the missionary Sisters embraced liberation theology. They further extended their role as educators from being schoolteachers to becoming community grassroots educators, making explicit the political dimension of everyday life."

As stressed earlier, the long 1960s opened doors to a new way of doing theology and to a process of resignification of mission grounded in practice as well as in analytical approaches emerging from that practice. That is made clear in Chapter 6 by Bruno-Jofré and Zaldívar, "Ivan Illich, the Critique of the Church as *It*: From a Vision of the Missionary to a Critique of Schooling." Their work examines Illich's critique of the Church as *It*, the institutionalized Church holding self-serving worldly power, and Illich's conception of the missionary as one working for the Church as *She*, the Church as inspired by the Spirit.

The relationship between church and state is a central theme in this collection. Beginning in the mid-nineteenth century, the Church – the complex formation of a central universal Church, local churches, and congregations – developed powerful educational networks that interacted with the existing educational systems (Bruno-Jofré 2013). In the case of Spain, after a conflict-ridden relationship during the Second Republic (1931–9), and following the triumph of Franco in 1939, the Church became the educational system itself. Chapter 2 of this collection, Bernard Hugonnier and Gemma Serrano's "Going to the Past: A *Longue Durée* Analysis of Catholic Education and the State in France," carefully describes the conflict between the Church and the French republican state that led to migrations of religious to Spain, and also to Canada. Spain was often a bridge to missions in Latin America. France was the cradle of congregations working all over the world and particularly in Spain and Canada. Hugonnier and Serrano trace the positions taken by the anti-clericals, the republicans (and their pragmatic members), as well as the Catholics, in the "school war" between 1789 and 1959. Since 1959, Catholic schools were compelled to digest both the Debré law (1959), which gave the Catholic Church the right to create private schools as long as it complied with requirements, and the Vatican Council's *Declaration on Christian Education* (1966), which, as stated earlier, conveyed an unclear mission, all in the context of secularism. Hugonnier and Serrano argue that Catholic education became well-integrated in French society, but at a cost: "these schools do not contribute enough to changing the elite of society; on the contrary, for some people, they contribute to its reproduction, which is denounced by highly recognized sociologists in France. Hence, not only do Catholic schools at present not provide sufficient help to poorer students or contribute enough to their evangelization, but they also help the privileged to secure the best education."

A fascinating case study in this collection, about connections among the Church, education, and the state during Franco's time, is chapter 3 by

Carlos Martínez Valle, "Active Methods and Social Secularization in School Catechesis during the Franco Dictatorship (1939–1975): A Transfer in a Cultural System in Change." Martínez Valle examines the peculiar discursive intersections of active methods (including the discourses' reference to John Dewey's ideas) and religious education (catechism) in Francoism, in spite of the condemnation of active methods by Catholic integrists. He shows that while the Spanish academic establishment referenced authors from the progressive education tradition, grassroots catechists adopted and practised active methods from the Church's own tradition, such as the Life's Review and the debate circles. Martínez Valle's key point is that the adoption of practices is more complex than the reception of ideas or names, in that the former requires transformation of pre-existing praxis. Active methods also implied democratic attitudes, according to Martínez Valle. In the context of secularization and the necessary renovation of the social pastoral, the impact of Vatican II and the move towards openness was powerful in Spain, especially with respect to religious education. As for political impact, in William J. Callahan's words, "the principles inspiring National Catholicism (in Spain) were put into question by the Second Vatican Council" (Callahan 2000, 501).

Catholicism and Aboriginal education is a prominent issue in the history of the Catholic Church in Canada. The construction of the modern educational state reconfigured the process of colonization of Aboriginal peoples through "education," in a project in which religious agendas of salvation and redemption converged with the state's agenda. In this collection, the topic is addressed with two contrasting chapters. In chapter 12, "Balancing the Spirit in Aboriginal Catholic Education in Ontario," Lindsay A. Morcom explains that "changes in Church doctrine following Vatican II, as well as an upsurge in cultural pride in Aboriginal communities, have led to meaningful changes in how the Catholic Church regards and respects its Aboriginal adherents." Conversely, in chapter 13, "Indigenous Education as Failed Ontological Reconfiguration," Christopher Beeman argues that despite the paradigmatic shift created by Vatican II that led towards openness and connectivity, Christian education of Aboriginal people has never been a successful project. At the core of his argument is the claim that educational practices should address "the difference between those living Indigenously and those not."

The openness towards change and to the world – in part unexpected – generated by the Second Vatican Council in the context of the long 1960s encouraged new readings of the sacred as it intersected not only with "other" ideologies and belief systems, but also with "sinful" homosexual discourse. In chapter 14, the discourse is presented as part of artistic expressions of critical public pedagogy that aimed at transmitting new Catholic values to the public, in particular a re-reading of love for the excluded and the destitute. Filmmaker Pier Paolo Pasolini has been influential in conveying such recreated Catholic values to the public, using film as a pedagogical tool. William Pinar's examination of Pasolini's work in "'The Scandalous Revolutionary Force of the Past': On Pasolini's *The Gospel According to Saint Matthew*" leads us to think in new ways about the relationship between religious renewal and public pedagogy, a topic often neglected but fundamental to our understanding of the formation of subjectivities. Critical public pedagogy thus understood is in line with a broad notion of education and the search for ways to open public dialogue on issues of relevance such as human rights and cosmopolitanism.

The scholars who collaborated in this volume – mainly historians, theologians, sociologists, educational theorists, and philosophers – examine experiences and historical scenarios that show the specificity of the reception and adaptation of Vatican II resolutions within the Church's own globality. The Second Vatican Council documents appear as enabling tools to deal with changes that had become imperative. We hope the reader will enjoy the interdisciplinarity of this collection, as well as the courage of mind displayed by its protagonists and scholars alike.

NOTES

1 Connection Grant of the Social Science and Humanities Research Council, file no. 611-2014-0050. Award Holder: Professor Rosa Bruno-Jofré (Queen's University). Co-applicant: Dr Pauli Dávila (University of the Basque Country). Collaborators: Dr Elizabeth M. Smyth (University of Toronto), Dr Luis M. Naya (University of the Basque Country), and Dr Gonzalo Jover (Complutense University of Madrid). We acknowledge the financial contribution from the Garaian Group, Facultad de Filosofía y Ciencias de la Educación, Universidad del País Vasco, to the production of this book. Additionally, the editors are grateful for the financial contribution to the production of this volume made by University of Deusto through the eDucaR-Deusto Research Group.

2 Visit http://www.ehu.eus/es/web/garaian/home.

3 Visit http://educ.queensu.ca/their.

4 For information about and images of the displayed works at the art exhibition that accompanied the symposium, visit http://onewomancaravan.net/ConnectionExhibitionCatalog.html.

5 "Vatican II 50 Years On: The New Evangelization," 26–9 June 2012, Leeds Trinity University College and the Centre for Catholic Studies, Durham University (UK) (https://www.dur.ac.uk/theology.religion/ccs/archives/september11); "Vatican II after Fifty Years," 11–12 October 2012, Georgetown University, Washington, DC (https://president.georgetown.edu/vatican-II-dialogue.html); "Revisiting Vatican II: 50 Years of Renewal" international conference, 31 January–3 February 2013, Dharmaram Vidya Kshetram, Bangalore, India (http://www.catholicethics.com/news/vaticanII50yearsofrenewalreport); "The Irrepressible Energy of the Spirit: Vatican II and beyond," 12–14 April 2013, Chestnut College, Philadelphia (http://www.mainlinetoday.com/Main-Line-Today/Calendar/index.php/name/Chestnut-Hill-College-Vatican-II-Conference/event/14722); "Vatican II 50th Anniversary Conferences," 12 January 2012 – 27 June 2013, Research Centre: Vatican II and 21st Century Catholicism, Saint-Paul University, Ottawa, Canada (http://ustpaul.ca/en/vaticanII-50th-anniversary-conferences_988_668.htm); "Our Inheritance: Vatican II at 50. The Post-Conciliar Generation Looks at the Next Half Century," 9–10 March 2015, Fordham Center on Religion and Culture, Fordham University, New York (http://www.fordham.edu/info/20095/center_on_religion_and_culture/165/upcoming_events); "The Nun in the World: A Transnational Study of Catholic Sisters and the Second Vatican Council," 6–9 May 2015, CUSHWA, University of Notre Dame, London Centre, England (http://cushwa.nd.edu/news/46133-call-for-papers-the-nun-in-the-world-a-transnational-study-of-catholic-sisters-and-the-second-vatican-council); "International Colloquium: Male and Female Religious and Vatican II," 12–14 November 2014, organized by LARHRA, Université de Lyon; CERCOR-EPHE, FR; KADOC-KU Leuven, Centro Studi e Richerche sul Concilio Vatican II (Pontifical Lateran University); with support from The 'École française de Rome, The Belgian Historical Institute in Rome, The Academia Belgica, Rome (https://agenda.kuleuven.be/nl/content/male-and-female-religious-and-vatican-ii); and "Lived History of Vatican II Conference," 24–6 April 2014, University of Notre Dame, Notre Dame (http://cushwa.nd.edu/events/the-lived-history-of-vatican-ii).

6 All references to "Church" indicate the Catholic Church.

7 The Council of Trent established the obligation of teachers to teach the Christian (Catholic) doctrine and of bishops to control what the teachers taught and the books they used. Julio Ruiz Berrio, "El oficio de maestro en tiempos de Cervantes," *Revista de Educación* 1 (2004): 11–26.

8 See Enrique García Hernán, *Ignacio de Loyola* (Madrid: Taurus, 2013).

9 Subsequently, Pope Pius V issued decrees (*Circa Pastoralis* [1566] and *Lubricum Vitae Genitus* [1568]) by which women claiming religious status were expected to be cloistered. Laurence Lux-Sterritt and Carmen M. Mangion, "Introduction – Gender, Catholicism, and Women's Spirituality over the *Longue Durée*," in *Gender, Catholicism, and Spirituality: Women and the Roman Catholic Church in Britain and Europe, 1200–1900*, ed. Lux-Sterritt and Mangion (London: Palgrave Macmillan, 2011), 1–19.

10 "The early history of the Ursulines epitomizes a growing female desire to undertake action within the Catholic Reformation. Founded in 1515 in Brescia by Angela Merici (1474–1540), the Company of Saint Ursula was approved by Paul III in 1544. In 1582, the Milan Archbishop Carlo Borromeo organized them into congregations, where the members lived together as laywomen with an apostolic and educational focus on girls. This uncloistered half-way house between lay and religious soon provided the model for an establishment in Avignon (1592), where Françoise de Bermond (1572–1628) procured Clement VIII's authorization to teach the Christian doctrine to girls and to women. The Ursuline movement rapidly spread across France and by the end of the century, there were an estimated 320 communities across the realm." Laurence Lux-Sterritt, *Redefining Female Religious Life: French Ursulines and English Ladies in Seventeenth-Century Catholicism* (Burlington: Ashgate, 2005), 3.

11 "Mary Ward's wish to develop an international Society of Jesus for Women took the ideal of female ministry further than the more localized endeavours of the French Ursulines. Yet, there remained some similarities with the endeavour of the first Ursulines *congrégées* of France: they too proposed to adapt the 'mixed' life of the clerks regular, to a female community. Although they did not claim to imitate any male congregation as openly as Ward emulated the Jesuits, they nevertheless worked closely with the Society and presented a profile which did not comply with the established definitions of female religious life." Lux-Sterritt, *Redefining Female Religious Life*, 38.

12 See Alexander Sedgwick, "Jansen and the Jansenists," *History Today* 40(7) (1990): 36–42; Françoise Hildesheimer, *Le Jansénisme, L'histoire et l'heritage* (Paris: Petite Enciclopédie Moderne du Christianisme, Desclée de Brouwer, 1992), 8–10.

13 The Sisters of the Infant Jesus, previously known as the Congregation of the Holy Infant Jesus or the Dames of Saint Maur, were founded in Paris in 1675.

14 This congregation was founded in 1691.

15 See David Armitage, "What's the Big Idea?: Intellectual History and the *Longue Durée*," *History of European Ideas* 38(4) (2012): 493–507.
16 See James C. Albisetti, "Catholics and Coeducation: Rhetoric and Reality in Europe before *Divini Illius Magistri*." *Paedagogica Historica* 35(3) (1999): 666–96. http://dx.doi.org/10.1080/0030923990350306.
17 The concept of the long 1960s is taken from Arthur Marwick, *The Sixties: Cultural Revolution in Britain, France, Italy, and the United States, c. 1958–1974* (Oxford: Oxford University Press, 1998).
18 See Leslie Woodcock Tentler, ed., *The Church Confronts Modernity: Catholicism Since 1950 in the United States, Ireland, and Quebec* (Washington, DC: Catholic University of America Press, 2007).

REFERENCES

Berger, Peter. 2014. *The Many Altars of Modernity: Toward a Paradigm for Religion in a Pluralist Age.* Berlin: de Gruyter. http://dx.doi.org/10.1515/9781614516477.

Bruno-Jofré, Rosa. 2013. "Introduction – Catholic Teaching Congregations and Synthetic Configurations: Building Identity through Pedagogy and Spirituality across National Boundaries and Cultures." *Paedagogica Historica* 49(4): 447–53. http://dx.doi.org/10.1080/00309230.2013.799498.

Callahan, William J. 2000. *The Catholic Church in Spain, 1875–1998.* Washington, DC: Catholic University of America Press.

Cesareo, Franceso C. 1993. "Quest for Identity: The Ideas of Jesuit Education in the Sixteenth Century." In *The Jesuit Tradition in Education and Missions: A 450-Year Perspective,* edited by Christopher Chapple, 17–33. Cranbury, NJ: University of Scranton Press.

"Declaration on Christian Education (*Gravissimum Educationis*)." 1966. In *The Documents of Vatican II,* edited by Walter M. Abbott, SJ, 637–52. New York: American Press.

Ebaugh, Helen Rose. 1993. "The Growth and Decline of Catholic Religious Orders of Women Worldwide: The Impact of Women's Opportunity Structures." *Journal for the Scientific Study of Religion* 32(1): 68–75. http://dx.doi.org/10.2307/1386914.

Gascoigne, Robert. 2009. *The Church and Secularity: Two Stories of Liberal Society.* Washington, DC: Georgetown University Press.

Lux-Sterrit, Laurence. 2005. *Redefining Female Religious Life: French Ursulines and English Ladies in Seventeenth-Century Catholicism.* Burlington: Ashgate.

O'Malley, John W. 2013. *Trent: What Happened at the Council.* Cambridge, MA: The Belknap Press of Harvard University Press.

Parra, Carlos Hugo. 2012. "Standing with Unfamiliar Company on Uncommon Ground: The Catholic Church and the Chicago Parliament of Religions." PhD diss., University of Toronto.

Rodgers, Daniel T. 2011. *The Age of Fracture.* Cambridge, MA: Harvard University Press.

Taylor, Charles. 2004. *The Secular Age.* Cambridge, MA: Harvard University Press.

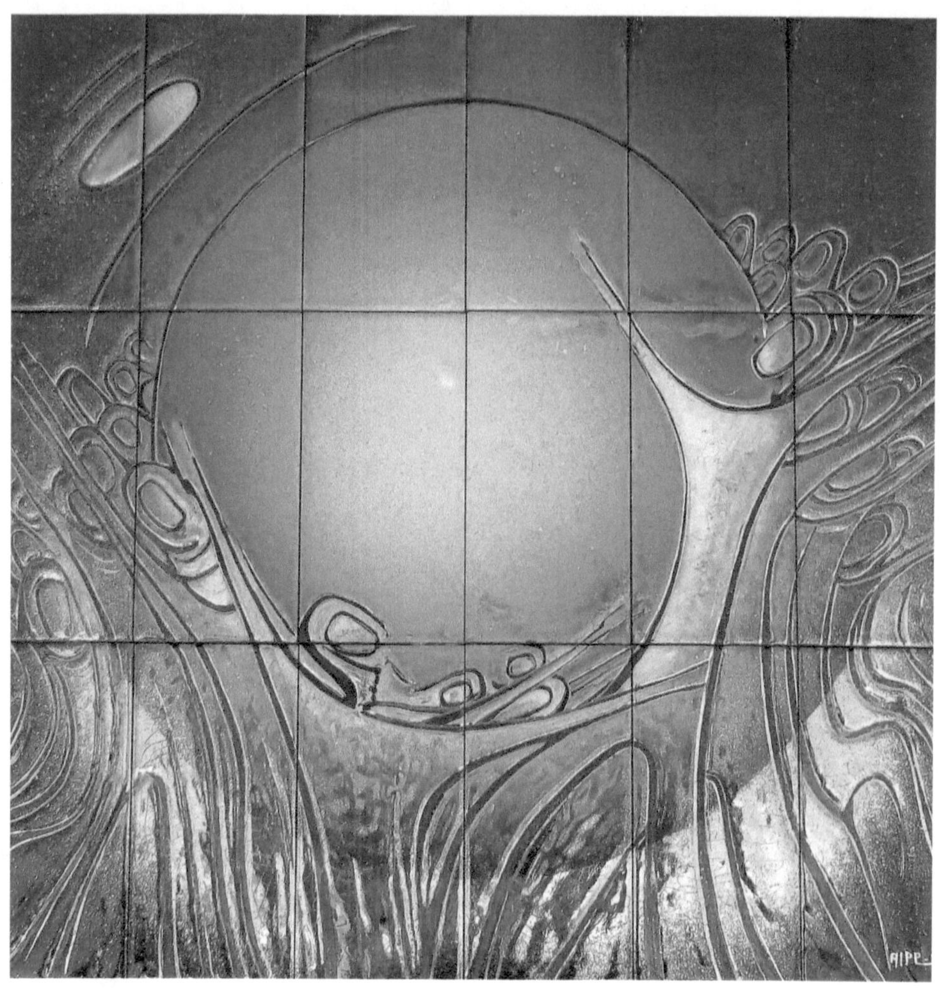

"MAGNIFICAT (Lucas/Luke 1: 46–55) no. 13." Ceramic tilework by María Cruz Bascones.

PART ONE

The Theological Framework: From Objectivity to Subjectivity and the Varied Strands

1 From Objectivity to Subjectivity: Changes in the Nineteenth and Twentieth Centuries and Their Impact on Post-Vatican II Theological Education

MICHAEL ATTRIDGE

Introduction

The 1879 encyclical *Aeterni Patris* of Pope Leo XIII marked a turning point for Catholic education in the closing decades of the nineteenth century (Maritain 1946, 134–54). The Pope's encyclical would have a lasting impact on the Catholic Church right up to the Second Vatican Council, more than eighty years later. The subject matter of *Aeterni Patris* was not new. It was the culmination of a theological movement that had been launched earlier in the century and that would take hold and flourish until Vatican II. Although the encyclical had been intended to instruct those in formation for the Roman Catholic priesthood, its reach was much longer: *Aeterni Patris* would shape Catholic thought and education in the twentieth century more broadly (Gleason 1999; McCool 1989a, 5; Shook 1971, 161, 211).

This chapter has three goals: (1) to sketch the outline of the movement known as neo-Thomism, a particular form of a broader movement of the nineteenth century known as neo-Scholasticism, and to consider its growth, its influence, and the characteristics of its method; (2) to explain some of the factors influencing change in the twentieth century that would lead to the end of neo-Thomism at Vatican II; and (3) to present something of the nature and plurality of theological method today, fifty years after Vatican II.

Securing Objectivity: The Rise of Neo-Thomism in the Nineteenth Century

Neo-Scholasticism was not entirely new; it was a new form of the old.[1] Its origins were in scholasticism, which arose in the Middle Ages and was named after the style of theology used by the scholastic theologians of that period. In the history of theology, the scholastics are known for the method by which they ordered theological terms and relations from the earlier centuries of Christian thought. Among these medieval thinkers, the Dominican Thomas Aquinas in the thirteenth century is especially renowned. His best-known work is the *Summa Theologiae*, widely considered one of the classics of Western philosophy. According to Gerald McCool, "the scattered streams of the Church's patristic tradition were unified in clear formulas of St Thomas' Aristotelian science of theology, and through that same science the Church's heritage of faith could be handed down securely to future generations" (McCool 1989a, 1). Neo-Scholasticism was the nineteenth-century revival of the scholastic method, and Thomas's works were considered by its adherents to be the "perfect scientific expression" of that, which was necessary to cure the ills of the age (McCool 1989a, 5).

By the dawn of the nineteenth century, the scholastic approach had all but disappeared from Catholic theology. The new philosophies of the Enlightenment had overshadowed the earlier scholastic method. The first blow to the medieval approach came from France. Thomas's system had relied on Aristotle's metaphysical science. According to this system, first principles were God's revelation, which existed outside the self. However, the seventeenth-century French philosopher René Descartes (1596–1650), through his famous "*cogito ergo sum*," persuaded many that the individual mind could find truth within itself. This created a separation between external objective Revelation and internal human reason. One could now speak of subjectivity and of the individual. As this Cartesian system moved into the foreground, the Thomistic system moved into the background.

The second blow came from Germany in the eighteenth century from Immanuel Kant (1724–1803). Against the Thomistic arguments of God's objective and external revelation, Kant argued that only one's "moral and practical reason was able to posit the existence of God" (Boersma 2009, 36). This was in direct opposition to the traditional notion of supernatural Revelation. As Hans Boersma notes, "it was certainly difficult to reconcile the immanentism of the Kantian moral universe with the Catholic demand for divine revelation" (ibid., 37). An approach to religion that takes its point of departure from the subjective, immanent, and moral needs of human beings is "diametrically opposed to a theology that begins with objective, external and propositional revelation" (ibid., 36).

In the nineteenth century, Catholic theologians began to incorporate Descartes and Kant, and three schools of philosophy emerged within Roman Catholicism – traditionalism, semi-rationalism, and ontologism – each of which attempted to reconcile faith and reason (ibid., 36–41; McCool 1989b, 37–128). All of them would be condemned during the nineteenth century for not having dealt properly with the relationship between faith and reason, and their very existence would strengthen the magisterium's argument for the need to revive the work of Thomas. From the standpoint of Church authorities, these newer Cartesian and Kantian philosophical systems were "confusing, to say the least to theologians who had been trained to deal with these topics through a model of nature and supernature constructed upon the Aristotelian categories of substance and accident" (ibid., 136).

The neo-Thomist movement was also strengthened in 1849 by the establishment of the conservative, Jesuit-run Roman journal *Civiltà Cattolica,* launched at the request of Pope Pius IX. The Pope had desired that a scholarly journal be created that would influence the cultural and social life of Italy. He looked to the Jesuits, whose academic reputation was already well known, to establish the periodical and provide the content. According to McCool, the editorial team of the journal had "access to the Pope and possessed his confidence." Moreover, their vision was clear: "replace all existing systems of Catholic theology with a single system: neo-Thomism" (ibid., 136). Thus in the decades that followed, condemnations were forthcoming, with two influential neo-Thomist Jesuit philosophers, Matteo Liberatore and Joseph Kleutgen, actively arguing two essential points: (1) traditionalism, semi-rationalism, and ontologism were philosophically and theologically erroneous; and (2) neo-Thomism could meet the standard of modern scientific philosophy and theology, and solve the problems of faith and reason (ibid., 138).

When Pope Leo's *Aeterni Patris* was published thirty years after the founding of *Civiltà Cattolica,* the path of neo-Thomism became secured at the highest level of the Church. Giacchino Pecci, as the newly elected Pope Leo XIII, had been a strong proponent of neo-Thomism for more than fifty years. The nineteenth century had been a difficult one for the Church. The Pope intended his pontificate "to be a time in which the Church, abandoning the defensiveness of Pius IX, would reach out once more to the modern world and win back a good measure of its influence on Europe's intellectual, political and social life" (McCool 1989a, 6). The new philosophies of the age had created doubt, which resulted in difficulties for religion and society.

The best way to deal with these difficulties was "to return to the sound philosophy and theology common to the Scholastic Doctors whose finest exponent was St Thomas" (ibid., 8).

The debate between Cartesian and Kantian-influenced philosophy and theology on the one hand and the Aristotelian, neo-Thomist system on the other would continue in the closing decades of the century. Antonio Fumagalli's final remark in his lecture delivered at the Milan Major Seminary in 1903 encapsulates the spirit of the time: "To the cry ... 'back to Kant' let us answer defiantly with the cry of Leo XIII 'Back to Thomas'" (Fumagalli 1903, 400). The culmination of the debate would occur with the Modernist crisis and result in the condemnations of Modernism – the "synthesis of all heresies" – from Rome in 1907 with the issuance of *Lamentabili Sane Exitu* from the Holy Office and later that year Pius X's encyclical *Pascendi Dominici Gregis*.

The style of neo-Thomism at the end of the century can be described with relative clarity. Descartes and Kant had introduced philosophies that led to individual, personalized, and subjective approaches to theology with indeterminate, unpredictable, and unstable outcomes. Against this, the neo-Thomists understood their system to be stable and predictable. Objectivity was the key. As Gabriel Daly writes: "The system was designed to demonstrate and defend an objective order of divine facts and teachings" (1980, 7). Against "the vacillations and unpredictabilities" of their opponents, "most Roman Catholic theologians were convinced that this firm and methodological objectivisation constituted the characteristic strength of Catholicism" (ibid., 7).

Changing World: Growing Plurality in the Pre-Conciliar Period

In the decades following the promulgation of *Aeterni Patris*, *Lamentabili*, and *Pascendi*, one can broadly distinguish two tracks within Catholic theology. The first was the status quo, namely, the neo-Thomist approach – objective, immutable, and ahistorical. Methodologically, the approach was deductive in that it began with abstract concepts that were understood as forming Christian belief and behaviour. This was the approach promoted at the official, magisterial level of the Church and reflected in the "Roman" manuals of theology used during the twentieth century to educate candidates preparing for priesthood. The second track was historical and contextual, responsive to changes in society and culture as well as to the new century's intellectual and philosophical currents. Methodologically, this second track was inductive in that it began with the human person and with experience and then looked for broader concepts and principles that might be discerned from them. This was the approach taken by some theologians and scholars, especially in the Catholic universities in the French, German, and Dutch-speaking world from the 1920s onwards. The first track would continue until the Second Vatican Council, when, as McCool concludes, it reached its terminus (McCool 1989a, 230). The second, which would be endorsed and reflected in the conciliar teaching, has shaped the post–Vatican II theological landscape of the past fifty years. We will look at the post-conciliar period in a later section. For now, let us consider the period after Modernism and leading up to Vatican II.

Francis Schüssler Fiorenza notes two influences in the twentieth century that would lead to a crisis within neo-Thomism. Both caused shifts to more contemporary approaches to theology. The first was an increased awareness of the relevance of history and how it shapes human thought. When applied to theology it "led to the recognition of the historical character of theological affirmations." In other words, if theological statements are historically conditioned, they are subject to change. They are therefore neither eternal and objective, nor immutable. The second influence involved a new understanding of the relationship of philosophy to theology. Philosophy was no longer viewed as secondary or as simply a tool for theologians – the handmaid of theology, as it was once called. As noted by Schüssler Fiorenza, "the development of transcendental, phenomenological, hermeneutical and existential philosophy affected a shift" (2011, 25–6). Philosophy *shaped* theological reflection instead of merely justifying its arguments. A full treatment of the relevant factors and individuals that influenced the changes in twentieth-century theology is not possible within the scope of this chapter. However, an outline of some of the broader elements is necessary.

The growth in historical awareness in the late nineteenth century brought about a change for many in thinking about sources in theology. If the language of Church teaching is historically conditioned, then the way things are now may not be how they always have been. An awareness of history prompted theologians in the 1930s and 1940s to re-examine the Church's tradition. Scholars began to look back at the early sources of Christian belief and practice and ask what these might have to offer our understanding of theology today. Three movements in particular from this time are worth noting for their impact on twentieth-century theology. The first was the biblical movement, started in the seventeenth century by Protestant scholars, which encouraged a reading of the Bible in its historical context. In the Catholic Church, this approach would not take hold until the end of the nineteenth century and the beginning of the twentieth, especially with the work of the Dominican scholar Marie-Joseph Lagrange (1855–1938) and with the founding of the École Biblique in Jerusalem (Nichols 1998, 115–19). Lagrange's use of the historical-critical method was ahead of its time in some ways within Catholic theology. Support for its use would not come at the official level until the encyclical of Pius XII, *Divino Afflante Spiritu*, in 1943.

A second movement in the return to the sources approach, called "ressourcement" because of its use by the French Dominicans and French Jesuits in the 1930s and 1940s, is the liturgical movement. The idea that prayer and the worship life of the Church was a source for theology goes back to the early centuries of Christianity. The fifth-century theologian Prosper of Aquitaine coined the axiom "*Lex orandi, lex credenda*" – that is, the law of praying gives rise to the law of believing. Thus, prayer or the liturgical life of the community was a source for theological teaching. Over the centuries, this notion was lost. In the nineteenth century the Benedictine abbot Dom Prosper Guéranger drew the Church's attention back to the importance of liturgy; some decades later, the liturgical movement began under the inspiration of Dom Lambert Beauduin (ibid., 107–10). In the twentieth century the Benedictine monk Odo Casel (1886–1948) would argue that the Liturgy was a response to God's revelation and therefore "should be its principal stimulus to theological reflection." Once again, the theologians were ahead of the magisterium. Not until Pius XII's encyclical *Mediator Dei* in 1947 did the Church recognize the importance of the liturgical movement in a formal way.

The third movement that highlighted the importance of history and that shaped the way theology was done in the decades leading up to Vatican II involved the attention given to the early Christian authors. Historically minded theologians in the nineteenth century became interested in reading the earliest sources of Christian thought. Instead of relying on the scholastic theologians of the Middle Ages, including Thomas, they were interested in the thinkers who had influenced these medieval theologians. This helped them understand and interpret the later writers; it also offered them a deeper understanding of the larger Christian tradition. This "patristic" movement was aided greatly by the French priest Jacques-Paul Migne (1800–75), who published for widespread use in a multi-volume set the works of all Latin and Greek Church writers from the first century through to the Middle Ages. Although better critical editions have appeared since, Migne's work made the patristic writings easily accessible to a wide audience. A return to the patristic sources was an obvious feature of the "ressourcement" movement and helped ground, historically, notions of revelation and faith against their ahistorical expression by the neo-Thomists. As the twentieth-century French Jesuit theologian Jean Daniélou argued, we need to understand the richness and breadth of the entire Christian tradition. As Nichols put it, "the faith of the Church ... needs many cultures and epochs for its full ... expression" (1998, 120–3). Neo-Thomism's emphasis on timelessness was out of touch with twentieth-century philosophy. By contrast, as McCool writes, "patristic thought ... was very open to the modern concern for the person, social unity, and history" (1989a, 209). It was essential to return to the earliest sources of Christianity and link them to modern philosophy and thought.

Each of these movements – the biblical, the liturgical, and the patristic, all three of which were tied to an increased awareness of the importance of history – would have a lasting impact on twentieth-century theology, even to the present day. *Aeterni Patris*, *Lamentabili*, and *Pascendi* all envisioned and promoted a more or less singular philosophical system based on Thomas Aquinas. That system's purpose was as much to advance the integrity of a uniform approach as it was to quell the plurality of philosophies since the Enlightenment. But the centre would not hold. The twentieth century would see not only the independence of philosophy from theology, but also the influence of multiple philosophical approaches on theological thought leading to new theological methodologies. In the next section we will explore five approaches to contemporary theology. For now, though, we will look at how Thomism evolved during the twentieth century, leading eventually, as McCool writes, "to the undermining of the 19th century conception of the 'wisdom of the Angelic Doctor,' which had inspired *Aeterni Patris*" (McCool 1989a, 3).

Four Thomists who were more or less contemporaries in the early part of the twentieth century are worth mentioning. Each had a role to play in the internal evolution of Thomism in the century that followed (ibid., 3). They are Étienne Gilson (1884–1978), Jacques Maritain (1882–1973), Pierre Rousselot (1878–1915), and Joseph Maréchal (1878–1944). While each was influential, only the work of the latter two would inspire successors who would shape post-conciliar approaches to theology. The relevance of the former two would be more limited in duration.

Historical research on Thomas grew during the early decades of the twentieth century. Foremost among the historians of this area of study was Étienne Gilson, who was neither sympathetic nor hostile to neo-Thomism but more interested in Cartesian and post-Cartesian philosophy.[2] Early on, Gilson was encouraged in his studies towards investigating the scholastic origins of Descartes's philosophy. As a historically minded scholar, he did not start his investigation with one or another school of thought but began directly with the works of Thomas himself. His research led him to conclude that the later fifteenth-, sixteenth-, and seventeenth-century commentators of Aquinas – Cajetan, Suárez, Báñez, and John of St Thomas – had misread Thomas and therefore misinterpreted him. And, as he pointed out, these were the ones upon whom the neo-Thomist authors of *Aeterni Patris* had relied.[3] The commentators had read Thomas's theological works and commentaries on Aristotle and had equated the Angelic Doctor's philosophy with that of the ancient philosopher. As such, they had separated philosophy from the context of theology, something Thomas had not done. Christian philosophy, in order to work properly, must "operate inside the theology which brought it into being and which nourishes its vitality" (ibid., 170). For Gilson, none of the commentators were properly Thomists. To be authentic was "to return to the Christian philosophy of St Thomas in the form in which he himself presented it in his theological works. To be a Thomist meant to be a disciple of St Thomas and of no one else" (ibid., 195).

Jacques Maritain lived almost as long as Étienne Gilson. But unlike Gilson, who worked as a historian, Maritain saw himself as a speculative philosopher. He influenced Catholic social thought and educational theory in the twentieth century, and his reflections on aesthetics, politics, culture, and education were widely read.[4] Maritain was introduced to Thomas Aquinas through the commentators of Cajetan and John of St Thomas, and throughout his life Maritain would remain faithful to their approaches to Aquinas. He sought to unify all knowledge through their systems and was so successful at doing so in the twentieth century "that the corpus of his writings represents Neo-Thomism's most successful attempt to achieve the goal of *Aeterni Patris*" (ibid., 117). Maritain's system was centred on the notion of concept. The difficulty, though, was that modern theology – influenced by history, phenomenology, existentialism, and so on – was becoming more complex than objective conceptualism would allow. By the mid-twentieth century "the Aristotelian sciences of metaphysics and theology, which Maritain had defended, could no longer give the Catholic faith the conceptual expression through which the modern mind could understand it properly" (ibid., 212). Maritain was deeply committed to neo-Thomism. But Gilson had discovered through his research not a single system of Thomism but a plurality, one that included the commentators upon whom Maritain has based his work. Gilson never said so explicitly, but according to McCool, Gilson's own criteria would have meant that the Thomism of Maritain – found for example in one of his most important works, *The Degrees of Knowledge* – was not an authentic Thomism (ibid., 227). By the time of the Second Vatican Council, "the Thomism of Maritain had ceased to influence of the progress of theology" (ibid., 3).

By contrast, the work of Pierre Rousselot has had a lasting impact on twentieth-century theology.[5] One wonders what further contributions he might have made if his life had not ended suddenly in 1915 during the First World War, when he was only thirty-seven. Rousselot was a historian and a theologian. He was also a Thomist, in that he read and was influenced by Aquinas's metaphysics. However, he was not in agreement with the neo-Thomists, especially with regard to their view of the act of faith. For neo-Thomists, if the evidence before someone can provide certainty that a truth is revealed by God, then the person must assent to that truth. Faith, therefore, is assent to a revealed, external, and objective truth. The neo-Thomists of Rousselot's time would acknowledge that in practice, many ordinary believers were incapable of determining the reasonableness of the act of faith. In such cases, as the well-known neo-Thomist Cardinal Louis Billot had said, they would be responsible for "taking things on authority" (Holstein 1965, 94). They would have to rely on the authority of parents, pastors, and so on. For Rousselot, the problem was that this undercut human freedom, which for him was essential. In the situation above, the person was obliged to believe. As McCool writes, for Rousselot humans need to be free to seek God. The problem with neo-Thomism was that "scholastic 'intellectualism' and its 'extrinsic' apologetics failed to do justice to the role of freedom in the human person's acceptance of faith" (McCool 1989a, 60). Rousselot was interested in addressing the problems of the day, which were grounded in the experience of the subject. The neo-Scholastic approach did not accomplish this. In separating himself from the neo-Thomists, Rousselot had distinguished himself from the Thomism of the earlier commentators. Thus, in Rousselot, the plurality of Thomism in the twentieth century had begun.

Joseph Maréchal outlived Rousselot by almost thirty years.[6] They were contemporaries. Maréchal influenced Rousselot, but so did Rousselot influence Maréchal. Maréchal's work led him to the conclusion that human beings as creatures desire to be in communion with God, the Creator. They are intrinsically ordered in this way: "The natural 'eros' of every finite agent moves him/her to 'return to God' by 'becoming like

God.' In other words, each finite agent strives to achieve his/her own proper perfection by participating in the perfection of the Creator to the full measure of the person's own specific essence" (ibid., 87). In his lifetime, Maréchal would bring together the transcendentalism of Kant with the metaphysics of Aquinas, resulting in a new school of thought known as "Transcendental Thomism," which would have a lasting impact on theology to the present day. Francis Schüssler Fiorenza writes: "As a theological movement, this effort was powerful and effective because it neither jettisoned the past out of fascination with the modern nor rejected the modern out of nostalgia for the past. Rather it opened a way to bring Thomas' theology in contact with modern philosophy' (2011, 28).

The period of the twentieth century leading up to Vatican II was remarkable for many reasons. Intellectual currents such as historical consciousness, an emphasis on subjectivity and experience, and the separation of philosophy and theology were developing. New schools of thought were emerging alongside growth in the social and human sciences. At the same time, the social and political landscape was rapidly changing, influenced by such dramatic, even tragic events as two world wars, the rise of communism, the Holocaust, rivalry between two superpowers, the Cold War, the assassinations of world leaders, decolonization, and the Cuban Missile Crisis. Each of these, in a variety of ways, would inform Pope John XXIII's decision to call the Second Vatican Council.[7] With regard to both content and method, Vatican II was a turning point for Catholic theological education. From the standpoint of content, Catholic theologians readily divide the twentieth century into two periods, before and after Vatican II. The Council had such a powerful impact on Catholic theology that its content post-Vatican II was substantially different from before. From the standpoint of method, Vatican II marked the end of Neo-Thomism and the transition to much greater plurality, found in a variety of approaches. In the final section of this chapter, I describe five post–Vatican II approaches to Catholic theology over the past fifty years and identify a number of influences.[8] I conclude with some observations regarding characteristics of Catholic theological education today.

Approaches and Influences in Theological Education after Vatican II

One characteristic that would mark modern theological method most clearly was the turning away from the object and towards the subject. Pre-twentieth-century Catholic magisterial theology began with that which was external to the human person – eternal, ahistorical, and immutable truth, communicated through the Church's official teachings. Once grasped, this truth was to have a normative influence on the believer. However, beginning in the nineteenth century, philosophers and theologians following Descartes began to reflect on history and human subjectivity in relation to God's revelation in the world and to the human person's response in faith. In the twentieth century, theologians sought to correlate the insights of modern philosophy inspired by Descartes and Kant with Thomism. The results would have a profound impact.

As mentioned earlier, Transcendental Thomism brought together the transcendentalism of Kant with the metaphysics of Thomas. Although the method originated with Joseph Maréchal, the philosophy behind it was not new. In the scholastic period, "transcendental" referred to a term or category that applied to everything; for example, "goodness" applied to God, to humans, and to all of creation. In the modern period, for Kant, transcendentalism referred to human experience, which considered the "conditions and possibility of knowledge through an analysis of human cognition" (Schüssler Fiorenza 2011, 29). Maréchal's transcendentalism combined these two: it incorporated Kant in that it considered the subjectivity of knowledge, especially knowledge of God's revelation; and it incorporated the scholastic understanding in that it directed the believer's knowledge of revelation towards the infinite. The result was a method that considered "the unlimited dynamism of the human intellect striving to grasp not just specific objects of experience but the meaning of the totality of reality" (ibid., 29).

The most influential and renowned proponent of Transcendental Thomism was Karl Rahner (1904–84), who was influenced by both Maréchal and Martin Heidegger (1889–1976).[9] Rahner's starting point was human freedom and the experience of the infinite. He understood human persons to be fundamentally oriented towards the infinite and absolute mystery of God. This orientation is "not only constitutive of human nature, but also results from God's historical self-communication" in and to the world (ibid., 29). Rahner was a Thomist, but he differed from Thomas, most fundamentally in his starting point (Rahner 1974, 94). Thomas, following an Aristotelian approach, started his *Summa Theologiae* with the existence and nature of God. His was thus a theocentric method. Rahner started with human persons, their cognition, and the universal human desire for knowledge and meaning. His was an anthropocentric model. Thomas's method moved from God to human persons, whereas Rahner's sought to relate anthropology to the content of Christian beliefs such as revelation, salvation, Christology, church, and sacraments. For Rahner, "anthropology constituted ... the starting point as well as the constant reference point of theological reflection" (Schüssler Fiorenza 2011, 31). Rahner's theology has been criticized for being excessively human focused. At the same time, it has been developed in relation to linguistic and cultural theory, as well as political and liberation (especially feminist) theology. Be it from the standpoint of critics or not, there is no doubt it has been highly influential. Moreover, the shift from a God-centred to a human-centred approach is one of the most important characteristics of modern, Catholic theological method and education.

A second approach in modern Catholic theological education is hermeneutical theology. Certainly, every approach in theology engages in hermeneutics insofar as it interprets such things as scripture, the tradition of the Church, creeds, liturgy, and magisterial teaching. What distinguishes hermeneutics from transcendentalism is its emphasis on language. Transcendentalism focuses on human experience, and within this framework, language is the tool used to express this experience. This developed from an earlier view whereby doctrines themselves were central to theology. However, the development in hermeneutical theory located language even prior to experience, such that "language does not just express but also constitutes experience" (ibid., 33). This insight has been influential in theology and has developed especially through the work of such philosophers as Hans-Georg Gadamer (1900–2002) and Paul Ricoeur (1913–2005). Gadamer argued in favour of the authority of classic texts – those that have endured the test of time – as important and influential for present understanding. In this view, one would fuse together the "horizon" of past traditions with one's own in the present, in such a way that the classic would be incorporated into it. Ricoeur developed Gadamer's work by relating explanation to understanding (Ricoeur 1977; Ricoeur 1984–8). Whereas Gadamer's hermeneutical understanding combined the past text with the present, Ricoeur emphasized a structural analysis of the text in order to gain a deeper, critical interpretation of it (Schüssler Fiorenza 2011, 34). In his construction of the systematic theological task, theologian David Tracy (b. 1939) has used both Gadamer's hermeneutical approach and appreciation of classical texts, specifically within the Christian tradition, and Ricoeur's work on structural analysis (Tracy 1981; 1987). Especially important for Tracy is "the explanatory modes of historical-critical, literary-critical, and social-critical analysis as complementary to interpretive modes of understanding" (Schüssler Fiorenza 2011, 34).

The hermeneutical approach is not above criticism. As Schüssler Fiorenza explains, a crisis may arise in the hermeneutical approach when it is discovered that the past tradition or experience is found to be lacking. In such a case, hermeneutics is inadequate. What is necessary is "to go beyond interpretation to a reconstruction of either tradition or experience," since the theological enterprise is not fundamentally about interpretation, but rather about investigating and revealing truth (ibid., 35).

A third approach in contemporary Catholic theology can be referred to as "analytical approaches." Two of these in particular have been widely recognized. The first is the use of models, which I will not spend much time on. The second is what has been called meta-theory, which I will focus on in more detail. The models approach is often identified with the work of Avery Dulles (1918–2008), who worked to arrange concepts within theology according to categories, most notably on the Church and Revelation (Dulles 1987, 1992). What is useful about this approach is that it clearly presents a diversity of views while at the same time showing their interconnectedness. This makes possible mutual and cooperative interaction among adherents of different models. This has been useful not only within Roman Catholicism but also between Christian churches engaged in the modern ecumenical endeavour. The obvious limitation in such an approach relates to how well it can categorize concepts without distorting their meanings in order to fit the model.

The other approach is associated with the Canadian theologian Bernard Lonergan (1904–84). Lonergan's work focused on identifying the characteristics of human cognition common to all human beings, prior to considering how this relates to the theological task (Lonergan 1970). It is therefore a meta-theory of human cognition. Lonergan argues that the process of knowing takes place in four successive steps: experiencing, understanding, judging, and, finally, making a decision. These steps, he points out, are common to all disciplines. When it comes to the task of theology, he applies his theory – analogous to the cognitional steps – as follows: research (gathering data), interpretation (understanding the data), history (which allows for the data to be judged), and dialectic (clarifying and deciding). At this point, once a decision has been made, a second stage is employed that reflects the task of the theologian. Following the four steps of cognition, but in reverse order, the theologian now moves as follows: foundations (the decision taken), doctrinal theology (judgments of truth), systematics (understanding), and communications (experience, especially in the practice of theology).

Important in the steps of this meta-theory is the notion of conversion that coincides with the knower taking a decision. Conversion can take place in three areas: intellectual conversion, in which the knower does more than just take a look; moral conversion, in which the person judges that something is truly meaningful and good; and religious conversion, in which the person embraces a level of transcendence that seeks ultimate meaning and value. As such, Longeran's approach shares strong characteristics with Transcendental Thomism. His work has been criticized for falling too heavily on the side of subjectivism, or reducing significant theologians and concepts to "abstract epistemological categories" (Schüssler Fiorenza 2011, 38). Karl Rahner argued that Lonergan's meta-theory is not a theological method but rather, as the title of his work in the area indicates, a method in theology (Rahner 1972, 194). As such, it is more concerned with cognitional structures than with theological method per se.[10]

The fourth approach is the method of correlation, identified in the work of the twentieth-century theologian Paul Tillich (1886–1965) (Tillich 1951–63). This method seeks to relate two things to each other. For Tillich this could pertain to such things, including in theology, as statistical correlation (data), logical correlation (concepts), or real correlation (things or events). His method has been described as both varied and complex (Schüssler Fiorenza 2011, 42).

In contemporary Roman Catholic theology, the method of correlation has been used widely by as diverse a group of theologians as Edward Schillebeeckx, Hans Küng, Joseph Ratzinger, Rosemary Radford Reuther, and David Tracy, whose approaches share both similarities and differences. In fact, many today maintain "that a method of correlation best expresses the theological task" since much of theology involves the correlation of two data sets or poles (ibid., 42). For Edward Schillebeeckx, the correlation is between two sources of theology – on the one hand, the tradition of Christian experience, and on the other, contemporary experience. The purpose is to allow the Christian story of the past to impact present experience in order to "allow the story of Christ's salvation to become for us an offer of salvation that critically corrects modern attitudes of individualism and possessiveness" (ibid., 43).

Hans Küng prefers to use the term "critical confrontation" instead of critical correlation, even though the approach is similar to that of Schillebeeckx. For him, the task of theology is to relate the Christian tradition of the past – especially the historical but living Jesus – to the present situation. Küng does not follow Schillebeeckx in arguing that the modern utilitarian experience is in need of conversion. Instead, for him "the proliferation of bureaucracies and a lack of individual freedom" are what need to be addressed and corrected (ibid., 44). Küng has been especially critical of the institutional Church and various offices, such as the papacy and the episcopacy, since Vatican II. Joseph Ratzinger seeks to correlate faith and reason through three levels: first in the relation of philosophy and theology, which correlate for example on the question of human mortality, by asking about human origin, destination, and meaning; second, in the way that faith advances ontology when it professes the existence of God; and third, in that theology incorporates the element of love through faith that seeks to move the person to truth in God (Ratzinger 1995; Schüssler Fiorenza 2011, 44–5). Rosemary Radford Reuther has used correlation in her feminist theology, but as a prophetic principle that seeks to liberate. She correlates issues of race, class, and gender, and, more recently, environmental and global concerns, with diverse traditions and texts in order to address oppression (Radford Reuther 2005). She writes: "Feminist theology that draws on biblical principles is possible only if the prophetic principles ... imply a rejection of ... every use of God to justify social domination and subjugation" (Radford Reuther 1983; 2007; Schüssler Fiorenza 2011, 45). Finally, David Tracy's position is that theology's task is to mutually and critically correlate "an interpretation of the Christian tradition with an interpretation of the contemporary situation" (Grant and Tracy 1984, 170). Thus, Tracy considers the twofold criteria of appropriateness to the tradition, which judges every subsequent theological statement in light of the apostolic witness in the Scriptures, and the criteria of intelligibility to the situation, which allows the classic event "to have a disclosing and transformative impact on the situation" in the present (Schüssler Fiorenza 2011, 46).

Although widely used and accepted within theology, limitations of the correlation method have been identified. For example, it is not always possible to correlate something of the past with something of the present. The terms used might be the same, but the concepts behind them, which are tied to specific cultures, may be different. Also, as Schüssler Fiorenza notes, correlation does not sufficiently take into account the need to critique the tradition by "reexamining the experiences and affirmations themselves" (2011, 47). It is with this in mind that I turn to the fifth and final approach in contemporary Catholic theological education.

The last approach is liberation theologies, which can refer to a number of theological movements such as Latin American liberation theology, feminist theology, black theology, and Asian theology, or any movement that criticizes oppression and advances liberation. Although used by diverse groups, it has some common elements. All liberation theologies begin with an analysis of the concrete situation and identify oppression, alienation, and discrimination. All of them acknowledge that the current situation is not how things are supposed to be. The next step is to search the tradition for what led to the oppression and critique those elements. Finally, the liberation theologian retrieves elements of the tradition that have been neglected, silenced, or forgotten as part of the constructive theological task. These could include "forgotten religious symbols, neglected ecclesiastical practices, and ignored experiences" (ibid., 49). History is often told by the victors. Liberation theology seeks to bring to the fore the stories that were forgotten and the voices that were silenced. Liberation theology is a theology of praxis, both as a criterion and as a goal. It involves action and a way of life, and it leads to further action and a transformation in the lives of those affected and liberated.

Conclusion: Openness to the Future

These five approaches to contemporary theological education are useful to present not only insofar as they describe ways in which theology is being done today, but also because they indicate a plurality within a particular field of discourse. It is obvious that the way in which theology is done has changed over the past two hundred years – broadly speaking, from singularity to plurality. One might also argue that there has been a move from a position whereby theology acts as though it stands over the divine, transcendent God claiming a position of certitude in knowing who God is and how God operates, to a position of humility where God stands over us and where the task of theology is only imperfect and analogous as we seek to understand and move more deeply into the mystery of faith. There has also been a decentralization of control over theology: it has shifted from the hands of the official magisterium to the hands of the broader theological community. The struggle between a singular, centralized theological approach and a plurality of approaches continues to this day and is at the centre of many of the warnings and silencings of theologians in recent decades. But beyond these observations, it is also now useful to conclude by reiterating some of the influences that have brought about these changes and highlighting characteristics of contemporary theological education.

The twentieth century was like no other in the history of the Church. The seeds of change were planted in the centuries beforehand. The Protestant Reformation of the sixteenth century, the Enlightenment of the seventeenth and eighteenth centuries, and the political revolutions on the eve of the nineteenth century each had a profound impact on the Church's religious, intellectual, and socio-political identity. The ecumenical moment of the early twentieth century precipitated a change whereby it is almost unthinkable today to do theology responsibly without the involvement of others in the wider Christian context. The role of philosophy in relation to theology has changed from one of instrumentality and subservience to one of dialogue and mutual interrelationality. Modern philosophies such as existentialism, personalism, and phenomenology have greatly shaped and informed the discipline of theology today. The separation of the Church from the state and the corresponding diminishment of power experienced by the former have meant that the Church no longer has formal control over political and social change. Both types of change are now beyond the reach of magisterial authority. As a consequence, broader cultural and political forces have affected theological education over the past century more profoundly than ever before. A growing number of theologians today argue that appropriating the insights of social scientific research in theology is foundational, perhaps even constitutive (Ormerod 2005). But over and above each of these broad influences in theology is the even broader influence of history and historical consciousness in theology. Scholars in disciplines outside of theology often wonder why the historical approach is still so often used in theology. The response to such questions must be twofold. First, in a field of study as old as theology, the appropriation of historical awareness is still relatively new. Much of the tradition remains in need of historical-minded study. Second, given that the discipline of theology involves an object that is also outside of time, there is a perennial challenge to remind some theologians that God's revelation is mediated in and through historical realities. For this reason, history is operative in theology in a way that it is likely not in other fields of study.

Finally, I want to highlight elements that are characteristic of a modern approach to theological education. The meta-theme of this chapter has been the change in the past two centuries from objectivity to subjectivity. The turn to the subject as a starting point has been one of the most important developments in theology, in my view. But other characteristics too have been important. A rediscovery of the nature of the human person primarily as dynamic, relational, and free – not static, abstract, or constrained by blind obedience – has been important. Human experience is now valued in theology. Attention to experience and especially the importance of relationality have increased awareness of the need for collaboration in the work of theology. When coupled with historicity, the turn to the subject has meant that mutability, changeability, and an openness to the future are features of a contemporary approach rather than the closed and static system of the past. It has also meant that theology is attentive to the context in which the individual believer or believers are located. Subject-centred and contextual theologies are now vital starting points in theology, ones that facilitate race, class, and gender analysis. Awareness of self and attention to otherness have contributed greatly to ecumenical and especially inter-religious theology in recent decades.

The above-mentioned characteristics are not exhaustive of that which influences theology today, but they certainly illustrate its plurality. Theology seeks to understand and communicate, albeit imperfectly, the mystery of God. As theologian Robert Doran has recently noted, questions arise in every age and "the sum of the questions always exceeds either actually or potentially the sum of the resources presently available to answer them" (2012, 7). Perhaps, put simply, theology today seeks to address questions while at the same time posing new ones. This is different from in the past, when theology purported only to have answers.

NOTES

1 For an excellent overview of nineteenth-century neo-Scholasticism, see McCool (1989b).
2 For a summary of Gilson's contributions, see McCool (1989a), 167–78, 179–99.
3 Gilson claimed that his own view of philosophy was the same as what Leo XIII had proposed in his encyclical. However, as McCool notes, Cajetan, Báñez, Suarez, John of St Thomas, and others were behind the work

of Kleutgen and Liberatore, who were the architects of *Aeterni Patris*. According to Gilson's own criteria, the Thomism of the encyclical is not an authentic Thomism. "Gilson was able to agree with *Aeterni Patris* because he understood the encyclical to be saying what in fact it never says: that to be a Thomist is to adhere with absolute fidelity to the way of philosophizing St Thomas employed in his theological works." See McCool (1989a), 195–6.

4 For a summary of Maritain, see McCool (1989a), 114–32, 133–60.

5 For a summary of Rousselot, see McCool (1989a), 139–58, 159–86.

6 For an overview of Maréchal, see McCool (1989a), 87–113.

7 For an excellent article explaining the socio-political factors that gave rise to the need for Vatican II, see Schloesser (2006), 275–319.

8 Regarding the following section, I am indebted to Schüssler Fiorenza for his excellent summary of contemporary theological method. See Schüssler Fiorenza (2011), 26–50. Note: these approaches are not mutually exclusive. They are theoretically distinct. However, elements of each are often combined in their actual usage by theologians today.

9 For a fuller understanding of Rahner's transcendentalism, see Rahner (1970), 287.

10 For Lonergan's work on method, see Lonergan (1972).

REFERENCES

Boersma, Hans. 2009. *Nouvelle théologie and Sacramental Ontology: A Return to Mystery*. Oxford: Oxford University Press. http://dx.doi.org/10.1093/acprof:oso/9780199229642.001.0001.

Daly, Gabriel. 1980. *Transcendence and Immanence: A Study in Catholic Modernism and Integralism*. Oxford: Clarendon Press.

Doran, Robert. 2012. *Missions and Processions*, vol. 1: The Trinity in History: A Theology of the Divine Missions. Toronto: University of Toronto Press.

Dulles, Avery. 1987. *Models of the Church*. New York: Doubleday.

– 1992. *Models of Revelation*. Maryknoll: Orbis.

Fumagalli, A. 1903. "Le indedie de una nuova scienza." *La Scuola Cattolica* 31: 400.

Gleason, Philip. 1999. *Contending with Modernity: Catholic Higher Education in the Twentieth Century*. Oxford: Oxford University Press.

Grant, Robert M., and David Tracy. 1984. *A Short History of the Interpretations of the Bible*. Philadelphia: Fortress Press.

Holstein, Henri. 1965. "Le Théologien de la foi." *Recherches de Science Religieuse* 53(3): 86–125.

Lonergan, Bernard. 1970. *Insight: A Study of Human Understanding*. New York: Philosophical Library.
– 1972. *Method in Theology*. New York: Herder & Herder.
Maritain, Jacques. 1946. *St Thomas Aquinas: Angel of the Schools*. Trans. J.F. Scanlan. London: Sheed and Ward.
McCool, Gerald. 1989a. *From Unity to Pluralism: The Internal Evolution of Thomism*. New York: Fordham University Press.
– 1989b. *Nineteenth-Century Scholasticism: The Search for a Unitary Method*. New York: Fordham University Press.
Nichols, Aidan. 1998. *Catholic Thought Since the Enlightenment: A Survey*. Pretoria: University of South Africa Press.
Ormerod, Neil. 2005. "A Dialectic Engagement with the Social Sciences in an Ecclesiological Context." *Theological Studies* 66(4): 815–40. http://dx.doi.org/10.1177/004056390506600404.
Radford Reuther, Rosemary. 1983. *Sexism and God-Talk: Toward a Feminist Theology*. Boston, MA: Beacon Press.
– 2005. *Integrating Ecofeminism, Globalization, and World Religions*. Toronto: Rowman & Littlefield.
Radford Reuther, Rosemary, ed. 2007. *Feminist Theologies: Legacy and Prospect*. Minneapolis: Fortress Press.
Rahner, Karl. 1970. "Transcendental Theology." In *Sacramentum Mundi: An Encyclopedia of Theology*, edited by Karl Rahner et al., 287–9. New York: Herder and Herder.
– 1972. "Some Critical Thoughts on 'Functional Specialties in Theology.'" In *Foundations of Theology: Papers from the International Lonergan Congress*, edited by Philip McShane, 194–6. Notre Dame: University of Notre Dame Press.
– 1974. "Reflections on Methodology in Theology." In *Theological Investigations*, vol. 1., translated by David Bourke, 68–114. New York: The Seabury Press.
Ratzinger, Joseph. 1995. *The Nature and Mission of Theology: Essays to Orient Theology in Today's Debates*. Translated by Adrian Walker. San Francisco: Ignatius Press.
Ricoeur, Paul. 1977. *The Rule of Metaphor: Multidisciplinary Studies of the Creation of Meaning in Language*. Toronto: University of Toronto Press.
– 1984–8. *Time and Narrative*. 3 vols. Translated by Kathleen McLaughlin and David Pellauer. Chicago: University of Chicago Press. http://dx.doi.org/10.7208/chicago/9780226713519.001.0001.
Schloesser, Stephen. 2006. "Against Forgetting: Memory, History, Vatican II." *Theological Studies* 67(2): 275–319. http://dx.doi.org/10.1177/004056390606700203.

Schüssler Fiorenza, Francis. 2011. "Systematic Theology: Tasks and Methods." In *Systematic Theology: Roman Catholic Perspectives*, 2nd ed., edited by Francis Schüssler Fiorenza and John P. Galvin, 1–78. Minneapolis: Fortress Press.

Shook, Laurence K. 1971. *Catholic Post-Secondary Education in English-Speaking Canada: A History*. Toronto: University of Toronto Press.

Tillich, Paul. 1951–63. *Systematic Theology*. Chicago: University of Chicago Press.

Tracy, David. 1981. *The Analogical Imagination: Christian Theology and the Culture of Pluralism*. New York: Crossroad Publishing.

– 1987. *Plurality and Ambiguity: Hermeneutics, Religion, Hope*. San Francisco: Harper and Row.

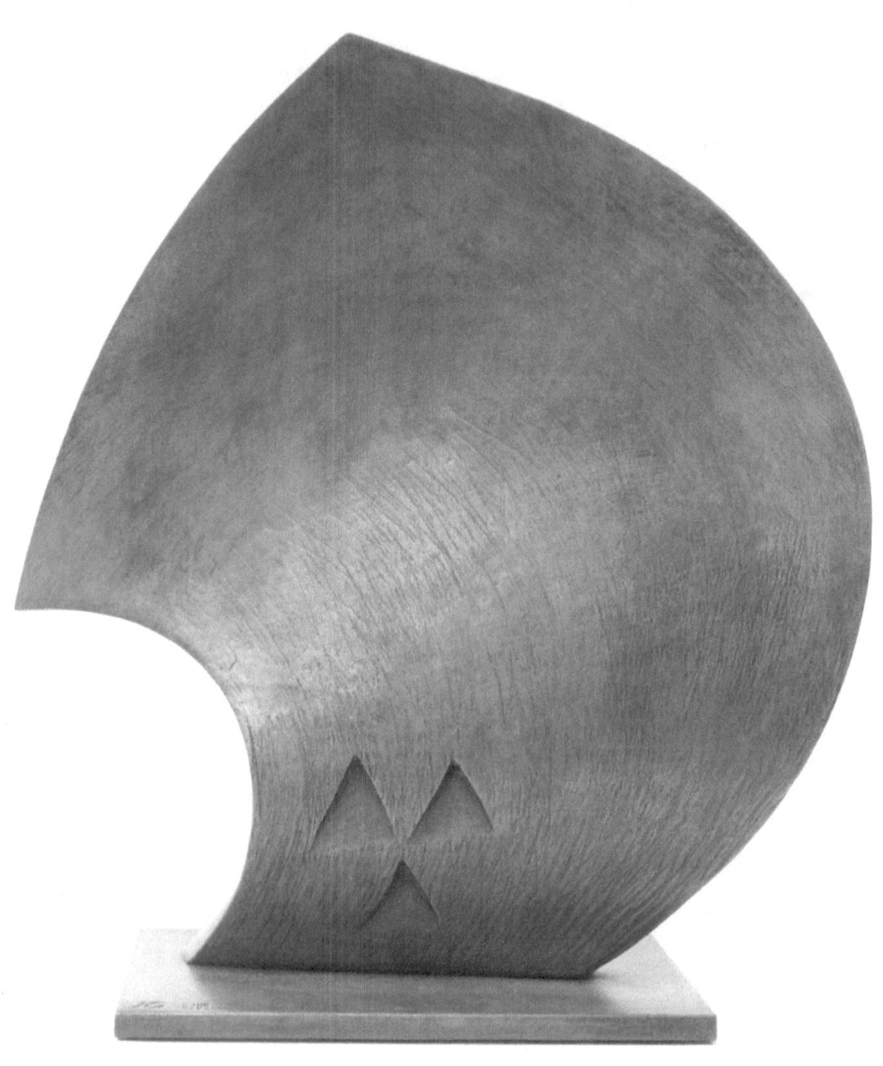

“Tu Melodía / Zure Doinua / Your Tune.” Sculpture by Joaquín Gogorza.

PART TWO

The Relationship between Church and State

2 Going to the Past: A *Longue Durée* Analysis of Catholic Education and the State in France

BERNARD HUGONNIER AND GEMMA SERRANO

Introduction

All religions have a natural interest in education. The Catholic Church is no exception. This was underlined by Pope Pius XI in the encyclical *Divini Illius Magistri* (31 December 1929), which stated:

> In fact, since education consists essentially of preparing man for what he must be and for what he must do here below, in order to attain the sublime end for which he was created, it is clear that there can be no true education which is not wholly directed to man's last end, and that in the present order of Providence, since God has revealed Himself to us in the Person of His Only Begotten Son, who alone is "the way, the truth and the life," there can be no ideally perfect education which is not Christian education.

The doctrine contained implicitly in this encyclical is threefold: first, Catholic education is indispensable to all human beings, otherwise they risk losing their faith; second, the mission of the Catholic Church is to provide such an education to all children; and third, parents who do not give their children a Catholic education may be betraying their faith.

The encyclical referred to above was published at a time when the desacralization of schools had already begun – hence the efforts by the Pope to stop this trend or at least slow it down. In addition, questions were being posed in some countries regarding the validity of the mission of the Catholic Church. This was notably the case in France, with regard to which the following question can be asked: Is there evidence that from its inception Catholic education provided education to *all* children, regardless of their social origin? The question is a valid one, because at the present time Catholic education in France mainly benefits students from affluent families. Hence these questions: Was this the case before? And why is it the case today? The following short history of Catholic education in France aims to address these specific questions.

This history is full of events and incidents. But three prominent dates stand out:

- The French Revolution of 1789 and its aftermath, during which the prominent role long played by the Catholic Church in French education was rejected.
- The 1905 Law, which set forth the separation of Church and state.
- The 1959 Debré Law, which recognized Catholic schools as part of the Republican education system and ended a long period of "school war."

Accordingly, this short history of Catholic education in France will be organized around these three dates.

From the *Ancien Régime* to the Revolution

In France, the period before the Revolution of 1789 is referred to as the *Ancien Régime*. Formal education was first established in France by Charlemagne, who became King of the Franks in 768. The educational system was centralized at first in a palace school and then eventually spread to monasteries. At that time and for the next several centuries, this form of education was a preserve of the elites.

The system remained elitist until the twelfth century, when it branched into two systems. The first of these provided education through small local primary schools was intended for working-class children (especially boys), who were taught how to read and write and to "know, love and serve God." The second was reserved for the nobility and for society's bourgeois elite, and offered a more thorough education (primary, secondary, and higher education) provided by tutors, often from the clergy. This education was mainly for boys. In both of these newer systems, the instructors were under the authority of a bishop. This two-tier system lasted until the sixteenth century.

After the Protestant Reformation that began in 1517, Protestant religion and education gained importance in several parts of France, such as Aquitaine. This spurred the Catholic Church during the Council of Trent (1545–63) to launch a Counter-Reformation. Among other things, the

Council decided to streamline the Church's institutions and to improve its administration; it also encouraged evangelization by the Catholic Church, in particular through the parishes; and, in response to the growing importance of Protestant education at that time, it granted the clergy more power to stimulate education through Catholic institutions.

In the mid-sixteenth century, educational activities increased, inspired by the Renaissance. Until that time, as noted earlier, education had been largely the preserve of the affluent. Towards the end of the sixteenth century, however, Saint Jean-Baptiste de La Salle created Free Church schools for poor children. Also, the Congregation of Brothers of Christian Schools introduced learning in classes rather than through individual instruction, and education in French rather than in Latin. These two innovations revolutionized education in France. Classroom education was immediately recognized as a much more effective and efficient system, one that also facilitated human relationships and thus provided a valuable social dimension. In the seventeenth century, the French language was not yet universal; many vernaculars were in use in different parts of France. Teaching in French – the language of the aristocracy and the middle class (one million people out of a total of 20 million) – was viewed as indispensable to nation-building and economic expansion.

Until the end of the seventeenth century, Catholic and Protestant schools coexisted. Then in 1695, Louis XIV abolished the "Edit de Nantes," a 1598 law that had extended Protestants the freedom to exercise their religion and to educate their children accordingly. This brought about the destruction of all Protestant schools. From that year on, the Catholic Church enjoyed a quasi-monopoly on education in France.

This long period from 768 to 1695 – almost a millennium – thus presents the following characteristics: At first, education was for the elite, the nobility. Over time, education gradually reached out to the bourgeoisie and to some of the working class, mainly boys. There were some attempts to provide education for the poor, but these efforts were rather rudimentary and were geographically limited. This sort of education was provided and supervised by the Catholic and Protestant Churches. In the early sixteenth century, the latter gained sufficient importance that it provoked a strong reaction from the former (during the Council of Trent). This competition between Catholics and Protestants continued until 1695, when Protestant education was prohibited; in effect, this awarded the Catholic Church a quasi-monopoly over education in France. At that time, education was viewed largely as a means to supply both state and Church with the bureaucratic officials they required.

From the Revolution to the 1905 Law of Separation between State and Church

The French Revolution of 1789 rejected the *Ancien Régime*, including the prominent role played by the Catholic Church in education. Education was not mentioned in the Declaration of the Rights of Man and of the Citizen; it was, however, included in the first constitution as follows: "Public instruction common to all citizens shall be created and organized, free as regard the education parts that are indispensible for all people and of whose establishments will be gradually distributed in relation with the organization of the kingdom."

Before the revolution, schools had been funded mainly by the Church's cash endowments and farmlands. The revolutionary government seized these endowments and properties and dismissed priests and Church-controlled teachers. Local governments were expected to take over, but many schools closed or struggled after a 90 per cent reduction in income.

Under the *Ancien Régime*, public education had been limited to primary education; at the time of the revolution, however, a system of public secondary schools (*écoles centrales*) was established. The government paid the teachers' salaries, and committees of teachers ran the schools. To train teachers, a normal school was founded in Paris. Some religious-based private (primary and secondary) schools were tolerated, but to attain an enviable position in the state bureaucracy, one had to have attended a public school.

The result was disastrous: municipalities rapidly ran out of money to pay teachers – that is, when they could find any: there were very few of them, and they were very poorly trained. In response, officially or not, religious orders began to offer an education with the same class bias as before the revolution – that is, education largely for the nobility and the bourgeoisie, and mostly for boys.

To address this problem, Napoleon signed an agreement (Concordat) with Pope Pius VII in 1802 that allowed some religious elementary schools to be re-established. However, they would have to share a significant amount of responsibility with local municipalities that were in charge of elementary schools. The most significant change was that for the first time in French history, elementary schools were now under state control, which made teachers civil servants, paid and supervised by public authorities. Indeed, the Napoleonic decree of 1808 established a rigorous state monopoly in education, over vigorous protests from Catholic bishops, who wanted freedom of instruction.

All education establishments now had to be authorized by the Imperial University, a body created by Napoleon in 1808 and charged exclusively with public education. The law declared that "no one may open a school or teach publicly without being a member of the Imperial University and a graduate of one of its faculties." This was a compromise with those who wanted to suppress all private schools.

In the decades following the Napoleonic era (1815–48), education policy was highly politicized between those who wanted schools to be controlled by the Catholics again and those who contended that education must be secular, free of Church interference. During the Second Republic, the Guizot Law of 1833 led to the creation of primary schools for boys (public or private) in every French commune – a crucial expansion of education (Gontard 1959). Inevitably, this resulted in poor and working-class students attending public schools while students from affluent families attended private Catholic schools, which also held a monopoly over girls' education.

In the 1850s, the Falloux Laws extended the Guizot Law: now, every town had to have a girls' school; in effect, this established universal primary schools in France. The same laws also allowed Catholic orders to supervise some primary schools. In addition, the laws gave the right to teach without a diploma to the clergy and members of ecclesiastical orders. Finally, the laws placed private schools under the authority not only of the mayor but also of the priest. By 1865, private schools, both lay and Catholic, at the secondary level were enrolling more pupils than the public system. The Falloux Laws had brought about an era of cooperation between Church and state that would last until the Ferry Laws.

The Separation between Church and School

The radicals who passed laws during the Third Republic in 1881 and 1882 contended that a principal reason for the German victory during the Franco-Prussian War of 1870 had been the higher quality of German education. France's education minister, Jules Ferry, an anti-clerical, launched what is remembered to this day as a revolution: free, compulsory, secular education. Religious education was forbidden in all schools,[1] and religious orders could no longer teach in them. In addition, the state appropriated funds from religious schools to build more public schools. In this way, the Ferry Laws created the modern republican school system.

The importance of the Ferry Laws should not be underestimated. When they were first passed, both the Catholic Church and employers were strongly opposed to them: at that time, eight out of ten French workers were engaged in agriculture, coal mining, or public works – activities that did not require literacy. "Is it not enough to listen to their boss's instructions during the week and the priest's sermon on Sunday?," asked those who opposed the new laws. Ferry and the Republicans wanted to end all the privileges attached to social status and to erase the inequalities in education that stemmed from social origin (Ozouf 1963). Their objective was equal access for all to all social goods. In their view, the sons of labourers should have access to the same schools as the sons of magistrates, and the latter should learn about the lives of the former. For Ferry, a "Republican education" was the only way to build national unity (Meirieu and Guirand 1997). The Catholic Church, for its part, rejected as unacceptable the collective emancipation and the promotion of individualism implied by the Ferry Laws. In the aftermath, the positions of the two camps became more strongly entrenched, while more moderate Republicans gradually shifted their support towards the most anti-clerical Republicans. It was clear to Ferry and his supporters that the time had come to separate the Church from France's schools (Chevallier 1981). This date (1881–2) marks a key moment in the history of Catholic education in France.

The Separation of Church and State: The 1901 Law

During the first decade of the twentieth century, the confrontation between Republicans and Catholics reached a climax. In March 1904, after intense pressure from the Republicans, a law was introduced prohibiting members of religious orders from teaching. This led to the closing of 14,404 out of a total of 16,904 "religious" schools. As a consequence, in July 1904, France and the Vatican broke off diplomatic relations. In December 1905 the law on the separation between Church and state was passed.

This law, which reflected the strongly anti-clerical climate of the time, was especially impactful in that it led to the closing of most religious schools, notably Catholic schools, which had always played a crucial role in French education. The law set out the secularist principle (*principe de laïcité*), while stipulated that the state should stay neutral in religious affairs, that citizens should be free to practise any religion they wanted, and that the state was to exercise power over the Church.[2]

The secularist principle meant, first, that religion was to be confined to the private domain and that an individual's freedom to belong (or not) to a religious group was guaranteed. It also meant that the state would not formally recognize any religious group, nor would it provide financial support to any religion. In addition, it meant that religion would not be part of the public school curriculum. Finally, it meant that no religious insignia were to be displayed in public schools. However, the law did set out that the state could financially support private schools, provided that they did not force religious education on students or discriminate between students on the basis of their religion (there was an exception for the Alsace-Moselle region).[3]

In February 1906, Pope Pius X responded by condemning the separation principle; this led the French government to prohibit any religious ceremony. This tension would last many years, with neither side willing to compromise. Finally, during the First World War, with the Vatican's growing acceptance of the situation, a sort of reconciliation between Catholics and the Republic took hold. This made possible the re-establishment of diplomatic relations in 1921 and a long-lasting "controlled" peace between the two camps.

Tensions rose again in 1945, after the Second World War, when the French legislature passed a law that ended financial support to religious schools. These tensions would remain until 1959, when the Debré Law ended the school war, which by then had lasted 170 years.

The School War Examined

This short history of Catholic education in France can be configured as a few key questions around which most of the disputes took place: Should public and private Catholic schools be allowed to teach confessional religious education? Could teachers be clerical? Could private schools be financially supported by the state? Could private schools impose tuition fees? Should state or Church authorities supervise private schools? Should private school teachers have the same background as public school teachers?

There were essentially three camps (see Table 2.1): the anti-clericals, the Republicans, and the Catholics. Most of the anti-clericals were revolutionary leaders, who were not necessarily from the poorest sectors of the population. They contended that the Church had always been the ally of the *Ancien Régime* and that it was time to reject theological and ecclesiastical authority and to replace it with universal reason, which should now be the guide for all behaviour. In their view, no compromise could ever be found with the Church. Their first preference was that there be no

Table 2.1 Summary of positions in the school war, 1789–1959

	Anti-clericals	Republicans	Catholics
Should public and private Catholic schools be allowed to teach confessional religious education?	No	In public schools: no. In private schools: yes.	Yes
Could teachers be clerical?	No	In public schools: no. In private schools: yes until 1867; no after that.	Yes
Could private schools be financially supported by the State?	No	Yes until 1867; no after that.	Yes
Could private schools impose tuition fees?	No	Yes	Yes
Should state or Church authorities supervise private schools?	State	Both until the Ferry Law; state only after.	Church
Should the state or the Church train private school teachers?	State	Both until the Ferry Law; state only after.	Church

Catholic (or any other religious) education in France. Any schools operated by religious groups should be strictly supervised and controlled by the state, with no financial support; furthermore, all teachers should be non-religious, and no religious education should be provided.

The Republicans were pragmatists. They quickly realized that the revolution, as far as education was concerned, did not have the means to finance its dreams: the municipalities had no money, there were no schools to train new teachers, there were not enough volunteers to become teachers, and there was not enough money for schools' upkeep. At the same time, religious teachers could be paid much less; also, they were available and willing to teach and had the vocation; also, they were well trained, experienced, and of proven competence. Besides all of that, religious orders provided education for girls, who had been largely neglected by public schools. To cap things off, religious orders offered free education to poor children (Mayeur 1981). So the Republicans tended to compromise, and to be much less stringent than the anti-clericals.

The anti-clericals and the Catholics (see Table 2.1) did not modify their positions over time; the Republicans did. For instance, regarding state financial support for private schools, the Republicans favoured it until the 1867 law but opposed it thereafter. And the same situation prevailed regarding whether teachers could be clerical. Again, the Republicans changed their position regarding the supervision of private schools and the training of private school teachers: in both cases, after the Ferry Law in 1867, the Republicans decided that these should be the purview of the state.

The school war was also a war of words and attitudes: in public textbooks, the name of God was expurgated; a public teacher was not expected to attend church, and if he did, a promotion might be problematic; and a public teacher could not send his children to a Catholic school. According to the other side, a school without God was a school of the devil. Such a school deceived children's intelligence, perverted their will, and distorted their consciousness.

The 1959 Debré Law and the Situation Since

In 1959 the Debré Act was voted into law. It allowed the French government to sub-contract secular instruction to private schools that had signed an agreement with the government. Under this contract, private institutions, religious or not, could open schools, which the state would again subsidize provided that they hired quasi-civil servants as teachers and respected the national curriculum.

Three main circumstances explain the change in climate that enabled the Debré Law to be passed in 1959:

- First, the confrontation between the state and the Catholic Church with regard to education had gone on for so long that many felt a compromise should be found, to improve relations.
- Second, the Debré Law offered a compromise. On the one hand, the right of the Catholic Church to establish private schools and to develop its own educational project was recognized. On the other, strict conditions ensured that teachers in those schools would be quasi-civil servants, that such schools would implement the national curriculum, that religious education would be not mandatory, and that Catholic schools would not discriminate against students on the basis of their religion. Without those strict conditions, the Republicans would not have accepted the compromise. The Catholic Church was wise to accept the terms of the contract.
- Third, France's situation in the world had changed: the colonial era was ending and the French Empire was in decline; a new Europe was being built, with a new vision of education; and doubts were rising that communism would solve the problems now faced by the education system (Hippolyte 2009).

Were the objectives of the Debré Law achieved? Resoundly yes, if the objectives were to end the education wars between the Republicans and the traditionalists; to improve the quality of education; to enhance cooperation between the public and private systems; and, finally, to have Catholic education accept the secularist principle whereby it would not impose religious education in its schools, was obliged to accept all students irrespective of their religion, and had to accept their liberty of conscience (Bellengier 2009).

Since the Debré Law and the Vatican Council, Catholic schools have been digesting this law, as well as the conciliar declaration *Gravissimum Educationis*, which specified its own "particular" missions. In 2009, the fiftieth anniversary of the Debré Law, those concerned (the Catholic education system, the episcopacy, historians, legal experts, and the major witnesses of such change) raised the question anew, launching research into the reception of the law and of the conciliar declaration. So, what can be said today, both about these receptions and about what remains to be accomplished?

For all the differences in perspective, analyses of the relationship between state and private education[4] institutions are in almost complete agreement that the law brought an end to the school war, and that for parents, denomination is no longer the main criterion when they choose a school for their children. The ensuing development of Catholic education has raised questions about the resulting contractual relationship. Thus, given the tensions generated by the murky legal notion of "particular quality," some have voiced concerns about the logic of separation and competition.

These observations question the specificity of Catholic schools, since the gap between private and public seems to have been reduced. This brings to the surface existing social divisions, as well as the difference between "good schools" and others. Moreover, the mutual ignorance between actors in the state school system and those in the Catholic school system underscores the need for a rapprochement and for a sharing of educational practices. This mutual ignorance is even more alarming when it comes to educational traditions.

On the fiftieth anniversary of the Debré Law,[5] the report *State and Private Schools after Debré* reached the following conclusions regarding its implementation and some changes observed in Catholic education.

Appeasement in Conflicts over the Debré Law

Researchers and experts all agree: the Debré Law was a political compromise. The result was not what had been hoped for, and at first glance, discontent on both sides seemed likely to undermine its implementation. Nevertheless, it helped resolve educational issues and halted the decline of private schools, thus becoming – thanks to its longevity – a kind of "shared legacy of the nation"[6] as well as an "insurance for the future" (Girard 2009, 16). The changes made to it over more than half a century did not alter its general framework.[7] Some attempts to revise that framework could have led us to believe that schools would re-engage in warfare. Those attempts failed; they did, however, serve as a reminder of how fragile the balance was (Langouet 2012; Toulemonde 1988; Battut, Join-Lambert, and Vandermeesrch 1995).

Indeed, the logic of competition and mutual ignorance still holds, despite exceptions such as the involvement of teachers and representatives of private schools on examination panels and the use of private facilities as examination centres: "the legal and regulatory change is complex but, as a whole, is leading towards separation, whereas the sociological and cultural change leads towards rapprochement" (Nau, 2011).

Denomination Does Not Determine Family Preference

There has been a profound change: it seems that parents no longer base their choice of school on denominational factors, as was the case when the law was passed. Instead, they exercise freedom: "in such a context, where the religious question is no longer central regarding collective affiliations and identities, secularity solely reduced to educational use might have shown its face from another time. French society does not regard school, public and private education, as it used to. The issue of liberal education has above all become a question of freedom, of fundamental freedom, that one must stand up for" (De Labarre 2010; Institut CSA 2009; Perrineau 2009, 61–3).

Although terms such as quality, attentiveness, close supervision, individual follow-up, discipline, tolerance, and rigour help define Catholic schools, all still question the religious specificity of such an education and the apparent dilution of its identity.

Agnès van Zanten distinguishes between three choices of orientation. Schools can focus on reflexive development, instrumentation, or the child's blossoming. The latter two choices view the Catholic school as a harbour in troubled times, a place of excellence that supports personal development in a calm, homogeneous environment. Also, the parents' cultural, social, and religious views are carefully considered (Van Zanten 2012). Parents' associations acknowledge that "school zapping" and "school shopping" influence their choices. They also point out that the sociological and qualitative gaps between schools are greater than the distinction between public and private (Delhaye et al. 2011).

Among Catholic schools, "family loyalty and disloyalty" (Toulemonde 2011, 1181–6) gauges the tensions among the institution's mission, its management, and the market (Da Costa and Van Zanten 2011, 305). These tensions lead us to consider that the success of Catholic schools with regard to families' choices can foster educational and social segregation. As Prost (2013, 15) writes: "Religion is diluted. Social superiority remains, hardly reduced. Despite the wide diversity of its schools and local environments – certainly wider than that of public schools – private education, as a whole, cannot escape its legacy. To me, this hallmark, confirmed by the use families of privileged background make of the [Catholic school], prevents them from playing a direct role in the reduction of inequalities."

It is important to ask why Catholic schools have been popular and successful. Many parents clearly recognize that the Catholic school tradition is good for their children, even when they don't fully understand why. What, then, accounts for the quality of those schools?[8] Can it be explained solely by their finances, by how they recruit their staff and choose their pupils, or by how they train their teachers? These questions are all relevant.

The Development of Catholic Education

At the start of the 2013 school year, France's Catholic education system comprised 8,970 schools and 2,042,588 pupils.[9] According to some, the unique qualities that French education laws allow these schools are largely a function of the centralized system within which these schools operate. According to Toulemonde,

> the "individual" autonomy of each establishment tends to be limited to the benefit of collective decisions taken by "private education" and its executives: a powerful pyramidal structure, parallel to that of the state administration, tends to be set up. We witness a tendency opposite to the change public education is undergoing, that is to say: private education, after a phase of extreme decentralization and autonomy of its establishments, is now in a phase of a certain "centralization," whereas public education, after undergoing complete centralization, now encounters a phase of decentralization and autonomy of its establishments. (2009, 1171)

The centralization/decentralization conundrum also raises the problem of teachers' training. Specifically, what impact does it have on the teaching profession and, more to the point, on how the different systems recruit their teachers? Worth noting here is that Catholic education, although it serves different educational communities, is marked by a shared spirit. As Berruer notes, "Catholic education is not a hierarchy where school principals would be managers in charge of executing orders coming from a superior. The School Principal is the facilitator of the educative community in order for each actor to be able to assume his/her own prerogatives" (2009, 33).

"Proper Function"

The murky legal notion of "proper function" has generated controversy in public debate, as well as in Catholic schools themselves. It is still being debated, raising questions about the link between "proper function" and the principles of secularity, neutrality of education, and the responsibility of the subject.

Article 1 of the Debré Law states: "In private establishments that have signed the appropriate contracts, teaching subject to associate agreement is under state control. While retaining its proper function, the establishment must provide teaching in total respect of freedom of conscience. All children, with no distinction of origin, opinion or belief, have access to this."[10] What, then, are the different conceivable hermeneutics?

A first reading of the above article distinguishes sharply between two obligations – to teach in a way that completely respects freedom of conscience, and to welcome everyone – and the proper function. Teaching is to be secular and neutral (although the latter is not mentioned in the law), and proper function is to be expressed in the world view of the establishment, although it is "outside" teaching per se.

But who is accountable for each part? The proper function comes under the jurisdiction of the mission expressed to the schools by the Church, while requirements related to teaching itself fall under the agreement signed with the state. This interpretation, which assigns a double-responsibility to Catholic schools – that of the mission, and that of the agreement – is fertile ground for disagreements, contradictions, oppositions, harmony, compromise, and so on.

Because of this distinction, some posit the following: that the "proper function" contradicts the law's provisions; that Catholic schools, because of this, as they evolve with society, encounter difficulty following the

Church's instructions; and that bishops connive to regain the control that the state has long been pulling from their grasp.[11]

The "Proper Function" in French Catholic Education

How has Catholic education interpreted and responded to its mission based on the law? Highly pertinent here is paragraph 8 of the Vatican II declaration *Gravissimum Educationis*:

> But its proper function is to create for the school community a special atmosphere animated by the Gospel spirit of freedom and charity, to help youth grow according to the new creatures they were made through baptism as they develop their own personalities, and finally to order the whole of human culture to the news of salvation so that the knowledge the students gradually acquire of the world, life and man is illumined by faith. So indeed the Catholic school, while it is open, as it must be, to the situation of the contemporary world, leads its students to promote efficaciously the good of the earthly city and also prepares them for service in the spread of the Kingdom of God, so that by leading an exemplary apostolic life they become, as it were, a saving leaven in the human community.

Gravissimum Educationis did not generate a passionate debate, even though the definition of the "proper function" is to be found here. The fundamental principles of Christian education amounted to an extension of other texts on education, in particular *Divini illius Magistri* (Casella 2007; Hubert 1995).

The Declaration did not cause a schism in how Catholic education was perceived in France, either before or after its promulgation. Christianity's presence in education, as a means to provide a vital service to society, has raised fundamental theological questions: What *is* the Christian mission? And how can Christianity affirm its identity while acting in a plural world? All of the texts produced by Vatican II tried to answer these questions. But the purpose of this chapter is not to review the reception of *Gravissimum Educationis* in France or the impact of educational questions on Vatican II as a whole (Grace 2013); it is, rather, to determine which pastoral application and which interpretation of "proper function" is now being promoted by the French Catholic education.

The educational statute of 1992 has inspired a multitude of interpretations, depending on how one reads it (Statut de l'Enseignement Catholique). A straightforward reading of the foreword would have us distinguish between two entities in Catholic education: the civil structure and the Christian institution (no. 1). The civil body is similar to any educational institution (dedicated to the nation and to society, referring to the law of 1959, no. 2). The "proper function" (no. 3) is given an ecclesial definition, which, in nos. 4 and 5, leads us to an educational project that must meet the Catholic expectations of the bishop and of those schools where the educational community, drawing on Christian faith, is both part of the educational project and involved in Church service (no. 6), and knows its responsibilities (no. 7). According to this straightforward reading, the Catholic school is an ecclesial subject that furthers the national interest. These two organisms are not antagonistic, given that the ecclesial body "institutionally takes part in the nation's responsibility towards teaching and education."

But when we distinguish between two services – service dedicated to the Church (no. 6), and service dedicated to the nation (no. 2) – the key to our interpretation may lie in the complicated interweaving of these two services, which could possibly dilute one to the benefit of the other. According to this reading, the "proper function" would be up to the establishments. It would be an option held by Catholic education, disconnected from the service of the nation. Catholic schools, as they apply the proper function, might be required to consider pastoral care as this free place outside the bounds of education. This is a position that no. 6 of the 1992 statute (service of the church) fights against: "the Catholic school is therefore by itself a place of evangelism, of authentic apostolate, not by means of pastoral activities, parallel or extracurricular, but thanks to the very nature of its action directly oriented towards educating the Christian personality."

The cultural transformations that followed the Second World War changed a "pastoral of transmission" or "pastoral supervision" (which used to prevail in schools where the majority of pupils were believers) into a "sowing pastoral." This refers to a practice of evangelism that consists in the seeding of ground that is then left to sprout on its own. The practice also becomes one of a "welcoming pastoral care" that imposes nothing, thus threatening to "undervalue[e] the mystery of faith."

The introduction to the 1992 text (no. 2) states that "Catholic education cannot renounce the freedom to offer the message and demonstrate the values of Christian education. It should be clear to all that displaying and offering is not tantamount to imposing." We can see here the "pastoral of offering" that, in 1996, bishops would invite from Christians (Les évêques de France 1996). This offering differs from implanting; rather, it looks like an initiation to the Catholic faith.

A final reading places the educational project (no. 4) at the centre of the educational process. It is face to face with nos. 1 and 7 (civil structure and Christian institution), nos. 2 and 6 (service to the nation and to the Church), and nos. 3 and 5 (specific characteristics and educative community). The interpretation key is not bifocal; rather, it places at the centre the educative goal as the "unifying principle," and reiterates that loyalty to the project relates to the Gospels and to the teaching of the Catholic Church (Moog 2012, 85–9).

What about the statute of June 2013? Does it lend itself to plural readings? From what pastoral context did it inherit? Or was it the driving force? Contrary to that of 1992, the regulation was written jointly by the bishops and Catholic education officials and completely rebuilds the latter. It contains six parts, of which we will consider only the first, "The Catholic School in the Educative Mission of the Church," which serves as the foreword.

At first glance, the elements that distinguish the 2013 from the 1992 statute are the *absent* ones: there is no mention of a double service or of a double structure within the school; the law of 1959 is not explicitly mentioned; and the expression "proper function" appears only once and its definition is altered. In the 2013 regulation, the proper function is referred to as "qualified educative offer" (no. 18). What reinterpretation of the law and of the statute of 1992 can be made from this? We mention three elements.

First, Article 17 states that "the ecclesial nature of the school is inscribed in the heart of its identity as school institution." This "permeates and models each moment of its educative action, is a basic part of its own identity and a focal point of its mission." As described in this chapter, one can no longer assert that there are two missions or two organisms in Catholic education, each with a discrete duty: one towards the society and the nation, the other towards the Church. The reading of the 1959 law includes teaching within the "proper function." Hence, the educative mission and the school institution considered as an ecclesial subject constitute a whole.

The 2013 regulation provides an alternative definition of proper function: there is an educative program qualified by the Gospels. Article 18 states: "This qualified educative program is formulated in the educative project of each school; it constitutes what the law designates as the specific characteristic."

Sections 3, 4, and 5 of that section describe the qualified educative program: its foundation, mode, and means of transmission, as well as its nature. The source and origin of this educative program is Christ, who is the foundation of the educative project (Articles 22–5). As for the mode, it refers to a program that does not separate education from Christ. This reference to Christ cannot be viewed as outside school routine, since the school is founded on Christ. Thus, unity of such an educative project is based on the non-separation between "learning time and education time, between time for knowledge and time for wisdom. The diverse disciplines not only represent knowledge to acquire but also values to assimilate and truths to discover" (Article 21).

The means to implement such educational programs are provided by various actors in society: society (i.e., the local diocese), the school principal, and the Church all call everyone to serve this task (Articles 33–5), whose intent is to uphold the dignity of the individual, and also social cohesion.

Service here is Christological, in its ecclesial meaning. We are no longer in a reading that would confine the associate school and make it different from what it is: an ecclesial subject that founds its educative act in Christ and, in its public aspects, dedicates itself to people by accomplishing services of general interest.

The Educative Proposition Legitimates the Association Agreement with Educational Public Service

Neutrality, freedom of conscience, and openness to all pupils are all part of the approach taken by Catholic education. Catholic schools by their very nature are open to all pupils (Article 38). The Gospel is linked to freedom of conscience (Article 37); for the sake of love of truth, it develops critical thinking. In this way, Catholic schools contribute to and take part in educating the nation. As partners, they cooperate and maintain a dialogue with the other parties, all of whom respect one another's roles (Articles 12–18).

Do these aspects modify our interpretation of the 1992 statute? Possibly they do not, because broadening our awareness of the relationship between the school and its founder, Christ, does not cause a rupture. Continuity is also ensured through Catholics' interpretation of the phrase in the 1959 law "while keeping its proper function," which, for them, includes the school's teachings.

Regarding the pastoral approach, according to one sociological analysis, some wondered whether the present process would be part of a Catholicism of identity rather than what is called a Catholicism of dialogue (Portier 2012). We are no longer in the era of "the end of Catholicism" (Hervieu-Léger 2003; Roy 2012). The fading of religion but not of belief (Gauchet 2014) raises new questions about the role of Catholic education in society.

The main consequence of the Debré Law has been that Catholic education is now well integrated into French society. Education in Catholic schools today is highly regarded and is sought after by many parents, from all religions, who appreciate these schools' programs, their climate and discipline, the quality of their teachers, and the higher performance of their students.

The law that provided parents with school choice increased social stratification, for private schools had a tendency to select students from privileged classes. This provoked a sharp reaction by the French left in 1984, leading 10 million citizens to sign a petition to repeal the Debré Law. The government attempted to reverse the law by proposing the creation of a "large educational public service" that would encompass public *and* private schools. But after huge demonstrations in June 1984, it withdrew the proposal.

Since 1984, the relationship between the republican and Catholic education systems in France has not changed, apart from a law passed in 2004 that banned the wearing of any "ostentatious religious symbols" – such as veils, crosses, or turbans[12] – in state schools, and a 2013 Ministry of Education charter, displayed in every school, that has reaffirmed the secularist principle. Notably, the charter recalled that pupils must be "protected from all forms of religious proselytising."[13]

Over the years, the Catholic Church has increased the number of schools in its system and welcomed more and more students. In 2015, 16.9 per cent of French students attended a private school (i.e., 2,051,700 out of 12,140,800). There were 8,435 Catholic schools in France, compared to 282 Jewish schools and 30 Muslim schools.

Conclusion

Catholic schools were first established in the sixth century and gradually expanded until by 1695 they enjoyed a monopoly, after Protestant schools were banned. They reached their peak of influence at the time of the French Revolution. Since then, relations between the state and Catholic education have been difficult, to say the least. "School wars" prevailed for 170 years among the anti-clericals, the Republicans, and the Catholics. Those wars reached a first climax at the time of the Revolution in 1789, when the government seized the endowments and properties of the Church and dismissed priests and Church-controlled teachers. A second peak occurred in 1881–2 when the Ferry Law established free, compulsory, and secular education in France, leading to a separation between the Catholic Church and education. This was followed by a 1905 law that formally separated the state and the Church. The school wars continued until the Debré Law in 1959, which, born out of a difficult compromise, brought the conflicts an end. Today, Catholic schools are well established in France (they teach 17 per cent of all school students), and their quality is fully recognized.

Yet Catholic schools still face challenges. Two main issues can be identified. The first is to overcome the weight of secularism – the "holy ignorance" of religions within schools. This will be addressed through sessions on religious culture, an awakening to faith as well as an investment in inter-cultural and inter-religious dialogue. According to the document "Educating to Intercultural Dialogue in Catholic Schools,"

> Education contains a central challenge for the future: to allow various cultural expressions to co-exist and to promote dialogue so as to foster a peaceful society. These aims are achieved in various stages: (1) discovering the multicultural nature of one's own situation; (2) overcoming prejudices by living and working in harmony; and (3) educating oneself "by means of the other" to a global vision and a sense of citizenship. Fostering encounters between different people helps to create mutual understanding, without meaning a loss of one's own identity. (Congregation for Catholic Education 2013).

In France, this is a complex situation because the implementation of the principle of *laïcité* is scrupulously monitored by the state and by civil society.

The second challenge is the following: the main characteristics of French Catholic schools, since their introduction fifteen centuries ago, has been that these schools tend to attract mostly wealthy students. This contrasts with what could be expected from them – for example, what Saint Jean-Baptiste de La Salle did in the Free Church schools for children from poor families. This should change, not only because the role of the Church is to support the disadvantaged but also because in educating these students, the schools would be playing a role in their evangelization, which is often lacking. In other words, one can ask: Have Catholic schools, through the centuries, with some exceptions, been fulfilling their mission? Should they not have a distinct preference for the poor instead of for the rich?[14]

For that reason, the education offered by Catholic schools should be made more accessible to disadvantaged students. Accordingly, Catholic schools should establish themselves in the areas where these students live – that is, away from city centres, in poorer neighbourhoods. However, this is not necessarily permitted by the state. Catholic schools could also try to attract disadvantaged students, at the risk of displeasing affluent parents and losing some wealthy students – but is that contrary to the schools' real interest? A major consequence of this situation is that these schools do not contribute enough to changing the elite of society; on the contrary, for some people, they contribute to its reproduction, which is denounced by highly recognized sociologists in France. Hence, not only do Catholic schools at present not provide sufficient help to poorer students or contribute enough to their evangelization, but they also help the privileged secure the best education. This call is a challenge for the new millennium:

> The girls from poor families that were taught by the Ursuline nuns in the 15th Century, the boys that Saint Joseph of Calasanz saw running and shouting through the streets of Rome, those that De la Salle came across in the villages of France, or those that were offered shelter by Don Bosco, can be found again among those who have lost all sense of meaning in life and lack any type of inspiring ideal, those to whom no values are proposed and who do not know the beauty of faith, who come from families which are broken and incapable of love, often living in situations of material and spiritual poverty, slaves to the new idols of a society, which, not infrequently, promises them only a future of unemployment and marginalization. To these new poor the Catholic school turns in a spirit of love. Spurred on by the aim of offering to all, and especially to the poor and marginalized, the opportunity of an education, of training for a job, of human and Christian formation, it can and must find, in the context of the old and new forms of poverty, that original synthesis of ardour and fervent dedication which is a manifestation of Christ's love for the poor, the humble, the masses seeking for truth. (Congregation for Catholic Education 1997)

NOTES

1 According to Article 2 of the 1881 law, "the public primary schools will hold one day free, apart from Sunday, allowing parents to give, if they wish, their children a religious education outside from school buildings. Religious education is optional in private schools."

2 The secularist principle was so important in France that it was laid down in the 1958 Constitution of the Fifth Republic, which states in its first article: "France shall be an indivisible, secular, democratic and social Republic. It shall ensure the equality of all citizens before the law, without distinction of origin, race or religion. It shall respect all beliefs. It shall be organized on a decentralized basis."

3 In Germany and Britain, religious education is more or less a standard ingredient of the curriculum. In both countries, religious moral issues are considered to be essential in order to educate citizens and build up identity. In Britain, religious education is compulsory and is mainly based on Christianity, but other religions are also recognized and taught. By contrast, in Germany, the idea of a Christian genealogy shines through.

4 Different expressions are in use: private education, private establishment under contract, private establishment associated with the state by contract, Catholic educational establishment, establishment for Catholic education, Catholic school, Catholic education, and so on. What is at stake in using one or the other is quite clear. In this chapter, the expression belonging to the ecclesial field will be used indistinctly and predominantly: "Catholic education" or "Catholic school."

5 There are very few studies. Some of them are Edmond Vandermeersch, *École: Église et laïcité: La rencontre des deux France. Souvenirs autour de la loi Debré* (Paris: L'harmattan, 2008); Bruno Poucet, ed., *L'état et l'enseignement privé: L'application de la loi Debré (1959)* (Rennes: Presses Universitaires de Rennes, 2011); Poucet, *La liberté sous contrat: Une histoire de l'enseignement privé* (Paris: Fabert, 2009); Bernard Toulemonde, "Le cinquantenaire de la loi Debré: Qu'est devenu l'enseignement privé?," *Revue de Droit Public* 5 (2011): 1158–87; Enseignement Catholique, ed., *50 ans après le vote de la loi Debré: 25 après le vote de la loi Rocard. Histoire, actualité et perspective*, Actes des journées Académiques et des journées nationales 2009/2010, 17 December 2009; Liberté d'enseignement et participation aux politiques publiques d'éducation: 17 décembre 2009, La Sorbonne, http://www.enseignement-catholique.fr/ec/divers/18355-libertenseignement-et-participation-aux-politiques-publiques-dcation-17-dmbre-2009.

6 "This point ought to be firmly reminded historically, since fifty years later one tends to forget it: the Debré bill does not belong to anyone, or rather, the Debré bill belongs to neither part other than that of the Republic which imposes it on them in order to make nation and consolidate the State." Bruno Poucet, "La loi Debré une histoire en question," in *L'état et l'enseignement privé: L'application de la loi Debré (1959)*, ed. Poucet (Rennes: Presses Universitaires de Rennes, 2011), 31.

7 Regarding law issues, ruptures, and modifications of contractual logic, as well as the return and renewal of the Debré bill in the 1980s, see Bruno Poucet, *L'enseignement privé en France* (Paris: PUF, 2012), 49–74.

8 "The 8,970 Catholic schools that in France provide nearly 20 per cent of students with schooling (that's to say 2,042,588 students) are not unanimously chosen for their Catholic characteristics. However, the parents underline the following appealing factors of our establishments: the attention paid to each person, the quality of the support given to children and youth, the seriousness of the supervision, the place given to the parents and the human quality of our establishments. This shows that, without being aware of it, many parents appreciate the strong points of an educative tradition based on the consideration of each and every one. This also compels schools to question their identity and their nature." Answer of the Catholic school to the questionnaire of the Congregation for the Education of the Faith, July 2014.

9 See http://www.enseignement-catholique.fr/ec/images/stories/hs/eca359-chiffres-cles-2013-2014.pdf.

10 See http://www.legifrance.gouv.fr/affichTexte.do?cidTexte=JORFTEXT000000693420.

11 The debate following Toulemonde's presentation demonstrates this point. Bernard Toulemonde, "La question du contrôle et de la gestion des enseignants du privé," in *L'état et l'enseignement privé: L'application de la loi Debré (1959)*, ed. Bruno Poucet (Rennes: Presses Universitaires de Rennes, 2011), 113–29.

12 See http://www.theguardian.com/world/2013/jul/22/frances-headscarf-war-attack-on-freedom.

13 See http://www.telegraph.co.uk/news/worldnews/europe/france/10296500/France-unveils-controversial-secularism-charter.html.

14 According to François Dubet, there is in France a certain preference for inequality: "While ancient school inequalities depended on large social and cultural categories as well as on unequal access to secondary education, new school inequalities are due to small initial inequalities that mount up and multiply to create great inequalities at the end of the pathway." Thus, the "inequality preference" is to be countered by a preferential option for the poor.

REFERENCES

Battut, Jean, Christian Join-Lambert, and Edmond Vandermeesrch. 1995. *1984: La guerre scolaire a bien eu lieu.* Paris: Desclée de Brower.

Bellengier, Ferdinand. 2009. *"Une loi d'apaissement." Enseignement catholique actualités.* Hors-série Novembre.

Berruer, Claude. 2009. "Le caractère propre comme contribution spécifique de l'enseignement catholique au service public d'éducation." In *In 50 ans après le vote de la loi Debré: 25 après le vote de la loi Rocard. Histoire, actualité et perspective*, edited by Enseignement Catholique. Paris: ECA.

Casella, Francesco. 2007. "Punti nodali della riflessione pedagogica dalla *Divini Ilius Magistri* alla *Gravissimum Educationis*." *Orientamenti pedagogici* 54(2): 293–304.

Chevallier, Pierre. 1981. *La séparation de l'Eglise et de l'Ecole*. Paris: Fayard.

Congregation for Catholic Education. 1997. *The Catholic School on the Threshold of the Third Millennium*, no. 15. Vatican City.

– 2013. *Educating to Intercultural Dialogue in Catholic Schools: Living in Harmony for a Civilization of Love*. Vatican City: Introduction.

CSA. 2009. *50 ans après la loi Debré, quel regard les français portent-ils sur la liberté d'enseignement?* http://csa.eu/index.aspx?recherche=les%20fran%C3%A7ais%20et%20l%27enseignement%20priv%C3%A9.

Da Costa, Sylvie, and Agnès Van Zanten. 2011. "L'enseignement privé entre mission, management et marché." In *L'état et l'enseignement priv:. L'application de la loi Debré (1959)*, edited by Bruno Poucet, 291–307. Rennes: Presses Universitaires de Rennes.

De Labarre, Éric. 2010 (6 June). "Discours à l'APEL." http://sitecoles.formiris.org/userfiles/files/sitecoles_2265_1.pdf.

Delhaye, Jean-Paul, Christine Allain, Philippe Vrand, et al. 2011. "Regards croisés des parents d'élèves de l'enseignement public et privé." In *L'état et l'enseignement privé: L'application de la loi Debré (1959)*, edited by Bruno Poucet, 227–36. Rennes: Presses Universitaires de Rennes.

Gauchet, Marcel. 2014. "Le désenchantement désenchanté." In *Charles Taylor: Religion et secularization*, edited by Sylvie Taussig, 73–83. Paris: CNRS.

Girard, Fernand. 2009. "*50 ans de la loi Debré*." In *50 ans après le vote de la loi Debré: 25 après le vote de la loi Rocard. Histoire, actualité et perspective*, edited by Enseignement Catholique. Paris: ECA, 2009.

Gontard, Maurice. 1959. *L'enseignement primaire en France, de la Révolution à la loi Guizot*. Paris: Les Belles Lettres.

Grace, Gerald. 2013. "From *Gravissiumum Educationis* (1965) to *The Catholic School* (1977): The Late Flowering of Aggiornamento in Catholic Education Thinking." *Pastoral Review* 9(3): 22–7.

Hervieu-Léger, Danièle. 2003. *Catholicisme, la fin d'un monde*. Paris: Bayard.

Hippolyte, Simon. 2009. *"Trois piliers pour éduquer": Enseignement catholique actualités*. Hors-série Novembre.

Hubert, André. 1995. "L'évolution de la pensée pontificale sur l'éducation, de Pie XI à Paul VI." In *Pédagogie chrétienne, Pédagogues chrétiens*, edited by Guy Avanzini, 501–7. Paris: Éd. Don Bosco.

Langouet, G. 2012. "L'enseignement privé sous contrat: continuité, diversification et stabilité." In *L'état et l'enseignement privé*, edited by Br. Poucet, 169–81. Paris: Presses Universitaires de France.

Les évêques de France. 1996. *Proposer la foi dans la société actuelle. Lettre aux catholiques de France.* Paris: Cerf.

Mayeur, Françoise. 1981. *Histoire de l'enseignement et de l'éducation*, vol. 3: *1789–1930.* Paris: Perrin.

Meirieu, Philippe, and Marc Guirand. 1997. *L'école ou la guerre civile.* Paris: Plon.

Moog, François. 2012. *A quoi sert l'École Catholique.* Montrouge: Bayard.

Nau, X. 2011. "Le statut de l'enseignant, cristallisation des enjeux de pouvoir dans l'enseignement privé sous contrat." Enseignement Catholique, *50 ans après le vote de la loi Debré. 25 après le vote de la loi Rocard. Histoire, actualité et perspective*, II. L'association à l'État, 9. Dossier no. 346.

Ozouf, Mona. 1963. *L'école, l'église et la République, 1871–1914.* Paris: Colin.

Perrineau, Pascal. 2009. "La société française face à la question scolaire." In *In 50 ans après le vote de la loi Debré: 25 après le vote de la loi Rocard. Histoire, actualité et perspective*, edited by Enseignement Catholique. Paris: ECA.

Portier, Philippe. 2012. "Pluralité et unité dans le Catholicisme français." In *Catholicisme en tensions*, edited by Céline Baraud, Frédéric Gugelot, and Isabelle Saint-Martin, 19–36. Paris: EHESS.

Prost, Antoine. 2013. "L'enseignement privé prisonnier de son héritage." *Revue Projet* 2(333): 33–41.

Roy, Olivier. 2012. *La sainte ignorance.* Paris: Seuil.

"Statut de l'Enseignement Catholique." 1992 (14 May). *Enseignement catholique actualités* 210.

Toulemonde, Bernard. 1988. "Réconcilier le public et le privé." In *Petite histoire d'un grand ministère: L'éducation nationale*, 247–63. Paris: Albin Michel.

– 2011. "Le cinquantenaire de la loi Debré. Qu'est devenu l'enseignement privé?" *Revue du droit public et de la science politique en France et a l'etranger* 5: 1181–6.

Van Zanten, Agnès. 2012. "La pluralité des motifs du choix des établissements privés catholiques par les familles des classes moyennes urbaines." In *L'état et l'enseignement privé: L'application de la loi Debré (1959)*, edited by Bruno Poucet, 183–99. Rennes: Presses Universitaires de Rennes.

3 Active Methods and Social Secularization in School Catechesis during the Franco Dictatorship (1939–1975): A Transfer in a Cultural System in Change

CARLOS MARTÍNEZ VALLE

Religious Education and Educational Active Methods

While it might at first appear to be a contradiction in terms, Spanish society achieved its modernization and secularization during the Franco dictatorship (1939–75), under profoundly Catholic and often anti-modern governments. These governments, the Catholic Church, and the educational establishment that was placed in high academic positions by the government after the Civil War purges looked for means to halt or control societal modernization and secularization. Some members of that establishment saw educational reform – in particular, active pedagogical methods – as one such means. It is possible to exemplify this interest in "active methods" (hereafter abbreviated as AMs) by examining reception of John Dewey, who was considered one of the field's most important theorists.

After the Spanish Civil War, Dewey was frowned upon by the victorious coalition of Fascists and the fundamentalist Catholic Church because of his political and educational ideas, in particular his "naturalism," which had been condemned in the 1929 encyclical *On Christian Education* (*Divini Illus Magistri*) (Article 59ff). Yet after the early 1950s, with the transformation of the Spanish government from a totalitarian to an authoritarian dictatorship, he was quoted more and more often in Spanish educational discourse, even in relation to religious teaching. The interest of the Spanish academic establishment in Dewey and AMs for reforming religious teaching is striking, given that Dewey was accused of trying to "root the idea of spirit out of minds" (Galino 1951). Besides that, religious education was, in fact, a catechesis – in other words, it had a clear denominational-confessional, proselytizing character. Yet until

1967, compulsory catechesis was not an informal education subject of the sort provided elsewhere by the parishes; rather, it was simply another school subject, one that included a syllabus and assessments.

From 1939 to 1975, catechists could choose among different intellectual traditions that proposed different active methods. Progressive Education, the tradition to which Dewey belonged, was one option. It proposed, among other AMs, Kirkpatrick's Project Method. The Catholic social pastoral movements (which worked out a set of AMs, including the *Révision de vie*, or Life Review) and Latin American approaches to popular education (in particular, after the mid-1960s, Freire's critical pedagogy) were possible alternatives. But as discussed in the next section, even when some of these currents were religious, the adoption of AMs raised problems, and not only for Spanish traditional Catholicism. AMs were also problematic from a general religious perspective, for they were based on a naturalistic and immanent conception of the human being and the world that fostered secularization.

The study of the adoption of AMs in school catechesis links issues of intellectual history, educational transfer, and the transformation of educational praxis, all of which will be examined here. First, the chapter discusses the construction of religion in a "secular age" that compelled the adoption of implicitly secularizing practices (active methods) in the teaching of religion. Second, traditional Catholic images of the human being as inherently weak or even sinful, related conceptions of education as a doctrine based on transcendental principles, and the Catholic rejection of naturalism (the basis of AMs) had together led to a rejection of AMs in Spain long before the period under study (Colom and Rincón 2004). This chapter therefore analyses the process of adoption of AMs that were at odds with the Spanish Catholic (educational) culture. Finally, I argue that any adoption of foreign practices requires changes in social structures and key beliefs – here, the Second Vatican Council provides the means – as well as the transformation of previous practices. In the case under study, the process of reception/adoption led to the rejection of the Progressive Education AMs and the adoption of the social pastoral ones.

The following section sketches the radical transformation that secularization introduces, in terms of the way believers understood and lived religion. This was exemplified in the need to adopt secularizing teaching methods for the catechesis. The problems posed to religious teaching by the secularizing nature of AMs, which made their adoption for catechesis difficult, are also analysed. Later sections deal mainly with the slow transformation of catechetic practices and discourses following a synchronic structure.

Here, the chapter is divided by decades, for the praxis and discourses show no particular turning points. The chapter concludes with reflections on the three main issues broached above, as well as some insights into the debates over the teaching of catechesis in state schools – debates that are still being waged in Spain, even after forty years of democracy.

Secularization, Active Methods, and Religion

In order to discuss how secularization transformed ways of living the Catholic faith in Spain, it is necessary to consider the form of the secularization of Spanish society. One strand of the modernization/rationalization paradigm of secularization posits that social-functional differentiation separates other social sub-systems from religion. This separation gives these social sub-systems autonomy and leads to the seclusion of religion to the private sphere; it also causes a decrease in the public significance given to religious belief and organizations (Bruce 2011; Casanova 1994; Dobbelaere 2004; Gorski 2000; Luhmann 1997; Tschannen 1991). However, the official status of the Spanish Catholic Church did not change even after the Law 44/1967 (Jefatura del Estado, 1967), "which regulated the implementation of the civil right to religious freedom." Catholic symbols, rites, and festivities continued to fill public spaces, including schools, during Franco's dictatorship. This impeded the transformation of school catechesis into a scientific, historic-comparative subject.

Another strand of the same paradigm describes secularization as a weakening belief in religious teachings and a distancing from religious culture – what could be called "conscience secularization" (Pérez-Agote 2007; Tschannen 1991). Conscience secularization implies more than disbelief or non-belief. It also means a change in the believers' ways of living religion, for secularization makes religion only one option among others – and religion is not always the easiest option (Taylor 2007; Tschannen 1991). Furthermore, conscience secularization implies a transformation of *Weltanschauung* (world view), in particular, of underlying anthropological conceptions. With worldliness as its foundation, secularization substitutes transcendent experiences and horizons of realization/plenitude with immanent ones. In other words, secularization changes anthropological conceptions; instead of a human being who blossoms by accessing transcendence and contemplating God, we encounter a more active human being who manifests her or his immanent powers through action and through the production of themselves and the world (Taylor 2007).

This latter secular perspective pervades AMs. Instead of viewing education as guided by the transcendent norms and models of the virtuous human being, AMs aim to foster worldly, problem-solving, adaptable individuals (Bernstorff 2009). The adoption of AMs in catechesis could thus constitute an antinomy, for this would imply adopting an instrument that fosters an opposite (immanent) human image.

The social secularization of Spanish society – a process that was consolidated during the period under study in this chapter (Pérez-Agote 2007) – involved diverse forms of anti-clericalism, atheism, and disbelief. Catechists felt that religion (Catholicism) was no longer universally known and informally taught in one's environment and by one's experience. So they felt a need to replace old catechisms and the hermeneutical method with participative methods, in order to educate in the faith those who had never lived in a religious universe (Taylor 2007). Their dilemma was that applying these methods would transform (secularize) their religion.

The adoption of AMs in catechesis had to overcome other problems related to the above-mentioned secular character of AMs. Educational activism presupposes that children learn while doing, whereas by its very nature, a great part of religion – in particular, revealed dogma – is not accessible through sensible experience and can plainly contradict such experience. The Church's magisterium – that is, the authority of the pope and the bishops to interpret both the revealed Scripture and Tradition (the *depositum fidei*, or the faith's deposit) – implied the necessity of what the Spanish academic establishment called "hetero-formation" – that is, frontal instruction by an authorized teacher, something that directly contradicted "self-" or "auto-formation," a key aspect of AMs.

Beyond dogma, AMs were a problem for catechesis because they have a clear, but only formal or procedural, moral determination. In other words, AMs reject top-down imposed morals, the idea being that children should develop their own rules and regulate themselves; from a religious perspective, this introduces a moral relativism. Furthermore, participative self-regulated groups tend to foster flat hierarchies, empowerment, and democratic ideas and practices.

Another problem in the relationship between catechesis and AMs is that the most consistent AMs imply the creation of things; thus the question is "what" can be created out of and for learning religion. The social pastoral tradition had an answer to this problem, for it conceived liturgy (as communion) and communitarian work and life as central performative affirmations of the faith and as active instruments for achieving (learning) it. Indeed, contemporary theology conceives both liturgy and communitarian work and life as re-enacting the bond (*re-ligare*, to bind again) with God and the community and, therefore, as containing the whole religion (Boyer 2001; Campbell and Moyers 1991; Harpur 2004). From a sociological perspective, Wilson (1988) maintained that religion is a community resource and that secularization is related to *Vergesellschaftung* (socialization), or the transformation of the community into a society. It follows that catechesis should reconstruct the community though liturgy and community work. However, this understanding of liturgy and community work and life (as discussed below) was a "secularizing" departure from traditional Catholic conceptions. Because liturgy (as communion) and community work and life took place outside the classroom, social pastoral educators developed AMs that were closely connected with liturgy and community work and life, but that were suitable for social pastoral education. These AMs included *le Sillon* (the sofa) and the Life Review.

After the War: Catholic Fundamentalism and Fascism

Culture wars around the secularization of society and schools did much to ignite the Civil War (1936–9). The victorious Falange, a fascist/nationalist group, and the integrist (fundamentalist) Church shared similar negative views of human nature, which allowed for a discourse coalition between both. The integrists emphasized that human beings were wicked and had fallen as a result of original sin and thus had a failed nature (*servo arbitrio*, or enslaved will); as a consequence, they were deterred from their elevated destiny by their base instincts and immoderate desires, which impeded salvation and social life. The fascists, for their part, maintained that greed and lust were behind the Republic's distributive politics, which had provoked the war. Politics and education needed, then, to restrain people's instincts and foster habits of continence, imposing the rejection of the self, or abnegation, for the sake of both the Fatherland and the Church (García Hoz 1941; Guerrero 1945 Leirós 1973; Ruíz 1968).

Humiliation and mortification were the nucleus of García Hoz's ascetic fighting pedagogy (*Pedagogía de la Lucha Ascética*, 1941), which viewed the Civil War and the repression that followed as educational instruments sent by God to straighten out the Spanish people's disordered passions. Renunciation and continence continued to be central to Hoz's (1962) educational proposals, as reprints of *La Tarea profunda de Educar* show.

These works shared similar principles with the encyclical *Divini Illius Magistri* (Article 59ff), which explicitly condemned naturalism, anthropological optimism, and confidence in the bounty of human nature. Following the encyclical, Catholic integrists condemned AMs at various catechetical congresses from 1926 on (Montero 1988; Viñao 2004).

In *The Teaching Active Method* (*El Método Activo de la Enseñanza,* 1960), Romero Marín, chair of social pedagogy at Madrid University, explained the reasons for rejecting Progressive Education AMs. He declared that whatever their prestigious supporters contended, AMs could not end the need for a strong authority to instil rationality in children. This idea, which was central to the Spanish educational tradition, was based on "an exaggeratedly pessimistic conception of human nature, that views in it only disordered instincts" (16).

Integrism (fundamentalism) requires traditional catechesis. However, fundamentalism coexisted in the 1940s with other, more moderate Catholic currents and positions. Two scholars are important to a discussion of these moderate positions that permitted the questioning of traditional catechesis: Zaragüeta and Tusquets. The Basque neo-Scholastic theologian Juan Zaragüeta (1883–1974) studied with Mercier and developed his career before the war. Joan Tusquets (1901–98) was a Catalan priest, an informer for the fascists, a maker of lists for reprisal, and Chair of General Pedagogy at the University of Barcelona. He founded *Formación Catequística* (*Catechetic Training*) and *Orientación Catequética* (*Catechetic Orientation*), the field's most important journals. Both scholars were aware of the challenges of secularization: modern society has lost its religious unanimity; scepticism or indifference defined the new social context. Their works (Tusquets 1944; Zaragüeta 1941) exemplify the problems inherent in the transfer and adoption of foreign ideas – in new-institutionalist terms, of rationalized educational myth (in this case, the AMs). In other words, complications develop as foreign ideas collide with the intellectual resistances and filters of the educational systems (here, the authors) that are receiving those ideas (Meyer and Rowan 1977).

Both Tusquets (1944) and Zaragüeta (1941) departed from Stieglitz and Göttler with their contention that AMs can be beneficial for religious teaching. Tusquets even criticized Stieglitz's and Munich's methods (Jedin 1981) for not drawing on children's experiences and not allowing them to take part in the process and express freely, in a personal way, what they learn. He contended that Progressive Education AMs (Decroly's centres of interest and "Dewey's method [*sic*]") were compatible and indeed "added to Stieglitz's Method a social surplus needed for a true religious life" in Catholicism, which was marked by liturgy, ritual popular piety, and community life. Notwithstanding the two scholars' high praises, Progressive Education AMs were difficult for them to understand and implement.

Tusquets maintained that Dewey's method consisted of "proposing the children do a work collectively and, once accepted, plan it. Working this way, the pupils search for and acquire *the knowledge of the lesson*" (1944, 34, emphasis added). Zaragüeta defined AMs not as a heuristic procedure (i.e., intellection was not its main feature), but as a method based in the "highest degree of initiative by the pupil who, stimulated and oriented by the teacher, explores and discovers by his own effort *the horizon of the discipline*" (1941, 21, emphasis added). Also, Zaragüeta did not mention any other product of the classroom than the pupils' responses. So it is clear that neither author understood the interdisciplinary character of AMs, and that both considered all methods of learning in which the students were not mere passive receptors to be AMs.

Zaragüeta and Tusquets criticized Progressive Education AMs for their practical problems, in that they were inadequate for fulfilling the nationally defined curriculum and were unsupportive of traditional forms of discipline. So Tusquets praised Progressive Education AMs for their social surplus, but he also divided classes, following the Jesuit tradition, into competing hierarchically organized groups of ten students, thereby creating discipline through competition. In this regard, Tusquets's proposals contradicted the proposals of progressive educators. Furthermore, the methods they proposed didn't produce anything else but the pupils' presentations in the class.

For both Tusquets and Zaragüeta, the main concern not met by Progressive Education AMs was that, since transcendent truths are not reachable through experience and are revealed only to the Church, the Church still needed to exercise its magisterial role. In other words, considering human nature and reason, religious pedagogy ought to use hetero-instruction (i.e., the explaining of the truth by a teacher) and vicarious learning. Yet Tusquets's acceptance of students' free expression did signal a more lax approach, given that one problem when teaching religion is that theology has a highly nuanced and precise terminology; thus free non-esoteric parlance can lead quickly to unorthodox meanings.

The two scholars also had difficulties accepting the principles of social pastoral AMs. Zaragüeta's sacramental-dogmatic conception of religion viewed belief as a cognitive faculty and religion as a system of transcendental-supernatural truths and grace. Thus he understood religious instruction as the means to teach a series of hypothetical utterances. In this way, he distinguished teachers from neophytes and viewed liturgy mainly as a worship and a grace sacrament; for him, the celebration or recreation of the community of believers was only a by-product. The means he proposed for teaching religion translated this traditional "frontal" didactic conception to the use of printed sermons; observations of nature and religious monuments, which invited believers to know and praise the Lord; and engravings of biblical characters that fostered the vicarious learning of ethics.

In 1946, Tusquets published "The Religion Explained to the Little Grownups," arguably the most detailed catechetic work of the time. In it, he quoted Progressive Education authors and AMs and accepted that children's psyches proceed from concrete sensations to symbolic, abstract theory – a basic position of AMs – but he also underscored that religious life consists in transcending the physical world. Indeed, he based this work on an AM developed by the social pastoral catechists: the study circle (Tusquets 1946).

However, Tusquets's adaptation of the study circle transformed its active character, in that the book proposed themes for debates and directed them through an initial reflection, a conclusion, a recapitulation, and a proposal for putting into practice the resolutions. Also, the didactic devices included images and graphics, illustrating the connection to the traditional standard *Catechism Explained with Graphics and Examples* (Llorente 1937), which was reprinted at least until the mid-1960s.

So notwithstanding their pleas in favour of, in particular, Progressive Education AMs, García Hoz, Tusquets, and Zaragüeta followed traditional methods; they considered hetero-instruction necessary, and they proposed activities of a merely intellectual nature that maintained the boundaries of the disciplinary taxonomies and had no productive aspects. The academic establishment was therefore unable to accept, understand, or apply AMs during the 1940s.

The 1950s

The regime's "opening" – that is, its transformation from a totalitarian dictatorship into an authoritarian–technocratic one in the early 1950s (Linz 2009) – brought a relaxation in censorship. This opened the door for some (albeit ambivalent) attention to, for instance, Dewey as an "ethno-typical North American educator" (Fermoso 1970; Iriarte 1957;

Tusquets 1968). Works by the Catholic educationalists Planchard (1949), de Hovre (1951), and Redden and Ryan (1961) were translated into Spanish around this time. Although these followed the encyclical *On Christian Education* (*Divini Illus Magistri*), their evaluations of Progressive Education AMs accepted some of their aspects for education (catechesis). Even so, the academic educational establishment[1] continued to lean on the same philosophical options predominant in the prewar academy: neo-Thomism, hermeneutic phenomenology, vitalism–existentialism (Bergson, Jasper, Marcel), Scheler's axiology, neo-idealism (Natorp), historicism, and personalism (Colom and Rincón 2004; Orden 2008; Vilanou 1999).

This apparent diversity was moderated by common principles that regulated the acceptance of different philosophical currents than those mentioned above (Schriewer and Martínez Valle 2003). The basic view of human nature that constituted the filter was the conservative one – that children were incomplete (albeit free-willed and rational) and needed to be educated, that is, freed from base instincts and passions through transcendent values, norms, and models (axioms). This would allow the child to flourish – to reach morality (virtues) and wisdom and thereby become a fully developed human being and achieve happiness (beatitude). For the educational establishment, contemplation more than action was the true human objective. Education was for them a "moral deliberative practice," a changing casuistic art or conversation, directed in a teleological way by exogenous ends and values that could not be fully grasped and directed by scientific knowledge (Damseaux and Solana 1967; Fermoso 1970; Tusquets 1951). For them, education was a doctrine, praxis guided by transcendent axioms (Galino 1951, 1961; Gonzalo Calavia 1955, 1966; Pacios 1947; Palmés 1953; Millán Puelles 1963). These principles, very similar to those held by the "moderate" academics of the 1940s, Tusquets and Zaragüeta, were implemented through a Hebartian pedagogy that contrasted with those on which AMs were grounded. During this period, this contrast determined how AMs were intellectually processed.

In 1950, the fourth *Congreso Nacional de Catecismo* (Catechism National Congress) emphasized the need to seek more effective methodologies. Minister of National Education Ibañez Martín (1950), after ratifying the Church's magisterial power and the state's subsidiary role, pleaded for new educational methods in catechesis. He maintained that religion should not be conceived as another school subject aimed at the formal acquisition of knowledge and that it should use specific methods for activating specific abilities and feelings. He seemed to be rejecting the old hermeneutical method, even while remaining committed to teacher-centred education (Ibañez Martín 1950). The same hopes for methodological change and dearth of methodological proposals (except for a vague nod to the importance of experience for teaching religion and morality) are evident in other publications of the 1950s (see Alonso 1957; Gil 1957).

In 1948, the *Spanish Journal of Pedagogy* (*Revista Española de Pedagogía*) launched a series on didactic reform with an article by García Hoz, followed by one from Tusquets in 1951, among others. For García Hoz (1948) the fundamental objective of this reform, which should include the introduction of some AMs, was to "instill in pupils' souls the ideals of cooperation, social accord or understanding, mutual aid and good will." For the social sciences he proposed a syllabus that reflected the weight given to religion in school curriculum and the academic establishment's interest in fostering participation in communitarian religious activities as catechetic instruments. At the core of the syllabus was a "questionnaire," which pupils were to pass on to relatives and neighbours. It was aimed at fostering pupils' participation in class as well as knowledge of their communities' pious practices and associations, such as masses, pilgrimages, and brotherhoods.

In his taxonomy of teaching methods, Tusquets (1951) considered AMs to be part of social methods. In his view, such methods would benefit pupils mainly by fostering cooperative work as they set and pursued their personal and social objectives. Tusquets, who was in charge of drawing the parameters for the reform of catechesis, dealt with the Progressive Education's AMs in very general and imprecise terms and did not follow García Hoz's intuition regarding the possibilities of liturgy and pious practices as AMs.

Even for this small discursive adoption of AMs, the Spanish education system first required AMs to be rehabilitated through Christianization. This was accomplished by creating genealogies that were both epistemological instruments and arguments from authority (*ad verecundiam*) claiming the orthodoxy of AMs. Romero Marín (1960) and Tusquets (1951), among others, made lists of those who had propounded AMs before they were heretically radicalized by Rousseau and progressivism, including Plato, the Church's doctor Aquinas (in *De Magistro*, or *On the Teacher*), and the *Ratio Studiorum* (*The Jesuit's Plan of Studies*) or Pestalozzi. Romero and Tusquets understood AMs within their own mental frames. Thus activism was related, following Llorente (1928), to the maieutic or "intuitive method" (Romero Marín 1960; Tusquets 1957). This was also the case in France, where Colomb's work (see below) was criticized as Platonizing (Molinario 2010). However, maieutic and intuitive methods are far from being AMs, for they imply only intellectual work. This makes one wonder whether Romero and Tusquets in fact moved beyond the methodological proposals of the Stieglitz method, which proposed the intuitive presentation of the theme, the explanation, and the application to life (Jedin 1981).

Furthermore, the basic religious presuppositions of the education establishment collided with core stances of active methods regarding transcendent ideas/values and epistemology (interests and wills, inductivism, or the value of experience). Even in his later works, García Hoz (1960, 45) pointed to this problem: given that "the notion of ultimate cause has lost its prestige," positivistic educational philosophy emphasized that when determining educational processes and objectives, society was the last ground on which to solve educational problems.

The 1960s: Functional and Political Differentiation within the Catechesis and the Church

Accelerating socio-demographic changes, urbanization, and industrialization (*Vergesellschaftung*), and the related cultural transformations (social secularization), increased the pressure for new catechetic concepts and didactics to ensure people's obedience to the Church and the regime (Sánchez 2003). The 1960s saw a gradual rediscovery of Progressive Education. Pleas for more active education began to emanate from various official research and educational institutions (del Pozo and Braster 2012).

Next to modernization and the relaxation of censorship, the ideological change that did the most to influence academic discourse was the Church's *aggiornamento* (bringing up to date) and Second Vatican Council (1959–65). In 1967, the Episcopal Commission of Teaching began holding regular meetings where new orientations and formulas were proposed; this development pointed to an increasing functional differentiation of catechetic pedagogy. The introductory discourse by the president of the Teaching Episcopal Commission mentioned the influence of the Second Vatican Council (*Decree on the Ministry and Life of Priests* [*Presbyterorum Ordinis*]), Article 22; *Pastoral Constitution on the Church in the Modern World* (*Gaudium et Spes*), Articles 1–11, 21–2) (I Jornadas 1967; Pope Paul VI 1965). The presentations mentioned some reasons for the secularization: the capacity of people to create their own, secure human world

(Norris and Inglehart 2004), pluralism, and the influence of science and of a culture of questioning authority. The authors of the presentations were also aware that pupils rejected catechesis.

Although the speeches of the Catholic hierarchy given at the I Jornadas called for adapting the message to the modern man, following the motto of the *aggiornamento*, their ideas were moderate and traditional, involving their references (Llorente, Cardinal Newman, or Pius X), their conception of hierarchy (the Bishop was the only full pastor), and Christianity (which, for them, was not a philosophy or a value system but a form of dogmatic knowledge), and their view of human nature. In accordance with this conservatism, the presentations proposed a "renewed kerigmatic" catechesis (*kerigma* meaning "the apostolic proclamation of salvation through Jesus Christ") – that is, one focused on announcing Christ's salvation, which would require a teacher-centred method and reject AMs. Consistent with this approach, they sketched out two methods. The first was a dialogic method through which the pupils could express and communicate their faith. The second was an amalgam of history and an appeal to "inferior faculties" (such as the senses, feelings, sensibility, and aesthetics) that would bring pupils to religion and faith. During these meetings, the hierarchy treated liturgy mainly as a specific "language" for transmitting the truth.

The grassroots catechists of the meeting's working groups (I Jornadas 1967) had a different perspective from those of the hierarchy and the academic establishment. Although no direct accusations were made regarding the Church's responsibility for secularization, some criticized its inactivity, as it relied on the national schoolteachers for doing the clergy's jobs, and pleaded for more pastoral planning and coordination. They criticized the hierarchy's legal and dogmatic conceptions of religion and catechesis, as well as its reduction of morals to sexual continence. They also fiercely attacked the academic character of the catechesis, which was based on memorization and bore no relation to the pupils' experiences, emotions, and wills – or to the community, the liturgy, or the Bible. They maintained that all of this was impeding the Church's ability to gain new believers and fortify the faith of existing believers. These are the earlier doubts I have found among catechists regarding the convenience of having a confessional religious subject in schools. The meeting's working groups were closer to Vatican II's proposals, in that they defended a catechesis linked to experience, community, and social needs. The socio-cultural provenience of these grassroots catechists explains the catechetical instrument they proposed and these criticisms: the Life Review.

The Life Review was an AM for popular education created by Joseph Cardijn in the 1920s. It proposed group analysis of daily experiences and problems of any participant. This involved judging these problems from an evangelical perspective, then adopting a common stance and planning a sequence of actions to solve them. Life Review would compel participants to think and act together in addressing a wide range of experiences (social problems) and would raise their awareness of socio-political issues. This AM, the most democratic and horizontal of the methods developed by the social pastoral movement, was very important for fostering a new social conscience within the Church, and quite possibly to the decision to organize the Second Vatican Council. Some of its features (e.g., its democratic communitarian practices, the relevance it assigned to experience, and its transformative practical objective) made it not only an active method but also a complement to liturgy (communion) and social work. Some of the works about Life Review recommended that it be celebrated connected with the mass (Bonduelle 1965; Maréchal 1960a; Royo 1964). Life Review was introduced in Spain in the 1950s (Bonduelle 1965; Grupos de apostolado obrero 1958; Maraval 1970; Maréchal 1960b; Martínez 1968; Royo 1964) by the HOAC (Workers Brotherhood of the Catholic Action) and the JOC (Young Catholic Workers) and was officially approved by the JACE (Youth of the Spanish Catholic Action) for all its groups in 1960. So although all of these associations had been created by the Catholic hierarchy and Acción Católica (Catholic Action) to evangelize Catholic workers and youth, the use of Life Review led to their increasing turn to the left; their social engagement, including civic education; and their break with the conservative Catholic Action in the early 1970s (Fullana and Montero 2003; López 1995). This progressive turn contributed to a radical transformation in some sectors of the Spanish Church (Montero 2009; Domínguez 1985). Clearly, Life Review is a perfect example of how practices influence ideas and theory, for it changed the catechesis and even ideas about its place in the school system. In the mid-1960s it began to be transferred from informal social pastoral education to the school catechesis, challenging both traditional catechetic methods and Progressive Education AMs.

The 1970s

In 1971 the translation of Colomb's *Catechetic Pedagogy Manual* (*Manual de Pedagogía Catequética*) appeared. It was based on a positive image of an active human being and Dewey's concept of experience, and for those reasons had been controversial in late-1950s France (Colomb 1971; Duperray and Ponson 1994). This work arguably had little influence on catechetic methodologies; even so, its positive view of human nature was shared by many Spanish catechists, some of whom (III Jornadas 1971) rejected traditional apologetics that justified God by pointing to the weakness of human beings. Just like Colomb, who maintained that human nature flowers through the opening to transcendence and stressed the religious relevance of this-worldly experience, these Spanish catechists did not follow the Church's traditional dualism and viewed human beings and the world as interdependent. Indeed, anti-dualism is a basic principle in Progressive Education AMs.

The second Jornadas (1971), "The Future of Education and the Future of Humankind" ("El Futuro de la Educacion y el Futuro del Hombre"), examined the chances taken by and the risks of the influential 1970 *Ley General de Educación* (General Education Law), which called for the adoption of Progressive Education AMs in schools and emphasized conceptions of the active human being. Contributions by grassroots catechists continued to raise criticisms of traditional catechesis as apodictic, speculative, and detached from real life. Although some of them mentioned Dewey, many proposed another social pastoral AM: *le Sillon*. "The Sofa," which can be viewed as an intermediate step in the social pastoral evolution from the Catholic Workers' Clubs to the Life Review, involved discussion circles focused on issues proposed by the participants themselves, and had a flat hierarchy (Sangnier, 1906).

The presentations of the third catechetical meeting in 1971, "The Spanish Catechesis Facing the Legal Reform and the Cultural Change" (III Jornadas 1971), accurately diagnosed the religious crisis arising from the "dissolution of the traditional images of the whole world" (1970, 23). For the participants, religion had lost its status of "unquestioned previous evidence" (47). It therefore required a transformation in catechesis, for the environment was not propitious for religious messages, making it difficult even for catechists to understand, live, and manifest their faith.

Most of the lecturers (III Jornadas 1971) fiercely criticized the Church and the Catholic schools for distancing people from the Church and for refusing to adapt to the new world. They judged both the Church and the schools in terms of the obstacles they posed to a living faith and human freedom – obstacles such as the curia's control of rites and thoughts that maintained laity as minors; the rigid and ugly aesthetic taste; and the religious schools' lack of both Christian spirit and intellectual creativity, as well as pedagogical innovation and freedom. Proposed solutions included rejecting any cultural and moral monopoly and serving the poor instead of forging alliances with elites. The lecturers also proposed the "deinstitutionalization" of Catholic schools in order to open them to society, as well as the education of a Christian youth devoted to social change, with independent judgment, and resilient in manifesting and explaining its faith in hostile environments.

Some presentations (III Jornadas 1971) pleaded for Progressive Education AMs (Decroly's Interest Centres and Freinet's school press) while maintaining that, although they were often quoted, only a few authors and teachers knew about them, and even fewer used them, because they involved more work than traditional methods. The pedagogy professor Julio Ruiz Berrio clarified the meaning of Progressive Education AMs: teachers become guides, students become self-organized groups, textbooks are not used, and knowledge is acquired through content areas instead of traditional subjects. Some of the other participants (III Jornadas 1971), all religious people, defended a "renewed kerigmatic" catechesis and a didactic based on the "inferior faculties" (i.e., the senses).

Some presentations (III Jornadas 1971) pleaded for a combination of the Sofa and the Life Review because catechesis was impossible without real faith experiences and communion with brothers. They recommended creating discussion groups that would include readings, debates, programs, and social intervention activities for creating community. The presenters were aware of the problems posed by their proposals, especially the challenges they posed to the Church. Thus, their recommendations, if followed, would have given students access to the Gospel and allowed them to question traditional ideas and to seek more evangelical and communitarian forms of living.

Two years later, the IV Jornadas (1972), "The Faith Education in Adolescents" (*La Educación de la Fe en los Adolescents*), gathered presentations in favour of both "renewed kerigmatic" and social pastoral catechesis. This brought to the surface the division within the Spanish Church. Proponents of the "renewed kerigmatic" catechesis, led by Elias Yañez, a member of the Bishops' Conference, defended their stance by arguing that the methodological problem had been solved, and that catechesis should rely on theology and on Church theologians and should spurn the conversion of liturgy into what they viewed as folkloric participative shows. Consistent with the methodology they proposed, they maintained that Catholicism should be part of the official school curriculum.

On the other side of the issue, grassroots catechists (including Demetrio González), as proponents of the social pastoral catechesis and therefore also of Life Review, defended their belief that Christian vocation implies social consciousness and the creation of community, which is both the means and the objective of active education. They consistently rejected the agreements between the Vatican and the dictatorship, as well as school catechesis. Indeed, the possibility that a secularizing didactic method, such as AMs, could strengthen the effectiveness of religious teaching led catechists to *plead* for secularization – in this case, as a functional differentiation between school and religion (IV Jornadas 1972; VI Jornadas 1976).

Conclusion

The secularization of the Spanish society increased from the late 1950s onward, as a consequence of modernization, urbanization, and increases in life security and educational level, to the point that children no longer experienced religion as part of their lived environment. This lack of natural relation with the religious culture and faith forced the Church to transform the teaching of religion in order to recreate a religious universe. The academic educational establishment began to voice the need for AMs in school catechesis in the 1940s. The 1961 *Encyclical on Christianity and Social Progress* (*Mater et Magistra*) – and even more fundamentally, the Second Vatican Council (1962–5) – encouraged the *aggiornamento* (the bringing up to date) of teaching methods in ways that corresponded to the logical demands of AMs. The *Pastoral Constitution on the Church in the Modern World* (*Gaudium et Spes*, Article 22) and the *Decree on Ecumenism* (*Unitatis Redintegratio*, Article 2.6) (Pope Paul VI 1965, 1964) stated, differentiating the doctrinal substance from its presentation, that the *depositum fidei* should be studied and expounded through modern methods and forms; they considered the Church's magisterium to be predominantly pastoral and emphasized its re-enactment in believers' lives.

The correspondence between the Second Vatican Council's teachings and AM (Life Review) requirements and effects can be explained by the increasing importance Life Review held for the Church. This suggests that Life Review could have been instrumental in the summoning of the Council. This study has shown that practices have the capacity to mould and change ideas, as attested by the interrelated expansion of the Life Review and leftist social stances in the Church. The use of this form of AM caused broad sectors of the Church to argue for social pastoral methods as well as for a religion lived for the needy and destitute. The more active the methods, the more democratic they were.

Although the academic educational establishment that worked on catechesis quoted the Progressive Education tradition (e.g., Dewey, Freinet, and Decroly), many school catechists adopted, albeit slowly, AMs from the Church's social pastoral education: the Life Review or the Sofa. There were some plausible reasons for this adoption. Spanish lay and religious authors did not fully understand Progressive Education AMs. Many Spanish catechists equated them with Platonism, accusing them of immanentism. Until the late 1960s, when some methods that can be considered truly active began to be implemented, educators viewed all methods that differed from "frontal" teaching as active – especially those that placed attention on the student's psychology.

The marginalization of the Progressive School AMs was also an outcome of the secularization of university education faculties that abandoned catechesis as an intellectual object and of the emergence of social pastoral education and catechists. Also, the adoption of new practices (school AMs) require the transformation of pre-existent praxes. The slow transformation within social pastoral education – from Recreational Circles to debate circles, the Sofa, and Life Review – exemplifies the need for gradual reform. Progressive Education AMs – which were defended by academics, not practitioners (catechists) – remained at the proposal level and were never implemented. Furthermore, the official status of school catechesis hindered its own transformation. In the event, reform would actually emerge from a non-institutionalized area where secularization was more strongly felt: social pastoral education.

Perhaps due to censorship, I have not found explicit references to Latin American Popular Education AMs. Some mentions of a development of "social communities" in the "Meetings of Educational Pastoral" (II Jornadas 1971) could refer to either Life Review or the AMs of Latin American popular education.

Not all catechists adopted social pastoral AMs. By the end of the period, many catechists still contended that systematic theology, not didactics, should shape how religious content was transmitted (Alberich 1991; Montero 2011). The reaction to new forms of catechesis fostered the development of "renewed kerigmatic catechesis" as a highly traditional form of catechesis. This reluctance to adopt AMs is understandable, for that adoption would have implied the transformation of religion.

Secularization in general construes religion as politics' "other"; it redefines religion and changes the conditions in which it is lived by believers (Asad 1999, 2003). Increasing secularization forced the Church to use AMs to (re)create a religious universe. These new methods then transformed not only the practices of the believers but also their understanding of hierarchies, faith, and ritual. These changes were partly in line with the proposals of Vatican II, but they can also be understood as secularizing.

Those who used Life Review required increasingly direct access to the Bible and easier explanations of the *depositum fidei.* Correspondingly, they also stressed a more open and communitarian conception of the Church and the Christian life. Closely related to this was the discursive change from an intellectual conception of religion to a felt and lived religion that could plausibly be expressed in the shift in emphasis from the *fides quae creditur* (the faith *in which* one believes) to the *fides qua creditur* (the faith *with which* one believes). Social pastoral AMs, debate circles, and Life Review fostered a more democratic and participative understanding and valuing (in the discourses, at least) of liturgy and community. The understanding of liturgy went from stressing its sacramental character to a performative manifestation of the religion with God and its community – that is, from liturgy to communion. All of these transformations implied a less hierarchical and more participative Church, as well as a translation of its culture from canon to morals and community. This favoured the further development of ecclesial grassroots movements.

But the clearest manifestation of the secularizing changes that occurred in the period, which can also be understood in relation to the gradual adoption of AMs, was the transformation of the underlying understanding of human nature. The idea of a worldly human being, which Taylor (2007) associates with secularism, experienced growing acceptance. In the late Franco dictatorship, some authors rejected dualism and considered work and activity (immanence) to be as important as contemplation or abnegation (both aspects of transcendence), and as central for believers.

In the later years of the dictatorship, some authors criticized the official or elite-oriented Church and religious schools. They contended that the Church should focus on social pastoral work, and they pointed out that the official status of the Church and the presence of a compulsory confessional-denominational religion subject in state schools was impeding the required catechetic reforms as well as the transmission of a living faith. At the end of the day, the main instruments and objectives of social pastoral AMs – the debate circles, the Sofa, and the Life Review – were found to be more relevant outside schools: in community life and work, and in the communion. Thus the adoption of implicitly secularizing AMs led many catechists to ask for more (functional) secularization and the removal of catechesis from the school system.

NOTES

1 Most of the authors I am dealing with in this section were university staff. High-ranking civil servants at the Ministry of Education, another form of establishment, hold different educational ideas and stances.

REFERENCES

I Jornadas. 1967. *I Jornadas Nacionales de Estudios Catequéticos: Por una formación religiosa para nuestro tiempo.* Madrid: Marova.

II Jornadas. 1971. *II Jornadas de Pastoral Educativa: Futuro de la educación y futuro del hombre.* Madrid: Bruño.

III Jornadas. 1971. *III Jornadas de Pastoral Educativa: La catequesis española ante la reforma pedagógica y el cambio cultural.* Madrid: Bruño.

IV Jornadas. 1972. *IV Jornadas de Pastoral Educativa: La educación de la fe en los adolescentes.* Madrid: Bruño.

VI Jornadas. 1976. *VI Jornadas de Pastoral Educativa: Educación de la fé y compromiso cristiano.* Salamanca: Ediciones San Pío X.

Alberich, Emilio. 1991. *La catequesis en la Iglesia.* Madrid: CCS.

Alonso, Praxedes. 1957. *Pedagogía catequística,* 3rd ed. Barcelona: Vilamala.

Asad, Talal. 1999. *Religion, Nation State, Secularism.* Princeton: Princeton University Press.

– 2003. *Formations of the Secular: Christianity, Islam, Modernity.* Stanford: Stanford University Press.

Bernstorff, Florian. 2009. *Darwin, Darwinismus und Moralpädagogik.* Kempten: Linkhardt.

Bonduelle, Jourdain. 1965. *Situación actual de la revisión de vida.* Barcelona: Nova Terra.

Boyer, Pascal. 2001. *Religion Explained.* New York: Basic Books.

Bruce, Steve. 2011. *Secularization: In Defence of an Unfashionable Theory.* Oxford: Oxford University Press. http://dx.doi.org/10.1093/acprof:osobl/9780199654123.001.0001.

Campbell, Joseph, and Bill Moyers. 1991. *The Power of Myth.* New York: Anchor Books.

Casanova, José. 1994. *Public Religions in the Modern World.* Chicago: University of Chicago Press.

Colom, Antonio J., and Juan C. Rincón. 2004. "Epistemologia neoidealista y fracaso fundacional del saber educativo." *Teoría de la Educación* 16: 19–47.

Colomb, Joseph. 1971. *Manual de Catequética.* Barcelona: Herder.

Damseaux, Eugenio, and Ezequiel Solana. 1967. *Historia de la Pedagogía.* Madrid: Escuela Española.

de Hovre, Frans. 1951. *Pensadores pedagógicos contemporáneos.* Madrid: FAX.

Dobbelaere, Karel. 2004. "Assessing Secularization Theory." In *New Approaches to the Study of Religion*, edited by Peter Antes, Armin W. Geertz, and Randi R. Warne, 229–53. Berlin: De Gruyter.

Domínguez, Javier. 1985. *Organizaciones obreras cristianas en la oposición al franquismo.* Bilbao: Mensajero.

Duperray, Georges, and Christian Ponson. 1994. "Colomb, Joseph." In *Dictionnaire du monde religieux dans la France contemporaine*, edited by Mayeur, Jean-Marie and Yves-Marie Hilaire, 123–4. Paris: Beauchesne.

Fermoso, Paciano. 1970. *Filosofía de la educación.* Madrid: Compañía Bibliográfica Española.

Fullana, Pere, and Feliciano Montero. 2003–4. "Los modelos educativos juveniles del movimiento católico en España." *Revista Historia de la Educación*: 33–51.

Galino, María Ángeles. 1951. Prologue to and "Estudio de los pedagogos españoles contemporáneos." In *Pensadores pedagógicos contemporaneous*, edited by Frans de Hovre. Madrid: Fax.

– 1961. *Introduction to Filosofía católica de la educación.* John D. Redden and Francoise Aloysius Ryan. *Filosofía católica de la educación.* Madrid: Morata.

García Hoz, Victor. 1941. *Pedagogía de la lucha ascética.* Madrid: Bolaños y Aguilar.

– 1948. *Elementos para un programa de enseñanzas sociales.* Madrid: Revista Española de Pedagogía.

– 1960. *Principios de pedagogía sistemática.* Madrid: Rialp.

– 1962. *La tarea profunda de educar.* Madrid: Rialp.

Gil, Antonio. 1957. *Estudios pedagógicos modernos.* Málaga: Denis.

Gonzalo Calavia, Leónides. 1955. *Pedagogía, metodología general y organización escolar.* Madrid: Omnia.

– 1966. *Pedagogía.* Madrid: Paraninfo.

Gorski, Phillip. 2000. "Historicizing the Secularization Debate: Church, State and Society in Late Medieval and Early Modern Europe, ca. 1300 to 1700." *American Sociological Review* 65(1): 138–67. http://dx.doi.org/10.2307/2657295.

Grupos de Apostolado, Obrero. 1958. *Al encuentro de Cristo en el otro por la revisión de hechos de vida obrera.* Madrid: Estades.

Guerrero, Eustaquio. 1945. *Fundamentos de pedagogía cristiana.* Madrid: Razón y fe.

Harpur, Tom. 2004. *The Pagan Christ: Recovering the Lost Light.* Toronto: Thomas Allen.

Ibáñez Martín, José. 1950. "Discurso en el Congreso Nacional del Catecismo (4. 1950. Valencia)." *Revista nacional de educación* 98: 79–95.

Iriarte, Joaquín. 1957. "Una filosofía con sede en los rascacielos." *Razón y Fé* 6(713): 549–60.

Jedin, Hubert, ed. 1981. *The History of the Church*, vol. 10: *The Church in the Modern Age*. London: Burns and Oates.

Jefatura del Estado. 1967. Ley 44/1967, de 28 de junio, regulando el ejercicio del derecho civil a la libertad en materia religiosa. https://www.boe.es/buscar/doc.php?id=BOE-A-1967-10949.

Leirós, Sara. 1973. *Pedagogía hispano-cristiana en su dimensión espiritual*. Madrid: Mundo Negro.

Linz, Juan J. 2009. *Totalitäre und autoritäre Regime*. Postdam: Weltrends.

Llorente, Daniel. 1928. *Tratado elemental de pedagogía catequística*. Valladolid: Martín Sánchez.

– 1937. *Catecismo explicado con gráficos y ejemplos*, 4th ed. Valladolid: Casa Martín.

López, Basilisa. 1995. *Aproximación a la historia de la HOAC, 1946–1981*. Madrid: HOAC.

Luhmann, Niklas. 1997. *Die Gesellschaft der Gesellschaft*. Frankfurt am Main: Suhrkamp.

Maraval, Juan. 1970. *Actividades apostólicas de las religiosas y "revision de vida."* Bilbao: Mensajero.

Maréchal, Albert. 1960a. *La revisión de vida*. Barcelona: Nova Terra.

– 1960b. "La revisión de vida en los primeros años cincuenta." *Aportes: Revista de Historia Contemporánea* 20(57): 22–35.

Martínez, Francisco. 1968. *Principios fundamentales sobre la revisión de vida*. Zaragoza: Berit.

Meyer, John W., and Brian Rowan. 1977. "Institutionalized Organizations: Formal Structure as Myth and Ceremony." *American Journal of Sociology* 83(2): 340–63. http://dx.doi.org/10.1086/226550.

Millán Puelles, Antonio. 1963. *La formación de la personalidad humana*. Madrid: Rialp.

Molinario, Joël. 2010. *Joseph Colomb et l'affaire du catéchisme progressif*. Paris: DDB.

Montero, Feliciano. 1988. *Propaganda católica y educación popular en la España de la Restauración*. Tours: l'Université de Tours.

– 2009. *La Iglesia: de la colaboración a la disidencia (1956–1975)*. Madrid: Encuentro.

– 2011. "La iglesia dividida." In *De la cruzada al desenganche: la Iglesia española entre el Franquismo y la Transisión*, edited by Manuel Ortiz Heras and Damián A. González, 51–76. Madrid: Silex.

Norris, Pippa, and Ronald Inglehart. 2004. *Sacred and Secular: Religion and Politics Worldwide*. Cambridge: Cambridge University Press. http://dx.doi.org/10.1017/CBO9780511791017.

Orden, Rafael V. 2008. "La formación de una Escuela de Filosofía." In *La Facultad de Filosofía y Letras de Madrid en la Segunda República*, edited by S López-Ríos Moreno, 212–23. Madrid: SECC.

Pacios, Arsenio. 1947. *Filosofía de la educación.* Madrid: Orbe.

Palmés, Fernando M. 1953. *Prologue to Pedagogía cristiana y experimental, by León Barbey.* Barcelona: Subirana.

Pérez-Agote, Alfonso. 2007. "El proceso de secularización en la sociedad española." *Revista CIDOB* 77: 65–82.

Planchard, Émile. 1949. *La pedagogía contemporánea.* Madrid: Rialp.

Pope Paul VI. 1964. *Decree on Ecumenism (Unitatis Redintegratio).* http://www.vatican.va/archive/hist_councils/ii_vatican_council/documents/vat-ii_decree_19641121_unitatis-redintegratio_en.html.

Pope Paul VI. 1965. *Pastoral Constitution on the Church in Modern World (Gaudium et Spes).* http://www.vatican.va/archive/hist_councils/ii_vatican_council/documents/vat-ii_cons_19651207_gaudium-et-spes_en.html.

del Pozo, María del Mar, and Sjaak Braster. 2012. El movimiento de la Escuela Nueva en la España franquista (España, 1936-1976). *Revista Brasileira de História da Educaçao* 12 (30): 15–44.

Redden, John D., and Françoise A. Ryan. 1961. *Filosofía católica de la educación.* Madrid: Morata.

Romero Marín, Anselmo. 1960. *El Método Activo de la Enseñanza.* Madrid: Bolaños y Aguilar.

Royo, Eugenio. 1964, *Acción militante y revisión de vida.* Madrid: Popular.

Ruíz, Manuel. 1968. *Hacia una pedagogía de la obediencia cristiana.* Madrid: Studium.

Sánchez, Fernando. 2003. *La España del Siglo XX.* Madrid: Istmo.

Sangnier, Marc. 1906. *Une méthode d'éducation démocratique.* Paris: Au Sillon.

Schriewer, Jürgen, and Carlos Martínez Valle. 2003. *World-Level Ideology or Nation-Specific System Reflection?* Lisbon: Educa.

Taylor, Charles. 2007. *A Secular Age.* Cambridge, MA: Harvard University Press.

Tschannen, Oliver. 1991. "The Secularization Paradigm: A Systematization." *Journal for the Scientific Study of Religion* 30(4): 395–415. http://dx.doi.org/10.2307/1387276.

Tusquets, Joan. 1944. *Pedagogía catequística para seglares.* Barcelona: Lumen.

– 1946. *La religión explicada a los mayorcitos.* Barcelona: Lumen.

– 1951. "La función catequística del maestro." *Revista Española de Pedagogía* 36: 20–46.

– 1957. "La nueva metodología catequística francesa para el parvulario." *Revista de Educación* 67: 37–41.

– 1968. *Teoría y práctica de la pedagogía comparada.* Madrid: Magisterio Español.

Vilanou, Conrad. 1999. "Pensamiento y discursos pedagógicos en España (1898–1940)." In *La educación en España a examen.*, edited by Julio Ruiz Berrio, 19–57. Zaragoza: Fernando el Católico.

Viñao, Antonio. 2004. *Escuela para todos.* Madrid: Marcial Pons.

Wilson, Bryan. 1988. "Religion as a Community Resource." *Perspectives on Culture and Society* 1: 81–100.

Zaragüeta, Juan. 1941. *Pedagogía de la religión.* Madrid: Espasa-Calpe.

4 Turning Need into a Virtue: The Adjustment to the Educational Demands of the Religious Congregations: The Case of De La Salle in the Basque Country, Spain

PAULÍ DÁVILA AND LUIS M. NAYA

Introduction

The educational work of religious orders and congregations throughout the twentieth century can be defined by two characteristics: an ability to adapt to the social environments that surrounded them and to meet the educational needs of the community, and the creation of an internal discourse that matched the new and changing realities of the Church at that time. This chapter aims to illustrate these two characteristics through the actions (and reactions) of the male religious congregations with the strongest presence in Spain and the Basque Country: the Institute of the Brothers of the Christian Schools (De La Salle). To that end, we analyse (1) the evolution of the Lasallian educational institutions throughout the twentieth century, noting their attention to local, social, and educational needs, and (2) the renewal of discourse following Vatican II in terms of the Brothers' role as teachers. These two phenomena will explain part of the success experienced by some religious institutes (orders and congregations) dedicated to education.

One of the most widely established theses in the historiography of Spain's religious institutes dedicated to education speaks to the ability of these institutes to adapt to the social contexts in which they were established (Dávila et al. 2009; Ostolaza 2000). That flexibility allowed most of them to continue the successful educational endeavours for which they were known. In the same vein, the establishment of religious institutes served as a modernizing element during the industrialization and modernization process in Spain and the Basque Country (Louzao 2011). However, the subject has barely been studied from the perspective of general historiography, the history of the Church, or education (Bartolomé 1997; Callahan 2000; Lannon 1987).

Along with the above thesis, we address another that is related to the changes that took place within the religious institutes as a result of Vatican II, focusing on the De La Salle congregation. The thesis of internal renewal, which had consequences for both the internal approaches taken by the religious institutes and the incorporation of new teachers and scholastic reforms, is well established. The changes benefited from a discourse in which the renewed charism of the Founder and a return to the congregation's origins explained the evolution that started with charism and moved to the Lasallian family. In this sense, Vatican II played a central role in offering theoretical tools that made this "reconversion" viable. This transformative process produced the desired effects; given the shortage of Brothers dedicated to teaching and the scarcity of vocations, the "shared mission" brought laypeople, including teaching staff and families, into the same discourse.

In the final third of the twentieth century, the phenomena of adaptation and adjustment were strengthened, which made it possible for there to be educational institutions in which the "brand" of a religious institute could endure despite the limited presence of religious teaching staff. In this sense, Vatican II made its contribution by defending the idea that we are all the Church and that laypeople should play a greater role in religious and educational duties. In focusing on these two phenomena through the lens of the De La Salle congregation, we observe a model in which adapting to the environment and adjusting the discourse explain the success of religious education in the Basque Country.

Adaptation to Social and Educational Needs

The secularization that Europe experienced throughout the twentieth century was marked by particular characteristics in the case of Spain (Pérez Agote 2012; Vanderstraeten 2014).[1] The various levels of conflict in Spain between the Church and the state were constant, though not continuous. In a certain sense, the Second Spanish Republic (1931–9) was the ultimate expression of this conflict, in that it proclaimed itself to be secular and expelled the Jesuits (de la Cueva and Montero 2009). In the first third of the twentieth century, two events gave rise to the role that religious teaching and education by religious institutes came to have (Dávila and Naya 2011). First, the state launched a series of policies and strategies that gave it greater control over education (thus the *Estado docente*, "teaching state") (De Puelles 2007; García Tejedor 1985, Viñao Frago 2004). Second, the Church began to engage in unifying action through various institutional alliances. Faced with secular policy, the Church adjusted its actions throughout this period, leaving behind its traditional isolation and seeking joint action (Faubell 2000). The organization of ecclesiastical congresses and the rise of Catholic Action in 1903 involved focusing efforts on the prelates as well as significant personalities in Catholicism (Callahan 2000). Over time, Catholic Action transformed itself into a movement that defended the Church and fostered a Catholic political right that was determined to organize the masses (Montero 2007). The rise of Catholic circles and Catholic-leaning unions completed this complex Church organization. The founding in 1930 of the Federation of Friends of Education (*Federación de Amigos de la Enseñanza* [FAE]), which represented the religious institutes, had a clear purpose: to unify Catholic activities. One of the FAE's promoters, Marianist Domingo Lazaro, noted that "we lack in Spain a Catholic general staff, in education as in all else" (Salaverria 2003, 243). The federation's objective was to gain that power for the Church, and it succeeded in unifying Catholics in the area of education.

During the Franco regime (1939–75), the feuding between the state and the Church gave way gradually to collaboration and consensus. However, this cannot be said of the entire Franco era, as made clear by the expressive title of a recent work, *From Crusade to Disengagement* (Botti 2008; Montero 2000; Ortiz and González 2011). At the beginning of the Spanish Civil War, the Church forged the myth of a "crusade"; but by the 1960s and 1970s, it started to distance itself from the Franco regime. This was the result of the process of secularization, the progressive politicization of the clergy, and accommodation to the principles of Vatican II. In this sense, the early years of the Franco regime can be seen as a "golden age": after a policy of subsidiarity was established in the 1945 Primary Education Act and the Concordat of 1953 was signed, there was an expansion of primary and secondary schools run by religious institutes. Beginning in the 1960s the monolithic image of the Church began to weaken – there were worker priests, objections from the Basque clergy, and so on. Vatican II explains the tensions and internal divisions within the Spanish Church, between those who supported Vatican II and those who opposed it. The same split occurred in the political arena, between the Francoists and their opponents (Montero 2011).

In this context, religious schools began to spread. In the 1950s, different religious institutes were expanding throughout Spain. The principal institutes were the Jesuits, the Salesians, the Marists, and the Lasallians, who built up a presence at various levels of education, especially in secondary and vocational training (Dávila and Naya 2011). After 1975 their presence in public schools began to grow as a result of the educational reform of 1970. The strongest evidence of this shift is the evolution in secondary education: "in 1950, there were only 119 public schools, compared to the 625 secondary schools run by religious institutes. This imbalance between the public and private education sectors was not new, and it resembled the predominant status prior to 1931. The orientation toward class that was characteristic of religious schools during the 1920s hardly changed during the 1940s and 1950s" (Callahan 2000, 353). In the 1960s, some who had connections with Opus Dei and who promoted technocratic approaches took up posts in government ministries; this drove an expansion of public secondary schools to the detriment of religious schools. While all the changes demanded by modernization and economic development were taking place, the institutes took heed and adapted themselves to meet the needs of the middle class by providing schools that charged fees, as well as the needs of the working class by providing vocational training. These were two areas that the state had not paid sufficient attention to, in terms of legislation and of building new schools. The De La Salle congregation provides a good model for explaining this phenomenon.

De La Salle: Evolution of the Institute

The De La Salle Brothers opened their first school in Spain in 1878 and permanently established themselves in the country upon their expulsion from France in 1904 (Bedel 2006; Cabanel 2005; Cabanel and Durand 2005; Delaunay 2005). The De La Salle Brothers' reception led to a growth spurt. The Lasallian congregation created an extensive network of primary, vocational, and secondary schools across the country (Gallego 1978; Gil 1997), particularly in the provinces bordering France, possibly with the idea that one day they would be able to return there (Dávila 2011). In 1904, there were forty-seven communities (groups of Brothers dedicated primarily to teaching) in Spain, constituting a total of 381 Brothers and 12,763 students. By 1913, the situation had changed substantially; there were 132 communities, 1,245 Brothers, and 26,026 students (Dávila et al. 2009). Thus within ten years the number of students had doubled and the number of communities had tripled, despite the anti-clergy political climate in Spain at the time. During that period, the communities consisted mostly of French Brothers, although little by little Spanish Brothers began to join various districts, due to new vocations and the training of Brothers native to Spain in the various novitiates that had been created for that purpose. This led to a process of "Hispanicization" in the communities, which had clear repercussions for the evolution of De La Salle in Spain (Dávila 2011).

The victory of Francoism allowed the Lasallians to establish themselves permanently and to experience steady growth. Like many other institutes, the Lasallians experienced a period during which they fully identified themselves with National Catholicism and expanded their network of schools throughout Spain (Dávila et al. 2009). The Church's support of and collaboration with the Franco regime and the passage of legislation that favoured religious education benefited religious schools; this led to a flourishing of schools at all educational levels (Faubell 2000; Viñao Frago 2004). This development can be explained by the capacity of the Lasallian schools to adapt to changing social and educational contexts. The situation remained stable for the Lasallian congregation until 1947, at which point it underwent another period of significant growth, lasting until 1967. As a result, the 142 communities (compared to 132 in 1930) and the 39,143 students that existed in 1947 had grown to 200 communities and 78,315 students by 1967. However, after 1967, the number of communities began to decline, and by 1977, there were just 181.

During the 1970s, two external events occurred, resulting in a new period of adjustment. The first was the impact of Vatican II, which emphasized a return to the charism of the Founder, which in turn meant a return to the institute's original advocacy of educating the poor. In Spain, as in other countries, this message was interpreted by Catholic schools as referring to the "option for the poor" (Griega 2007). The second event consisted of a series of changes related to (1) legislation (the General Education Act of 1970); (2) demographics (more students were entering the education system); (3) economic development and a certain degree of modernization; and (4) growing political unrest. In the case of the Basque Country, besides these external factors, there were others factors internal to the congregation itself: (1) the inadequacy of the De La Salle schools located in the Basque region, which had stopped carrying out their function due to the growth of the public schools and the *ikastolas* (schools where the primary or sole language of instruction is Basque); (2) the increase in the number of years of schooling, which gave rise to greater access to secondary education (a level of education that had been little valued by Lasallians due to the connotations of educating a particular social class), which offered a diploma to the general population and spurred the working classes to attain this level of education; (3) the decrease in the importance of religious rituals and the crisis experienced by the Basque Church, which found itself in conflict with other dioceses in Spain over questions of national identity; and (4) the decline in the number of religious vocations and the gradual substitution of Brothers by secular teachers, both male and female (Dávila et al. 2009). In the case of the Lasallians, their adaptation to social needs can be seen in three areas: secondary education, vocational training, and Basque language.

Prestigious Schools and Secondary Education

In this context, the De La Salle congregation also chose to run prestigious schools, albeit to a lesser extent than other institutes. Educating the upper and middle classes made it possible for the Brothers to operate their free schools, sometimes even within the same facility. Some of the schools that stand out in this regard are Bonanova in Barcelona, Maravillas in Madrid, Lourdes in Valladolid, and Paterna in Valencia (Gallego 1978). In the Basque Country, notable schools are Santiago Apóstol in Bilbao, San Marcial in Irun, and La Salle and San Bernardo in San Sebastián. The latter is especially relevant, for this was the famous St-Bernard School that had been transferred from Bayonne, France, and that operated in San Sebastián from 1905 to 1928, the period during which the French Brothers were exiled (Lissarrague 1999). The San Bernardo School was for many years the flagship of the Brothers of the Christian Schools in the province of Guipúzcoa, and it had a great influence on other schools in the region (Dávila et al. 2009). It was a boarding school that attracted students who went on to secondary education and advanced commercial training. In this latter arena, the incorporation of innovations in commercial training also entailed an advance in the teaching and learning methods, and these offered a model that soon spread to other schools within the congregation, both in Spain and in other countries (Dávila et al. 2012).

When the San Bernardo School was moved back to France, this type of education was no longer offered in San Sebastián, so in 1946 the La Salle School opened, explicitly declaring itself the successor of San Bernardo; the school still exists. Another of the school's distinguishing features was that it remained a boarding school, welcoming students from various backgrounds, in terms of both their geographic origins and their training. The success and prestige of this school was continuously demonstrated both by the number of students enrolled and by the broad range of training it offered.

The De La Salle boarding school closed in 1981 owing to a variety of academic, social, and organizational factors. By that time "secondary education institutions were being established in towns ... In the final year of operation, only 40 students were enrolled in the boarding school ... The freer attitude that was introduced in the middle of the 1970s was incompatible with the environment of austerity and discipline and the work that was characteristic of our school, which until that moment had been accepted as the most natural thing in the world" (Garitano 1997, 48). In addition to these factors, we must take into account the position taken by the provincial chapters (1968, 1969–71, 1973) in their discussions of whether there was a need to keep operating these kinds of boarding schools for the children of the elite families in the province of Guipúzcoa. This reflected the pervasiveness of the decisions taken by the General Chapter in 1996.

Popular Education and Vocational Training

The Lasallian Brothers were most active in the field of vocational education (Dávila et al. 2013). During the Franco regime, their congregation had the most vocational schools: in 1944, 22 per cent of the twenty-seven schools that were in the Church's hands in the Basque Country were run by the De La Salle Brothers (the rest were run by Jesuits, Marists, and Salesians). The De La Salle schools were concentrated in Guipúzcoa and in a number of towns in Bilbao's industrial belt (Dávila et al. 2012). The locations of the congregation's schools were a response to the towns' growing industrialization and to calls by industrialists, boards of trustees, and municipal bodies for schools to be opened in particular locations.

Some schools chose to offer a *Bachillerato Laboral* (Occupational Baccalaureate); others offered a stream in Professional Initiation, which was tied more closely to primary education. At one point, this type of diploma was offered in some towns in Guipúzcoa: Zumarraga, starting in 1965 (although after 1952 it was at the apprenticeship level); Eibar, starting in 1964; and Zarautz, starting in 1965. In addition, these schools taught courses in commerce, as was the case at Los Ángeles in San Sebastián starting in 1953 and at La Salle in San Sebastián starting in 1959. In 1954, the school in Beasain began to offer a stream in industrial, commercial, and vocational initiation; in 1953 the school in Zumarraga established a Professional Apprentices' School, as did the school in Andoain (1945–73). The school that most clearly dedicated itself to vocational training from the start was the Professional School of Irun. All of these vocational studies programs were established at a time when the state paid little attention to this type of education. After the General Education Act was passed in 1970, these kinds of schools became regulated by the state (ibid.).

The success of this type of vocational training was guaranteed, for many students were able to find employment in the flourishing industrial sector, in banks, and in private companies. Many companies requested from particular schools specialized training that met their industrial and business needs; sometimes the demand was so great that students were hired even before they had finished their studies (Dávila et al. 2009).

Making Teachers and Schools Basque-Speaking

Another area in which we can observe the capacity of the De La Salle Christian Brothers to adapt to the social environment is the incorporation of the Basque language into scholastic activities. This required a process of "euskaldunization" (becoming Basque-speakers), in which the Brothers became speakers of Basque, particularly during the 1970s. In the first third of the twentieth century, it was already possible to observe the Visiting Brother recommending that the Brothers speak to their students in Basque, despite the language of instruction being Spanish. Moreover, the De La Salle Christian Brothers' publishing house, Bruño, published textbooks in Basque, which the Brothers themselves wrote. During the Franco regime the situation changed, and the role of Basque in schools underwent three distinct phases. In the first, which lasted until the mid-1960s, it was confirmed that teaching Basque-speaking students in Spanish was not sufficiently effective owing to their relative lack of proficiency in Spanish. In the second, from the 1960s to the 1970s, classes were taught in Basque on a voluntary basis, and some Brothers began to learn to speak, read, and write in Basque. In the final phase, there was a clear preference for teaching in Basque most of the time, in alignment with the sociolinguistic environment in which some schools were embedded. It is also worth noting that parallel to this process, some schools engaged in activities related to Basque culture and the fostering of the Basque language (ibid.).

Table 4.1 Composition of teaching staff at the De La Salle schools in Guipúzcoa, 1960–2000

	1960		1970		1980		1990		2000	
	N	%	N	%	N	%	N	%	N	%
Brothers	100	**83.33**	95	**43.98**	74	**29.84**	80	**21.79**	55	**13.68**
Secular men	20	**16.66**	117	**54.17**	111	**44.76**	130	**35.42**	129	**32.09**
Secular women	0	**0**	4	**1.85**	63	**25.40**	157	**42.78**	218	**54.23**
Total	120	**100**	216	**100**	248	**100**	367	**100**	402	**100**

Source: *Bajo el signo de la Educación.*

Adjusting Discourse to the New Nature of the Church

A second pillar that supports the enduring nature and success of the Brothers' schools is that they adjusted their pedagogical approach and renewed their discourse to accommodate the new requirements of the Church, especially during the Franco era. The Brothers' traditional discourse remained virtually unchanged until the 1960s (Valladolid and Dávila 2012); even the training received by those who aspired to become Brothers remained invariable (Comte et al. 2014). But after Vatican II, the Lasallian discourse changed. Before we examine these consequences, basing our analysis on the congregation's own texts, it is worth noting that their schools continued to be successful despite the progressive decline in the number of Brothers who taught.

Table 4.1 shows the changes that took place over four decades: a 70 per cent reduction in the number of Brothers who taught, a 16 per cent increase in secular male teaching staff, and the introduction of secular female teaching staff, whose numbers progressively increased to their current level, comprising over 50 per cent of the total teaching staff.

This helps us understand how the new discourse was used. Vatican II accommodated the increased presence of secular teachers – that is, it turned necessity into a virtue. The necessity was the incorporation of laypeople into the educational endeavor; the virtue was the strengthening of the Lasallian charism. All of this took place under the aegis of post–Vatican II postulates. To this renewal of charism and of the pedagogical discourse were added the concepts of "shared mission," which opened the mission to laypeople, and of "religious family," encompassing the charism and the apostolic mission of each religious institute (Botana 2008). This was, without doubt, a moment of crisis during which charism was the vehicle for building a new religious identity that fit the new situation in which the Church found itself (Álvarez 2001; Consejo Internacional de Estudios Lasalianos 2005).

In tandem with this process, the decrease in the number of religious vocations at De La Salle schools can be observed. There were sixty-five vocations between 1942 and 1965, divided as follows: three brothers, twelve priests, twenty-one seminarians, and twenty-nine other religious institutes.[2] The period of greatest vocational recruitment was 1940 to 1970. Note, however, that only a minority of these recruits were for the De La Salle Brothers. Other congregations experienced similar declines. In the second half of the twentieth century, the decline of the religious institutes was due to two factors operating more or less successively: a marked decrease in the number of new recruits, and a strong increase in the number of brothers and sisters who were leaving (Vanderstraeten 2014, 505).

Clearly, this shift should be framed in the discourse of the religious institutes, since this phenomenon affected all of them. In other words, faced with a new educational reality, a new pedagogical discourse had to follow. The recommendations in Vatican II allowed a return to charism without a loss of identity, while also allowing for renewal, adjustment to changes, and the incorporation of laypeople into the teaching endeavour.

Consequences of Vatican II and *accommodata renovatio*

There are a number of well-known studies on the consequences of Vatican II (Escudero 2014; Lamb and Levering 2008; Ruiz de Galarreta 2012; Unzueta 1995). However, it is worth highlighting how *accommodata renovatio* was implemented in the case of the De La Salle Brothers, especially after the Declaration of 1967, which became the backbone of Lasallian renewal. Vatican II's proposals for *aggiornamento* marked an important turning point for all the religious institutes that had to apply *accommodata renovatio* to religious life. With regard to the De La Salle congregation, the document that most precisely expresses this renewal is *The Brothers of the Christian Schools in the World Today: A Declaration*, approved in 1967 as part of the 39th General Chapter. The Declaration's importance was such that the 40th General Chapter (1976) reaffirmed its validity with regard to the mission of the Brother (Hermanos de las Escuelas Cristianas 1977, 227–311). The challenge the institute faced after the General Chapter in 1966 was to contribute to the necessary renewal of the school in a way that "would help bring into being a school that is capable of training men in the 20th century" (Gil 1994, 332). Other decrees adopted as part of this chapter affected the daily life of the Brothers; to maintain the lay nature of the institute, female students were allowed to enrol in the schools; also, Brothers were no longer required to change their names upon entering the institute and were allowed to wear clothing other than the official uniform. The importance and repercussions of Vatican II within the Lasallian Institute are demonstrated by the example of a "postcounciliar Brother" who advocated a renewed apostolic commitment (Gallego 1969) and a vision of the school from a Lasallian educational approach (García Carrasco 1969). Even in more recent times, there has been an insistence on these approaches and on the renewed vision of the Brother relative to popular Christian education and from the Lasallian perspective (Villalabeitia 2014).

However, this renewal caught the congregation at one of the lowest points in its history, as indicated by the testimony of Michel Sauvage (Comte et al. 2014), who wrote about this era with a certain bitterness, noting the contradiction in which the Brothers found themselves.

> On one hand, there was implicit recognition of their apostolic and educational work; on the other there, was a decline in vocations: Due to numerous causes, during the 1970s the Institute underwent significant hemorrhaging, losing Brothers in several countries. At the same time, the number of new members fell almost everywhere, such that in some cases the attrition was total ... The statistics impassively announced each year that the Institute continued losing numbers and was ageing: all of this made it very painful for the leadership, who had to make the Brothers aware of the extent of a phenomenon that affected all the rest of the religious orders and the diocesan clergy. (Comte et al. 2014, 24–5)

This crisis affected both male and female congregations.

This was a crucial moment for Lasallian identity, for Vatican II required the congregation to renew its own rules. The General Chapter of 1966–7 was "the decisive event that ushered we Brothers into a new era" (Comte et al. 2014, 308). This General Chapter is considered within Lasallian history to be of great significance, for one of its central themes was the "option for the poor" and adapting to the social needs of the times: "the De La Salle Brothers' calling is to give themselves entirely to God, in service of educating the poor" (Alpago 2000, 387). Over the course of the General Chapters that followed (1976, 1986, 1993), this Lasallian characteristic was reaffirmed; it was noted that the institute's aims were those of a community of Brothers assembled for the purpose of educating the poor in a changing world and in a Church in flux (ibid.).

The Brothers of the Christian Schools in the World Today: A Declaration (1967)

The importance of the 1967 Declaration is directly linked to Vatican II. It was later shown that the text was authored by Michel Sauvage. As he himself stated, the text was the result of discussions that took place during the Chapter of 1966, to which he "only" contributed his "pen." Indeed, many of the concerns that greatly occupied him at the time are reflected in the Declaration (Comte et al. 2014). Regardless, the text is well structured and sound in that it addresses several of the Lasallian Brothers' characteristics at that time: (1) loyalty to the Founder, (2) knowledge of the signs of the time, (3) the Brothers' vocation, (4) religious life (communal and apostolic), (5) serving the poor through education, (6) the teaching of faith and human formation, and (7) the educational activities of the Brothers. Thus it is understood that the Declaration reflects three of the Vatican II texts that affect religious life: *Lumen Gentium*, which addresses the nature of the religious figure in the world; *Perfectae Charitatis,* which is a call to deep renewal; and *Gravissimum Educationis,* which addresses the issue of what Christian education should be. As Saturnino Gallego (1978, 730–1) points out, these three texts "hit our targets" as De La Salle Brothers.

Of the above aspects, the ones that most interest us are those related to service to the poor, education in faith and in human formation, and educational renewal. In terms of *serving the poor* though education, the congregation's fidelity to the principles laid out by the Founder is clear, reminding them that "an orientation toward the poor is an integral part of the Institute's aims" (Hermanos de las Escuelas Cristianas 1977, 265); this meant that reaching out to the poor needed to include a gradual transformation of some schools and a renewal of others. This recommendation, in practice, was fulfilled with less resolution than hoped. Along the same lines, the Declaration suggested that the increase in vocations be directed towards "towns that find themselves on the path to development" (ibid., 272). Thus, this text is behind the changes that took place in secondary education, which entailed closing schools and directing new vocations towards developing countries, as was observed in the case of the Basque Country.

With regard to *teaching the faith and Christian formation,* the Declaration reiterated the Rules of 1705: "The aim of this Institute is to provide

Christian education to children." Nevertheless, both *Gravissimum Educationis* and the Declaration recognize the universal right to education as proclaimed by international bodies. The first also includes aspects of the Council's own reminder of the importance of evangelization and catechism in the apostolic activities of the Church. The vision of the Catholic school, as given in *Gravissimum Educationis*, is based on the Church's right to establish and promote schools. These centres should be educational communities moved by the evangelical spirit of freedom and charity where teachers, in their apostolate, are well trained to serve society. Thus, the Declaration urged the Brothers to carry out this work, particularly with the most vulnerable youths and adolescents. It also maintained that all catechists "today need to be introduced to the sciences of man" (ibid., 279), so Brothers should be well trained in this area.

In the same vein, within the Brothers' educational activities, the apostolate scholar should retain his importance since the Christian school "facilitates the exercise and effectiveness of catechism" (ibid., 287). However, the Declaration praised the *pedagogical renewal* observed among the Brothers, inviting them to participate in this pedagogical movement. The aim of the De La Salle schools is characterized by "the quality of their study programs and the seriousness of their training, as demanded by both their professional honor and their dedication to youth and society" (ibid., 289). The Declaration also pointed out the importance of the school community and the need for Brothers to cooperate in defending a pedagogy of freedom, which was believed to be as indispensible as education in faith, for "the Christian school wishes to impose as little as possible: it proposes, without forcing, the infinite possibilities that are offered by a life that follows Jesus Christ" (ibid., 293). As the Declaration laid out, all of this entailed new requirements for the training of teachers. Also, the Brothers should become more involved in non-scholastic activities in order to remedy education-related needs, making the schools places where everything converged.

Following the General Chapter of 1966 and the Declaration of 1967, implementation was carried out through the First General Chapter of Assistance in Spain and the District of Bilbao, both held in 1968 (Lasa et al. 1989). The first Chapter of the District of Bilbao dedicated itself to education and laid out a series of conclusions, including that the planning of schools should be conducted in accordance with "supporting the popular classes, promoting the working class and a return to the poor," following the directives of the General Chapter of 1966. In this regard, a "model organizational flow chart" was drawn up, which each school could adapt to its particular situation when forming a team for vocational and psychological guidance and special courses. In terms of the Brothers themselves, it was recommended that funds be provided so that some could obtain professorships at accredited educational institutions, particularly in Schools of Education. This reflected one of the conclusions given in the General Chapter of Assistance in Spain.

The following year, the District Chapter, held between 1969 and 1971, called for the creation of an Office of Education as "a requirement that is necessary for carrying out suitable planning for the District in the current moment." It also outlined the tasks that most urgently needed to be undertaken: establishing a psycho-pedagogical guidance service; training the teaching staff in modern teaching methods and activity guidance; starting a pilot school for basic education and another for bilingual education; and raising teachers' awareness of the value of leisure and training them in techniques to guide recreation. As we can observe in the chapter, the concerns of the District focused on questions related to organization, planning, and the Basque language.

The third chapter, which met between 1973 and 1974, again insisted on concrete methods for reviving, from the perspective of faith, the ministry of service to the poor. This principle was specified with respect to the schools themselves: it would be appropriate to reduce their number "in order to gain freedom and dedicate themselves to the most destitute, going beyond the requirements that were noted in the planning of the previous Chapter" (Dávila et al. 2009, 161). In this regard, the Visiting Brother, along with the District Council, "was to establish the means for orienting the schools in wealthy areas toward students with fewer economic resources" (ibid., 161). It was suggested that, in line with this action, communities be constituted in very poor areas. In this spirit of service to the poor, it was agreed that the schools would be "open to everybody and they would participate in the culture, language, traditions and activities of the town or neighborhood, in the pastoral activity of the parish or community, in literacy campaigns, and in intensive vocational training" (ibid., 161). Similarly, it recommended that the Brothers, in carrying out their educational work, be fully dedicated to the poorest of the poor; this included rehabilitating people with disabilities by attending to their ongoing education, helping immigrants integrate, and linking with the parochial, cultural, athletic, social, and labour organizations in their environment. To cap all of this off, the Brothers were asked to spend their days in complete dedication to their work. Their residences and lifestyles should resemble those of families with modest means.

To this end, the institute made some of its properties available to the lower classes as a part of its social service.

As we have seen, in the first three District Chapters (1968–74), the basic theme of their conclusions revolved around aspects whose importance cannot be underestimated given the political situation, the underlying religious approaches, and the educational reforms following the General Education Act of 1970, one consequence of which was the closing of several schools in Guipúzcoa. It is important to point out that during those years, a new direction was being forged within the De La Salle Institute in the Basque Country, one whose starting point can be found in the General Chapter of 1966, which was itself the result of the far-reaching framework established by the Second Ecumenical Vatican Council.

Conclusion

One of the most important challenges for historians of religious congregations dedicated to teaching – in this case focusing on the Basque Country – is to explain how schools run by religious institutes have remained open for so many decades despite the conflicts in Spain between the Church and the state. We have highlighted two explanations: the ability to adapt to social, economic, and educational needs, and the adjustment to the Church's discourse of renewal.

In studying the case of the De La Salle schools in the Basque Country, we have determined that their successful educational practices, which resulted from their ability to adapt to social needs, took place on two educational levels. On one hand, they provided secondary education to the middle and upper classes at prestigious secondary schools, and on the other they provided vocational training to the working class, guaranteeing them a degree of social mobility and meeting the needs of various social and economic stakeholders. Furthermore, the De La Salle Brothers' interest in the Basque language at particular moments demonstrated their adaptation to the bilingual context of the Basque Country.

The De La Salle Brothers' adjustment to the dominant discourse of the Church following Vatican II also demonstrates that they have internalized the post-counciliar message. This adjustment is evident in *The Brothers of the Christian Schools in the World Today: A Declaration* (Hermanos de la Escuelas Cristianas 1977), which addressed issues related to the Brothers' vocation, education in faith, option for the poor, pedagogical renewal, and educational activities.

Thus the De La Salle Brothers' educational activities and their renewed discourse formed the two pillars that supported the Lasallian institution in the era in question. One cannot be explained without the other. In this particular case, we see how a change in the state of affairs required that they take on a new pedagogical discourse that better accommodated educational and pastoral needs. Vatican II is the hinge that allows us to understand the changes that occurred in the 1970s in most of the religious congregations devoted to teaching.

NOTES

This article is the result of a research project financed by the Spanish Ministry for Economy and Competitiveness, project number EDU2013-44129-P. The authors are members of the Group for Historical and Comparative Studies in Education, Garaian, recognized by the Basque Government, registry number IT 911-16, and of the Unity of Education and Research "Education, Culture and Society (UFI 11/54)" at the University of the Basque Country UPV/EHU.

The authors would like to thank Wendy Baldwin for her assistance in translating this chapter from Spanish to English.

1 For sociological approaches to the role of religious congregations, secularization, and modernization, authors such as Durkheim, Weber, Luckmann, and Berger should be kept in mind. In the case of Berger, the new approaches to pluralism and modernity do not invalidate previous approaches. See Peter Berger, *The Many Altars of Modernity: Toward a Paradigm for Religion in a Pluralist Age* (Berlin: De Gruyter, 2014).

2 De La Salle Archive, District of Bilbao, Box 255, file 10.

REFERENCES

Alpago, Bruno, FSC. 2000. *El Instituto al servicio educativo de los pobres.* Roma: Casa Generalicia FSC.

Álvarez, Jesús. 2001. *Carisma e historia. Claves para interpretar la historia de una congregación religiosa.* Madrid: Publicaciones Claretianas.

Bartolomé, Bernabé. 1997. *Historia de la acción educadora de la Iglesia en España. Edad Contemporánea.* Madrid: Biblioteca de Autores Cristianos.

Bedel, Henri, FSC. 2006. "An Introduction to the History of the Institute of the Brothers of the Christian Schools: 19th and 20th Century (1875–1928)." *Lasallian Studies* 11: 207–39.

Botana, Antonio. 2008. *Compartir carisma y misión con los laicos: La familia evangélica como horizonte. Vitoria/Gasteiz.* Madrid: Instituto Teológico de Vida Religiosa.

Botti, Alfonso. 2008. *Cielo y dinero. El nacional catolicismo en España 1881–1975.* Madrid: Alianza.

Cabanel, Patrick. 2005. "Panorámica general del exilio congregacionista." *Anuario de Historia de la Iglesia* 14: 97–108.

Cabanel, Patrick, and Jean-Dominique Durand. 2005. *Le grand exil des congrégations religieuses Françaises 1901–1914.* Paris: Les éditions du CER.

Callahan, William J. 2000. *The Catholic Church in Spain, 1875–1998.* Washington, DC: Catholic University of America Press.

Comte, Robert, Paul Grass, and Diego Muñoz. 2014. *La frágil esperanza de un testigo. El itinerario del H. Michel Sauvage (1923–2001).* Roma: Casa Generalicia FSC.

Consejo Internacional de Estudios Lasalianos. 2005. *El Carisma Lasaliano.* Rome: Hermanos de las Escuelas Cristianas.

Dávila, Paulí. 2011. "Las órdenes y congregaciones religiosas francesas y su impacto sobre la educación en España. Siglos XIX y XX." In *Francia en la educación de la España contemporánea (1808–2008)*, edited by José Maria Hernández, 101–60. Salamanca: Ediciones de la Universidad de Salamanca.

Dávila, Paulí, and Luis M. Naya. 2011. "La enseñanza privada religiosa en España: instituciones, políticas e identidades." In *Laicidade, Religiões e Educação na Europa do Sul no Século XX*, edited by Joaquim Pintassilgo, 367–92. Lisbon: Instituto da Educaçao.

Dávila, Paulí, Luis M. Naya, and Hilario Murua. 2009. *Bajo el signo de la educación. 100 años de La Salle en Gipuzkoa San Sebastián.* San Sebastián: Hermanos de las Escuelas Cristianas, Distrito de Bilbao.

– 2012. "The Educational Work of the De la Salle Brothers and Popular Education in Gipuzkoa in the Twentieth Century." *History of Education* 41(2): 213–33. http://dx.doi.org/10.1080/0046760X.2011.582046.

– 2013. "Tradition and Modernity of the De La Salle Schools: The Case of the Basque Country in Franco's Spain (1937–1975)." *Paedagogica Historica: International Journal of the History of Education* 49(4): 562–76. http://dx.doi.org/10.1080/00309230.2013.799500.

de la Cueva, Julio, and Feliciano Montero, eds. 2009. *Laicismo y catolicismo. El conflicto político-religiosos en la Segunda República.* Madrid: Universidad de Alcalá.

de Puelles, Manuel. 2007. *Política y educación en la España contemporánea.* Madrid: UNED.

Delaunay, Jean Marc. 2005. "Exilio o refugio en España (veinticinco años después)." *Anuario de Historia de la Iglesia* 14: 153–64.

Escudero, José Antonio. 2014. *La Iglesia en la historia de España*. Madrid: Fundación Rafael del Pino.

Faubell, Vicente. 2000. "Educación y órdenes y congregaciones religiosas en la España del Siglo XX." *Revista de Educación*, special issue: 137–200.

Gallego, Saturnino. 1969. *El Hermano posconciliar*. San Sebastián: Conferencia de Visitadores FSC.

– 1978. *Sembraron con amor. La Salle, Centenario en España (1878–1978)*. San Sebastián: Conferencia de Visitadores FSC.

García Carrasco, Joaquín. 1969. *La política docente. Estudio a la luz del Vaticano II*. Madrid: Biblioteca de Autores Cristianos.

García Tejedor, Teódulo. 1985. *La polémica sobre la secularización de la enseñanza en España (1902–1914)*. Madrid: Fundación Santa Maria.

Garitano, Luis. 1997. *La Salle, una presencia. Medio siglo de servicio en San Sebastián*. San Sebastián: La Salle Ikastetxea.

Gil, Pedro M. 1994. *Tres siglos de identidad lasaliana: la relación misión-espiritualidad a lo largo de la historia*. Roma: Casa Generalicia FSC.

– 1997. "Hermanos de las Escuelas Cristianas, lasalianos." In *Historia de la acción educadora de la Iglesia en España. Edad Contemporánea*, edited by Bernabé Bartolomé, 162–78. Madrid: Biblioteca de Autores Cristianos.

Griega, Maria del Mar. 2007. "The Education Battle: The Role of the Catholic Church in the Spanish Education System." In *International Handbook of Catholic Education – Challenges for School Systems in the 21st Century*, edited by Gerald Grace and Joseph O'Keefe, 291–310. Dordrecht: Springer.

Hermanos de la Escuelas Cristianas. 1977. "Declaración sobre el Hermano de las Escuelas Cristianas en el mundo actual (1967)." In *Reglas y Constituciones*. 40° Capítulo General F.S.C. 227–301. Madrid: Héroes.

– 1977. *Reglas y Constituciones. Libro de Gobierno*. Madrid: Hermanos de las Escuelas Cristianas.

Lamb, Matthew L., and Matthew Levering, eds. 2008. *Vatican II: Renewal within Tradition*. Oxford: Oxford University Press.

Lannon, Frances. 1987. *Privilege, Persecution, and Prophecy: The Catholic Church in Spain, 1875 1975*. Oxford: Clarendon Press.

Lasa, Martín, et al. 1989. *Distrito de Bilbao. 50 años en camino*. Bilbao: Hermanos de las Escuelas Cristianas, Distrito de Bilbao.

Lissarrague, André. 1999. *D'une rive à l'autre de l'Adour. Itinéraire d'un collège bayonnais Saint-Bernard*. Biarritz: Infocompo.

Louzao, Joseba. 2011. *Soldados de la fe o amantes del progreso: Catolicismo y modernidad en Vizcaya*. Madrid: Geuneve Ediciones.

Montero, Feliciano. 2000. *La Acción católica y el franquismo. Auge y crisis de la Acción Católica especializada*. Madrid: UNED.

– 2007. "Del movimiento católico a la Acción Católica. Continuidad y Cambio." In *La secularización conflictiva: España (1898–1931)*, edited by Merino Julio de la Cueva and Feliciano Montero García, 169–86. Madrid: Editorial Biblioteca Nueva.

– 2011. "La Iglesia dividida. Tensiones intraeclesiales en el Segundo franquismo. (La crisis postconciliar en el contexto del tardofranquismo)." In *De la cruzada al desenganche: la Iglesia española entre el franquismo y la transición*, edited by Manuel Ortiz and Damián Gonzalez, 51–76. Madrid: Silex.

Ortiz, Manuel, and Damián González, eds. 2011. *De la cruzada al desenganche: la Iglesia española entre el franquismo y la transición.* Madrid: Silex.

Ostolaza, Maitane. 2000. *Entre religión y modernidad. Los colegios de las congregaciones religiosas en la construcción de la sociedad guipuzcoana contemporánea 1876–1931.* Bilbao: Universidad del País Vasco.

Pérez Agote, Alfonso. 2012. *Cambio religioso en España: los avatares de la secularización.* Madrid: Centro de Investigaciones Sociológicas.

Ruiz de Galarreta, José Enrique, SJ. 2012. *El Concilio Vaticano II ¿Me importa algo hoy?* Madrid: Mensajero.

Salaverria, José M. 2003. *Domingo Lázaro (1877–1935): Un educador entre dos grandes crisis de España.* Madrid: PPC.

Unzueta, Angel María. 1995. *El Vaticano II en una Iglesia local recepción del Concilio Vaticano II en la Diócesis de Bilbao.* Bilbao: Universidad de Deusto.

Valladolid, José Maria, and Paulí Dávila. 2012. "Edición, introducción y notas a la Guía de las Escuelas de Juan Bautista de La Salle." In *Guía de las Escuelas dividida en tres partes*, by Juan Bautista De La Salle, 18–85. Madrid: Biblioteca Nueva-Siglo XXI,

Vanderstraeten, Raf. 2014. "Religious Activism in a Secular World: The Rise and Fall of the Teaching Congregations of the Catholic Church." *Paedagogica Historica: International Journal of the History of Education* 50(4): 494–513. http://dx.doi.org/10.1080/00309230.2014.904913.

Villalabeitia, Josean. 2014. *En los manantiales de la escuela popular cristiana.* Madrid: Ediciones La Salle.

Viñao Frago, Antonio. 2004. *Escuela para todos. Educación y modernidad en la España del siglo XX.* Madrid: Marcial Pons.

5 The Sisters of the Infant Jesus in Bembibre, León, Spain, during the Second Stage of Francoism (1957–1975): The School with No Doors

ROSA BRUNO-JOFRÉ

Introduction

It is almost commonplace for the people of Bembibre, León, Spain, to say that the town cannot be understood without considering the presence of the Sisters of the Infant Jesus, who established their apostolate there early in the 1960s. During a focus group meeting organized in the congregation's house in Bembibre by Sister Yolanda Busto Gómez, a past leader of various projects in the community, and still involved in many, it became evident that the mission of the Sisters of the Infant Jesus in that town has been construed by the townspeople as a beacon of change during the last two decades of Francoism.[1] One member of the community – not a religious person – nicely outlined the Sisters' approach: "They moved us from Catholicism to Christianity; nothing to do with Spanish Catholicism. The Sisters cleaned it [Catholicism] up."[2] The meaning of this statement is to be found in the context of Francisco Franco's regime (1939–75). The Franco regime, as Alvarez Bolado (1976) said, was a historical unitarian experiment having as protagonists the state and "a Church that dreamed of a Catholic and national consensus, through the political operation of a re-conquered state that brought back the spirit of a 'New Middle Age'" (10). The ideological confluence between the regime and the hierarchy of the Church,[3] aimed at monopolizing education, was clearly conveyed in the ideology of "national Catholicism," which provided the principles of the "new" education: it was to be confessional and highly politicized (Puelles Benítez 2010, 289; Ruiz Rico 1977).[4] This is the kind of Catholicism the focus group participant was referring to, dominant even as the regime moved into a technocratic phase from the late 1950s on, a time when important sectors of the Church reacted against the regime.

Using archival materials and oral narratives from several focus groups organized by Sister Busto Gómez featuring the perspectives of former collaborators, including teachers, parents, and priests, this chapter examines the Sisters of the Infant Jesus's mission in Bembibre and surrounding villages in the 1960s and 1970s. In order to examine the intentionality and resignifications characterizing the mission, I will take a transnational and trans-temporal approach to try to answer the following questions: What vision inspired the foundation of what would become the Sisters of the Infant Jesus, Saint Maur? What was the Church context of the 1960s that would motivate the Sisters to return to their roots? What were the socio-political conditions with which the congregation interacted during the second stage of Francoism? What was the school and community landscape created by the Sisters in Bembibre and Comarca del Bierzo between 1963 and 1975? How did the trans-temporal reappropriation of the original intuition of the founder – Nicholas Barré, O.M., a voice of French spirituality during the seventeenth century – mediate their apostolate in Bembibre during the renewal process after Vatican II? And, finally, how did the mission in Bembibre embody a resignification of Barré's original inspiration?

A Transnational and Trans-Temporal Journey: From Seventeenth-Century France to the Town of Bembibre in the 1960s

The Second Vatican Council's *Decree on the Adaptation and Renewal of Religious Life* (*Perfectae Caritatis*) was promulgated by Pope Paul VI on 28 October 1965. According to the Decree, the renewal of religious institutes should involve "the constant return to the sources of all Christian life and to the original spirit of the institutes and their adaptation to the changed conditions of our time" ("Decree" 1966, 2). This meant a spiritual return to the founder of the congregation, Nicholas Barré (1621–86), a Minim Friar, who in 1666 had established an Institute of Charitable Teachers – the future Sisters of the Infant Jesus – without vows or enclosure, and under the direction of a superior. The institute had as its mission the education (Christian instruction, reading, writing, and arithmetic) of poor girls, workshops for women, and sessions of religious instruction on festive days.[5] In this way, Barré was able to deal with the Church's exclusion of women from active apostolate, decided by the Council of Trent (1545–63) and the Pius V decrees of the mid-sixteenth century, which were still in effect in the seventeenth and eighteenth centuries.[6] The seventeenth century was a time of renewal in French theology. The encounter between politics and religion was now tainted by Gallicanism, Jansenism, and anti-Jansenism.[7] Some of the leading voices of that century, including Nicholas Barré, Jean Eudes, Vincent de Paul, Jean-Jacques Olier, Pierre de Bérulle, and Jean-Baptiste de La Salle, saw a need to open to the social needs of the world around them. Women religious without enclosure were acutely needed in the Catholic effort toward the educationalization of social problems of the time. To that end, in 1634, Vincent de Paul founded the Daughters of Charity with annual vows and no enclosure; in 1641, in Caen, Eudes founded the Union of Our Lady of Charity with a mandate to help marginalized women; and the Daughters of the Cross and the Daughters of St Genevieve had an apostolate in education and nursing with no vows.

Barré was a spiritual adviser to Jean-Baptiste de La Salle. In 1684, when the Teachers of the Charitable Schools for boys, a male congregation founded by Barré in 1681, failed to flourish, de La Salle received them in his home. In 1684, de La Salle founded the Institute of Christian Brothers, in order to provide free elementary and religious instruction in the vernacular to poor children. De La Salle's work is well-known, but not that of Barré, who, as just stated, had established the Schools of the Infant Jesus run by the Charitable Teachers as early as 1662 and soon after attached to them formative seminaries ("normal schools") for his teachers.

The schooling of the poor was a renewed response to the Protestant Reformation. Since the Council of Trent, the Church had become aware of the power of education to regulate life, secure faith, and avoid deviations from Catholic orthodoxy. In the seventeenth century, educationalization, and even pedagogization, of the faith was taking place to the extent that various congregations were developing methods to evangelize and instruct in the 3Rs through schooling, and women were becoming integrated into apostolic work despite papal restrictions.[8]

Notably, Barré's ideas regarding women were not different from the dominant ideas in the Church. This is evident, for example, in the means he devised to deal with the "weak" and "sometimes superficial" devotion of women and their desire to be flattered (Maximas 1997). Nonetheless, de La Salle and Barré put in operation principles of modern education that had emerged from the foundations of the Enlightenment's political and moral theories.[9] Thus, their work is connected not only to the ideas of Johan Amos Comenius (1592–1670), pedagogue and last bishop of the Unity of Brethren, but also to those of John Locke (1632–1704), a key figure in the Enlightenment. (This topic is largely neglected, but further discussion is beyond the scope of this chapter.)

In 1677, Barré wrote the statutes and regulations of the Christian and Charitable Schools of the Saint Infant Jesus to teach girls, as well as those of the Institute of Charitable Teachers, which later became the Sisters of the Infant Jesus.[10] He did not use terms such as "rules" or "constitutions," as was customary in the orders. Barré was submerged in a baptismal spirituality (the notion that Christian people can respond to the perfection received when they are baptized), which placed the Charitable Teachers close to laypeople. A value dominant in Barré's time in the seventeenth century was that life around the Church should become the central collectivity and place of reunion (Dupuy 1997). Today that notion can be construed as "presence in the world." It is also the case that Barré did not subordinate the Charitable Teachers to the priest: "The houses will never have or they could not have other superiors than that of the general order of the Church."[11] The aim of the Teachers was to be not their personal perfection, but the apostolate (ibid., 10), and they were to subordinate spiritual exercises to their teaching obligations. Timetables, organization of the class, punctuality, and use of the vernacular were important parts of those obligations. Above all, Barré expected them to share the insecurity of the poor to whom they were bringing Jesus Christ.

The Charitable Teachers had protectors from the nobility. Barré was known in the court, and Louis XIV asked for Barré's help for his College of St Cyr, as well as for assistance in preparing the Dames of St Louis with new teaching methods (Gelpí i Vintró n.d.). After Barré's death in 1686, two branches grew from the Charitable Teachers. On 27 July 1691, a royal decree established the separation. Rouen would be the mother house of the Sisters of the Infant Jesus, Providence de Rouen, and Paris would be the mother house of the Sisters of the Infant Jesus, Saint Maur (the Sisters studied in this chapter). The Rouen branch would take on a regional character; the Paris one would take on national and urban dimensions and would include private schooling. Both were congregations with vows. In the nineteenth century, the Sisters of the Infant Jesus, Saint Maur, established missions in Monaco, Spain, England, Malaysia, and Japan (Gelpí i Vintró n.d.). Not until quite late in 1866, however, did they receive pontifical approval as a congregation.

The mission in Spain was opened in Barcelona in 1860. It began with a small school but later became an influential institution. The work was eventually extended to Madrid (1904), Burgos (1891), Fuenterrabía (1904), and San Sebastián (1951). The congregation made a name for itself in education serving the middle-upper classes, although it also provided school services for the poor, as well as social services, in which the alumni collaborated, although by and large within the framework of charity.

The Sisters had navigated the turbulent waters of France that generated two exiles of French congregations, male and female religious, between 1880 and 1882, and between 1901 and 1914 (Cabanel and Durand 2005; Dávila Balsera 2011; Delaunay 2005). As the Sisters indicate, many members took refuge in Barcelona, leading to the opening in 1904 of two schools for girls of humble condition. Following their arrival and first mission in Spain in 1860, the congregation lived through the ending of the reign of Isabel II (1833–68), the reign of Amadeo de Saboya (1871–3), the short First Republic (1873–4), the Bourbon Restoration (1874–1931), the Second Republic (1931–6), the Civil War (1936–9) – at which time most of them went to France – and the era that the Sisters considered a return to normality: the Franco dictatorship and national Catholicism (Religiosas del Niño Jesús 1986).

The Sisters started the mission in Bembibre in 1963 during the second stage of the dictatorship, the stage that Viñao Frago (2014) places between 1957 and 1975 and which is variously known as "technocratic developmentalism" and "the final phase of national Catholicism." The regime opened a process of modernization while it continued "mutilating the process of cultural and political pluralism characteristic of modernity."[12] During this phase, modernization exposed the regime's limitations as well as its illegitimate character. Thus, from 1957 on, alongside the military, a strong presence of technical experts began to appear in the ministries, most of them associates of the Catholic right-wing secular institute Opus Dei, which aimed at the sanctification of the secular world (Payne 1984). In contrast, beginning in the early 1960s, important groups within the Church, the younger clergy, and Catholic militant workers' associations were becoming restless due to the political immobility and the lack of attention to social issues, including minimum salary (Callahan 2000, 502). This is evident in Catholic publications of the time. The magazine *El Ciervo*, for example, conveyed a Christian humanism inspired by the personalism of Emmanuel Mounier, to some extent the humanism of Jacques Maritain, and the experience of the *curas obreros* (worker priests), mainly of France.[13] As Alvarez Bolado (1976) put it, these sectors of the Church not only ceased providing legitimization to the overall project of Francoism, but started to erode it.

In the early 1960s, the regime's stabilization plan of 1959 had not appeased labour groups concerned with the plight of workers, including the *Hermandades Obreras de Acción Católica* (Workers' Brotherhood of Catholic Action) and the *Juventud Obrera Católica* (Catholic Workers Youth). Instead it was the 1961 encyclical *Mater et Magistra* (John XXIII, 1961), issued by Pope John XXIII (1958–63) to address social issues within the framework of progress, that inspired laity and clergy (Callahan 2000, 421). Within this context, labour conflicts and strikes, as well as mobilizations by university students, reached a high point in the 1960s. Worker priests, a type of apostolate suspended by Pope John XXIII in 1959, also had an impact, both on the Church and on the community (Sánchez Recio 2003). *Abside*, a Jesuit magazine, published an article in 1956 describing the worker priests' experience in a tile factory in Tudela de Navarra, in which it was noted that more than thirty seminarists, nineteen employees of the dioceses, nineteen Jesuits, and a Dominican Father had been employed there as workers (Martín Tejedor 1956).[14]

Meanwhile, the Second Vatican Council (1962–5) had brought a profound shift in the positioning of the Church *vis-à-vis* other faiths and the world itself. Baum (2011) summarizes this shift, writing that the Church redefined its relationship with outsiders, moved to dialogue and cooperation, recognized social justice as an imperative of the Gospel and consequently of spiritual life, and acknowledged the need to reinterpret its teachings in response to the historical present (362). Briefings and meetings related to Vatican II generated new understandings and openness among sectors of the clergy and laity, thus repositioning the Sisters with respect to plurality of views and the search for justice. As they were an international congregation – even having their novitiate situated in Paris (in whole or in part, depending on the time) – the Sisters had also been exposed to developments in various parts of the world.[15]

But perhaps one of the projects that had a most unintended effect is the call made by Pope John XXIII to religious congregations in August 1961: that they send 10 per cent of their membership to Latin America (Casaroli 1961).[16] Consequently, the Sisters of the Infant Jesus opened a mission in Peru and, like many other international congregations, came into contact with liberation theology, grassroots movements, and cultural developments emerging from Latin America. As mentioned during one of the Bembibre focus groups, in the late 1960s and early 1970s, the Sisters read liberation theologians like Gustavo Gutiérrez and critical pedagogues like Paulo Freire. At the same time, Vatican II's "Declaration on Religious Freedom (*Dignitatis Humanae*)" (1966) stated that "the right to religious freedom has its foundation in the very dignity of the human person" ("Declaration" 1966, 679). After pressure from political and civil groups and intense debates over the Declaration, the Organic Law of Religious Freedom (*Ley Orgánica de Libertad Religiosa*) of 1966 was passed; but the law was made compatible with the confessional character of the Spanish state as proclaimed in its fundamental laws (López Alarcón 2000).[17] The seed was planted for the opening of new spaces.

In 1962, on the three hundredth anniversary of the founding of the Sisters of the Infant Jesus, the congregation had 1,735 religious distributed all over the world in 74 communities, was in charge of 142 schools, and had 93,000 students (Gelpí i Vintró n.d.). However, it was clear by 1965 that the Spanish province of the congregation was not growing but diminishing, while the number of lay teachers was increasing. (But the congregation's report also noted that there was a new community in Bembibre.)[18]

In the 1960s, enabled by the directives of Vatican II and responding to the political and social realities framing their renewal, the congregation and its Spanish province gave new meaning to the original commitment to the poor as well as to Barré's pedagogical and ecclesiastical tenets. This time the congregation's language was one of social justice and openness to the world, evident in their documents.[19] The letter calling for the Extraordinary Chapter of 1968 said that it aimed "to revise the constitutions to allow the congregation to be a 'living testimony' of Christ out in the world of today and work efficiently toward the Kingdom of God."[20] Clearly, Vatican II's *Pastoral Constitution on the Church in the Modern World* (*Gaudium et Spes*) (1966) had a great impact on the congregations.

The mission in Bembibre yields a fascinating scenario in which the Sisters encountered plurality from a frame of reference that progressively exhibited freedom, initiative, change, and openness, thereby generating unexpected configurations of ideas and practices. These practices conveyed new ways of articulating ideas, work, and experience across difference, often embedded in contradictory directions. This apostolic experience had an inspiration rooted in Barré's conceptions, transported and recreated through time and place, as discussed below.

The Insertion in Bembibre: The School with No Doors

In 1963 the Sisters opened their mission in Bembibre, province of León, Partido de Ponferrada, in the Comarca del Bierzo, a coal-mining zone, in a rented house at Avenida De Villafranca 68. The existing schools – a national school (public elementary) and three private academies that prepared students to pass the exam for secondary school courses – could not meet the local demand. The mines had attracted migrants from Asturias, Galicia, Extremadura, and Portugal to the zone; in the 1970s, Bembibre also received people from Cabo Verde, and in the 1980s, families from Pakistan and Vietnam. When the Sisters arrived in 1963, there were 6,141 *de jure* inhabitants and 6,072 *de facto*; by the 1970 census, these figures had risen to 9,011 and 8,477, respectively. The 1950 census had indicated a population of 4,760 *de jure* and 4,777 *de facto* inhabitants (Instituto Nacional de Estadística, 2016).[21] The need for schooling in Bembibre was evident in the wholehearted way the town, at every level, received the school and the Sisters. When the *Colegio del Niño Jesús* (School of the Infant Jesus), a parochial school, started classes on 3 September 1963, 140 girls aged five to nine were enrolled (four more girls would be accepted that year). The school had five women religious teachers (*Sint Unum* 1963, 12). The Sisters contended that there was a need for at least five hundred places for students.[22] By 1965, the number of students the school could accommodate had reached only 166 (at the elementary and junior high school levels), while the number of students in all of the schools of the Spanish province was 3,379.[23]

The educational policy of the regime in the 1960s was characterized by a preoccupation with ensuring elementary education that was in line with the development plan (*Plan de Desarrollo*) and creating a minimally qualified working force, since the illiteracy rate had reached 17.1 per cent in 1963 (Ministerio de Educación y Ciencia 1969; Puelles Benítez 2010).[22] Access to schooling was conditioned by geographical location – rural areas were neglected – and social class. Puelles Benítez (2010), quoting the *Libro Blanco de la Educación* (White Book of Education), states that for every 100 students who started elementary education, 27 went to the elementary bachelor (middle school or junior high) and only 18 passed it; 10 out of the 100 passed the senior bachelor (*bachillerato superior*) (330).

The narrative of the founding of the Sisters of the Infant Jesus in Bembibre has taken on myth-like dimensions. It tells us that over time, the congregation received postulants from the province of León who had expressed a desire to open a house in León. The Superior had said that there would be a foundation if they had seven Sisters from León. In 1962, after achieving that number and paying a visit to Comarca del Bierzo, the congregation decided to establish a foundation in Bembibre. The reception of this news was very positive. The Bishop of Astorga, Marcelo González, said: "Come as soon as possible ... But over time you should commit yourself to an apostolate beyond private schools [schools with fees] ... We should be more interested in the working classes. It is enough that you put in writing that you will honour this commitment" (Gelpí i Vintró n.d., 137). It was 1962. The conditions were there for a renewed apostolate, one that would radicalize itself in the field.

When, in May 1963, two Sisters went to Bembibre from San Sebastián to familiarize themselves with the state of the work in the new mission, they reported that

> a large crowd of mothers, fathers, sisters, brothers ... our Sisters, and children came to say good bye at the train station ... They all brought presents ... We got into the train loaded with presents and were saying good bye when a mom came with a little lamb alive. The train departed and we had the little lamb in our arms. What to do? Passengers were not allowed to travel with animals! We emptied a basket full of presents and placed there the "petit agneau." He did not bother us at all during the night and from time to time Mother Marie-Mercedes caressed him maternally. (*Sint Unum* 1963, 10)

Sister Yolanda Busto Gómez, who went to Bembibre in 1968 after her noviciate in Paris, attributed the character of the mission in Bembibre to the changes brought by Vatican II. When, during the community focus group, some participants indicated that Bembibre began in 1962, at the same time as Vatican II, she responded that "there was a climate of change, and during the sessions of Vatican II we had meetings, discussions with specialized people within the Church, [and we] received information." This is not surprising, since the *nouvelle théologie* had reached everywhere, and in particular, the new generations. As often happened, however, the changes created division within the congregation at large, and some Sisters thought it was horrible to leave "the big collegiate to go to the peripheral neighborhoods or to villages."[23]

The Spanish and local context generated conditions for a new approach in which residuals from the congregation's old habits were redefined or abandoned after the Vatican II process of renewal. During one of the focus groups, Sister Busto Gómez said: "We came from a very elite school in Madrid, in Chamberí, where the girls took piano lessons and horse riding." At first the Sisters in Bembibre were addressed as Mother: "Mother Pilar, Mother I don't know what; suddenly the Sisters told us don't call them Mother and to use their birth names."[24] Lucía Gil Ballenas, who had come to teach in 1966, at a time when the students were addressed as Ms X, Ms Y, and treated as Usted (the formal "you"), recounted: "To teach a girl 8 years old and to call her Ms X was not my way, but I had to adhere to the ways of the centre. We placed bands on the students at the end of the course. It started with that class bias but it changed rapidly, the glove was turned inside out."[25]

The "Mothers" removed the habit in 1969 (although not all of them at the same time). They did not keep the title, either. The notion of extending a middle-class education to the people had been challenged not only by the process of going back to the roots but also by the reality of the locality itself. The Sisters in Bembibre, albeit from different positions, opened new avenues from the start: when the parish was going through political turmoil during the first years of the mission – following the parish priest falling out with his associate priest, Don Emilio, who was considered a revolutionary – the Sisters supported one or the other. (As punishment, Emilio was removed from Bembibre by the Bishop of Astorga and sent to another village; instead, he went to Madrid and left the priesthood.[26]) The mission took the route of commitment to change with the people; the traditional ideological framework for religious life that had taken shape over the years was set aside, and a new one emerged. Bembibre provided a rich setting for this redirection.

There was something unique in the Bembibre mission, in line with the congregation's renewal efforts. The mission took shape along the way: the school, the day care, boarding for girls, integration with the parish, pastoral work with those on the margins, building relationships with the people, and perhaps, most importantly, taking the school to the street (*Sacamos la escuela a la calle*), hence making the school a public space for the community.

The orientation of the mission was well established by 1968: openness to the needs of the community, social options for the poor, "no intention to compete with the State but to provide what was needed," and a commitment to improve the community's standard of living. The return to Barré's principles led to a dramatic shift away from the Black Ladies (*Damas Negras*), as they were known in Madrid and Barcelona, founders of large upper-class schools. It is clear that in Bembibre the Sisters adopted the notion of popular schools with a sense of autonomy, concentration on pedagogization of the faith, openness to everybody, and the intention to use education for the public good. All of those values were rooted in their studies of Barré and then recontextualized in the process of living the radicality of the Gospel as the Sisters assumed it.[27] A comment by Sister Busto Gómez is telling: "There is a chapter in the book with Barré's work where we are called to freedom. He wrote, 'free for this,' 'free for the other.' We need to be free, but docile to the spirit, like a feather in the hands of a writer."[28] This is a powerful comment, given that the Spirit in the Tridentine tradition assumed by the congregations had been mediated by the institutionalized Church.

The Sisters developed a powerful network with the mayor of the town, the clergy, and members of the community, and interacted with the state in trying to obtain support for their work. They applied their principles in various ways. The fees were adjusted to the student's ability to pay; there were no fees in the old building (1963–7). In 1964, the school started a junior high school program (*bachillerato elemental*), but the girls had to go to the *Instituto de Bachillerato Gil y Carrasco* in Ponferrada for examinations. The *bachillerato* was given official status in 1967, thus increasing the number of lay teachers and personnel, and consequently making it necessary to charge high fees. For this reason, in 1972, after the *Instituto de Bachillerato Gil y Carrasco* opened in Bembibre, the Sisters closed their program.

In 1967, the school moved to new facilities built by the congregation and received a *patronato* (funding) for four units (grades one to four). Both religious and lay teachers became public teachers. In 1971, following the new General Law of Education of 1970, the boarding component of the school became a home school (*escuela hogar*) funded by the state. In 1973, the school was reclassified for General Basic Education and received full state funding, which brought an end to fees for the higher grades (Religiosas del Niño Jesús 1986, 56–8). That year, the name of the school changed to *Colegio Virgen de la Peña*. By that time the school had 594 students, including those in nursing (day care), kinder, elementary or primary, elementary bachelor, and junior high school, as well as those taking accounting and mechanography (typewriting) in the evenings and those attending sewing lessons.[29] The Sisters found the new Law of Education useful for their work, especially because of its extending of formal education, its emphasis on the relationship between education and work, and its openness to pedagogical change.

A significant amount of participation and discussion, parent involvement, and creative extra-curricular activities took place at the school in Bembibre. In the focus group meetings organized by Sister Busto Gómez, the emphasis on group work, hands-on activities, consideration of the special gifts of each student (a Barré principle), projects with the community, and providing the space and means for creativity (also valued by Barré) were also mentioned at various points. (However, the focus groups, even those involving the teachers, did not provide much information about educational theories and practices of the time.)

What did it mean to take the school to the street or to have a school "with no doors," an expression used by a participant at one of the focus groups? It meant what the Sisters called "incarnation in the community," and also the emergence of a unique dynamic between the Sisters and the laypeople. This was achieved in collaboration with the priests, but not in subordination to them, and in relation to the overall pastoral project. The "presence" of Barré in this mission cannot be overstated. The Sisters worked closely with the priests with whom they shared their pastoral work, even as they had some differences. This is how Sister Busto Gómez described it:

> From the beginning, our approach was: we, in the school, provided teaching services with our own ideology, but the school was integrated with the people and we were integrated with the church (parish). We never had a chaplain; it was a matter of principle. We never had a chaplain because we did not want one; we went to religious services in the church or churches. We did parish catechesis even if it was in the school ... We struggled on occasions to change or to transform the direction of the local church, but we never did *una capilla aparte* [a separate church][30]

Tomás, a priest who participated in the focus group, commented that "there was also a sector that did not look upon your way of doing things favourably."[31] He was referring to the fact that not all the clergy and not all the priests in the area agreed with the direction taken by the Sisters. Tomás, a supporter of the Sisters, was the first priest of the parish of Santiago Apóstol, in the poor neighbourhood of Socuello, close to the train station, where the Sisters started work in 1975 – the year they divided the community between Bembibre and Socuello. Arturo, also a parish priest, talked of the municipality of Bañeza and resistance to change:

> I humbly confronted a traditionalist situation (I call it of the JONS, *Junta Ofensiva Nacional Sindicalista* [Offensive National Unionist Junta], a totalitarian extreme right group that merged with the Falange). I took what I learned and my experience here to my parish and I had many problems starting with other priests, and priests and people related to Opus Dei ... Here we met every week, we had the Eucharist in the school around a table, without ornament; the one who presided wore the shawl.[32]

Tomás added:

> They [the Sisters] were so "incarnated" in the problematic of the neighbourhood, they had the nursing school, but also the house open to everybody, anyone could go to visit, people who were ill, people who had needs. It called the attention of many because the first house where you lived was very humble [*pobre*]. They were "incarnated" even in the way they lived.[33]

The Sisters offered practical courses in Socuello, as part of the attempt to provide an alternative to those who could not work in the mines any longer or who wanted something different. However, the Sisters did not neglect catechesis and related activities. Overall, they created a correspondence between life, the Gospel, and the Eucharistic celebration.

The school in Bembibre embodied Christian life in line with the re-creation of the Sisters' own history. It was a house for young people, including those attending other schools, and it was the centre of life in the town. It was the place where children could go and play; catechesis took place in the school for everyone who wanted to attend; the gymnasium, the only one in town, was open for community use and for sports events; the neighbourhood association met in the school (at one point, Sister Busto Gómez was the group's secretary). For the Sisters, these associations were part of their pastoral work; but during Franco's regime, the associations also played a political role. Furthermore, in the basement of the school, clandestine meetings took place with people who were involved or would later be involved in the Spanish Socialist Workers' Party or in the United Left, and who came not only from Bembibre but also from Ponferrada and other places.[34] There were also connections with the Workers Brotherhood of Catholic Action (*Hermandades Obreras de Acción Católica*). In short, the Sisters provided a physical space that had profound political and social dimensions. In the 1980s, Muslim believers from Pakistan also found in the school a space for their cultural activities and faith, and before them so did Vietnamese families.

The *Instituto Gil y Carrasco* did not have a dining room, so students from villages around Bembibre came to eat at the Sisters' school; they brought their food and sat at a table; others paid some kind of pension, and still others stayed in the school and studied in whatever space they could find. "There were no problems and we were 300 in the dining room."[35] The school organized carnivals, discussion groups for young people, groups of girl hikers, and camping activities. The Sisters introduced their students, interns, and other young people to writers such as the Communist

Chilean Nobel Prize winner poet Pablo Neruda (banned by Franco), and to music from the Chilean protest folk group Quilapayún, Violeta Parra, and Victor Jara (who was later killed during the Pinochet coup). By doing so, they were demonstrating the connection of the ebullient Latin American political reality with their mission. For the boarders, Sister Busto Gómez provided recordings of The Beatles and other countercultural expressions of the "global long 1960s" (Marwick, 1998).

The Sisters and the priests also participated in feasts of the nearby villages and towns, and they danced and sang until dawn with the people. One or another Sister would have family in those places, and they would all have meals together. Sometimes personal friendships developed between families of priests and Sisters. But the Sisters and the priests were not just having a good time; they worked together on catechesis, including a new catechesis developed by Arturo, two Sisters, and others.[36]

Some of the narrations in the focus group were based on memories of political repression in the early 1970s. For example, in the mining town of Matarrosa, there had been a priest "like Emilio" named Javier, who organized pastoral events, including some in which groups of young people sang protest songs. The narrator ran into trouble with the *Guardia Civil* (police) while protecting the young people he had transported to Matarrosa.[37] He was accused of not collaborating with the regime.

During the early 1970s, the rhythm of life was intense: pastoral work, school work, community involvement, puppetry for the public in the market square, as well as theatre. Bembibre had had a theatre tradition that was reawakened by some of the Sisters in the early 1970s. Sister Busto Gómez and Paco Frades, a theatre person, along with a teacher from the *Instituto Gil y Carrasco* and young people from the area, worked on theatre, with the school (the *Colegio*) as the centre of activities. One of the collaborators in the focus group said that his first contact with the Sisters had been at a mass for young people celebrated in the chapel of the school: "That was the germ, where we began to get to know each other because there was nothing in Bembibre. Well, going to a youth mass was different than a mass where the priest talked and people listened … It was another thing. There we met Yolanda, started to talk and we went into theatre."[38] The theatre group performed expressionist theatre, with an emphasis on concepts and expressions, as well as mime. The presentations attracted large numbers of people and filled theatres. The group produced plays from R. Tagore, Antonio Machado (adaptations), Frank Baum, Emile Esbois, Beatriz Tanaka, and plays or compositions authored by the group, among many others.[39]

It is not surprising that the Sisters became threaded in the memory of the town as bringing light and life to the community, and providing a space to engage in artistic, spiritual, and even political expressions. They engaged in many other projects not discussed here, including "Project Hombre," aimed at helping drug addicts in the community.[40]

Conclusion

The mission in Bembibre revealed a scenario in which its school played a public role beyond denominational concerns, at the same time as providing a testimony for a way to live the faith that can be traced to the origins of the congregation and the French spirituality of the seventeenth century. The pastoral work, out of necessity, became intertwined with the dynamics, desires, and contradictions of the second stage of Francoism, as well as with the social difficulties of a mining region.

The reading of the Vatican II documents and its implementation by the Sisters were mediated – once they went to the original inspiration – by Barré's heritage, and nourished by the process of renewal of Catholic spirituality and their lived experiences. Vatican II became an enabling force leading to a process of change and renewal that would take place outside the Vatican walls.

The mission created a popular school that became the centre of collective life, brought back recontextualized notions from Barré's writings, and embraced his view that Sisters were not expected to be subordinated to priests. Barré's emphases on the individuality of the student, creativity, and involvement by people were recreated in Bembibre. This particular scenario provided the conditions of possibility for a unique apostolate. Thus, it seems clear that the founder's principles were latent in the cultural heritage of the congregation, and that they acquired new political and social tones during their rediscovery and application in their new setting.

Towards the end of a focus group, Sister Busto Gómez read a piece written by Father Matías, parish priest in Bembibre, describing the Sisters and the relevance of Barré in this period of their life.

> How do I see the Religiosas del Niño Jesús in my parish? Due to differences that existed between the priest and the associated priest [this has to do with Father Emilio] in which some of the Sisters took positions, I was told to be on guard and observe. There were criticisms for their full openness and for their collaboration with the priest in the region. I observed that some in the parish were scandalized by their mannerism and way of dressing which

contrasted with what they knew when they first came, the black habit, veil, white *coiffe*. There was a metamorphosis from the Black Ladies. This is the pleasant experience I have of them. I believe that they have re-discovered the true charisma of Nicholás Barré.

NOTES

This research was made possible by an Elliott grant from the Faculty of Education, Queen's University. I would like to thank Dr Gonzalo Jover, who provided the connection with the Sisters. Our original intention was to work on this together, but his administrative obligations did not make it possible. My thanks also to the readers Jon Igelmo, Carlos Martínez Valle, and Eva Krugly-Smolska for their input.

1 Sister Yolanda Busto Gómez played a leading role in Bembibre and the region in various capacities as teacher and community organizer, as religious. She requested that this chapter not emphasize the significance of her role. I respect her will and her vows of humility.
2 Focus group organized by Sister Yolanda Busto Gómez, in the residence of the Sisters of the Infant Jesus, Bembibre, León, Spain, November 2013. The group included parents of former students.
3 All references to "Church" indicate "Catholic Church."
4 National Catholicism reached its highest point with the ministry of Ibañez Martín (1939–51).
5 See "Estatutos y Reglamentos de las Escuelas Cristianas y Caritativas," in *Nicolás Barré: Obras completas* (Barcelona, Spain: EDIM, 1977). The Estatutos were written in 1677.
6 In 1563 the Council of Trent defined women devoted to religious life as enclosed, denying them the opportunity to conduct apostolic work outside the cloister. This was followed by Pius V's *Circa Pastoralis* (1566) and *Lubricum Vitae Genitus* (1568), which made enclosure a prerequisite for female communities claiming religious status. It has been argued, however, that enclosure was not so hermetic. See Laurence Lux-Sterrit and Carmen M. Mangion, "Introduction: Gender, Catholicism and Women's Spirituality over the *Longue Durée*," in *Gender, Catholicism, and Spirituality: Women and the Roman Catholic Church in Britain and Europe, 1200–1900*, ed. Lux-Sterrit and Mangion (London: Palgrave Macmillan, 2011), 1–19.
7 See Joseph Bergin, *The Politics of Religion in Early Modern France* (New Haven: Yale University Press, 2014). In the mid-seventeenth century, the papacy

condemned propositions contained in a theological treatise by Flemish bishop Cornelius Jansen titled "Augustinus" (1636). The controversy needs to be understood in the context of debates over the relationship between God's grace and human free will that shook the foundations of Christendom during the Reformation. In "Augustinus," Jansen intended to restate the fourth-century Catholic position on Grace, advanced by Saint Augustine. Jansen insisted on the crippling impact of Original Sin on human will, which needed to be motivated by grace. The movement that emerged, which also contained modernist elements, was seen as a threat to both Rome and Versailles. See Alexander Sedgwick, "Jansen and the Jansenists," *History Today* 40(7) (1990): 36–42, esp. 36. Jansenism is often conflated with moral rigorism. Contemporary authors have interpreted Jansenism as favouring the rights of the individual consciousness, advocating direct contact with the Bible, a major role for women, and the understanding of the Church as an assembly of the faithful. See Françoise Hildesheimer, *Le Jansénisme, L' histoire et l'heritage* (Paris: Petite Encyclopédie Moderne du Christianisme, Desclée de Brouwer, 1992), 8–10. As for Gallicanism, Susan Smith, RNDM, wrote: "Gallicanism is best defined as a complex of ecclesiastical and political doctrines and practices which sought to restrict papal power in the French Catholic Church, and which advocated that the Pope be subject to ecumenical councils. By the nineteenth century Gallicanism had lost much of its appeal, and instead Ultramontanism (lit. 'beyond the mountains'), which strongly emphasised papal authority and centralisation of church structures, became the dominant ideology." Susan Smith, RNDM, *Call to Mission: The Story of the Mission Sisters of Aotearoa, New Zealand, and Samoa* (Auckland: David Ling, 2010), 272.

8 I am not using the concepts of educationalization and pedagogization in the sense that Frank Simon, Marc Depaepe, and in particular Tom Popkewitz and Daniel Tröhler use them in their examination of the educational state and transnational institutions in the twentieth and twenty-first centuries. See Smeyers, Paul, and Marc Depaepe, eds., *Educational Research: The Educationalization of Social Problems* (Educational Research 3) (Dordrecht: Springer, 2008).

9 De La Salle Schools have been well analysed. This is not the case with the Charitable Teachers. See Enrique García Ahumada, "350 años del natalicio de San Juan Bautista de La Salle," *Annuario de Historia de la Iglesia* 11 (2002): 375–81; José María Valladolid and Paulí Dávila. *Estudio crítico, notas y bibliografía a la edición en español de la* Guía de las Escuelas (Madrid: Biblioteca Nueva-Siglo XXI, 2012); and Paulí Dávila, Luis M. Naya, and

Hilario Murúa, "Tradition and Modernity of the De La Salle Schools: The Case of the Basque Country in Franco's Spain (1937–1975)," *Paedagogica Historica* 49(4) (2013): 562–76.

10 See "Estatutos y Reglamentos de las Escuelas Cristianas y Caritativas," in *Nicolás Barré: Obras Completas*, 170–222. Barcelona: EDIM.

11 This statement appeared in the statements (constitutions) of 1662 (Dupuy 1997).

12 See also Gilverto Sánchez Recio, "Inmovilismo político y cambio social en los años sesenta," *Historia Contemporánea* 26 (2013): 13–33.

13 In Barcelona, in 1943, influenced by French *nouvelle théologie*, the Hermandad de Cristo Trabajador (Brotherhood of Christ Worker) started its work.

14 An interesting analysis is Manuel Azcárate, "Curas-obreros en España," *Nuestra Bandera, revista teórica y política del partido comunista de España* 44–5 (May–June 1965): 57–65.

15 Until 1999, French was the official language of the congregation, although they used Spanish in their provincial administration.

16 The call was addressed to North American congregations. However, given the cultural affinity, some Spanish congregations sent new missions. Spanish congregations had a history of missionary work in Latin America; the Sisters of the Infant Jesus did not.

17 See Mónica Moreno Seco, "El miedo a la libertad religiosa: Autoridades franquistas, católicos y protestantes ante la Ley de 28 de junio de 1967," *Anales de Historia Contemporánea* 17 (2001): 351–63.

18 *Informe de la Provincia de España para leer en el Capítulo Provincial que tiene lugar en Barcelona.* 20 March 1965. Mother House, Archive of the Religiosas del Niño Jesús (hereafter, ARNJ), Madrid, Spain.

19 This is clear in the documentation related to the Spanish province, particularly after the Extraordinary Chapter of the Congregation that took place in 1968. See also Actes du Chapitre, 1ère Session 1968. ARNJ, Madrid, Spain.

20 Soeur Justin Deleuze, Supérieure générale, letter to Mes bien chères Filles. 8 December 1967. ARNJ, Madrid, Spain.

21 See also Ángel Ferrero Carracedo and Yolanda Busto Gómez, "Plan de actuación de atención a inmigrantes en los colegios públicos 'Menéndez Pidal' y 'Santa Bárbara de Bembibre,' C.P. 'Menéndez Pidal' y C.P. 'Santa Bárbara.'" Bembibre, León, March 2003. Document provided by Yolanda Busto Gómez.

22 The situation was expounded later in the so-called *Libro Blanco de la Educación* (White Book of Education) that preceded the 1970 General Law of Education (Puelles Benítez 2010).

23 Sister Yolanda Busto Gómez, in a focus group with community members, Sisters of the Infant Jesus, residence house, Bembibre, León, Spain, 18 November 2013.
24 Lucía Gil Ballenas, in a focus group with teachers led by Sister Yolanda Busto Gómez, Sisters of the Infant Jesus, residence house, Bembibre, León, Spain, 18 November 2013.
25 Lucía Gil Ballenas, in a focus group with teachers led by Sister Yolanda Busto Gómez, Sisters of the Infant Jesus, residence house, Bembibre, León, Spain, 18 November 2013.
26 Sister Yolanda Busto Gómez, in a focus group with community members, Sisters of the Infant Jesus, residence house, Bembibre, León, Spain, 19 November 2013.
27 *Group Padre Barré, Líneas Pedagogicas de Nicolas Barré, fundador de las Religiosas del Niño Jesús.* ARNJ, Madrid, Spain.
28 Sister Yolanda Busto Gómez, in a focus group with priests, 20 November 2014. This statement reflects Sister Yolanda's own reading of Barré.
29 "Comunidad de Bembibre 1973–1974." Document provided by Sister Yolanda Busto Gómez.
30 Sister Yolanda Busto Gómez, in a focus group with priests, 20 November 2014.
31 Sister Yolanda Busto Gómez, in a focus group with priests, 20 November 2014.
32 Sister Yolanda Busto Gómez, in a focus group with priests, 20 November 2014.
33 Sister Yolanda Busto Gómez, in a focus group with priests, 20 November 2014.
34 Sister Yolanda Busto Gómez, in a focus group with community members, Sisters of the Infant Jesus, residence house, Bembibre, León, Spain, 18 November 2013.
35 Sister Yolanda Busto Gómez, in a focus group with community members, Sisters of the Infant Jesus, residence house, Bembibre, León, Spain, 18 November 2013.
36 Sister Yolanda Busto Gómez, in a focus group with community members, Sisters of the Infant Jesus, residence house, Bembibre, León, Spain, 18 November 2013.
37 Focus group with collaborators, organized by Sister Yolanda Busto Gómez, 20 November 2014.
38 Focus group with collaborators, organized by Sister Yolanda Busto Gómez, 20 November 2014.
39 Information provided by Sister Yolanda Busto Gómez via email to Rosa Bruno-Jofré, 27 March 2015.
40 Sister Yolanda Busto Gómez was involved in this project. Personal communication.

REFERENCES

Alvarez Bolado, Alfonso. 1976. *El experimento del nacional-Catolicismo, 1939–1975.* Madrid: Editorial Cuadernos para el Dialogo.

Baum, Gregory. 2011. "Vatican Council II: A Turning Point in the Church's History." In *Vatican II: Canadian Experiences,* edited by Michael Attridge, Catherine E. Clifford, and Gilles Routhier, 360–78. Ottawa: University of Ottawa Press.

Cabanel, Patrick, and Jean-Dominique Durand. 2005. *Le grand exil des congrégations religieuses Françaises 1901–1914.* Paris: Les éditions du CERF.

Callahan, William J. 2000. *The Catholic Church in Spain, 1875–1998.* Washington, DC: Catholic University of America Press.

Casaroli, A. 1961. "Appeal of the Pontifical Commision to North American Superiors." Appendix in G.M. Costello. *Mission to Latin America: The Successes and Failures of a Twentieth-Century Crusade,* 273–81 (Maryknoll: Orbis Books, 1979).

Dávila Balsera, Paulí. 2011. "Las órdenes y congregaciones religiosas francesas y su impacto sobre la educación en España, siglos XIX y XX." In *Francia en la educación de la España contemporánea (1808–2008),* edited by José María Hernández Díaz, 101–57. Salamanca: Ediciones Universidad de Salamanca.

"Declaration on Religious Freedom (*Dignitatis Humanae*)." 1966. In *The Documents of Vatican II,* edited by Walter M. Abbott, SJ, 672–97. New York: The American Press.

"Decree on the Adaptation and Renewal of Religious Life (*Perfectae Caritatis*)." 1966. In *The Documents of Vatican II,* edited by Walter M. Abbott, SJ. New York: American Press.

Delaunay, Jean-Marc. 2005. "Exilio o refugio en España (veinticinco años después)." *Anuario de Historia de la Iglesia* 14: 153–64.

Dupuy, Michel. 1997. "Introduction: El pensamiento de Nicolás Barré en su contexto, vida de Nicolás Barré." In *Obras Completas de Nicolás Barré,* 9–14. Barcelona: Hermanas del Niño Jesús.

Gelpí i Vintró, Núria. n.d. *El imprevisible soplo del espíritu. Historia de las Religiosas del Niño Jesús. Nicolás Barré en España, 1860–1897.* Barcelona: Editorial Claret.

Instituto Nacional de Estadística (INE). 2016. "Censo de Población y Vivienda. Pcia de León." http://www.ine.es/intercensal/intercensal.do?search=1&cmbTipoBusq=0&textoMunicipio=Bembibre&btnBuscarDenom=Consultar+selecci%F3n&L=1.

John XXIII. 1961. "On Christianity and Social Progress (*Mater et Magistra*)." Libreria Editrice Vaticana. http://w2.vatican.va/content/john-xxiii/en/encyclicals/documents/hf_j-xxiii_enc_15051961_mater.html.

López Alarcón, Mariano. 2000. "Problemas que afronta la ley de libertad religiosa de Espana y soluciones que ofrece para los mismos" (Universidad de Murcia). *Anales de Derecho* 18: 223–42.

Martín Tejedor, Jesús. July 1956. "Jesuitas de a pie." *Abside: Revista de Faith y Pensamiento* 1(2): 8–9.

Marwick, Arthur. 1998. *The Sixties: Cultural Revolution in Britain, France, Italy, and the United States, c. 1958–1974.* Oxford: Oxford University Press.

"Maximas para toda clase de personas." 1997. In *Nicolás Barré: Obras completes,* 287–351. Barcelona: EDIM.

Ministerio de Educación y Ciencia. 1969. *La educación en España: Bases para una política educativa.* Madrid.

"Pastoral Constitution on the Church in the Modern World (*Gaudium et Spes*)." 1966. In *The Documents of Vatican II,* edited by Walter M. Abbott, SJ, 199–309. New York: American Press.

Payne, Stanley G. 1984. *Spanish Catholicism: An Historical Overview.* Madison: University of Wisconsin Press.

Puelles Benítez, Manuel de. 2010. *Educación e ideología en la España contemporánea,* 5th ed. Madrid: Tecnos.

Religiosas del Niño Jesús. 1986. *Nuestra historia: Provincia de España.* Madrid.

Ruiz Rico, J. 1977. *El papel politico de la Iglesia Católica en la España de Franco.* Madrid: Tecnos.

Sánchez Recio, Glicerio. 2003. "Inmovilismo político y cambio social en los años sesenta." *Historia Contemporánea* 26: 13–33.

Sint Unum (no. 69). 1963 (September).

Viñao Frago, Antonio. January/March 2014. "La educación en el Franquismo (1936–1975)." *Educational Review* 51(51): 19–35. http://dx.doi.org/10.1590/S0104-40602014000100003.

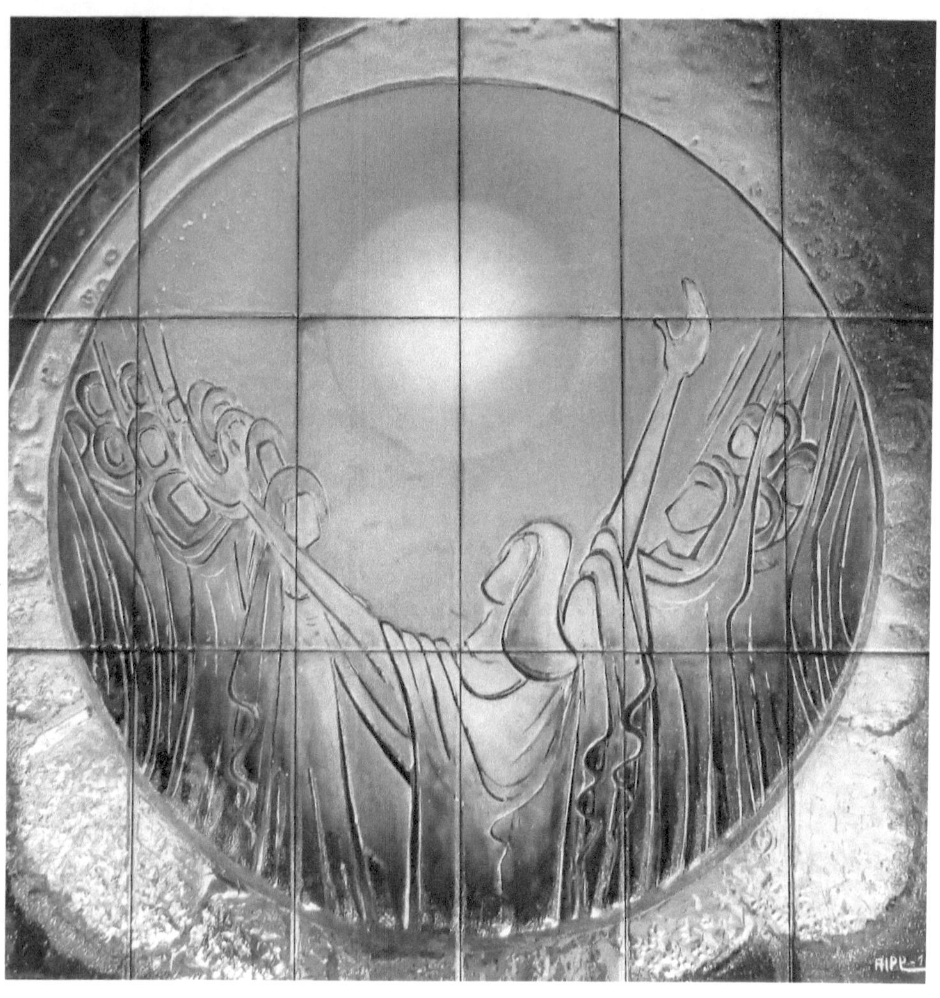

"MAGNIFICAT (Lucas/Luke 1:46–55) no. 5." Ceramic tilework by María Cruz Bascones.

PART THREE

The Processes of Resignification of Missions

6 Ivan Illich, the Critique of the Church as *It*: From a Vision of the Missionary to a Critique of Schooling

ROSA BRUNO-JOFRÉ AND JON IGELMO ZALDÍVAR

Introduction

As David Cayley writes, Ivan Illich,[1] from the start of his ordained life, had distinguished two forms of the Church, which he called the Church as *She* and the Church as *It*. He saw the Church as *She* as the repository of tradition and the living embodiment of the Christian community, the mystery, the kingdom among us. By contrast, he considered the Church as *It* to be a self-serving worldly power, one in whose side Illich was to become a thorn (Cayley 2005, 4). This distinction is fundamental to understanding Illich's work in Cuernavaca, Mexico. There, Illich founded a network of centres that would play a role in the formation of missionaries going to Latin America after 1961. In fact, between 1961 and 1965 (inclusive), a total of 408 missionaries attended the sessions offered by the *Centro de Investigaciones Culturales* (Center for Cultural Research [CIC]) in Cuernavaca, of whom 130 came from Canada, 240 from the United States, and 28 from Europe.[2] (There are no numbers for the years 1966 to 1969.) CIC had a counterpart in Anápolis first, and later in Petrópolis, Brazil, the *Centro de Formação Intercultural* (Center for Intercultural Formation [CENFI]). Many of the missionaries served as teachers, while others were involved in alternative educational projects and did community work, often accompanying people in their struggles for social justice. Education was more than just a subject learned in the missionaries' formation: more than half of the participants would go on to work in educational projects.

The centres offered formative courses: spiritual formation, intercultural studies, educational issues, and extensive political and socio-economic components, as well as courses for learning Spanish. The participants were mainly those involved in the Papal Volunteers for Latin America Program (PAVLA), a lay apostolate program approved by the Vatican in 1960, and members of congregations responding to John XXIII's 1961 appeal to religious congregations to send missionaries to Latin America. The American hierarchy and the Vatican converged with the process of the modernization of Latin America led by the United States as a response to the Cuban Revolution.

In this chapter we examine the principles guiding the formation of missionaries, in light of Illich's distinction of the Church as *She* and *It*. We argue that while the papal programs conceptualized "mission" as ecclesiocentric – that is, as responding to the needs of the Church as identified by the Church as an institution, the Church as *It* – Illich conceived of the formation of the missionary as a missionary working for the Church as *She*, inspired by the Spirit.

While Illich's approach was reignocentric, the centres he ran did not produce a direct critique of the Church as *It* until 1964. The critique gradually took shape, intellectually as well as institutionally via the organization of the centres, during a process of radicalization of Illich's thought, culminating in his writing "The Seamy Side of Charity" and "The Vanishing Clergyman" in 1967. That process was part of a constellation of changes that characterized Cuernavaca, ideologically and intellectually, in the late 1950s and the 1960s (Bruno-Jofré and Igelmo Zaldívar 2016). The Church there, led by Bishop Sergio Méndez Arceo, had begun a liturgical, aesthetic, social, and cultural *aggiornamento* even before the Second Vatican Council (Vatican II) (1962–5). The renovation of the Cathedral of Cuernavaca, which began in 1956, is a good example of those changes.

Various influences converged and intersected in Illich's development during his time in Cuernavaca, including his neo-Thomist formation and the influence of Jacques Maritain; his close relationship with Méndez Arceo; his collaborations with social psychoanalyst Erich Fromm, a neighbour and friend; and his friendship with Gregorio Lemercier, close friend of Méndez Arceo, prior of the Benedictine monastery *Santa María de la Resurrección* in Santa María de Ahuacatitlán (Lemercier was also committed to social services and brought psychoanalysis to his monks). Also influential were Illich's notion of "poverty" as central to missionary formation, a stance adopted since his time in Puerto Rico; his reaction to US policies in Latin America and their links to the Church; and his early exposure to liberation theology and grassroots movements in Latin America. Vatican II had a tremendous impact on Latin America, where it was largely read through liberation theology as conveyed in the 1968 Medellín documents. It legitimized a new way of doing theology. However, while Illich and his centres provided spaces for the early development of liberation theology (Smith 1991, 120), Illich cannot be identified with it, since he situated himself outside modernism and embraced neither the dominant ideology of progress and emancipation nor Marxist ideas.

Illich's view of what was going on in the Second Vatican Council helps us understand his theological, and consequently, his political and cultural stands. In a recent book, Todd Hartch (2015) wrote:

> Illich participated in the most important Catholic meetings of the century, the second and third sessions of the Second Vatican Council. He did meet Latin American theologians there but, more importantly, the experience seems to have influenced his later attitudes toward church authorities. He served as an advisor to the committee of four cardinals, led by Leo Joseph Suenens of Belgium and including Grégoire-Pierre Agagianian of Armenia, Giacomo Lercaro of Italy, and Julius Dopfner of Germany, who were appointed by Paul VI to moderate the council. After meeting with this group, who were seen at the time as "highly progressive," every day during the second session (fall 1963) and the third session (fall 1964), Illich told Suenens, "I'm leaving now. Yesterday you proved to me that his Council is incapable of facing the issues which count, while trying hard to remain traditional" ... He came to believe that Church officials had been so infected by the plague of institutionalization that they were incapable of thinking and acting in a truly Christian manner. (64–5)

We can distinguish four phases in the life of the centres. The first spanned from 1961 to 1964, and included the reception of the first missionaries to CIC and CENFI, centres financed by Fordham University and the Latin American Bureau of the National Catholic Welfare Council (NCWC). The second phase lasted from 1964, when Illich dismissed the board and took control of the structure of the centres and their publications, to 1966, when in October he asked Bishop Méndez Arceo of Cuernavaca for permission to merge the centres into one – the *Centro Intercultural de Documentación* (Center for Intercultural Documentation [CIDOC]) – and to move it to Rancho Tetela. The third phase starts at the end of 1966, when the CIDOC, now in Rancho Tetela, ceased to offer residence to missionaries, and the conflict with the Vatican began; this phase ended in February 1969, when the *New York Times* and *Excelsior* of

Mexico published an "inquisitorial" questionnaire that the Vatican had sent to Illich and that Illich forwarded to those newspapers. The fourth phase started in 1969, a time that signalled the highest point of the conflict with the Vatican, and ended in 1976, when Illich decided to close the CIDOC on 1 April of that year. During this last phase, the CIDOC functioned as an independent academic centre with its own resources generated by teaching Spanish classes, and as a centre of documentation on Latin America, offering services to researchers from prestigious American universities (Igelmo Zaldívar 2011, 512). In this chapter we focus on the first three phases.

As stated earlier, Illich's resignification of the notion of missionaries during his time in Cuernavaca was related to his critical vision of the Church as *It*. The development of his notion of missionary encompasses the radicalization of his thought that eventually culminated in a conflict with the Vatican, after which Illich shifted his critique from that of the Church as *It* to that of secular institutions like schooling, while referring to the Church as *It* only in analogy. In other words, by shifting to a critique of the secular, he was able to talk from his faith without revealing that it was the source of his words; this was a way to deal with the silence imposed on him by Rome.[3]

Resignifying the Role of the Missionary in the Church as *She*

In the 1950s, the Holy See had already attempted to build Catholic inter-American cooperation, although from the top down. John XXIII had put Archbishop Antonio Samoré in charge of Latin American issues. Samoré had overseen the organizing of the 1955 Eucharistic Congress in Rio de Janeiro, from which the *Consejo Episcopal Latinoamericano* (Latin American Episcopal Council [CELAM]) emerged. He had also been instrumental in organizing the First Inter-American Conference (2–4 November 1959) called by the Holy See, hosted at the Georgetown University School of Linguistics and presided over by Cardinal Richard Cushing of Boston. The eighteen bishops who met there had as their goals building pan-American collaboration, mobilizing and coordinating efforts from Canada and the United States, and strengthening the Church in Latin America (Garneau 2001). This pan-American approach was an attempt to identify and address social problems from a centralized, top-down perspective. The Holy See was responding in the main to the Cold War–related crisis identified in Latin America – "the advance of communism" – though equally worrisome was the spread of

Protestantism. The missionary work appeared rooted in specific political and social projects embedded in the language of the Cold War. Cushing, an anti-communist crusader, emphasized the importance of promoting the social doctrine of the Church and healthy social reforms to counter the spread of communism.[4]

A number of Latin American bishops expressed their discomfort with Cushing's views and the overall official approach. This was the case with Dom Hélder Pessoa Câmara, Archbishop of Rio de Janeiro, who would later help Illich organize a centre in Petrópolis. Câmara replied to Cushing that the urgent problem was not communism, but rich people's egotism and their blindness to poverty (Câmara, qtd in Garneau 2001, 680).

In 1960, Illich opened the centres in Cuernavaca. In 1961 – the year we identify as the beginning of the first phase of the centres – he began receiving missionaries from PAVLA and from congregations responding to John XXIII's call (Bruno-Jofré and Igelmo Zaldívar 2014). Initially, Illich was not against the papal project; in fact, as stated earlier, he was financially supported by the Latin American Bureau of the NCWC.[5] However, Illich had his own vision of the role of the missionaries, even as his network of centres remained an integral part of Cushing's and Maryknoll director of the Latin American Bureau of the NCWC John Considine's projects for Latin America (until 1964). So when Illich became the executive director of the CIF – the production hub of the centres' written materials – and founded the CIC, he not only chose the place where Méndez Arceo was the bishop (Cuernavaca) but also instrumentalized his own notion of missionary within a Church he conceived as *She*.

From very early, Illich resignified the understanding of mission and missionary, grounded in his notion of the Church's apostles as announcers of the Gospel and inspired by the Pauline epistles. According to Illich's early vision of the missionary's role, missionaries should incarnate themselves in the culture rather than becoming agents of their own culture, having "poverty" as a central virtue (CIF 1963). Illich linked missionary "poverty" to feelings of weakness and dependency on the role of others; he saw it as part of a process in which the missionary divests herself from values and assumptions to meet the other. Illich also referred to the spiritual "poverty" upon which the universality of the Church is built, across difference. It was originally a Church without the pitfalls of institutionalization of central values such as hospitality and charity.

There is a mystical element in Illich's notions of love and incarnation: "love urges us to become like those we love." From this perspective, missionaries "seek to become like the people they are sent to adopt, yet do not cease to be sons of their native country" (CIF 1961). The Incarnation, Illich wrote, is the infinite prototype for missionary activity (CIF 1963). Love is at the core of the apostolate, and it should be its intentionality; it is the coordinate force behind Illich's discourse, and can be encapsulated in the notion of "poverty" of the missionary mentioned above. Illich's understanding of mission naturally led to a critical view of the Church's involvement in the American political project of modernization.

Even the early years of the centres should be viewed in line with Illich's notion of missionary for a Church as *She*, a space where the missionaries acquired a special awareness of the spiritual formation they needed to engage in the apostolate in a foreign culture (Fitzpatrick, 1963). Dom Placide Pernot (1962), who spent time in Cuernavaca, wrote that at the centre, intellectual and scientific work, while very important, was secondary to the spiritual formation that generated a profound inspiration. The centre had an intense spiritual life. The preparation for a process of adaptation to the missionary field in Latin America was understood not as instrumental for professional efficacy, but as a testimony of gratuitous love. Studies of the profane, Pernot wrote, would help missionaries to reach spiritual poverty, a sense of freedom in love, and a more profound and more authentic sense of their mission in the Church.

In the second phase of the centres (1964–6), Illich fully concentrated on his critical view of the Church as *It*. Cuernavaca provided a space where the Church (as an institution), from the mid-1950s on, and under the leadership of Méndez Arceo, had started to construct a means to relate to God from a Latin American standpoint – that is, from poverty, pain, dependency, and injustice. Meanwhile, the centres had also become a hub of alternative views for change. At this point, the formation of the missionary for a Church as *She* was not enough in Illich's view, because the missionaries were still serving the Church as *It*. Grego (2013) writes that St Matthew 4:1–11, in which the Spirit leads Jesus into the wilderness to be tempted by the devil, after he has fasted for forty days and forty nights, was an important reference for Illich. In this passage, the devil tempts Jesus with three forms of power – economic, psychological, and political (the devil takes him to a mountain to tempt him with power over the kingdoms of the world). Illich believed, Grego says, "that renouncing power was a critical part of the way that Jesus revealed" (92). The attempt by the official Church to institutionalize the Gospel, as well as tradition – which incidentally was important to Illich, and he was willing to recognize his own ambiguity about this – had prompted Illich, by his own account, to use the Latin adage *corruptio optimi quae est pessima* (the corruption of the best is the worst) (Cayley 1992, 242).

Equally relevant in Illich's approach was St Luke 10:25–37, which contains the parable of the Good Samaritan, Jesus's story about an outsider who helps an injured Jew and thereby embodies the possibility of mutual belonging beyond created barriers. Illich claimed that "the Samaritan parable was scandalous for the Pharisees to whom it was presented, because the Master told them who your neighbour is is not determined by your birth, by your condition, by the language which you speak, but by you" (Cayley 2005, 207). According to Charles Taylor's (2007) interpretation of Illich's notion of *corruption*, it began to develop after the Church started to erect a system to secure mutual belonging, incorporating a code, a set of rules, and a set of disciplines aimed at internalizing those rules, as well as constructing an organization and bureaucracy to ground them (739). In summary, Illich was always profoundly faithful to the Church as *She*; he developed this idea further by positioning the notion of missionary for a Church as *She* in relation to a critique of the Church as *It*, and to a critique of educational institutions. The latter becomes relevant given the involvement of the Church in education in Latin America.

Many of the missionaries were teachers who became involved with Catholic education in Latin America, a region that at the time was characterized by its division along profound class lines. Out of the 408 missionaries who attended Cuernavaca, 48 went to specialized education and 156 to general education, 45 to health services, 60 to social work, 28 to technical work, and 71 to direct evangelization (CIF 1965). Themes of education and schooling seem to have weighed heavily in the minds of the participants.

Educating Missionaries

The *CIF Reports* serve as an important reference to understand the approach to missionary formation. The *Reports* show that in the first two years, from 1962 to 1964, the centre's materials introduced a notion of the missionary rooted in the Gospel and exhibiting a preoccupation with authenticity, self-awareness, and motivation. This preoccupation reveals an influence from psychoanalysis, to which Illich was exposed through his friends Erich Fromm, Gregorio Lemercier, and Sergio Méndez Arceo.[6] Méndez Arceo and Lemercier took the issue of the relevance of psychoanalysis to faith to the fourth period of the Second Vatican Council in September 1965 (Méndez Arceo 1968). According to them, psychoanalysis could be used to purify vocations. Méndez Arceo and Lemercier also questioned what they saw as a purely sociological approach, in disregard of an anthropological perspective, taken by the Council. In their view, modern human beings were more self-aware, self-conscious, and associable, and tended to rationalize their positioning vis-à-vis the Absolute. With psychoanalysis, they claimed, human beings became aware of themselves (Bruno-Jofré and Igelmo Zaldívar 2016, 12).

From the start, the *Reports* were seen by some readers as oriented towards a political critique of the North, although, by and large, the materials used were rather conventional.[7] However, from 1964 on, there is a rupture. That year was key in the radicalization of Illich and the centres. In February, Illich appointed himself editor of the *Reports* and announced a change in their design and content; instead of curriculum materials for the seminars with missionaries, there would be selected articles on Latin America written by critical-minded politicians, writers, activists, religious people, and educators. After this point, the articles represent an eclectic kaleidoscope, including alternative, grassroots, radicalized experiences and political reflections, all of which were at odds with notions of change that had been supported by some sectors of the Church hierarchy.

The centre became independent; its board – which included John Considine – was discontinued. A new editorial committee was formed, composed of Illich and his close employees and friends, Valentina Borreman (director of the CIDOC) and Benjamin Ortega.

The first two volumes of the *Reports,* which came out prior to 1964, coincide with the phase we identified as the first phase of the centres, 1962–4. These volumes contain materials that are in line with the rhetoric of the Cold War, the concern with Cuba, an analysis of Catholic education in Latin America, and studies regarding the need to extend Catholic education at a time of demographic changes in the congregations, as shown by a decline in vocations. They also display a concern with the process of adaptation of the Church's structures to contemporary societal demands, with specific references to schooling, technology, and the uses of reason and freedom. They include a call for "a proper proportion" between theology of redemption and theology of incarnation, which is "clarified" in a gendered language as "a matter of appreciating the passive and active, the 'feminine' and 'masculine' character of man [*sic*] and his society" (Brison 1962). That statement is in line with the inherited Greek (Aristotelian) tradition of positioning the woman as the just man's passive "underling" – a theory adopted by Thomas Aquinas and the scholastic tradition (Boutin 1991, 9). Such language and its ideology sustains the exploitation of women and, ironically, the patriarchal model of the Church as *It*.

In the early *Reports*, education is presented as key to socio-economic development adapted to the age of technology "in a continent so young as Latin America" (Brison 1962). Note here that "young" appears to mean *immaturity* in relation to the North. Another important notion is that of schools as "pluralistic," referring to their ability to offer many more services than the typical school program. The language used in the *Reports* was rooted in the official American project for Latin America and, as noted earlier, in the gendered approach of the Catholic Church. As for the US initiative Alliance for Progress (AFP), it was examined from the perspectives of various political forces in Latin America, including different notions of revolution (Marxist, Reformist – such as that of the Christian Democratic Party – and John F. Kennedy's notion of revolution), and to dissenting critical views within the Church. In an analysis of the AFP, Dom Hélder Pessoa Câmara is quoted as saying: "Liberty is only a name, a sound for the two thirds of mankind [*sic*], without houses, without clothes, without food, without a minimum of education and above all without human conditions" (Center for Intercultural Research 1963). Overall there is a conventional anti-communist, capitalist, North American–oriented approach with strong gendered connotations.

However, after the mentioned rupture in 1964, the content and political language of the *Reports* changed dramatically, towards a critique of the Church as *It*, although admittedly not towards a critique of the patriarchal character of the Church as *It*. Clearly, the new language was related to a reading of the various grassroots movements and alternative views emerging in Latin America, the political and cultural revolts of the 1960s in the United States, and the overall social movements of the global 1960s.

The very first volume of the *Reports* after Illich's coup (i.e., his dismissal of the board in 1964) opened with an article titled "Subversion through Catholic Education?" written by Marina Bandeira (1964), executive director of the Radio School System run by the Bishops of Brazil, a component of the Basic Education Movement (*Movimento de Educaçao de Base* [MEB]). The article introduces the MEB and the events surrounding the confiscation of the primer *Viver E Lutar* in 1964 by the conservative governor of the state of Guanabara, Carlos Lacerda. Bandeira's article represented education not as a service offered by the Church but as a tool for subversion. Notably, it was published before the end of Vatican II.

Another signal of Illich's radicalization was that he republished an article on psychoanalysis by Gregorio Lemercier (1965) titled "A Benedictine Monastery and Psychoanalysis." Given the aforementioned relationships between Illich, Méndez Arceo, Lemercier, and Erich Fromm, the decision to republish that article in *Reports* was no accident. Fromm attempted to frame Freud's discoveries in humanism by situating them as a search for criticism and uncompromising realism (Bruno-Jofré and Igelmo Zaldívar 2016, 11). The preoccupation with psychoanalysis did not involve addressing the gender issue or questioning the patriarchal character of the Church as *It*, but it seems grounded in vocational issues (purification of vocations) and sexual concerns.

In previous works (Bruno-Jofré and Igelmo Zaldívar 2016) we have discussed the content of the *Reports* in the second phase in more detail; here, we will merely stress that they included reproductions of articles from the most distinguished figures of the time. Those figures brought a rainbow of voices reflecting the complexity of Latin American reality. They ranged from Salvador Allende, Adolfo Gilly, and Augusto Salazar Bondy, to sociologist Pablo Gonzalez Casanova, François Houtart, Dom Hélder Pessoa Câmara, and anthropologist Rodolfo Stavengahen, among many others.

The missionaries going through their formation at the centres were exposed, then, to critical alternative voices; also, many more in the field were receiving the *Reports*, which were widely distributed in Latin America. Interestingly, at the end of 1966, when the Cuernavaca centres were merged and moved to Rancho Tetela and the CIDOC ceased to offer residence to missionaries, future missionaries continued attending the CIDOC, due to the success of the Spanish classes and their attraction to alternative views.

During the third phase (late 1966 to February 1969), Illich's gradual radicalization culminated in an open conflict with the Vatican with the publication on 21 January 1967 of "The Seamy Side of Charity" in *America*, a Jesuit magazine, and on 16 June 1967 of "The Vanishing Clergyman" in *Reports* (it was first published on 7 June of the same year in the Chicago magazine *Critique*). Illich's strongly voiced criticisms, which began with that of the involvement of the Church with American policies towards Latin America in "The Seamy Side," were compounded by his questioning of Church rules, in particular celibacy, in "The Vanishing Clergyman."

After an investigation, Illich was called to Rome in June 1968. On 8 January 1969, the Vatican's Sacred Congregation for the Doctrine of the Faith *(Sacra Congregatio Pro Doctrina Fidei)* included a prohibition on religious congregations sending their members to the CIDOC for training in Spanish and other courses (Juicio al Padre Illich, 1969).[8]

While the CIDOC continued flourishing, the conflict with the Vatican silenced Illich's critique of the Church as *It*. The CIDOC became a civic centre, a space for academic debate over alternative ideas on culture, politics, and socio-economic matters; education became the central focus. Until 1969, missionaries had been allowed to attend the CIDOC; however, after the publication of the Vatican's questionnaire in the *New York Times*, it became unclear whether they were still allowed to do so ("Illich Goes His Own Way," 1969). The Vatican took a hands-off position regarding Illich and the CIDOC, given that those attending the centre did so as individuals.[9]

Even before being called to Rome, Illich was writing about education, using an analogy of schools as *It* for the Church as *It*. Three texts can be construed as transitional towards Illich's *Deschooling Society* (1971). The first was "The Futility of Schooling in Latin America," originally published in *Saturday Review* in April 1968 (Illich 1968a). In line with his critique of the Alliance for Progress and the Church's involvement in US policies conveyed in his 1967 "The Seamy Side of Charity"(Illich 1967a), in "The Futility of Schooling" Illich (1968a) critiqued the role of schooling in the so-called movement towards "progress" as an attempt to extrapolate an institutional model based on meritocracy, serving a modern middle class rather than the Latin American urban proletariat and the traditional landless rural masses. In the article, he also revisited an idea expressed in "The Seamy Side" – that the transplantation of people and institutions left little space for creative local solutions.

The second text we identify as part of the transition is "La Escuela, esa Vieja y Gorda Vaca Sagrada; en America Latina Abre un Abismo de Clases y Prepara a una Elite y con ella el Fascism" (The School, That Old and Fat Sacred Cow: In Latin America It Opens an Abyss between Classes and Prepares an Elite and with Her, Facism), published in the Mexican magazine *Siempre* in August 1968 (Illich 1968b). Notably, Illich refers here to the international seminars on education at CIDOC, in which missionaries still took part. The article contains his personal conclusions about the seminars. Illich portrays the teacher as a missionary of the school and an agent who has been successful because the colonial missionary prepared the way for the peoples' acceptance of the school's mission. Illich described the school as a "rite of passage" monopolizing education, the temple where "progressive initiations" take place. Illich goes on to say that we forget that the school is a historical phenomenon linked to industrial development (1968b, 95). For Illich, in the same way that faith is more than the Catholic institution, education is more than schooling – a theme he would revisit. He writes: "Any society that makes human experience its centre of development – and this is the society that we look forward to and dream – needs to clearly distinguish between the process of instruction and the opening of the conscious of each individual, between training and the development of creative imagination" (95–9). At this point, Illich saw Paulo Freire's pedagogical approach to literacy and his theory of *conscientização* (consciousness-raising) as providing good examples of a non-structured educational process that would enable individuals to learn more about themselves by engaging in dialogue with other individuals from their environment.

In the third text, "La Metamorfosis de la Escuela" (The School's Metamorphosis), a speech delivered on 6 June 1969 and published in the Mexican newspaper *El Dia* on 2 July, Illich characterized school as a "secular church" belonging to a time that was nearing its end. Using a powerful analogy intended for a critique of the Church as *It*, he wrote: "The deschooling of education and the demythologization of the school need to be understood by means of an analogy with the secularization of Christianity and the demythologization of the Church" (Illich 1969, 148/5). He continued: "The 'service' to a system of production – irrelevant of what system – has always threatened the Christian prophetism of the Church in the same way as today it threatens the educational potential of the school" (148/6). We believe that Illich saw the missionary as an educatee imprisoned within the Church as *It*, and the educatee and the educator both as imprisoned within the School as *It*. In "La Metamorfosis," he also stated that schools of the time were being mistaken (*se confunde*) for *education*, just as the Church was mistaken for *religion*. Writing against the backdrop of the 1968 student protests in Mexico and in other parts of the world, he equated the protests with the large charismatic movements of the Church, without which reforms within the Church would not have happened.

The missionaries who passed through Cuernavaca – a total of 408, through 1965 – and those who attended afterwards (for whom there are no data) were exposed to the complex process of radicalization of Illich's thought and the environment of change that characterized Cuernavaca. It is evident that before the formal rupture with the hierarchy of the Church in 1967–8, the centres had opened a space for discussion and critique of social, political, and economic ideas regarding Latin America, along with a critique of the Church conceived as *It*.

Conclusion

Ivan Illich's critique of the institutionalized Church and his notion of the missionary need to be understood in relation to his intellectual background, including the neo-Thomism of Jacques Maritain. The radicalization of his thought must be situated in the context of transformative ideological configurations at work in Cuernavaca, and in particular, his consistent distinction from the start of two forms of the Church: the Church as *It* and the Church as *She*. According to Illich, the Church as *It* embodied self-serving worldly power, while the Church as *She* was inspired by the Spirit and embodied the mystery of the Church, as well as the community.

Love (becoming like those we love), incarnation (incarnating in the other's culture rather than serving as an agent of one's own), and "poverty" (a profound feeling of dependency on others) were central virtues that Illich aimed at cultivating in the missionary. Influenced by psychoanalysis, Illich pursued authenticity in the vocations. However, he came to realize that the virtues were not enough if the missionaries continued to serve the Church as *It*. We distinguished four phases in the life of the centres and in the thinking of Illich during his time in Cuernavaca. The first was from 1962 to 1964, when the centres were externally financed by Fordham University and the Latin American Bureau of the NCWC, and the formation of missionaries was within the domain of papal projects. The second, from 1964 to 1966 (inclusive), signalled a rupture with the American sponsors and fully conveyed a radicalization of approaches, the basis of the critique of the Church as *It*. The third phase lasted from the end of 1966 until February 1969, when Illich decided to publish a questionnaire sent to him from the Vatican. In this phase, he fully engaged in a critique of the institutional Church that culminated in his conflict with the Vatican, and in his consequent shift to transforming his critique of the Church as *It* into a critique of the school as *It*. Stated differently, his critique of schooling that started in 1968 and concluded with *Deschooling Society* (Illich 1971) was carried out in analogy to his critique of the Church as *It*. However, it is noteworthy that Illich did not think of approaching the school as *She* as he did with the Church, despite saying that the school had been mistaken for education just as the Church (as institution) had been mistaken for religion.

In "The Seamy Side of Charity" and "The Vanishing Clergyman," Illich (1967b) focused on critiquing the Church as an institution, as well as in terms of the blind spots he identified in the selection of issues by the Vatican II Council, such as celibacy and psychoanalysis. Although Illich critiqued the ideological involvement of the Church with American projects for Latin America and conveyed an anti-imperialist position, his ideas and work were not actually related to any of the political/ideological configurations dominant in the 1960s in Latin America. In contrast with liberation theology, Illich's texts have not been taken up by a political and social movement or served as points of reference. Therefore, while liberation theology became inserted in wider movements in Latin America, Illich's rupturist discourse only found some continuity in secular fields like educational theory.

NOTES

1 Ivan Illich was born in Vienna in 1926. In the 1940s, he attended the Pontifical Gregorian University. He completed his PhD in 1950 at the University of Salzburg with a thesis on philosophy of history. In the 1950s, he was engaged in pastoral work in New York, and between 1956 and 1960 he served as vice-president of the Pontifical Catholic University in Ponce, Puerto Rico. In 1961, he founded a centre in Cuernavaca, Mexico, as a formative ground for prospective Catholic missionaries and lay Catholics. In education, the name Ivan Illich is narrowly tied to his renowned book *Deschooling Society* (1971). This book featured a radical critique of modern education institutions, which were undergoing extraordinary expansion in the 1970s.

2 Information about the number of missionaries is available at Center of Intercultural Formation, *Progress Report Submitted to the Board of Directors, New York City, June 14, 1965*, Cuernavaca, Mexico. Daniel Cosío Villegas Library, El Colegio de México, Inventario 2007, folder 370.196 C 397d.n. We do not have numerical data regarding participants after 1965. From 1966 on, the connection with religious congregations was weakened; this was the last year that the CIC served as a boarding residence for missionaries preparing themselves to go to Latin America. A new structure developed with the creation of CIDOC, which was moved to Rancho Tetela on the outskirts of Cuernavaca. The CIDOC did not provide residence. It was a centre where workshops were delivered and Spanish classes were offered, and there was a large library with new materials on Latin America, including a large collection of pastoral information on Latin America after the sixteenth century. The CIDOC was visited by religious and lay people interested in Latin America.

3 See Rosa Bruno-Jofré and Jon Igelmo Zaldívar, "Ivan Illich's Late Critique of *Deschooling Society*: 'I was largely barking up the wrong tree,'" *Educational Theory* 62(5) (2012): 573–92, doi:10.1111/j.1741-5446.2012.00464.x; and Lee Hoinacki, "The Trajectory of Ivan Illich," *Bulletin of Science, Technology, and Society* 23(5) (2003): 382–9, doi:10.1177/0270467603259776.

4 See Richard Cushing, *Questions et réponses sur le communisme* (Sherbrooke: Apostolat de la presse, 1961).

5 Illich's creation of the CIF and its publications was fully supported by the Latin American Bureau of the National Catholic Welfare Council (NCWC), directed by Considine. The bureau, with funds from the council, provided Illich with $75,000 to initiate the project. See Matthew John O'Meagher, "Catholicism, Reform, and Development in Latin America, 1959–67," PhD diss., Department of History, Duke University, 1994, 377.

6 The involvement of Lemercier with psychoanalysis started when he had a hallucination on 4 October 1960. See Juan Alberto Litmanovich, "Las operaciones psychoanaliticas gestadas al interior del monasterio Benedictino de Ahuacatlitlán, Cuernavaca, Morelos, Mexico (1961–1964)" PhD diss., Universidad Iberoamericana de Mexico, 2008; and Henry Giniger, "A monastery in Mexico closed in dispute over psychoanalysis," *New York Times*, 6 September 1967, 15.

7 "*CIF Reports* is a service with a political platform. Our politics – let us be frank – is to get you involved [in] Latin America. We do not wish to shout with certain extremist groups in either North or Latin America. We only say that we are here, ready to report to you the thinking and activities that have been and are being generated by certain Christian revolutionaries in the Americas" (Brison 1963, cited in Bruno-Jofré and Igelmo Zaldívar 2016).

8 See *Sagrada Congregación para la Doctrina de la Fe*, 1969, Comunicado al Obispo de Cuernavaca, in CIDOC Cuernavaca, *Mexico "entredicho" del Vaticano al CIDOC 1966–69, CIDOC Cuaderno* (no. 37), 4/132–4/133; and A. Mauro, Carta circular al R. P. Arrupe, SJ, in CIDOC Cuernavaca, *Mexico "entredicho" del Vaticano al CIDOC 1966–69, CIDOC Cuaderno* no. 37 (1969): 4/157.

9 Sergio Méndez Arceo, in his pastoral letter of 21 June 1969 – after his meeting with the Pope – reported the positioning of the Vatican in relation to the conflict with Ivan Illich and the CIDOC. He wrote: "I wish to talk about my recent visit to the Pope. In the last years I have gone to see the Pope every year, not for the sake of doing it, although I meet with him with great satisfaction, but due to the internal urgency of ecclesial communication in the same way as Paul went so see Peter. Informing the details of my trip, I say that there had been a 'solution in principle' and

that *ad experimentum* those who had been banned could continue using the CIDOC. The will of the Pope was to undo a hurried prohibition that was issued in his name not allowing ecclesiastics and religious to attend CIDOC and participate in its activities ... A second issue is the pastoral preoccupation the Pope had regarding the priest Ivan D. Illich, who would not be forced to leave Cuernavaca immediately. Instead, it would be the pastoral task of the bishop to assure his faithfulness and priestly vocation." Sergio Méndez Arceo, in CIDOC Cuernavaca, *Mexico "entredicho" del Vaticano al CIDOC 1966–69, CIDOC Cuaderno* no. 37 (1969): 4/267–4/268.

REFERENCES

Bandeira, Marina. 1964. "Movimento de Educação de Base." A report given to the Catholic Inter-American Cooperation Program (CICOP), Chicago, 23 February 1964. [Reprinted in CIDOC Cuernavaca. 1970, *CIF Reports*, vol. 3, *April–December 1964, CIDOC Cuaderno* no. 38.]

Boutin, Lea. MO. 1991. *Women in the Church: The Pain, the Challenge, the Hope.* Aurora: Southdown Emmanuel Convalescent Foundation.

Brison, Peter. 1962, November. "Notes from the Editors of *CIF Reports.*" [Reprinted in CIDOC Cuernavaca, 1969. *CIF Reports*, vol. 1: *April 1962–March 1963, CIDOC Cuaderno* no. 36: 6/4.]

– 1963 (January). "Notes from the Editors of *CIF Reports.*" [Reprinted in CIDOC Cuernavaca, 1969. *CIF Reports* vol. 1: *April 1962–March 1963, CIDOC Cuaderno* no. 36: 8/5.]

Bruno-Jofré, Rosa, and Jon Igelmo Zaldívar. 2014. "The Center for Intercultural Formation, Cuernavaca, Mexico, Its Reports (1962–1976), and Illich's Critical Understanding of Mission in Latin America." *Hispania Sacra* 66 (extra 2): 457–87. http://dx.doi.org/10.3989/hs.2014.096.

– 2016. "Monsignor Ivan Illich's Critique of the Institutional Church, 1960–1966." *Journal of Ecclesiastical History* 67(3): 568–86.

Cayley, David. 1992. *Ivan Illich in Conversation.* Toronto: Anansi.

– 2005. *The Rivers North of the Future: The Testament of Ivan Illich.* Toronto: Anansi.

Center for Intercultural Formation (CIF). 1961. "Pope John XXIII, Feast of the Annunciation." In *Center of Intercultural Formation (CIF), Fordham University, Summer–Fall, 1961, Cuernavaca, Mexico; Anápolis, Brazil* (pamphlet). Cuernavaca, Mexico, manuscript. Daniel Cosío Villegas Library, El Colegio de México, Inventario 2007, folder 370.196 C 397d.

– 1963. *The Center of Intercultural Formation, CIF, 1962–1963. Cuernavaca, Mexico; Petrópolis, Brazil; Fordham University, N.Y.C.* Cuernavaca, Mexico, manuscript.

Daniel Cosío Villegas Library, El Colegio de México, Inventario 2007, folder 370.196 C 397d.
– 1965. *Progress Report Submitted to the Board of Directors, New York City, June 14, 1965.* Cuernavaca, Mexico, manuscript. Daniel Cosío Villegas Library, El Colegio de México, Inventario 2007, folder 370.196 C 397d.n.
Fitzpatrick, Joseph P., SJ. 1963 (Winter). "Fordham and the Challenge of Latin America." *Fordham Alumni Federation Magazine.* 3–5.
Garneau, James F. 2001. "The First Inter-American Episcopal Conference, November 2–4, 1959: Canada and the United States Called to the Rescue of Latin America." *Catholic Historical Review* 87(4): 662–87. http://dx.doi.org/10.1353/cat.2001.0153.
Grego, Daniel. 2013. "Thirteen Ways of Looking at Ivan Illich." *International Journal of Illich Studies* 3(1): 79–95.
Hartch, Todd. 2015. *The Prophet of Cuernavaca: Ivan Illich and the Crisis of the West.* New York: Oxford University Press. http://dx.doi.org/10.1093/acprof:oso/9780190204563.001.0001.
Igelmo Zaldívar, Jon. 2011. "Ivan Illich en el CIDOC de Cuernavaca (1963-1976). Un acontecimiento para la teoría y la historia de la educación." PhD diss., Universidad Complutense de Madrid.
Illich, Ivan. 1967a (21 January). "The Seamy Side of Charity." *America* 21: 88–91.
– 1967b (16 June). "The Vanishing Clergyman." [Reprinted in CIDOC Cuernavaca, 1967, *CIF Reports,* vol. 6: *January–June, 1967, CIDOC Cuaderno* no. 41: 6/13–6/30.]
– 1968a. "The Futility of Schooling in Latin America." *Saturday Review* 57–8 (20 April): 74–5.
– 1968b (August). "La escuela, esa vieja y gorda vaca sagrada: en America Latina abre un abismo de clases y prepara a una elite y con ella el fascimo." [Reprinted in CIDOC Cuernavaca, 1968, *CIDOC Informa Julio–diciembre 1968, CIDOC Cuaderno* no. 41: 95/1.] *Siempre* 78 (789): 30–4.
– 1969 (2 July). "La metamorfosis de la escuela: mensaje en ocasión de la graduación celebrada en el reciento universitario de Río Piedras, Puerto Rico." *El Día.* [Reprinted in CIDOC Cuernavaca, 1969, *CIDOC Informa Julio–diciembre de 1968, CIDOC Cuaderno* no. 44: 148/5.]
– 1971. *Deschooling Society.* New York: Harper & Row.
"Illich Goes His Own Way." *New York Times,* 2 February 1969, E5.
"Juicio al Padre Illich: Texto del interrogatorio al que lo sometió el Vaticano." 1969. *Excelsior* (Mexico), 3 February, 1, 16, 17.
Lemercier, Gregory. 1965. "A Benedictine Monastery and Psychoanalysis." [Reprinted in CIDOC Cuernavaca, 1970, *CIF Reports,* vol. 4: *January–December 1965, CIDOC Cuaderno* no. 39: 10/19–10/26.]

Méndez Arceo, Sergio. 1968. "Intervención conciliar, algunas observaciones al Esquema XIII." In CIDOC Cuernavaca, *Fuentes para el estudio de una diócesis,* vol 1: 4/154–8. Cuernavaca, Mexico. [The full text of Méndez Arceo's presentation is reproduced in Latin as it was written.]

Pernot, P., Dom. 1962 (March). *Le Centre de Formation Interculturelle de Cuernavaca, Extrait des Images de Toumliline.* Cuernavaca, Mexico, manuscript. Daniel Cosío Villegas Library, El Colegio de México, Inventario 2007, folder 370.197 C 3975.

Smith, Christian. 1991. *The Emergence of Liberation Theology.* Chicago: University of Chicago Press.

Taylor, Charles. 2007. *A Secular Age.* Cambridge, MA: Harvard University Press.

7 From Serving in the Missions at Home to Serving in Latin America: The Post-Vatican II Experience of Canadian Women Religious

ELIZABETH M. SMYTH

The history of women religious in Canada has been one of continuous missionary service. In 1639, members of two congregations of women religious voyaged from their European homelands to New France, to serve God through ministering to the colonists and Indigenous people. Under the leadership of Marie Guenet de Saint-Ignace, three sister-nurses who were members of the Augustinian Hospitaliers de la Misericorde de Jesus of Dieppe and three sister-teachers of the Order of St Ursula (the Ursulines), led by Marie de L'Incarnation, established the first convent-based hospitals and schools north of Mexico. Over the following five centuries, the tradition of missionary service continued, as Canadian and European communities of men and women religious, as well as members of pious apostolic societies and lay associates, continued to serve European, Canadian, and Indigenous peoples. Members of religious communities came as immigrants themselves, following their country folk as European colonial expansion reshaped the Canadian frontiers. Yet as early as the mid-nineteenth century, the mission fields of Latin America beckoned. In 1864, members of the Christian Brothers from La Prairie, Quebec, established a foundation at Port-au-Prince, Haiti. In 1875, members of Les Filles de la Sagesse journeyed from Ottawa and Montreal to establish a boarding school for girls in Port-au-Prince.

Missionary activities accelerated with the founding of *Consejo Episcopal Latinoamericano* (CELAM) in 1955 by the bishops of Latin America and of the Pontifical Commission for Latin America in 1958 by Pope Pius XII. Six Canadian bishops joined their brother bishops from the United States and Latin America in planning a concerted effort to support the growth of the Catholic Church in Latin America, launching umbrella organizations that would later create infrastructures to support missionary activities. The response to the decrees of the Second Vatican Council (Vatican II) further developed a Canadian presence in the mission fields of Latin America.

This chapter analyses the engagement of one community of Canadian women religious in the Latin American mission fields in the years following Vatican II. Through document analysis and oral histories, it explores how the Congregation of the Sisters of St Joseph of Toronto diversified their educational, health, and social services ministries in Latin American missions. This chapter also documents how the mission activities in the countries where the Sisters worked impacted their congregation at home. It is clear from the experience of this congregation that the response to the call to the mission fields of Latin America brought women religious into waters they had never imagined. They found themselves confronting civil authorities and placing their members directly in the path of death squads. Their leaders would have to confront fundamental questions of religious formation.

Theoretical and Historical Context

This chapter is nested within the Canadian historiography of the study of women religious, as well as the historical and theological literature on Vatican II and vow formation. As I have argued elsewhere, while the historiography of women religious in Canada has been uneven in its development, there are many opportunities to develop stronger theoretical underpinnings, applying multidisciplinary tools to enhance the scholarly discourse, and structuring a more robust methodological analytical framework (Smyth 2014). Dutch moral theologian Annelies van Heijst (2012) likewise calls for a more balanced historiography of women religious. She cautions that the constructs of feminist theology and women's history have not diminished but have in fact contributed to the long tradition of hagiography in the writing of the history of women religious. She challenges historians in general, and feminist historians in particular, to move beyond celebrating the achievements of women religious as a triumphalist parade of women worthies, in spite of the fact that they were trapped within a theological and institutional patriarchy. She argues that there are serious and highly problematic elements in the history of women religious that have their roots in the patriarchy in which women religious exist. For evidence to support her argument, van Heijst looks to the enthusiasm with which women religious embraced Vatican II, concluding:

> After Vatican II, they turned their traditional way of life upside down and the authoritarian lifestyle, which used to rely on blind obedience, was replaced by democratic interaction ... The military-like uniformity was exchanged for a personal lifestyle, in which emotional warmth and relationships were no longer taboo. New values of health – both mental and physical – and happiness were central, and nuns made efforts to be committed to issues of justice and peace, and to be close and supportive to those in need. (168)

Van Heijst's work provides a useful framework for analysing the experience of the congregation studied in this chapter, and aligns with that of other recent contributions to the fields of history and theology. Stimulated by the fiftieth anniversary of the calling of the Second Vatican Council, a number of historians and theologians have produced an array of fascinating studies that point to, among other features, the long period of reform that preceded the Council; the role that Canadians played at the Council; and the impact of the Council on theology, ecumenism, and religious life, perhaps best exemplified by chapters published in the bilingual volumes by Attridge, Clifford, and Routhier (2011).

Four key Vatican II documents frame the Congregation of the Sisters of St Joseph's missionary activities in Latin America. Each of these will be discussed in turn. In his aptly titled *The Rebirth of Latin American Christianity*, Todd Hartch (2014) neatly provides a contemporary historical backdrop for the experience of the Sisters of St Joseph in Latin America. Stepping back from *Decree on the Church's Missionary Activity* (*Ad Gentes*) – the final document of the Council, issued on its final day, 7 December 1965 – Hartch delves into the motivations underlying the creation of the Latin American missions. He argues that Pius XII "believed that the combination of a severe priest shortage and the challenges of urbanization, industrialization, Protestantism and Marxism had created a crisis that was too much for Latin America to deal with on its own" (171) and thus encouraged the American bishops to work together for the betterment of the Church in the Americas. With the strong support of his successor, Pope John XXIII, the First Inter-American Episcopal Conference was held at Georgetown University in Washington, DC, on 2–4 November 1959. Six Canadian bishops, as well as the Canadian apostolic delegate, were active participants and delivered several key interventions. Not surprisingly, the majority of the bishops were francophone and represented French or bilingual dioceses: Archbishop and President of the Canadian Catholic Conference (the predecessor to the Canadian Conference of Catholic Bishops), Paul Bernier (Gaspé); Archbishops Georges Cabana

Table 7.1 Foundations of Canadian religious congregations in Latin America, 1864–1966

Year	Number of foundations
1864	1
1864–1909	4
1910–19	1
1920–9	3
1940–9	26
1950–9	32
1960–6	127

Compiled by the author from tables produced by the *Office Catholique Canadien de L'Amerique Latine*. CSJTA. Note: figures include diocesan priests, lay apostles, and members of pious societies

of Sherbrooke and Marie-Joseph Lemieux (Ottawa); and Coadjutor Bishop Albert Sanschagrin (Amos). The bishops of two Ontario anglophone dioceses attended: Bishop John C. Cody of London and Auxiliary Bishop Francis V. Allen of Toronto. The episcopacies and dioceses of these latter two individuals would be significant for the Congregation of the Sisters of St Joseph, as would two initiatives that the Canadian bishops launched as a result of the Georgetown meeting: the Canadian Episcopal Commission for Latin America (CECAL) and the Canadian Catholic Office of Latin America (COCAL).

As Table 7.1 indicates, supported by CECAL and COCAL, Canadian involvement in Latin American missions grew exponentially in the 1960s. In fact, within a brief six years, the number of individuals involved more than doubled the number that the previous century had seen. At 735, women religious constituted 41 per cent of the missionaries serving in Latin America.[1] The distribution of the Canadian missionaries by country is documented in Table 7.2. The largest numbers were deployed in Haiti, followed by Peru, Brazil, Chile, and Honduras. As Garneau (2001) observed: "The Canadian Church reached its apex in the number of missionaries sent to Latin America in 1971, when there were 1,894, serving in twenty-three countries. This was an increase of 93.9% since 1958" (686). Thus, in response to *Ad Gentes*, Canadian missionaries built on those activities initiated in the 1950s.

The second Vatican II document key to the experience of the congregation analysed in this chapter is the *Decree on the Up-to-Date Renewal of Religious Life* (*Perfectae Caritatis*). Promulgated on 20 October 1965, *Perfectae Caritatis* accelerated the changes to religious life that had been initiated under the papacy of Pius XII. During his papacy, Pius XII had held the first

Table 7.2 Top Five Latin American missions where Canadian missionaries served in 1966

Country	Canadians serving (women religious)
Haiti	356 (225)
Peru	330 (154)
Brasil	289 (123)
Chile	178 (34)
Hondouras	115 (62)

Compiled from tables produced by the *Office Catholique Canadien de L'Amerique Latine*. CSJTA. Note: Figures include diocesan priests, members of lay apostolates, and pious societies.

international meeting of the Superiors General to discuss the challenges and opportunities for women religious available in the postwar world. Among the challenges set out were the educational needs of young sisters: they needed to be adequately prepared to enter the professions, especially in the domain of education. As well, practically and symbolically, the habit was in need of change. Veils and headpieces created health and safety risks. Damp and highly starched face pieces caused ear infections. Large and cumbersome veils were safety risks when operating motor vehicles, as many created blind spots. Extended sleeves were dangerous. Care of the habit, even with the advent of mechanized laundries, was time consuming. *Perfectae Caritatis* moved beyond these cosmetic and educational changes, mandating an examination of the origins, governance, and operations of the religious congregations. The document declared that religious were in fact members of the laity and removed the long-held understanding that theirs was a special status, occupying a third space between the ordained priestly caste and those non-vowed individuals who occupied the pews.

It is somewhat ironic that one outcome of Vatican II was that once again, as so often is the case in the history of the Roman Catholic Church, a collection of secular priests dictated to men and women religious how they were to live their lives in community. Women religious were charged with exploring their foundations and foregrounding their founding charisms, and they took this charge very seriously. These explorations, set within the social upheaval characteristic of the 1960s in North America, unleashed massive changes in religious life. In fact, it could be argued that Vatican II fundamentally changed the nature of religious life for the more than 60,000 Canadian women who were members of religious congregations in the 1960s.

The final document under discussion is the *Decree on the Apostolate of the Laity* (*Apostolicam Actuositatem*). Promulgated on 18 November 1965, it emphasized the role of the laity in the Church. The laity, defined as all baptized persons, was deemed to have an important role to play in the apostolic work of the Church. Priests and men and women religious were directed to work collaboratively with the laity, educating them as appropriate and supporting them as they too engaged in apostolic work.

The response to these Vatican documents changed the Sisters of St Joseph. *Perfectae Caritatis* led them to rediscover their founder, his "Little Design," and caused them to restructure their community governance. *Apostolicam Actuositatem* brought them into ongoing work with the laity. *Ad Gentes*, with its calls for a renewed commitment to missionary activity, brought them to Latin America. An examination of the mission in Guatemala – its origins, the decision-making that went into its founding, and the orientations of the community's apostolic endeavours – demonstrate the impact these three documents had on the Sisters of St Joseph of Toronto.

The Sisters of St Joseph of Toronto

The Sisters of St Joseph is a community of women religious engaged in education, social service, and health care. They were the second community to be established in Toronto, the Irish Institute of the Blessed Virgin Mary (the Loretto Sisters), a teaching order, being the first. The Sisters of St Joseph were established in LePuy, France, in 1650 by a Jesuit priest, Jean-Pierre Medaille, who gathered six women who desired to serve God through service of neighbour. Their mission would become the motto of the congregation. The women sought to live not as cloistered nuns but as active women, housed in small residences that accommodated up to ten. They dressed in the manner of respectable widows and soon were operating missions throughout France. Over the course of the eighteenth century, their governance, missions, and way of life became more formalized and institutionalized, with the community living under a constitution, engaging in reception and vows ceremonies, using a governance structure, and wearing standardized habits. After the French Revolution, Mother St John Fontbonne centralized the French communities at Lyons and re-established the congregation. In 1836, six Sisters journeyed from Lyons to establish the first North American foundation in Carondelet, Missouri. Its purpose was to provide a range of educational, social service, and health care initiatives, which grew to include a school for the deaf, parish schools, schools for young women, orphanages, and a hospital. From there, the Sisters spread, establishing foundations across the United States. From their foundation in Philadelphia, the Sisters of St Joseph established a foundation in Toronto in 1851. The Sisters came at the invitation of Bishop Armand de Charbonnel, a native Frenchman, who knew the Sisters of St Joseph from his years in central France. Mother Delphine Fontbonne, a niece of Mother St John Fontbonne, was the founding superior. Delphine led a peripatetic existence, serving in Carondelet and Philadelphia before establishing the Toronto community. The initial charge was for the Sisters to establish an orphanage, to meet the needs of children and the sick poor. The Sisters began teaching in parish schools in 1852, and by 1854 they had established a convent academy for girls and young women, which grew into a women's college at the University of Toronto. They expanded their social service activities to include homes for the infirm and elderly in 1857, and in 1892, with the founding of St Michael's Hospital, they established a network of hospitals and schools of nursing. Plans for a North American pontifical-style congregation, based in Carondelet, never came to fruition. The Sisters of St Joseph of Toronto, and the five congregations that grew from it – the Sisters of St Joseph of Hamilton (1852), of London (1868), of Peterborough (1881), of Pembroke (1910), and of Sault Ste Marie (1836) – were individually established as pontifical congregations over the course of the twentieth century.

Throughout the nineteenth and twentieth centuries, the Toronto community expanded across Canada, but it did not engage in overseas mission work until the 1960s. The priests of the Scarboro Foreign Mission Society (SFM) tried unsuccessfully to recruit the Sisters of St Joseph to serve with them in their Chinese missions. But finally, after establishing missions across Canada and serving many ethnically and racially diverse communities, in the aftermath of Vatican II, the community established missions in Guatemala.

Mary Estelle McGuire – in religion, Mother Maura (1900–79) – oversaw the congregation as General Superior from 1956 to 1968. Educated by the Sisters of St Joseph in their Toronto Academy, Mary Estelle graduated with a commercial diploma in 1918 and relocated to Montreal, where she worked in banking while earning a diploma in accounting from McGill University. She entered the community in 1921, enrolled in the Toronto Normal School, and taught at the congregation's schools in Toronto, St Catharine's, and Vancouver. She served as principal of the order's flagship school, St Joseph's College School. In 1945, she was assigned to St Michael's Hospital, where she served in a number of administrative roles and earned, in the words of her necrology, "a reputation as an astute business woman, initiating an ambitious period of reconstruction and modernization launching the first ever fund raising campaign for the hospital."[2] For her services in that domain, she was among the first recipients of the Order of Canada in 1967. As General Superior, she led the congregation through a decade of expansion. She oversaw the relocation of the mother house from its downtown Toronto location to a sprawling site known as Morrow Park in 1960. She also oversaw the congregation's initial implementation of the reforms of Vatican II. In 1968, at the end of her term as General Superior, the congregation was at its peak of 591 members: 526 fully professed Sisters, 48 junior professed, and 17 novices.[3]

Missionary activity was at the core of many community discussions during and after Vatican II. The notes of the Tenth General Chapter of 24–31 July 1963 record that the community expressed "openness to establishing a foreign mission if requested."[4] Mother Maura's correspondence indicates that indeed the community did receive requests to found missions. Her reputation as an eminently practical woman is verified by the approach she took to assessing where the community should engage. Writing to Father Roland Roberts SFM in August 1965 concerning the possibility of establishing a mission at Georgetown, St Vincent, West Indies, she posed a very specific set of questions:

> What is the most direct route to your mission?
> Would there be catechetical work in the parish?
> Is there suitable property where you would wish this mission located?
> Is there a contractor in the locality?
> What would be the best for durability – wood? Cement block?
> What type of climate?
> What is the situation politically in your locality?
> Would four Sisters be sufficient?

She hastened, "Father, I am not being 'choosey' [emphasis in original] but I think it is well to have definite answers to give ... I may have to do a selling job as there are some that think we should go to Peru, Brazil etc. I would like to go where we are needed and I feel there is real need where you are."[5] In the end, she decided to deploy her congregation elsewhere.

It was as a result of consultations with Bishop Alexander Carter (president of the Canadian Episcopal Commission for Latin America) and Fr Pierre Goyett that she made her decision. Fr Goyett was well placed to offer advice. He was a member of the *Société des Missions-Étrangères* – a Laval, Quebec-based order of priests that had been established in 1921 – and he served as the director of the Latin American Office of the Canadian Catholic Conference. Mother Maura learned that three countries had been identified as being in most urgent need of missionaries: Guyana, the Dominican Republic, and Guatemala. Writing to the community in October 1966, Mother Maura explained: "I found that Guatemala's need is most urgent, since the Church is organizing, in different countries to the south, teamwork to cover every apostolic angle." She argued that "the Eastern part of Guatemala is already occupied by two foundations of the Sisters of St Joseph of Canada – Hamilton and North Bay." Having been advised by Fr Goyette, she announced: "I think [it] wise to go and look over the situation."[6]

On 12 January 1967, Mother Maura, accompanied by Mother Assistant Raphael Kane, journeyed to Guatemala. Accompanied by Monsignor Conway McKee, the representative of the Canadian bishops, the Sisters visited potential mission sites in the diocese of Quetzaltenango. She wrote:

> Each day we sta[r]ted out very early and drove miles to visit different Missions to see if we could find where God wanted the Sisters of St Joseph of Toronto to serve Him and His poor ... Morales was the place that seemed to creep into our hearts. The area is a large one comprising towns and mountain sections inhabited by about 30,000 souls who have no permanent priests and, of course, no Sisters or anything of a Catholic nature.[7]

Ever observant to the political situation, Mother Maura recounted:

> Wherever we drove in Guatemala, we were stopped on the road about every five miles by soldiers with bayonets fixed. These were Government soldiers. The government at present is non-Communist, succeeding a Communist one, and on the alert for Communist guerillas. No one is above suspicion, not even priests and nuns.[8]

Mother Maura was observing the most recent chapter in the complex history of Guatemala. Its economic potential had attracted the interest of Europeans and Americans. Its Indigenous population laboured on coffee and fruit plantations. Mount (2013) described the country as one in which "72% [of the] arable land was owned by 2% of the population" (25), and as dominated by large conglomerates such as the United Fruit Company, which had "powerful connections in Washington" (25) – connections that played a major role in both internal and external politics. It was against this politically charged background that the bishops of Guatemala had reached out to their brother bishops worldwide to help them implement the Church's teachings on social justice, and in this context that the Sisters of St Joseph of Toronto's Guatemalan missions were established.

In spite of these ominous observations, a vision of what the community could do took shape in Mother Maura's mind. For the time being, the Sisters could live in the United Fruit Company compound on the edge of the town of Morales. From there, Mother Maura foresaw four Sisters: "a nurse, a teacher, a visitor and a catechist ... could become acquainted with the people and the locality and before long we would know the best location for us to build a permanent Convent with the facilities needed."[9]

Returning for a second visit, she wrote: "We started out early to view again our 'first love' at Benares and Morales, a drive of 200 miles. We went over all the ground again and we both felt that this was the place the Holy Spirit had chosen for us."[10] She reported to the congregation that when she informed the bishop of her decision, he "was genuinely happy and promised to see that our Sister Missionaries would have all the necessities of Religious Life supplied as far as possible by Canadian and American Missionaries."[11]

She continued: "Now for the important part of this letter – the personnel of our Guatemalan Mission-to-be." In the spirit of the reforms of Vatican II, and the reconceptualization of the vow of obedience, the Sisters would not be assigned under obedience to serve in the mission, but would be asked if they wished to volunteer to serve. Even as Mother Maura presented this option, she set forth a very candid analysis of the physical and spiritual challenges the Sisters would face. She described the challenging climate: very hot summers and four months of rain. She cautioned: "Naturally a Sister who finds heat unduly oppressive or rain unduly depressive would find it difficult and I do not think saying 'I will offer it up' would be the answer. Some naturally find heat and rain harder to bear than others."[12]

She presented the challenges she foresaw with unfamiliar food, an unsafe water supply, and an unstable power grid. After noting the lack of creature comforts, she concluded with five spiritual challenges that she had identified:

1. [T]he distance from our main Community
2. Loneliness
3. Repulsiveness of surroundings – diet etc.
4. This is no place for a moody person.

5. It is necessary that a great spirit of charity should exist among the Sisters themselves. They must have love for one another before they can give li[f]e to those [they] serve.[13]

In retrospect, this was a somewhat blunt assessment of what the community might face. But Mother Maura had failed to identify the greatest challenge the Sisters would encounter: engaging in social justice activism under a repressive regime.

The response of the community was enthusiastic. Some seventy-nine Sisters volunteered for the mission, and four were chosen, drawn from the fields of education, social service, and health care, all with experience in a broad spectrum of community life. Selected for the mission were Sister Tarcisius Stradiotti, stationed at Terrace, BC; Sister Mary Lois Barnett, stationed at Chilliwack, BC; Sister Mary Beatrice (Therese) Cleary, St Michael's Hospital, Toronto; and Sister Andrea Dumont, St Joseph's Hospital, Toronto, who would stay in Guatemala for the duration of the mission. Before leaving for Guatemala, the Sisters studied for nine months at the Scarboro Foreign Missions Latin American Institute at St Mary's, Ontario. Sister Andrea Dumont recalled their time at the institute: "We had been very well prepared ... to go down there not to impose our culture, but to make ourselves not needed ... [to] act as a catalyst for the people ... to train health workers from the villages" (Smyth and Wicks 2001, 186).

On 14 January 1968, the community bid farewell to the four Sisters at a Departure Ceremony held at St Michael's Cathedral and presided over by Toronto Archbishop Phillip Pocock. The Sisters who departed for Guatemala were all professional women, vowed religious who had experienced first-hand the changes of Vatican II. Their Departure Ceremony was the occasion for officially presenting to the outside world the modified habit, and the four missionary Sisters were the first to wear it. Discarding their serge habits modelled on French peasant dress, they boarded the aircraft in clothing appropriate to the tropics: white short-sleeved dresses and veils. In later years, options would include blouses and skirts, and even slacks. The missionary Sisters had participated in the extraordinary Chapters – congregational meetings mandated by the Vatican councils – during which discussions of the meaning of the vows that bonded them together, conceptualizing chastity, poverty, and obedience, had taken place. Collectively, the Sisters of St Joseph of Toronto decided: "We must let others see that a life dedicated to Our Lord is a happy life, that his [*sic*] companionship richly supplies for marital joys, that the inheritance of the earth is wealth enough and that doing His will is a happy privilege, not a constraint."[14]

As a community, these Sisters had participated in the debates concerning how to meet the needs of the times. Their conclusion: "Knowing that the world of today calls for adjustment of the changed conditions of these times, the Sisters of St Joseph feel that, in responding to new apostolic needs, we are rather deepening our traditions than surrendering them. Both Father Medaille and Mother St John, deeply concerned with all human misery, wanted to embrace whatever apostolic work was most pressing. Therefore we are happy to reach out to new works."[15]

Specifically discussing social problems, they were part of a community that declared: "Problems of poverty and social injustice have always distressed religious women. Some of our Sisters have felt drawn to missionary life in Guatemala or among the Indians of Canada and some to living among the poor in depressed areas ... by our efforts to find 'the solutions to the outstanding problems of our times,' both on a community and on an individual level we are continuing the spirit of our founder."[16] The four missionary Sisters carried with them to Guatemala a new way of living their vows in community. There was both continuity and change in their actualization.

Six months after the founding of the mission, and as was her custom as Superior General, Mother Maura reported to the congregation about the state of their mission. She wrote to the General Chapter: "The four Sisters are well, have weathered the climate, food and inconveniences and are gradually winning their way into the hearts and souls of the people. They are visiting the homes, instructing the children, the adults and caring for the sick as well as teaching preventive medicine."[17]

Ever the savvy businesswoman, she looked to the bottom line. She advised the Chapter of the financial obligations the congregation had undertaken, reminding the Sisters that "the Mission of Guatemala will not be self-supporting in the foreseeable future." One project the congregation had agreed to fund was the building of a permanent convent and dispensary.[18]

When surveyed as a whole, the history of the Sisters of St Joseph's Guatemala mission is one of struggle with the local authorities. In a sesquicentennial volume, Smyth and Wicks (2001) collected the oral histories of the Sisters who served in the Guatemalan mission. The Sisters documented how they experienced first-hand violence, brutality, and cruelty and had their own visions of what they were going to do challenged. They lived through earthquakes, and through coups. Sister Patricia Dowling reflected: "I was going to go and save the poor and help the poor [until] the Medellin Documents ... really changed the whole attitude on missionary work ... Our work was to conscienticize [*sic*] the poor and help the people realize their dignity and human rights ... Little by little I realized the poor were evangelizing me" (ibid., 184).

The Sisters' work in the area of human rights brought them into conflict with the government and the army – a conflict that escalated after the devastating earthquake of 4 February 1976. As part of the reconstruction process, the Sisters worked with the community for over a year in planning the building of 109 homes as well as a school, a church, and a market stall. Sister Andrea Dumont recalled that teaching "a decision making process was fundamental, due to the fact that people are often denied the freedom of shaping their own destiny. They become objects rather than subjects of their lives. Besides learning building skills, some attended workshops on Ecclesial Base Community, Liberation Theology and Community Building" (ibid., 185).

The Sisters were educating leaders, and this was a threat to the civil and military authorities. Their convent was firebombed. Father Tulio Maruzzo, the parish priest with whom they worked, and a catechetical worker with whom he was travelling, were brutally tortured and murdered. The Sisters debated among themselves what they should do. Sister Andrea Dumont recalled: "People were being murdered and tortured right left and centre. They would leave the body in town, exposed or on the side of the highway as a warning to other people ... The Bishop had forbidden anyone from coming to our Centre anymore because it put them in danger. So effectively we were paralyzed. On the other hand, we felt we could leave and they could not and if they needed support it was then. The people, themselves, said 'We don't need any more martyrs'" (ibid., 187).

Sister Patricia Dowling recalled: "I was torn between. Where is my obedience? If the rest are really representing the Congregation, do I obey the group and go with the group? Or do I obey the poor, our people? Do I obey our people who would want us to stay? Although by staying we also put in danger other people as well as ourselves" (ibid., 184).

The Sisters knew they were being spied on and that their phones were tapped. They communicated in code and suffered significant psychological stress. They also knew their lives were in danger. They openly planned for their death. Sister Andrea Dumont recalled: "We had agreed, as a team, that if we were taken, we would run so that they would shoot us because under torture you could not guarantee that you would not give the names of the catechists or that type of thing. We had talked realistically about the situation we were living in but we still did not want to leave" (ibid., 188).

However, with heavy hearts, the Sisters left in December 1981. All Sisters who served there were deeply touched by their experience. Sister Pat Connaughton asserted: "I received much, much more than I ever could possibly have given. They are wonderful people and they have suffered. They have suffered all their lives. They are born into it and they die in it. Yes, five hundred years of it" (ibid., 190).

After their return to Canada, some of the Sisters who had served in the mission continued to engage in missionary work, including working for the Inter-Church Committee on Human Rights in Latin America, returning to Latin America to engage in community development in Nicaragua, and working with Guatemalan refugees in other Central American countries. Neither the Sisters who served nor the larger community that supported them, financially and with prayers, would ever be the same. No Guatemalan women ever joined the community, but its former mission sites would remain central in their psyche.

Conclusion

The experience of the members of the Congregation of the Sisters of St Joseph in Guatemala highlighted the many ways in which engagement with the documents of the Second Vatican Council changed religious life even while preserving some of its core historical elements. For the community as a whole, their work in the Latin American mission field was merely one part of an active apostolate. It was service of God through service of neighbour. While the Sisters who went into the field did so as volunteers and not under the vow of obedience, they did so as delegates from their home community and with the financial, spiritual, and psychological support of their Toronto-based Sisters. The Canadian schools in which the Sisters taught, the hospitals in which they nursed, and the parishes in which they offered catechetical instruction were all brought into the mission activities through fundraising efforts and requests for prayers. Visiting missionary Sisters were guests of schools, hospitals, and service clubs. Articles appeared in the local secular and religious press. But unlike the missionaries of past times, the missionaries of the post-Vatican II era did not inspire young women to follow their lead and join the congregation.

The work of the religious communities in the aftermath of Vatican II reinforced the fact that the key constant in the lives of many of these communities is change. The overseas missions of this community moved the Sisters into dangerous territory that challenged both their faith and their assumptions, thus propelling them individually and as a congregation into a new era of religious life. Involvement in the mission fields compelled them to confront how their communities had reconceptualized their vows and their congregational charisms.

The 1976 words of Mother Mary Lenore Carter – who served as General Superior of the Sisters of Providence of Kingston during the period of Vatican II and who founded her congregation's Guatemalan mission – present a provocative reflection on which to conclude: "The Second Vatican Council, in striving for new and beautiful things did not envisage the weakening of religious life but a strengthening and deepening of our commitment and our manner of it ... The future is bright with hope."[19]

Would the members of the congregation studied here agree? This chapter has argued that the mission experience of the Sisters of St Joseph did put to the test the process mandated by the Second Vatican Council of adapting the vows, historical governance structures, and traditional charisms to the contemporary scene. The Guatemalan mission has disappeared *in situ*, yet it continues to live in the collective memory of the community, and its spirit has infused the congregation's activities in other locations. For some members of the congregation, their first-hand and virtual experience of the Guatemalan mission has led to political and policy activism on a larger international scale. Does this constitute hope for the future? Garneau (2001) thinks just the opposite, and concludes that the missionaries

> responded to the call of the Holy See as they understood it in 1959. That understanding was heavily influenced by the Cold War national and international ambience of the day ... Many individual missionaries, nearly on their arrival in some cases, would make their own judgments, causing many of them to embrace interpretations that led to deep-seated theological conflicts within the Church, locally and universally. The collapse of much of the missionary effort, as advocated by Popes Pius XII and John XXIII, was the result. (687)

The evidence presented in this chapter falls in between Mother Mary Lenore Carter's vision of hope and Garneau's vision of despair. With reference to the latter, perhaps the missionary activities advocated by the two popes deserved to disappear, and Gospel-linked social activism – as opposed to Cold War ideology – may in fact be the legacy of the Guatemalan mission.

NOTES

The author acknowledges the support of the Social Sciences and Humanities Research Council of Canada (SSHRC), and the leadership teams, members, and archivists of the Congregation of the Sisters of St Joseph of Toronto, and the Grey Nuns of the Immaculate Conception for their assistance in the research reported here.

1 Congregation of the Sisters of St Joseph of Toronto Archives (CSJTA), *Canadians in Latin America – February 1966*, typescript copy (Ottawa: Office Catholique Canadien de L'Amerique Latine, 1966.
2 CCSJTA, "McGuire, Mary Estelle (Maura)." Necrology.
3 McGuire, Mother Maura. n.d. [1968], "Superior Generals [sic] Report." Sisters of St Joseph for the Diocese of Toronto (Toronto: n.p.).
4 CSJTA, Finding Aid #7 – Governance, 19.
5 CSJTA, Guatemala – Generalate Corespondence, box 142, Mother Maura to Fr Roland Roberts, 31 August 1965.
6 CSJAT, Guatemala file, Mother Maura to the Sister Superiors and Sisters, 31 October 1966.
7 CSJTA, Generalate Files: Guatemala, box 142, Mother Maura to Sister Superiors and Sisters, 27 February 1967.
8 CSJTA, Generalate Files: Guatemala, box 142, Mother Maura to Sister Superiors and Sisters 27 February 1967.
9 CSJTA, Generalate Files: Guatemala, box 142, Mother Maura to Sister Superiors and Sisters, 27 February 1967.
10 CSJTA, Generalate Files: Guatemala, box 142, Mother Maura to Sister Superiors and Sisters, 27 February 1967.
11 CSJTA, Generalate Files: Guatemala, box 142, Mother Maura to Sister Superiors and Sisters, 27 February 1967, 4.
12 CSJTA, Generalate Files: Guatemala, Box 142, Mother Maura to Sister Superiors and Sisters, 27 February 1967, 5.
13 CSJTA, Generalate Files: Guatemala, box 142, Mother Maura to Sister Superiors and Sisters, 27 February 1967, 5.
14 CSJTA, 1968, "Response to the Spirit," 26–7.
15 CSJTA 1968–9, "The Love of Christ has gathered us together."
16 CSJTA, 1968–9, "The Love of Christ has gathered us together."
17 CSJTA, 1968, "Superior General's Report, 1968 Chapter," 601.11, file 12.
18 CSJTA, 1968, "Superior General's Report, 1968 Chapter," 601.11, file 12.
19 ASPK, Lenore Carter, 1976, 9–11 October, "The Superior as Spiritual Animator," Folder *Addresses and Newspaper Articles* 105.18-ADD.

REFERENCES

Attridge, Michael, Clifford, Catherine E., and Routhier, Gilles, eds. 2011. *Vatican II: Experiences canadienne/Canadian Experiences.* Ottawa: University of Ottawa Press.

Garneau, James. 2001. "The First Inter-American Episcopal Conference, November 2–4, 1959: Canada and the United States Called to the Rescue of Latin America." *Catholic Historical Review* 87(4): 662–87. http://dx.doi.org/10.1353/cat.2001.0153.

Hartch, Todd. 2014. *The Rebirth of Latin American Christianity.* New York: Oxford University Press. http://dx.doi.org/10.1093/acprof:oso/9780199844593.001.0001.

Mount, Graeme. 2013. "The Era of Bishop Alexander Carter (1958–1985): The Consolidator." *The History of the Roman Catholic Diocese of Sault Ste Marie.* https://zone.biblio.laurentian.ca/dspace/bitstream/10219/1999/15/Chapter_4.pdf.

Smyth, Elizabeth, M. 2014. "Worlds within Worlds: International Connections, Ecclesiastical Webs, and the Secular State." In *Women Educators, Leaders, and Activists: Educational Lives and Networks,* edited by Tanya Fitzgerald and Elizabeth M. Smyth, 51–7. London: Palgrave Macmillan.

Smyth, Elizabeth M., and Linda Wicks, eds. 2001. *Wisdom Raises Her Voice.* Toronto: Transcontinental.

van Heijst, Annelies. 2012. "The Disputed Charity of Catholic Nuns: Dualistic Spiritual Heritage as a Source of Affliction." *Feminist Theology* 21(2): 155–72. http://dx.doi.org/10.1177/0966735012462841.

8 Women Religious, Vatican II, Education, and the State in Atlantic Canada

HEIDI MACDONALD

In the 1960s, Atlantic Canada had the highest rates of Roman Catholicism outside Quebec. According to the 1961 Census of Canada, New Brunswick's population was 52 per cent Catholic, Prince Edward Island's was 45 per cent, Newfoundland's was 36 per cent, and Nova Scotia's was 35 per cent. Each of the four provinces provided, to varying degrees, a parallel slate of Catholic and public/Protestant social institutions. All provinces maintained at least some Catholic schools, and each had at least one Catholic post-secondary institution (Gidney and Millar 2012, 5). More than a dozen congregations of women religious from both within and outside the region provided the main workforce for these schools, and most colleges and universities had Sisters on their faculties.

However, beginning in the mid-1960s, the number of sister-teachers and sister-professors in Catholic schools, colleges, and universities in Atlantic Canada declined, and many of the schools and colleges closed or transitioned into public, non-denominational institutions. While the decline is often explained, as it is in Quebec, by the expansion of government into the educational sphere, a closer examination of three congregations' work in three of the four Atlantic Canadian provinces shows that the state usually supported Sisters' continued work in schools, but the decreasing membership in women's religious congregations and their shifting priorities after Vatican II made it impossible to continue staffing schools and post-secondary institutions at pre-Vatican II levels. Congregations recalibrated their service in the educational sphere based on their reduced workforces, newly developed priorities, *and* the goals of the state.

There is no doubt that provincial governments *were* encroaching on women religious's secondary and post-secondary teaching territory in an unprecedented way in the 1960s. However, this does not mean that the state pushed Sisters out of teaching. Two particularly relevant internal issues in the three congregations under study – the Sisters of St Martha (Prince Edward Island), the Sisters of Charity (Nova Scotia), and the Presentation Sisters (Newfoundland) – must also be considered.[1] First, along with all congregations of men and women worldwide, these four congregations were required by the 1965 Vatican II decree *Perfectae Caritatis* to reconsider their mission in light of the changing needs of the modern world. They were asked to work more directly with the poor, decrease their focus on institutional work, and assign work based on individual Sisters' talents and preferences rather than the needs of the congregation (*Perfectae Caritatis*, #2). This decree had the potential to significantly impact their work in education because more Sisters were engaged in teaching than in any other ministry. However, congregations *interpreted* the Vatican's directive to decrease institutional involvement in different ways.

The second internal factor was declining membership: between 1965 and 1975, the number of women religious in Canada dropped 32 per cent, from approximately 66,000 to 44,127. Feminism, anti-authoritarianism, consumerism, secularization, and other 1960s social factors reduced the appeal of the convent; fewer human resources then forced many congregations to withdraw from labour-intensive missions, including schools. The number of sister-teachers in Canada fell by 74 per cent between 1965 and 1975, from approximately 44,000 to 11,000 (Lessard and Montminy 1965, 295–6).[2] The downward trend was strongest in Quebec, where the largest number of women religious – approximately 75 per cent of the national membership – served, and where the Lesage government (supported by a majority of the population) targeted religious schools as part of the Quiet Revolution (Dickason and Young 2003, 336). Thus in Quebec, thousands of women religious left their convents (Christiano 2007; Gavreau 2007), and those who remained in religious life were often discouraged from teaching by restrictive government policies that sought to reduce the Roman Catholic Church's power in the province and end the clerical control of education (Christiano 2007, 29).

PEI – The Sisters of St Martha

The Sisters of St Martha were founded in 1916 as a diocesan congregation (MacIsaac 1991, 1–3). Other congregations operated in PEI, including the Congregation of Notre Dame, which ran four schools, but as the only diocesan congregation (until it achieved papal status in 1957) under the control of the Bishop of Charlottetown, the Sisters of St Martha were jacks-of-all-trades whose approximately 160 members in the early 1960s served in a variety of capacities on the island, including in several schools, two hospitals, two social welfare bureaux, and a university (Coady 1955, 30–1; Cullen 1969, 38–9; MacIsaac 1991, 23). During their Vatican II renewal deliberations in the 1960s and 1970s, the Sisters of St Martha de-emphasized their institutional commitments, including by taking into consideration a Sister's "inclination, education, knowledge, and training" before assigning her to a mission, and by supporting more Sisters' work assignments in unwaged positions, such as missionary work in Latin America.[3] At the same time they were making these decisions, the Sisters of St Martha experienced a 9 per cent membership decline between 1967 and 1976, from 160 to 139. Although the number of Sisters of St Martha seeking dispensations was well below national and regional rates, slowing entrance rates increased the percentage of members aged 70 and over from 17 per cent to 29 per cent between 1967 and 1973, signalling the trend of fewer Sisters able to work in institutions that had government-mandated ages of retirement, such as schools and hospitals.[4] Finally, at the same time the Sisters were implementing Vatican II renewal (which included decreasing their work in institutions) and experiencing a decline in membership, they were affected by provincial government initiatives aimed at several of their institutional missions, including St Dunstan's University.

St Dunstan's University was the Diocese of Charlottetown's pre-eminent social institution and PEI's only university until 1964. It was also the Sisters of St Martha's first mission: to provide domestic service for the priests and students of the college.[5] This domestic service assignment continued into the 1960s, by which time several Sisters were working in university administration and teaching on the faculty. The 1965 Royal Commission on Higher Education recommended the amalgamation of St Dunstan's with Prince of Wales College, the public college, which had just obtained university status. These two Prince Edward Island universities had roots in the 1830s and offered distinct and separate courses of instruction. The private, Roman Catholic St Dunstan's had achieved university status in 1917 in cooperation with Laval University and had begun conferring its own degrees in 1942, but not until 1951 did it begin receiving government funding (MacDonald 1984, 495–7). Prince of Wales, by contrast, came under government control in 1879, received public funding for capital and operating costs, and gained a reputation as a fine junior college, with PEI's only normal school until St Dunstan's gained one in 1957 (MacKinnon 1995, 57–8; McKenna 1982, 207). Each institution developed a niche and enjoyed relative independence. The more complicated post-secondary educational environment following the Second World War, which included the federal government's funding of veterans' educations and campus building improvements, spurred the provincial government's increased involvement in post-secondary education.

It became increasingly obvious that two post-secondary institutions were not sustainable in a province with a population of just 104,629 in 1961 (McKenna 1982, 208–10). When the premier announced that the Royal Commission on Higher Education had recommended amalgamating the province's two post-secondary institutions, he admitted that he was reluctant to force a union: "If either wished to continue its existence as a private institution, utilizing its own financial resources, the government certainly will not interfere. But let one thing be clear: the Government will support financially, with all the funds at its disposal, only a single public university in Prince Edward Island" (MacKinnon 1995, 213).

St Dunstan's University had struggled financially throughout its history. Now its board, which was chaired by the Bishop of Charlottetown and included several priests, recognized that the sooner they cooperated, the sooner St Dunstan's faculty, and especially its priest- and sister-professors, might be assured teaching positions and other concessions in the new university.[6] When St Dunstan's began playing offence, Prince of Wales was forced to play defence (McKenna 1982, 217). In fact, Prince of Wales's principal, Frank MacKinnon, who ended up resigning over the amalgamation issue, wrote a scathing account of the process three decades later. Referring to Premier Alexander Campbell's support for a single university, he commented: "Then and in the following months, his government gave the Roman Catholic Church everything it wanted and more. It let the Bishop's wishes and St Dunstan's standards push Prince of Wales and its much higher standards right out of the subsequent politics and into oblivion" (MacKinnon 1995, 110). If MacKinnon is correct, the provincial government did not push the PEI Roman Catholic Church out of higher education; it *accommodated* the Church's wishes in the new provincial university. Most notably, nine priest-professors and five sister-professors (all Sisters of St Martha) taught at the University of Prince Edward Island in its inaugural year and were paid government salaries. Three Sisters taught in the Department of Home Economics, one in Education, and one in Religious Studies.[7]

The Sisters' work in domestic service at St Dunstan's did not survive the amalgamation. They were only employed by UPEI during the transition to the new university, which was located on the former St Dunstan's campus. The explanation for not employing Sisters for the long term was that the publicly funded UPEI could pay its own cleaning and food services staff. The St Dunstan's board of governors fought to include the sister-professors in the new amalgamated university, but they made no effort to include the sister-domestics. In fact, according to Edward MacDonald, the sister-domestics were not even thanked by the St Dunstan's board or university administration for their five decades of service at minimal pay.[8] This oversight did not involve the provincial government pushing the Sisters out; it was the St Dunstan's board's own decision that the domestic Sisters would serve no intrinsic purpose at UPEI. The board had prioritized the high-status positions of Sisters who were professors, and who thus held great potential influence over their students, and saw little value in Sisters doing domestic labour. In fact, the image of Sisters doing domestic labour at an amalgamated university seems to have been one that the former St Dunstan's board wished to avoid.

It is significant that despite trends in other provinces towards non-denominational or secular education, the Roman Catholic Church secured five faculty positions for Sisters and an administration position in the registrar's office for a sixth Sister, as well as nine faculty and two staff positions for priests, in the negotiations to amalgamate St Dunstan's and Prince of Wales. However, with declining membership, the Sisters of St Martha could not sustain the sister-professor positions allotted to them in that amalgamation. The Sisters of St Martha were a small congregation whose resources had always been stretched, given that they served in schools, hospitals, social services, and domestic service. Even in 1970–1, the second year of UPEI's existence, one of the original five sister-professors, Sister Mary Ida, retired, and with no suitable Sister of St Martha to replace her, she was succeeded by Sister Marie Hagen, a member of the Quebec-based Congregation of Notre Dame.[9] Of the original five sister-professors, the Sisters of St Martha could only contribute Sister Bernice Cullen and Sister Irene Burge, professors in Religious Studies and Home Economics, respectively, for several more years. There is no evidence to suggest that the UPEI administration or any government policy discouraged the Sisters from teaching at UPEI. In fact, the Sisters of St Martha did not have enough highly qualified Sisters to maintain the number of positions they had been allotted at UPEI, and that is why they withdrew. They were forced to prioritize among their many commitments, perhaps chief among them the Charlottetown Hospital, which they did not relinquish until 1982.

Nova Scotia – Sisters of Charity

The Sisters of Charity, Halifax, were founded in 1849 as an offshoot of the New York Sisters of Charity, who had come at the request of the Archbishop of Halifax to educate the city's poor children (Sister Maura 1956, 1–2). Their work expanded into the fields of social work and health care. By the early 1950s the Sisters of Charity had staffing commitments in Canada, the United States, and Bermuda to eighty-six elementary schools, twenty-two high schools, six hospitals, and several residences for the aged and for children, as well as one First Nations residential school and one college for women (McKenna 1998, 76). The Sisters of Charity received on average more than fifty entrants annually between 1955 and 1965, drawn equally from the United States and Canada, and had a total membership of more than 1,700 by 1965, which made them not only the largest of the four congregations under study, but also the largest English-speaking congregation in Canada (Lessard and Montimy 1965, 380).

The Sisters of Charity's renewal process was particularly robust. An intense consultation phase began in 1966, followed by the submission of more than a thousand proposals to their Chapter of Renewal in 1968–9, the majority from provincial and regional chapters but also two hundred from individual Sisters.[10] Mother Maria Farmer challenged the Sisters to consider: "Are we ... honestly facing the problems that are keeping us from functioning at maximum efficiency for the good of the Church in this post-Vatican era? ... Do we tend to use too much of our income on ourselves? Our convents? For the upkeep of our motherhouse and institutions?"[11] Consequently, the Sisters divested many of their schools and hospitals in the United States and Canada, a decision that became tied not only to their revitalized commitment to working more directly with the poor rather than in institutions, but also to the new reality of rapidly decreasing human resources; more than four hundred Sisters received dispensations from the congregation in the decade after Vatican II (Anthony 1997, 166). The loss of almost one quarter of the congregation in such a short time immediately affected their capacity to staff institutions; it also had broader financial implications, for those who left took their salaries and pensions with them, and the congregation lost the investment in those Sisters' educations. The situation was exacerbated by the debt from the $7,000,000 mother house, built in the mid-1950s to house the congregation's headquarters, including designated space for 238 postulants and novices, whose actual numbers were under a dozen by the early 1970s (McKenna 1998, 72, 79, 214).

The 1969 Chapter of Renewal approved withdrawing from owning hospitals and educational institutions in principle, but qualified that its implementation "will be dependent on the need for funds to reduce debts and to provide an adequate pension program for all the sisters."[12] The most expensive institutions were the first to be scrutinized.[13] The Halifax Infirmary and St Elizabeth Hospital in Sydney, Cape Breton, were sold to the province in 1972 and 1975 respectively, for a total of $2,500,000 (McKenna 1998, 285–8, 293–5). With their high standards for accreditation, specialized professional staff, and large capital and equipment costs, these hospitals had been running at a deficit for years, even as government funding increased with the introduction of the Diagnostic Services Act in 1958 (Vayda and Deber 1992, 127). Another institution requiring an equally specialized and highly educated staff was Mount Saint Vincent University (MSVU), whose future was also questioned through a motion passed at the 1969 Chapter Meetings requiring that the university's holdings be presented "in full, even in minute detail."[14]

MSVU had grown out of Mount Saint Vincent Academy, a private girls' residential and day school, which the congregation founded in Bedford, Nova Scotia, in 1873 (Corcoran 1999, 11). Recognizing that their own sisters needed to earn bachelor's degrees in order to maintain their government-funded teaching positions in high schools, and the lack of Catholic universities that accepted women, Mother Maria Berchmans Walsh became determined that the Sisters of Charity provide that service for themselves as well as for other interested Catholic women (Corcoran 1999, 257; Shook 1971, 98). In 1921, the congregation negotiated an affiliation with Dalhousie University, whose professors travelled to MSVU to offer third- and fourth-year courses while sister-professors provided the freshman and junior courses. Meanwhile, seven sisters were sent to pursue PhDs in preparation for offering upper-level courses themselves. By 1924, thirty sisters had earned bachelor's degrees (half of them from Dalhousie under the affiliation arrangement), several had earned master's degrees, and four of the seven PhDs were complete. In 1925, the congregation secured college status and MSVU became "the first and only independent degree-granting college for women in Canada and in the British Commonwealth" (Corcoran 1999, 9).

From 1925 to 1935, Mount Saint Vincent College's annual enrolment was between 100 and 150, with Sisters usually outnumbering laywomen by two to one (Corcoran 1999, 353, table 3). Enrolment continued to rise in the 1940s and 1950s until it reached more than three hundred students, and the ratio of Sisters to laywomen reversed. In 1966, Mount Saint Vincent College achieved university status. The newly formed board of governors was predominantly lay rather than clerical, and eleven of the thirty-four full-time faculty were also lay.[15] The new president, and the only female president of a Canadian university, Sister Catherine Wallace, referred to "The Mount" as the Radcliffe of Canada (Corcoran 1999, 190). Under Wallace, the university passed through what the student newspaper called a "revolution in reverse," with the administration loosening a variety of rules. For example, it relaxed the dress code, allowed smoking in classrooms, and lifted evening curfews. These changes resulted in women's residence rules even looser than those at the secular Dalhousie University (Corcoran 1999, 193).

At the same time that the university was flourishing with regard to academic standards, identifying more openly with feminist principles, promoting partial secularization, and encouraging the admission of African Nova Scotian women (Corcoran 1999, 191–5), it was struggling financially.[16] Although it received provincial funding according to its provincially mandated post-secondary charter, the college and university had always been subsidized from the congregation's coffers and specifically from sister-teachers' public school salaries, which accounted for 75 per cent of the congregation's income.[17] By contrast, Halifax's men-only Catholic university, St Mary's, was owned and funded by the Archdiocese of Halifax, which paid the university's $250,000 annual debt payments in the 1960s (Shook 1971, 99). In the late 1960s, there was an unsuccessful attempt to amalgamate St Mary's and MSVU into one Catholic university to reduce the duplication of costs; however, the St Mary's board's proposal refused to accept the Sisters of Charity on equal terms, insulting the Sisters' experience, level of education, and ability to keep their own institution out of debt.[18]

By the late 1960s, the withdrawal of many sister-teachers and the decision of other Sisters to engage in unpaid work as per *Perfectae Caritatis*'s directive meant there was less income available to subsidize MSVU and other missions. There was no good financial argument for keeping the university open, but many Sisters argued that there were *other* good reasons, including that with the congregation's recent sale of so many schools and academies in both Canada and the United States, MSVU was now the only educational institution owned by the congregation, and thus a necessary link to the Sisters' original reason for coming to

Halifax in 1849: accessible education. Moreover, the financial situation had improved somewhat by the early 1970s: the two hospitals had been sold, enrolment had risen, the revitalized affiliation with Dalhousie had been settled, and affiliation with St Mary's was off the table.[19] In addition, although the congregation was attracting only a handful of entrants a year, most of those vocations were connected to MSVU, so closing it would have threatened to completely dry up the pool of new entrants.[20]

Over the next fifteen years, the congregation continued to rationalize its ownership of the university, emphasizing the crucial link between women's education and social justice (including gender equality). In 1968, the university's president, Sister Catherine Wallace, presented a brief to the Royal Commission on the Status of Women in which she declared that education was crucial to a woman's understanding of herself as a total person. The Mount had begun to specialize in part-time studies, which allowed married women with children to pursue post-secondary education. In a CBC interview following her address to the Royal Commission, Wallace emphasized women's right to choose to stay at home caring for children, *or* to leave the home for study or work: "No one should oppose an individual woman's decision. Women must have freedom without guilt."[21] A decade later, retiring president Sister M. Albertus affirmed that

> education [is] the great need of women at the present time. I think they have the natural qualities, the stamina and the courage, but I do think they need to be educated so that they have equal qualifications with men when it comes to a choice for a position. I honestly don't believe in token affirmative action. I think that women can go into decision-making positions and their education has to prepare them for that. They have to, for example, be given business admin skills, management skills, they have to understand what's involved in decision-making so that they can function equally to men.[22]

There is no evidence that the province ever discouraged the Sisters of Charity from operating MSVU. Any hesitancy came from the congregation itself and was connected to the loss of 25 per cent of its members between 1965 and 1975, the struggle to meet the debts it had accumulated in 1950s building campaigns, and the worry that St Mary's University's decision to go co-ed in 1968 would siphon off its potential Catholic female students. The university was financially unwieldy because of its physical plant costs and its need for highly skilled and thus well-paid employees (i.e., teachers); it would never be able to pay its way entirely through government grants and private donations. MSVU was controversial within the congregation, yet successive chapters held democratic votes that ultimately determined that Canada's only independent women's university was worth the challenges it presented to the congregation, for it symbolized their post-Vatican II recommitment to women's education as essential to gender equality.

After 1925, the year that Mount Saint Vincent achieved college status, the state appeared to support it to the same degree that it supported other Nova Scotian government-chartered post-secondary institutions. Successive presidents of Mount Saint Vincent were valued in regional and national post-secondary associations, with Sister Catherine Wallace having the greatest impact on the post-secondary landscape in the Maritimes, including as vice-president and president of the Association of Colleges and Universities of Canada in 1972 and 1973 and as the first chair of the Maritime Provinces' Higher Education Commission in 1974 (Corcoran 1999, 232–5; Wainwright 1992, 9, 15). If there was any group that failed to support the Sisters' efforts at MSVU, it was the archdiocesan-owned St Mary's University, whose board would not accept the Sisters of Charity as equal partners in a proposal for a federated Catholic university in 1967–8. Indeed, in 1968 St Mary's became a direct competitor of MSVU by going co-ed. Fortunately, the Sisters of Charity were able to secure a broad-based affiliation with Dalhousie University, whereby it was "related to Dalhousie, but not swallowed up" by it. St Mary's would have insisted on swallowing MSVU (Corcoran 1999, 164–8).

Like the Sisters of St Martha from PEI, the Sisters of Charity made strategic decisions to continue in some of their institutions and to divest themselves of others in the decades after Vatican II. While doing so was a financial challenge, the Sisters of Charity maintained ownership of MSVU because it aligned so well with their charism in women's education. By the time they gave the university to the board of governors in 1988, many post-secondary institutions run by women religious in other provinces had been closed for years, including Littledale College, which the Sisters of Mercy (Newfoundland) closed in 1974.[23]

Newfoundland – Presentation Sisters

A small group of Irish Presentation Sisters came to St John's in 1833 to set up a girls' school at the request of Bishop Michael Fleming.[24] Teaching was the Presentation Sisters' main mission in Ireland and Newfoundland,

and one they held to during the Vatican II renewal process. Four Sisters had come to Newfoundland in 1833; by the mid-1960s there were 370, all of them from Newfoundland. Like the other Atlantic Canadian congregations, the Presentation Sisters had strong entrance rates in the lead-up to Vatican II, with an average of twenty-one entrants annually between 1951 and 1960.[25] The congregation focused on elementary, high school, business, and music education. In 1961, its 229 teachers served in schools with a total of more than 20,000 students.[26] Incoming entrants usually studied teacher training at St Bride's College, Littledale, a Memorial University–affiliated junior college and normal school run by the Sisters of Mercy, another Irish congregation, which had engaged in teaching in Newfoundland since 1842.[27]

Like the other congregations under study, and as mandated by *Perfectae Caritatis*, the Presentation Sisters engaged in an intense process of renewal in the late 1960s. They rewrote their constitutions, modified their habits, and did away with outdated practices concerning permissions, but they never seriously considered weakening their focus on education. After studying the original charism of Nano Nagle – educating the poor – in the socio-economic context of the 1960s, the congregation determined that withdrawing from their work in institutions was, in fact, the opposite of what was required. In other words, their renewal explorations confirmed that their work in schools was benefiting students. Also, considering Newfoundland's denominational school system, and that the province had the poorest high school completion rates in Canada (Forbes and Muise 1993, 444; McCann 1994, 214), the Sisters argued that their influence and skills were badly needed. Newfoundland, as a colony, had endured a non-elected government for almost two decades, and it had only narrowly voted to enter Confederation with Canada in 1949, just sixteen years before *Perfectae Caritatis* was proclaimed.

The context in which the Presentation Sisters were asked to reconsider working more directly with the poor was different in Newfoundland, where poverty was more severe and widespread than in the other Atlantic Canadian provinces (Conrad and Hiller 2015, 241; McCann 1994, 214). Many Sisters believed they were already working "directly with the poor" by teaching in government-funded Catholic schools. As a submission by the congregation's Sisters in central Newfoundland to the General Chapter in 1967 explained: "Here in Newfoundland there is at present a serious shortage of qualified teachers, and Sisters are eagerly welcomed and sought after to fill teaching positions. (If a surplus of lay teachers existed the situation might be a different one.)"[28]

Affirming the demand for qualified teachers in the province, the chair of the Presentation Sisters' Committee on the Apostolate and Adaption in the Light of Vatican II cautioned against taking resources away from teaching to do new work: "There might be a tendency (concern) on the part of some Sisters to get so obsessed with their desires for renewal, as to project themselves into fanciful works of mercy, and so forget the fact that Providence has assigned to them a task in the Apostolate of teaching upon which depends their own sanctification and that of those committed to their care."[29] The same committee reinforced their recommendation a few months later, stating that sister-teachers should not yield their positions of authority, including as school principals, too readily to laypeople.[30]

As the congregation reconfirmed its dedication to teaching at the elementary and high school levels, it simultaneously refocused its energies on improving its sister-teachers' academic credentials based on its own needs assessment as well as the new policies of the Newfoundland Teachers' Federation, the provincial government, and school boards (Cadigan 2009, 215; McCann 1994, 17–18). Before the mid-1960s, the congregation had the freedom to conduct corporate hirings in government-funded Catholic schools; later in the decade, policies restricted this practice. Formerly the congregation would promise a certain number of Sisters to a school, but not specific Sisters. This evolved into specific Sisters having to qualify through a competitive process to be hired by the school boards. As the Mother General reminded the Sisters in 1967, "the schools are not ours." Instead of assigning Sisters, the Mother Superior could "merely nominate" sister-teachers to particular school boards, after which she had "no further right to interfere."[31]

Newfoundland sister-teachers had earned the nickname "intellectual shock troops," in that they went off-island to earn degrees at Atlantic Canadian institutions such as St Francis Xavier and MSVU, usually at summer school, and then returned to Newfoundland schools to teach for the regular school year. In the period after Vatican II, the congregation stepped up this practice, aiming for more sister-teachers with bachelor's, master's, and doctoral degrees. The numbers of Sisters with one, two, three, and four degrees was reported at every chapter in the 1970s and 1980s. It was a particular coup for the congregation when Sister Perpetua Kennedy, who had recently earned her doctorate, was hired at the provincial non-denominational post-secondary institution, Memorial University, in 1969, where she could have influence over students in the Bachelor of Education program.[32] The congregation similarly gained influence over government policy decisions; by 1973 they had five sister-teachers working throughout the province supervising religious education at the school board level and two sister-teachers working with the provincial Department of Education – one as a music consultant and one as an evaluation consultant.[33]

The province encouraged the congregation to deepen its collective teaching credentials and to participate in policy-making, but did not force it to do so. The Presentation Sisters judged that both adaptations would help them maintain their influence in provincial education. Other circumstances prevented the sisters from asserting themselves any more forcefully on the denominational school landscape, however. As early as 1967, because of resettlement and consolidation, the congregation was unable to meet requests for its labour in elementary schools as new central and regional high schools were opening (Cadigan 2009, 246).[34] By the time of its next general chapter in 1973, the loss of 20 per cent of members in just six years had made it impossible for the congregation to maintain its pre-Vatican II level of teaching commitments.[35] Concern was expressed at the 1973 interim chapter that with such small numbers working in nine of the twelve Catholic school boards, "sisters will sooner or later have to withdraw from schools where they are presently engaged."[36] The Mother General admitted in 1976 that the work of the congregation was not sustainable.

Newfoundland had a strong, government-funded denominational school system. It had been negotiated in 1927 and confirmed through Term 17 of the Articles of Confederation in 1949 (May 2003, 198–200). Within this system of seven parallel denominational school systems, as long as the sister-teachers maintained their credentials, they had a basic agreement that would allow them to continue in the school system for the foreseeable future. They also had a consensus within their congregation that continuing in the provincial school system for as long as possible was, in fact, the best use of their resources – this was where they could make the most impact. Their withdrawal from schools, starting in the late 1960s, was in proportion to their loss of members and the lack of new entrants to replenish the stocks of sister-teachers who had retired at the provincial mandatory age of sixty. By 1977, the Presentation Sisters' total membership was 264, one-third fewer than in 1967, a decline that outpaced that of the Sisters of Charity, Halifax. Moreover, in 1977, one-quarter of the congregation was over sixty, the provincially mandated retirement age for teachers.

As with the other congregations under study, the Presentation Sisters experienced a steady reduction in their numbers through the end of the twentieth century but nevertheless maintained a role in the educational sphere. When a referendum returned a vote of 73 per cent in favour of ending the denominational school system in 1997, the provincial government contended that the confiscation of existing school buildings across Newfoundland had been implied in that vote. The Presentation Sisters disagreed and joined the Sisters of Mercy – their counterparts in operating Holy Heart of Mary Regional High School, a large high school with state-of-the-art performance facilities – in suing the Department of Education in 2001. The Sisters explained: "This kind of intrusive, government action is an issue of fairness and justice, and has implications for the civil rights of every citizen of our province."[37] After almost five years, the province settled out of court on the eve of their court date, for more than $4,000,000, which the congregations have since used to fund a variety of charitable endeavours locally, nationally, and in Latin America. The two congregations successfully argued that they had been paying for the land and building over forty years, mainly through sister-teachers' salaries, and thus the confiscation was in violation of their individual rights to their wages under the Charter of Rights and Freedoms. Justice Leo Barry confirmed: "[There remain] unexplained failures by ministers and other government officials to respond (to the claim) in a prompt, or even polite fashion."[38] While no Sisters were teaching in the school by the time of the settlement, their success in court ensured that their role in education over the past century and a half would not be forgotten, nor would it be undervalued, as women religious's labour has long so often been.

Conclusion

These three case studies show that, compared to Quebec, Sisters in Atlantic Canada were not pushed out of the education system by the government. Rather, they recalibrated their goals in the 1960s and thereafter, according to the availability of human resources and the reformulation of priorities related to their founding charisms and the needs of their modern societies. At the same time, we see in all three examples a lack of appreciation for women religious's labour: St Dunstan's University's undervaluing of the domestic Sisters, whom they failed to thank after fifty years of service;[39] the archdiocesan board of St Mary's University's inability to conceive of sister-professors as equal to their own priest-professors; and the Newfoundland government's blindness to the labour of sister-teachers over almost two centuries.

NOTES

1 Many thanks to these three congregations for their generosity in allowing me to study their archives and conduct oral interviews, as well as to the Social Sciences and Humanities Council of Canada for their financial support. I originally planned to include a New Brunswick example so that all four Atlantic Canadian provinces would be represented, but space considerations did not allow this.

2 The number of teachers was calculated by adding the 30,855 Sisters Lessard and Montminy identified with two-thirds of the number they identified in the combined educators and hospitaliers category (2/3 of 22,301).

3 Sisters of St Martha Archives (SSMA), Minutes, Chapter of Affairs (extraordinary chapter), 15 July–5 August 1967 and 3–11 July 1968; and Minutes of Elections and Chapter of Affairs, 25 July 1973 (new binder), box 42B chapter minutes, apostolic works committee proposals, #2.

4 SSMA, chapter minutes 1967–8, Apostolate Committee Report, Report on Renewal, July 1973, box 42B, "Graph indicating Age of Professed Sisters as of 1 July 1967."

5 SSMA, box 10, no. 5, "Memorandum of Agreement between the Sisters of St Martha and St Dunstan's University," 1930.

6 The statement of acceptance was prompted by Prince of Wales College's concern about priest-professors being inappropriate in a non-denominational institution; the newly appointed University Prince Edward Island administration responded "that staffing positions be open to all qualified persons, whether lay or clerical, and that no qualified person will be excluded or treated prejudicially because of circumstances of race, creed, sex, or religious commitment" (McKenna 1982, 217).

7 Sister Mary Wisener worked for many years as a secretary in the registrar's office.

8 According to historian G. Edward MacDonald, neither the diocese nor the college formally thanked the Sisters: "apparently they just packed up and left without so much as a handshake." E-mail correspondence with Edward MacDonald, 5 February 1999.

9 Sister Marie Hagen remained at UPEI for seven years before leaving to study in Rome.

10 Sisters of Charity, Halifax, Archives [SCHA], Material in Preparation for the 11th General Chapter, File 1-3-4, "Memo to the Sisters from Mother Maria Gertrude, 13 Nov 1966."

11 SCHA, Material in Preparation for the 11th General Chapter, file 1-3-4, "Memo to the Sisters from Mother Maria, 1 August 67."

12 SCHA, Chapter 1976, box 24, files 1-5-12, "Proposal: That the Congregation keep MSV University."

13 SCHA, ch. 1976, box 24, files 1-5-12, "Proposal: That the Congregation Continue to Examine Its Commitment to Maintaining an Independent University for Women."

14 SCHA, Material from Community Service Commission, c. 1968–9, box 12, files 1-3-42-1-3-50, file 1-3-42, "Community Service Commission," 18 July 1969, 5.

15 By 1973–4, fifty-two of the seventy-six professors were lay. See Corcoran (1999), 219–20.

16 For example, unable to afford the cost of hiring lay staff, the congregation was forced to close the academy in 1972, just one year short of its 100th anniversary.

17 SCHA, Chapter of Renewal, July 1969, File 1-3-38, "Financial Report to the Second Session," 20.

18 In 1966–7, five of the twelve Sisters in Administration had PhDs and six had Master's degrees, while eleven of thirty-four sister-professors had PhDs and another twenty had Masters, which would have made it difficult for the St Mary's Board of Governors to argue that the Sisters' credentials were inferior. Mount Saint Vincent University Archives, *Mount Saint Vincent University Calendar*, 1966–7, 8–12.

19 SCHA, ch. 1976, box 24, files 1-5-12, "Proposal: That the Congregation keep MSV University"; and Corcoran, *Mount Saint Vincent University*, 153–66.

20 And because the Sisters of Charity operated Mount Saint Vincent College (later university) and their own normal school, they offered a wider range of career opportunities than many other congregations. See, for example, their 1950s vocation pamphlet, "Religious Vocation: Invitation to Happiness," which listed fifteen possible careers that might be pursued by members of their congregation.

21 Mount Saint Vincent University Archives, CA MSVUAAV-419, 426, CBC interview with Sister Alice Michael, 1968, http://archives.msvu.ca/atom/index.php/cbc-interview-sister-alice-michael.

22 SCHA, April 1978 clippings, "Mount Pres Recalls Career," *Chronicle Herald*, 21 February 1978.

23 Littledale was a normal school and junior college that closed in 1974. http://www.heritagefoundation.ca/media/728/report-st-brides-college-littledale.pdf.

24 "Beginnings: Presentation Sisters, Newfoundland and Labrador, Canada." http://www.presentationsisters.ca/begin.html.

25 Presentation of the Blessed Virgin Mary Archives [PBVMA], Profession register.

26 PBVMA, file 302.1967.10, "Superior General's Report (Chapter 1967)," 7.

27 "Our Story: About Us." http://www.sistersofmercynf.org/ourstory/default_gallery.cfm?loadref=6; "Heritage Foundation of Newfoundland and Labrador Building Report, St. Bride's College, Littledale." http://www.heritagefoundation.ca/media/728/report-st-brides-college-littledale.pdf.
28 PBVMA, file 302.1967.11, "A Brief on Religious Life in General presented by the Presentation Sisters of Central Newfoundland to the Sisters of the General Chapter of the Congregation, April 1967," 5.
29 PBVMA, file 302.1967.9, "Minutes of the Committee on the Apostolate and Adaption in the Light of Vatican II, 5th meeting of committee, [March 1967]"; Sister Mark, "Religious Instruction and Sexual Education," 2.
30 PBVMA, Sister Mark, "Religious Instruction and Sexual Education," 2.
31 PBVMA, file 302.1967.5, "Minutes, Opening Session," 3 July 1967.
32 PBVMA, "Report to Chapter by Superior General, 1967–73," 10.
33 PBVMA, "Report to Chapter by Superior General, 1967–73," 10.
34 PBVMA, file 302.1967.5, "Minutes of Second Preliminary Session of General Chapter, 30 June 1967."
35 Membership fell from 384 to 305 between 1967 and 1973.
36 PBVMA, file 302.1976, "Interim Chapter Minutes, Business Arising from Minutes, 19 August 1976."
37 *The Telegraph* (St John's), 26 April 2001, 4.
38 *The Telegraph* (St John's), 17 December 2005, A1; 7 December 2005, A3; 4 April 2006, A3.
39 This was rectified decades later with a plaque.

REFERENCES

Anthony, Geraldine. 1997. *Rebel Reformer Religious Extraordinaire: The Life of Sister Irene Farmer.* Calgary: Detselig Enterprises.

"Beginnings: Presentation Sisters, Newfoundland and Labrador, Canada." n.d. http://www.presentationsisters.ca/begin.html.

Cadigan, Sean. 2009. *Newfoundland and Labrador: A History.* Toronto: University of Toronto Press.

Christiano, Kevin J. 2007. "The Trajectory of Catholicism in Twentieth-Century Quebec." In *The Church Confronts Modernity: Catholicism in the United States, Ireland, and Quebec,* edited by Leslie Woodcock Tentler. Washington, DC: Catholic University of America.

Coady, Mary Jeanette. CSM. 1955. "The Birth and Growth of the Congregation of the Sisters of St Martha of Prince Edward Island." MA thesis, University of Ottawa.

Conrad, Margaret, and James Hiller. 2015. *Atlantic Canada: A History*, 3rd ed. Toronto: Oxford.

Corcoran, Theresa. 1999. *Mount Saint Vincent University: A Vision Unfolding, 1873–1988.* Boston: University Press of America.

Cullen, Ellen Mary, CSM. 1969 (rev. 1988). *A History of the Sisters of St Martha of Prince Edward Island*, vol. 1. Charlottetown: Sisters of St Martha.

Dickason, John, and Brian Young. 2003. *A Short History of Quebec*, 3rd ed. Montreal and Kingston: McGill-Queen's University Press.

Forbes, Ernest, and Del Muise. 1993. *Atlantic Provinces in Confederation.* Toronto: University of Toronto Press.

Gavreau, Michael. 2007. "'They Are Not of Our Generation': Youth, Gender, Catholicism, and Quebec's Dechristianization, 1950–1970." In *The Church Confronts Modernity: Catholicism in the United States, Ireland, and Quebec*, edited by Leslie Woodcock Tentler. Washington, DC: Catholic University of America.

Gidney, R.D., and W.P.J. Millar. 2012. *How Schools Worked: Public Education in English Canada, 1900–1940.* Montreal and Kingston: McGill-Queen's University Press.

Lessard, Marc A., and Jean-Paul Montminy. 1965. *The Census of Religious Sisters in Canada.* Ottawa: Canadian Religious Conference.

MacDonald, G. Edward. 1984. "'And Christ Dwelt in the Heart of His House': A History of St Dunstan's University, 1855–1955." PhD diss., Queen's University.

MacIsaac, Mildred. 1991. *The Story of the Sisters of St Martha, 1916–1991.* Charlottetown: Action Press.

MacKinnon, Frank. 1995. *Church Politics and Education in Canada: The Prince Edward Island Experience.* Calgary: Detselig Enterprises.

Maura, Sister. 1956. *The Sisters of Charity, Halifax.* Toronto: Ryerson.

May, Stephen. 2003. "The Terms of Union: An Analysis of their Current Analysis." *Royal Commission on Renewing and Strengthening Our Place in Canada.* http://www.gov.nf.ca/publicat/royalcomm/research/May.pdf.

McCann, Phillip. 1994. *Schooling in a Fishing Society: Education and Economic Conditions in Newfoundland and Labrador, 1836–1986.* St John's: Institute of Social and Economic Research.

McKenna, Mary Olga. 1982. "Higher Education in Transition, 1945–1980." In *The Garden Transformed*, edited by Verner Smitheram. Charlottetown: Ragweed Press.

– 1998. *Charity Alive: Sisters of Charity of Saint Vincent de Paul, Halifax, 1950–1980.* Boston: University Press of America.

Perfectae Caritatis: Decree on the Adaption and Renewal of Religious Life. 1965. http://www.vatican.va/archive/hist_councils/ii_vatican_council/documents/vat-ii_decree_19651028_perfectae-caritatis_en.html.

Shook, Lawrence K. 1971. *Catholic Post-Secondary Education in English-Speaking Canada: A History*. Toronto: University of Toronto Press.

Vayda, Eugene, and Raisa B. Deber. 1992. "The Canadian Health-Care System: A Developmental Overview." In *Canadian Health Care and the State: A Century of Evolution*, edited by C. David Naylor. Montreal and Kingston: McGill-Queen's University Press.

Wainwright, Lillian. 1992. "'Catherine Wallace: A Woman of Many Gifts.' *Folia Montana: Mount Saint Vincent*." *Alumnae Magazine* (Spring–Summer): 9–10.

Archives Consulted

Presentation of the Blessed Virgin Mary Archives, St John's, Newfoundland
Mount Saint Vincent University Archives, Halifax, Nova Scotia
Sisters of Charity Archives, Halifax, Nova Scotia
Sisters of St Martha Archives, Charlottetown, PEI

9 The Sisters of Our Lady of the Missions in Canada, the Long 1960s, and Vatican II: From Carving Spaces in the Educational State to Living the Radicality of the Gospel

ROSA BRUNO-JOFRÉ

Situating the Sisters of Our Lady of the Missions

The *Religieuses de Notre Dame des Missions* (RNDM) / Sisters of Our Lady of Missions was founded in Lyon, France, in 1861, by Euphrasie Barbier (Marie du Coeur de Jesus, 1829–93), at the crossroads of modernity and the Catholic Church's reaction to it (Hobsbawm 2012; Ollivier 2007; Wittberg 1994).[1] It has been argued that the Catholic Church encouraged the creation of active congregations that would disseminate Catholic values in a modernizing and secularizing world (Vanderstraeten 2014). At the time, several factors were particularly relevant in the newly emerging configurations in which congregations were being inserted, including the spread of industrial transformation, the widening of world markets, processes of colonization, the consolidation of the bourgeoisie as a new political and economic class, the ideology of progress, the increasing importance of the scientific method, and the impact of evolutionism. However, the modern world did not erase Christianity and personal piety, which was expressed in various ways including through educational pursuits that, in their Protestant strands, intertwined with the building of the educational state. Nor did it erase Catholicism and its local variants. Catholics negotiated with the state to find their own place in education. Discourses coexisted. Missions moved across the world, and the apostolate became naturalized in the new spaces; however, the missionaries kept the Catholic "truth" as a starting point for their apostolate, and this conditioned their interactions as they encountered different ways of being.

While Catholic enterprises were not necessarily a faithful reflection of the anti-liberalism and anti-modernism of the popes of the nineteenth century, they were still framed by those positions. The ultramontane ("beyond the mountains") view had dominated the First Vatican Council (1869–70) and was expressed in the "First Dogmatic Constitution on the Church of Christ (*Pastor Aeternus*)," which declared the infallible teaching authority of the Pope (Misner 2000; Smith 2010). Anti-modernist positions did not lose their momentum with Leo XIII (1810–1903) and were fully conveyed in the 1907 "Encyclical of Pope Pius X on the Doctrines of the Modernists (*Pascendi Dominici Gregis*)," in which the Pope condemned "modernism" as the "synthesis of all heresies" (Misner 2000, 1). That had serious consequences for the study of theology in general and for any historical study of the Bible and even on the incorporation of new educational theories.

The first constitutions of the RNDM, approved by the Vatican in 1890, stated their mission. Article 2 declared that the Sisters would devote themselves to the instruction and Christian education of children and women, above all in "infidel" and non-Catholic countries (McBride 2006, 2). That was clearly within the ethos of colonization and inspired by a theology of redemption. Thus constituted, the congregation spread across the globe, responding to the needs emerging in the missionary field – for example, the education of children of Catholic colonists. By the time of their arrival in Canada in 1898, the congregation had established an international network of houses spread over Europe, Asia, and Oceania (Development of the Sisters of Our Lady of the Missions 2011). Three years later, in 1901, the congregation left France as a consequence of the Associations Bill, which subjected religious associations to regulation and ensured the supremacy of civil power. The RNDM moved the mother house from Lyon to Deal (England).

In this chapter I make the case that teaching congregations – here, the RNDM in Canada – cultivated an educationalizing/moralizing Catholic culture in which Catholic schooling served as a tool for generating social, religious, and political spaces. (This dimension of the educationalization of the world is often neglected.[2]) However, it is also the case that socio-economic conditions and the ideological context changed after the Second World War, thus altering the setting of the RNDM's educational mission. Furthermore, beginning in the long 1960s, the internal life of the congregation underwent dramatic changes. I argue that the new experiences and the search for individual and collective identity that emerged were partly related to an encounter with pluralism at the time when the congregation was relativizing its own standpoint, following the Second Vatican Council's redefinition of the relationship with outsiders as one of dialogue and cooperation. Finally, I examine the crisis of the long 1960s[3] and its implications for the congregation.

I use as a heuristic tool the recent work of Peter Berger (2014), which brings to the forefront the notion of pluralism – "the co-existence of different worldviews and value systems in the same society" – as "the major change brought about by modernity for the place of religion both in the minds of individuals and in the institutional order" (ix). That notion is particularly useful, especially since Berger also rejects exclusive emphasis on secularization as an explanatory tool, allowing for a more nuanced explanation of the processes of differentiation and deinstitutionalization of practices (the latter was evident during the 1960s at the apostolates in what previously had been homogeneous communities).[4]

Educationalization of the World, the Catholic Dimension: The RNDM as a Teaching Congregation in Canada before Vatican II

The foundress of the RNDM, Euphrasie Barbier, attended Our Lady's Training College on Mount Pleasant Street in Liverpool, run by the Sisters of Notre Dame de Namur, and was influenced by their ideas on education. Barbier had been sent to England to learn English, the language of the colonies, during her time with the Sisters of the Calvary.

The Sisters of Namur's co-foundress, Julie Billiart (1751–1816), had an avowed mission to educate girls and women. Her focus was on universal and free Catholic education provided by trained teachers in well-organized rural schools. (Her congregation served the upper classes as well.) Teaching congregations like the RNDM had roots in this educationalized or pedagogized[5] Catholic approach, a response to the Protestant Reform that went back to statements from the Council of Trent (1545–63), which called on schools and teachers to provide a "true" Christian education. This approach was further developed in the seventeenth century, along with a renewed spirituality and a preoccupation with providing a Catholic education, including practical skills, to poor girls and boys. In fact, methods and approaches developed by both Jean-Baptiste de La Salle (1651–1719), founder of the Christian Brothers, and Nicholas Barré (1621–86), founder of the Sisters of the Infant Jesus, are part of this modern approach to education. The Society of Jesus (whose constitutions were approved in 1540), and their Jesuit-like vocation to proselytize in the world, were always points of reference for women religious, who were officially restricted to enclosures for three centuries, and had to find ways to enact their apostolate.

In the nineteenth century, after the upheavals of the previous century, active teaching congregations aimed at developing a Catholic moral and social order – and at keeping the flock, as well as including new populations in the Church – and were carving their own configuration of power in an educationalized and eclectic world.[6] They were often beacons of a questionable "civilizing" mission. The number of women religious grew exponentially in the nineteenth century. Catholic schools, when they did not encounter hostile (anti-clerical) laws, had to relate in some way to the educational state. This was precisely the situation in which the Sisters found themselves, when they were inserted into the Canadian reality. They were brought to Canada in 1898 by the ultramontane archbishop of St Boniface, Adélard Langevin, who questioned the existence of the common school and the central role of the state in educating Catholic children. Langevin also contested the liberal project (Bruno-Jofré 2005).

Euphrasie Barbier's letters of instructions to the teaching Sisters, and her own formative history in the second half of the nineteenth century, lead me to infer that her ideas on education were, probably vicariously, influenced by Johann Heinrich Pestalozzi (1746–1827) and Friedrich Froebel (1782–1852). Here I am referring to Pestalozzi's attention to the development of the senses and mind of the child, and to Froebel's notion of the intrinsically good and creative nature of the child and his emphasis on love. These ideas were circulating in Europe in the nineteenth century (Mumm 1992, 172).

The pedagogical sources the Sisters used were the same as the ones reaching the public schools, and the Sisters' limited teaching preparation was no different from that of the elementary teachers in Canadian public schools (Bruno-Jofré and Cole 2014). Thus, the core ideas that originally guided the Sisters were the centrality of the child, sensitivity to stages of development, discipline (but with no system of punishment), attention to the senses, and the provision of practical courses as well as instruction in music and the arts (McBride 2006). Over time, these conceptions became fairly nuanced in Canada and in other missions, as a result of the Sisters' teacher preparation in normal schools, and in many cases, in universities. But the Sisters' presence also needs to be understood in relation to the salvific mission of the Church, and also in relation to the concepts that made up the semantic field characterizing the Sisters' consecrated life and that populated the records of the congregation until Vatican II – concepts such as submission, obedience, humility, and sacrifice. The Canon Law of 1917 made their lives even more regulated. Beyond the Rule of Augustine, which governed the congregation, other regulations and prohibitions permeated the way the Sisters lived their spirituality (i.e., their beliefs and values pertaining to the spirit of the congregation), and these in turn became embedded in their teaching. The dogmatic stance was particularly evident in the teaching of religion, as is clear from the texts used for decades in high schools – texts such as *Bible Studies,* first published in 1881 but still in use in the late 1950s, and *Our Quest for Happiness: The Story of Divine Love* (Elwell 1951).

The RNDM's educational work, like that of any other congregation, was conditioned by the specifics of the locality – in this case, by their teaching apostolates, mainly in Manitoba and Saskatchewan. The RNDM was invited to Manitoba in 1898, in the aftermath of the political crisis known as the Manitoba School Question (1890–7), when, in 1897, public funding for confessional schools came to an end, along with the status of French as a founding language in the province. From the humble accommodations of their early days, the RNDM and other congregations moved to impressive buildings that peppered the prairie landscape as the "other" of modernity – an "other" that could not be, and was not, ignored.

The Sisters taught in public, private, parish, and separate (Catholic) schools, the latter in Saskatchewan and at a school in Ontario. Very early in the twentieth century, they opened foundations in Franco-Manitoban Catholic communities such as Grande-Clairière, Ste-Rose du Lac, St-Eustache, Elie, Letellier, and St-Joseph (Sister Mary of the Holy Trinity, n.d.). In French Canadian communities, teaching congregations developed a notion of the Catholic citizen as oppositional to the state. Schooling (even public) was used as a means to challenge assimilation and to assert a communitarian identity. Often, the teaching Sisters, the priest, and the members of the communities – through boards of trustees – were in charge of the local public schools. Over time, the schools became part of a provincial and national institutional network, as well as an instrument of collective action for the project of French Canada in minority settings outside Quebec (Martel 1997, 20). The existence of hundreds of school districts, each with a rather homogeneous community, facilitated challenges to the Department of Education and alternative notions of citizenship formation.

At the end of the nineteenth century, communities of immigrants, many of them Catholics of non-British origin, began to establish themselves in the Prairie provinces.[7] The RNDMs were ready to respond to the unique needs of these new immigrants. In English-speaking areas, the Sisters ran parish and private schools in English. In the city of Brandon, Manitoba, for example, they ran the St Augustine parish school (for grades one to eight) and St Michael's Academy (a private boarding secondary school), where they taught many girls, in particular new immigrants from Eastern European countries. At St Michael's they diversified the curriculum by providing practical knowledge, commercial courses, music classes, and sports. In the late 1960s, after school districts were consolidated and new policies were promulgated, the St Augustine parish school and St Michael's joined the Brandon School Division. For decades, the schools in Brandon played a role in the life of immigrant groups who searched for social recognition while building community identity (Bruno-Jofré 2015).[8] The congregation also had a parochial school in Winnipeg's West End. As with other teaching congregations, the Sisters' approach to teaching broke from the common school's approach of universality and of building a cohesive society through Anglo-conformity.

At private schools they opened for girls in Saskatchewan, the Sisters provided a much-praised space for Catholic girls, preparing them for work and family (within the Catholic tradition). The community valued the teaching of music and commercial skills. However, a number of private RNDM schools in Saskatchewan did not survive the process of change. These included the Sacred Heart Academy in Regina, founded in 1905, taken over by the Catholic Separate Board in 1965, and closed in 1969 after enrolment fell from 279 students in 1965, to 175 in 1966, and to 148 in 1968; Sacred Heart College, also in Regina, which had opened in 1926 and was awarded the status of junior college by the University of Ottawa, but was discontinued in 1949; and Marian High School, which opened at the former Sacred Heart College with the same name in 1955, moved to an adjacent building with the name Marian High School in 1963, transferred to the tax-supported Catholic Separate High School District in 1965, and was demolished in the 1990s. Deteriorating buildings, lack of necessary facilities, and a decline in the number of women religious as teachers were often mentioned as contributors to these changes of the late 1960s. Nevertheless, the Sisters continued teaching in the Separate Catholic School Boards in Saskatchewan.

A 1942 editorial in *Stella Orientis* (Editorial 1942), the annual graduate publication of Sacred Heart College, stated that the students "were shown the Catholic view on all matters, the rightness of the Church's mind, thus enabling us to uphold and defend our Christian Faith" (6). Likewise, *The Clarion,* published by the staff and students of St Michael's Academy in Brandon, contained this statement: "Teach us to walk in the footsteps of Jesus, our Divine Brother, by practicing the special virtues of youth, charity, obedience, purity, love of study and of sacrifice, Christian and all-conquering joy" (*The Clarion* 1953). These statements certainly fit within the framework of the official line of the Church before Vatican II. However, the context of the Sisters' work began to change in the postwar years, and this led to a dealignment not only with missionary aims but also with the universe of the religious – particularly in the long 1960s. Vatican II became a catalyst for these myriad changes. Meanwhile, the number of students attending (publicly funded) Catholic schools – schools that were well-entrenched in the system – did not decline.

The Global Crisis of the Long 1960s, Its Intersection with Vatican II, and the Resignification of Mission

Vatican II produced three documents related to religious life that had an impact on mission and on collective identity: (1) *Dogmatic Constitution on the Church* (*Lumen Gentium*), which situated religious life within the broader mission of the Church and extended the notion of fullness of Christian life to all faithful; (2) *Decree on the Appropriate Renewal of Religious Life* (*Perfectae Caritatis*), which focused on renewal in light of the original spirit of the congregation; and (3) *Gaudium et Spes*, which addressed the presence and activity of the Church in the world today. Also influential was *Ecclesiae Sanctae*, Paul VI's apostolic letter dealing with directives regarding the renewal (Paul VI, 1966).

Within the Church there was not only a liberal/conservative divide, but also a challenging relationship between radical politics and theology, expressed in the emergence of liberation theology in Latin America (quite extensive among Protestants as well). Tension was evident as well between new epistemologies and theology – as in the case of feminist thea/ologies, black theologies, and later, eco-theologies.

In the world outside the walls of the Vatican, the movements of the long 1960s, and the presence of a pluralism that invited "contamination," interaction, negotiation, and relativization, had reached the congregations and crossed paths with the renewal process launched by Vatican II.[9] This situated the Sisters in relative openness to the world and to its plurality of discourses and ways of being. In that context, the Sisters searched for their individual and collective identities, and the layers within, from a psychological and subjective standpoint. Former RNDM Provincial Superior Sheila Madden said of the process: "It was a year of people finding themselves and I think overtly for the first time in terms of a sexual orientation" (Sisters of Our Lady of the Missions, Leadership Discussion 2012, 5). All congregations now shared the drive to find both the self and the woman religious who had been lost in rules and regulation.

The documents from Vatican II and the ensuing process of renewal facilitated this new relationship with a plural world. The process led to the disintegration – and in some cases, reproposal – of missionary goals. An interesting example can be found in RNDM's missionary work in Peru; there, the Sisters opened a mission early in 1969 – a late response to the call from Pope John XXIII, but inspired by the directive from *Perfectae Caritatis* ("Decree" 1966) to revisit the original spirit and special aims of the congregation. In the complex interplay of locality and lived experience, the missionary Sisters embraced liberation theology. They further extended their role as educators from being schoolteachers to becoming community grassroots educators, making explicit the political dimension of everyday life. They generated a renewed understanding of mission well before the congregation at large did. The notion of salvation in liberation theology collapsed the distinction between sacred history and secular earthly history without making them synonymous; it also debunked the theology of redemption that had sustained their original notion of mission (Smith 1991). Beyond the contradictions and failings of the so-called Peruvian Revolution, the Sisters remained committed to social justice, even as important sectors of the Church moved away from liberation theology (and other sectors never accepted it). The Sisters asserted their own sense of living the radicality of the Gospel very early and were actually quite ahead of the generalate of the congregation (Bruno-Jofré and Jofré 2014). It was not until 1984 that the congregation as a whole embraced social justice and the "option for the poor," although it continued to hold on to an ecclesiocentric approach for a few more years (*Witnessing to the Gospel* 1984).

Teaching congregations encountered powerful challenges. They had to deal with drastic changes in the education system and with the sociopolitical change affecting their constituencies; at the same time, they had to revise their entire religious ethos and approach to religious education, while also addressing the declining number of vocations, which led to more lay teachers being placed in classrooms. The Vatican II document *Declaration on Christian Education* (*Gravissimum Educationis*) (1966) did not seem to be of great concern in the general or even the provincial chapters. The redirection of religious studies took on a life of its own, with involvement from the bishops and the boards of education – along with the laity and, of course, the Sisters. At the elementary school level, *The Canadian Catechism: Come to the Father* (1972) brought a new pedagogical dimension and renewed content; materials for high schools took more time to be developed.

Canada as an imagined community had taken root in the minds of the members of the Canadian Province of the RNDM. During the preparations for the Regular General Chapter of 1966, Provincial Superior Jeanne Roche positioned her argument against the centralized hierarchical governance of the congregation and asked for more autonomy by appealing to Canada's history and its progress from colony to nationhood. She wrote: "Please do not consider us either rude or rebellious. We are merely Canadian" (Sisters of Our Lady of the Missions, Leadership Discussion 2012). It was a time of rapid movement and overlapping intentionalities. By and large in North America, the political left, the countercultural movement, and the liberal social reforms of the 1960s were giving way to neoliberalism, which would become dominant towards the late 1970s. Neoliberalism was beginning to align the state with the free market; schooling was being revamped through a discourse of freedom and choice that generated a utilitarian understanding of education and new forms of social control. A new paradigm of education, *scientification* – still dominant today – relied heavily on cognitive psychology, which focused on research into mental activity as a form of information processing, research that had itself been inspired by cybernetics as well as by premises from the natural sciences (Rohstock and Tröhler 2014, 124).

In the 1960s, changes in education in various provinces in Canada – for example, in Manitoba and Ontario – included consolidations that eliminated hundreds of school districts. These changes also brought an end to the relative autonomy that had favoured the Sisters' educational work in various ethnic communities. In Saskatchewan, where consolidation had taken place in 1944, the Sisters had their private schools and also their place in the publicly funded separate (Catholic) schools; in 1964, the legislation was changed to extend tax support to public high schools, including separate high schools (Noonan 1998). The separate Catholic schools also absorbed some of the Sisters' private schools.

Furthermore, the RNDM, along with other congregations, played a relevant role – through their teaching in private and public schools and their parish work – in buttressing the identity of what Marcel Martel (1998, 3–5) calls the "French-Canadian nation" (Quebec and communities outside Quebec). However, the understanding of Quebec as the "basic polity" of French Canada in the 1960s, and the movement away from building a common identity for all French Canadians, created a new political and educational scenario. In 1969, the Canadian Province wrote that "Quebec has become anti-clerical. It offers a large field for the Apostolate" ("Process Verbal" 1969).

The context had changed, and adjustment was necessary. In 1964, the intended force behind the Sisters' narrative of Catholic education, their intentionality, still had as point of reference the 1929 encyclical of Pope Pius XI, "On Christian Education (*Divini Illius Magistri*)." This document had strong anti-modernist tones and a vision of education that did not fit with the 1960s, not even with new theological developments. An example is the argument that the congregation articulated in 1964 in the midst of financial problems, for a special agreement with the Separate School Board in Regina, Saskatchewan, regarding Marian High School and Sacred Heart Academy, both private schools. The agreement would have provided the schools with a per capita fee or with the payment of teachers' salaries and operational costs while the Sisters would still keep control of the schools. (This was prior to the integration into the separate system in 1965.) The schools followed the curriculum set by the provincial education department. In the proposal, the Sisters made their case by stating that:

> Inherent in the philosophy of the schools and in conformity with the Encyclical on Education by Pope Pius XI, is the belief that the ideal of Catholic education is best realized in institutions where at the high school level boys and girls are taught in separate institutions. Following this belief the Sisters over a period of sixty years have striven to establish girls' schools providing students with the means of enabling them to procure an academic training second to none and a spiritual formation in accordance with the philosophy and ideals of Holy Mother Church. (Views with regard to the Separate School Question, 1964)

Although the RNDM Canadian province had been sensitive to educational changes, the identity of the sister-teacher and their approach to the education of girls were not in tune with the times. Feminist writers had started to unveil patriarchal power. However, even as many Sisters felt uncomfortable with a "symbolic universe" that could not integrate new meanings and experiences, the writers of the proposal illustrated the schools' academic achievement by stating that more than ninety former pupils of Sacred Heart Academy had entered religious life, and that many others from the two schools were (at the time) successful Catholic professionals or businesswomen or Christian wives and mothers. To continue with that success, they needed support but also autonomy. The Sisters also pointed out that the number of students had diminished. That year (1964), as they documented, Marian School had enrolled 156 students, even though it had room for 320 (Views with regard to the Separate School Question, 1964). The journey towards resignifying the congregation's mission involved dealing with nested configurations of intentions and desires emerging at the provincial and central (generalate in Rome) levels, having the Vatican as frame of contention.

The Regular General Chapter of 1966 reiterated Chapter 1 of the constitutions, in which it was stated that the principal apostolate of the congregation was that of Christian education. It went on to say: "It is essential, therefore, that all the Sisters be thoroughly imbued with the spirit of the Church and well informed on papal documents concerning it, such as Pope Pius XI's encyclical letter *Christian Education of Youth* and Vatican II's *Declaration on Christian Education* and the *Decree on the Church's Missionary Activity*" (Congregation of Our Lady of the Missions 1966, 10). It is not surprising that the reference in the General Chapter to the 1965 Vatican II document *Declaration on Christian Education* (1966)[10] was placed in relation to the Pius XI (1929) encyclical on education (Congregation of Our Lady of the Missions 1966, 10), since that encyclical is often quoted in the Declaration. It should be noted, however, that the purpose of the Declaration in relation to the modern world is ambiguous – open to it, while at the same time defending "the traditional concept of the 'Catholic social order' wherein the Church determined the nature of the common good" (Stafford, in this volume, 215).

The General Chapter seems to be trying to come close to the congregation's original mission and vision at a time of drastic changes. It continues: "It is essential that the Sisters possess knowledge of the apostolate of education so as to understand and appreciate its greatness, its vastness, its primacy among the works of mercy. By the approval of the holy Church, our Congregation is ranked among missionary-teaching congregations and has, therefore, received from holy Church the mandate of helping in the salvation of souls by the apostolate of Christian education" (Congregation of Our Lady of the Missions 1966, 10). The Chapter stresses obedience in a traditional way: "moved by the Holy Spirit, they subject themselves in faith to their superiors, God's representatives" (ibid., 10).

The lived history of the Sisters challenged the statements of the 1966 Chapter. As mentioned earlier, *Perfectae Caritatis* ("Decree" 1966)[11] opened an unexpected door to the discovery of the self, in its rather modernist sense. As discussed by Heidi MacDonald (2017), between 1965 and 1975 the number of women religious in Canada fell 32 per cent, from 66,000 to 44,127. Sister Claire Himbeault, RNDM, Provincial Superior between 1971 and 1977, recalled that after Vatican II,

> a great number of Sisters were leaving for various reasons. Perhaps, it was that they for the first time saw that there was something else for them, that this was not really their place. So I found myself accompanying many of the Sisters as they made their discernment and lived it with sadness and pain. At the same time, it was really the right thing for many people, but I nevertheless felt it, felt the separation. (Sisters of Our Lady of the Missions, Leadership Discussion 2012, 2)

Sister Cécile Campeau, Provincial Superior between 1968 and 1971, reminisced that there was a great desire, or some desire, for greater freedom in every sense of the word, and a trend towards expanding education beyond just the teaching certificate, as well as an interest in various spiritualities. She added: “Many of us attended healing workshops” (ibid., 18).

Vatican II carried the Sisters to a new experience of religious life and consequently to a different understanding of mission and vision, one that they needed to articulate as a collective at a time when they had also begun to discover their own selves and desires, and when many were moving away from teaching. The focus was on personal development, but that went along with deep questioning, even of vows.

Patricia Wittberg writes that the Sisters’ religious language moved from theological constructs to psychological paradigms; however, the latter were not adequate to explain what was desirable to their life as religious. Wittberg contends that religious congregations suffered an alarming loss of identity and that they reacted in a defensive way, thus generating a self-defeating pattern. They crafted statements of mission or charism that were vague enough to encompass various interests, and this made it difficult to plan; they also emphasized an interpretation of community in terms of the members’ needs, instead of in terms of sustaining corporate commitments. In her study of US religious congregations, Wittberg made the case for the need of a coherent and lived ideological frame if a religious movement is to survive (1994, 256).

The Canadian Provincial Chapter of 1969 painted a realistic picture of the congregation: “In the time of Mother Foundress instruction was the great need of the people; in our time a broader educational apostolate may be the greater need. In our Canadian province we are being progressively freed from commitments in schools and so are able to widen our field of apostolic endeavour" ("Process Verbal" 1969). The minutes noted that "in many social and catechetical works the income is inadequate and teachers in paying positions are necessary to make such works possible" (ibid.). Similarly, in a report of April–May 1973, the Superior General after visiting Canada wrote with reference to the Sisters' apostolic and missionary activity: "We must not forget that *education* remains our primary *service* in the Church. There exists today a disaffection for teaching properly so called. However, I believe it still has an apostolic value and it continues to be an excellent means of reaching the young" (Ollivier 1973, 2). She asked "why so many years of study [were needed] to obtain necessary qualifications if afterwards the Sisters turn to other activities." The Superior General's words reinforced the congregation's understanding and redefinition of its educational role. She said: "To be sure, I do not envisage education in the restricted sense of the term. I am convinced that religious have roles to fulfil in pastoral catechetics and in works of a social nature such as Jean Vanier School, etc., and I fully approve them" (ibid., 2).

Several difficulties flowed from the international/transnational character of the congregation and the need to integrate the aspirations and visions of different provinces. The constitutions, even in their final version, reflected changes within specific parameters; the language of the oral narrations and even the various positions in the Chapters actually went beyond the language of the constitutions. In Superior Provincial Sister Cècile Campeau's words: "The congregation soon discovered that the constitutions which we had worked so hard at reflected very little of the spirit and the spirituality of our congregation. So the constitutions were soon replaced – I think in 1972" (Sisters of Our Lady of the Missions, Leadership Discussion 2012). In fact, the constitutions' *ad experimentum* of 1969 were amended in 1972 and 1975; eventually, the rule and the constitutions were approved by the Decree of 1979 by the *Sacra Congregatio Pro Religiosis et Institutis Saecularibus*, as a text defining the congregation's identity (Congregation of Our Lady of the Missions 1979).

A cursory reading indicates that the original core of the mission as established in Article 2 of the first constitutions – which stated that Sisters would devote themselves to the instruction and Christian education of children and women, above all in "infidel" and non-Catholic countries[12] – was reproposed in Article 58 of the new constitutions. Article 58 reads: "We share in the missionary task of the church principally through the works of Christian education. Other works in keeping with the mission and spirit of the congregation are also undertaken" (ibid., 40). The educational work that had been so prominent in the foundation of the congregation no longer defined its mission, although some of the Sisters would continue teaching for some time. The General Chapter of 1972, fittingly titled "Recreated in Hope," had changed the concept of education, which was so central to the spirit (charism) of the congregation, by making it very broad – partly because there were problems in identifying a common vision. At the Chapter, in her opening address, Marie Bénédicte, Superior General, posed a key question: "What is the meaning of our 'mission' in the church and in the contemporary world?" She continued: "We know that we cannot live it as we did in the past. We must review our missionary vocation in the light of new conditions of life and environment. New worlds are springing up everywhere and the church is not present in them" (Congregation of Our Lady of the Missions 1972, 4).

When discussing the principles behind the apostolate, the Acts of the Chapter made it clear that the primary service was education, especially in non-Christian and de-Christianized countries. This was followed by another principle: "As members of a 'pilgrim church,' we share its obligation to move, to be sensitive to the needs of our time, and open to the Spirit in our vision of the future" (Congregation of Our Lady of the Missions, 1972). The apostolates at the time were described as diversified as they included nursing, parish work, and other forms of social service. The account added that the congregation followed the trend of interpreting their primary work of education in its broadest sense (ibid.).

The General Chapter of 1984, *Witnessing to the Gospel: Beyond all Frontiers,* conveyed a sense of maturity in the recreation of the congregation's vision and mission. The Chapter challenged all RNDMs "to develop a world vision and to be ready to move out in response to the great needs of today's world, e.g., in the Pacific, Latin America, the Far East … to respond … to the changing needs of those around us" (1984, 3). Inculturation in every milieu was central in an apostolic plan that committed the Sisters to "on-going programmes for education and conscientization in the areas of social justice" (ibid., 9), as well as to "education and conscientization of the non-poor and non-oppressed to realize that structures that protect their interests are very often the cause of misery for the poor" (ibid., 11). The Chapter included a call to develop curriculum and justice and peace programs in the congregation's schools, in order to conscientize students and expose them to injustices in their own and others' societies. The Canadian Province embraced the General Chapter's recommendations and further developed a program with Native peoples, refugees, and the Peruvian mission (which was about to gain autonomy) (Provincial Chapter Canada 1986). The renewal did not end with the relinquishment of school teaching. The congregation became actively engaged with the world by generating new configurations of ideas that nested their own positioning, and assumed coexistence and interaction with emerging transformative perspectives in a more fluid social milieu, although they were still contending with the parameters of a gendered hierarchical institution.

The "Reflections of the Visitation to the Canadian Province" of 1989 conveyed a clear shift. The notion of Christian education had been considerably widened within the Province; a movement to reach out to the poor, the marginalized, and those suffering injustice had come into being; there was evidence of greater awareness with regard to the Natives and Métis; and overall, social justice issues were fully embraced. Moreover, the language of the needs of the Church was no longer there: the mission had become reignocentric rather than ecclesiocentric (Himbeault and Ross 1989).

Conclusion

The RNDM was founded as a teaching congregation in the "Age of Empire" (a term from Hobsbawn 2012), at a point when the Catholic Church was engaged in a reactive confrontation with modernity and liberalism, in a world in which the secular gained prominence and intertwined with the religious. For the Church, school teaching had been a means to build a Catholic social order, within the order of things at the time, and to keep its flock in the churches. The Church played a role in the educationalization of the world in a contesting yet parallel way while interacting (through curriculum, certification, and so on) with the modern educational state. The RNDM played a role in building a French Canadian identity beyond Quebec, in parish, private, and public schools in rural areas. The schools provided a space for social recognition and identity for Catholic immigrant children, mostly in Manitoba and Saskatchewan, although the work was extended to Ontario; they even delivered advanced education for girls and young women, particularly in Saskatchewan; and, along with other congregations, they delivered schooling from a Catholic perspective to Métis children in some of their schools, albeit while neglecting their identity.

Vatican II found the RNDM confronting a crisis: its instrumental mission could not address the changing reality, the education system had changed dramatically, and a decline in vocations was evident. The plural world, with its peculiar coexistence of various discourses, could not be confronted with a static notion of tradition and dogma. Vatican II brought the means to deal with that overwhelming context. Berger's (2014) theory of a paradigmatic shift, which emphasized the workings of pluralism, provides an explanation for the ensuing change that current theories of secularization do not. The RNDM, like other congregations, encountered pluralism at precisely the same time that the congregation was relativizing its own standpoint. The Sisters opened to the plurality of the world, not as the enemy, not limited by rules and regulations, but in a way that led to a cognitive process, leading to a new understanding of their mission. Their dialogue with the (not only plural, but also contradictory) world would help recreate their individual and collective selves. In tune with the circumstances of the time, the RNDM's constitutions expanded the notion of education beyond schooling. Subsequently, the Canadian Province of the RNDM moved away from school teaching. Its numbers decreased from 192 Sisters in 1965, including six novices and twenty-one temporary professed, to forty-two Sisters, and no novices or temporary professed, in 2015. However, they were part of an international congregation of 886 Sisters (although there had been 1,307 Sisters in the period 1959 to 1964), which reflected the new geographical map of the Catholic Church, and who were able to articulate a renewed mission and vision that had eco-spirituality and social justice at its core. (The latter is beyond the scope of this chapter, which centres on the teaching character of the congregation.) Briefly, while the constitutions broadened the notion of education, the Sisters discovered the self, and over many years cultivated new apostolates, despite and against inherent difficulties: they created a new collective identity.

NOTES

This chapter is part of a major research project funded by the Social Sciences and Humanities Research Council of Canada (SSHRC). I appreciate the comments made by Eva Krugly-Smolska and Suzan Poiraz on an earlier draft.

1 Ollivier provides a non-hagiographical account of Euphrasie Barbier's life and a good historical account of the foundation of the congregation.

2 The Catholic Church saw education as a means to keep the poor in the flock and, in many cases, to address poverty and social crisis resulting from wars, plagues, and so on. Some of the congregations even developed pedagogical approaches. Later, the congregations' educational work converged with processes of civilization and pedagogization of society that occurred in tandem with professionalization and expertise. Important work on pedagogization, although it does not touch the Catholic dimension, can be found in Smeyers and Depaepe (2009).

3 See Marwick (1998), 7.

4 For a discussion of secularization and the religious crisis of the 1960s, see Brown (2010).

5 I am appropriating the term "pedagogized" from Smeyers and Depaepe (2009), although the contextual framework is different.

6 For various approaches to the educationalization of social problems from a historical perspective, see Smeyers and Depaepe (2009) and Tröhler (2013).

7 "Almost half of all prairie residents at the start of the First World War had been born in another country, and the proportion was still 1 in 3 as late as 1931" (Friesen 1987, 244).

8 See *The Convent on Victoria and Lorne, Brandon* (n.d., 1).

9 Concepts taken from Berger (2014). However, here I don't discuss theories of secularization or the religious crisis of the 1960s. For this topic, see Brown (2010), McLeod (2007), and McLeod and Ustorf (2003).

10 The actual date of publication of the document by the Vatican is 1965.

11 The actual date of publication of the document by the Vatican is 1965.

12 "The Sisters may accept with the consent of the General Council, other works of charity" (Mary of the Heart of Jesus 1869, 265).

REFERENCES

Berger, Peter. 2014. *The Many Altars of Modernity: Toward a Paradigm for Religion in a Pluralist Age.* Boston and Berlin: De Gruyter Mouton. http://dx.doi.org/10.1515/9781614516477.

Brown, Callum. December 2010. "What Was the Religious Crisis of the 1960s?" *Journal of Religious History* 34(4): 468–79. http://dx.doi.org/10.1111/j.1467-9809.2010.00909.x.

Bruno-Jofré, Rosa. 2005. *The Missionary Oblate Sisters: Vision and Mission.* Kingston and Montreal: McGill-Queen's University Press.

– 2015. "The Situational Dimension of the Educational Apostolate and the Configuration of the Learner as a Cultural and Political Subject: The Case of the Sisters of Our Lady of the Missions in the Canadian Prairies," In *Education, Identity, and Teaching Sisters, 1800–1950*, edited by Deidre Raftery and Elizabeth Smyth, 160–81. London and New York: Routledge.

Bruno-Jofré, Rosa, and Josh Cole. 2014. "To Serve and Yet Be Free: Historical Configurations and the Insertions of Faculties of Education in Ontario." In *Teacher Education in a Transnational World*, edited by Rosa Bruno-Jofré and James S. Johnston, 71–95. Toronto: University of Toronto Press.

Bruno-Jofré, Rosa, and Ana Jofré. 2014. "Reading the Lived Experience of Vatican II: Words and Images, Contrasting with the Past, and Grasping the Spirit of the Times. The Canadian Province of the Sisters of Our Lady of Missions in Peru." *Historical Studies*, Canadian Catholic Historical Association, 81, 31–51.

The Clarion. Coronation Year 1953, St. Michael's Academy, Brandon, Manitoba. Invocation: O Immaculate Virgin, p. 3. Section D, shelf 5, green box, Canada 1949–1961, RNDM General Archives, Rome.

Congregation of Our Lady of the Missions. 1966. "Statutes of the General Chapter." Section H, shelf 2, box 4, RNDM General Archives, Rome.

– 1972. "Recreated in Hope: Acts of the Twentieth General Chapter." Section H, shelf 2, box 4, RNDM General Archives, Rome.

– 1979 (8 December). "Constitutions." Rome: Sacra Congregatio Pro Religiosis et Institutis Saecularibus.

"Declaration on Christian Education (*Gravissimum Educationis*)." 1966. In *The Documents of Vatican II*, edited by Walter M. Abbott, SJ, 637–52. New York: American Press.

"Decree on the Appropriate Renewal of Religious Life (*Perfectae Caritatis*)." 1966. In *The Documents of Vatican II*, edited by Walter M. Abbott, SJ, 466–82. New York: American Press.

Development of the Sisters of Our Lady of the Missions. 2011 (August). [Manuscript provided to author by Provincial Superior of the Canadian Province, Sister Veronica Dunne, Winnipeg, Manitoba.]

"Dogmatic Constitution on the Church (*Lumen Gentium*)." 1966. In *The Documents of Vatican II*, edited by Walter M. Abbott, SJ, 14–101. New York: The American Press.

"Editorial." *Stella Orientis* (yearbook). 1942. Regina: Sacred Heart College.

Elwell, Clarence E. (Rev. Msgr). 1951. *Toward the Eternal Commencement: Our Quest for Happiness: The Story of Divine Love.* Textbook Series for High School Religion, Book Four, for the Senior Years. Chicago: Mentzer, Bush & Company.

Friesen, Gerald. 1987. *The Canadian Prairies: A History.* Toronto: University of Toronto Press.

Himbeault, Claire, Superior General, and Moira Ross, Assistant General to the Sisters of the Canadian Province. 1989 (24 November). "Reflections of the Visitation of the Canadian Province, 12 September–12 November 1989." Box 01–04, files 12/14, CPSHSB.

Hobsbawm, Eric. 2012. *The Age of Empire, 1875–1914.* London: Abacus.

MacDonald, Heidi. 2017. "Smaller Numbers, Stronger Voices: Women Religious Reposition Themselves through the Canadian Religious Conference." In *Vatican II and Beyond: The Changing Mission and Identity of Canadian Women Religious,* edited by Rosa Bruno-Jofré, Heidi MacDonald, and Elizabeth Smyth. Kingston and Montreal: McGill-Queen's University Press.

Martel, Marcel. 1997. *Le deuil d'un pays imagine: Réves, luttes et dèroute du Canada français: Les rapports entre le Québec et la francophonie canadienne (1867–1975).* Ottawa: Les presses de l'Université d'Ottawa.

– 1998. *French Canada: An Account of Its Creation and Break-Up, 1850–1967.* Canadian Historical Association, Canada's Ethnic Group Series, booklet no. 24. Ottawa: Canadian Historical Association.

Marwick, Arthur. 1998. *The Sixties: Cultural Revolution in Britain, France, Italy, and the United States, c. 1958–1974.* Oxford: Oxford University Press.

Mary of the Heart of Jesus, Superior General of Our Lady of the Missions. 1869 (31 March). "Notes on the Beginning of the Congregation of Our Lady of the Missions, Its Development, Its Present State, and Its Special Aim. Translation of the Writing of Mother Mary of the Heart of Jesus," vol. 2, letter 261. Letters, section A, shelf 6, RNDM General Archives, Rome.

Mary of the Heart of Jesus, Superior General of Our Lady of the Missions. 1869 (31 March). Notes on the Beginning of the Congregation of Our Lady of the Missions, its Development, its Present State and its Special Aim. Translation of the Writing of Mother Mary of the Heart of Jesus, vol. 2, 1869, letter 261. Letters, section A, shelf 6, RNDM General Archives, Rome.

McBride, Maureen. RNDM. 2006. "'Our students must become valiant women!' Approaches to Education of Euphrasie Barbier 1829–1893, Foundress of Sisters of Our Lady of the Missions." Paper presented to RNDM Education Symposium, St Mary's College, Shillong, North East India, 26 January.

McLeod, Hugh. 2007. *The Religious Crisis of the 1960s.* Oxford: Oxford University Press. http://dx.doi.org/10.1093/acprof:oso/9780199298259.001.0001.

McLeod, Hugh, and Wener Ustorf, eds. 2003. *The Decline of Christendom in Western Europe, 1750–2000.* Cambridge: Cambridge University Press. http://dx.doi.org/10.1017/CBO9780511496783.

Misner, Paul. 2000. "Catholic Anti-Modernism: The Ecclesial Setting." In *Catholicism Contending with Modernity: Roman Catholic Modernism and Anti-Modernism in Historical Context,* edited by Darrell Jodock, 56–87.

Cambridge: Cambridge University Press. http://dx.doi.org/10.1017/CBO9780511520136.005.

Mumm, Susan E.D. 1992. "Lady Guerrillas of Philanthropy: Anglican Sisterhoods in Victorian England." PhD diss., University of Sussex.

Noonan, Brian. 1998. *Saskatchewan Separate Schools*, 2nd ed. Muenster: St Peters Press.

Ollivier, Marie-Bénédicte, RNDM. 1973, 26 May. Report of the Visit to the Canadian Province, Regina, Saskatchewan, box 13, file 9, CPSHSB.

– 2007. *Missionary beyond Boundaries: Euphrasie Barbier, 1820–1893.* Translated by Beverly Grounds, RNDM. Rome: Institute Salesiano Pio XI.

"Pastoral Constitution on the Church in the Modern World (*Gaudium et Spes*)." 1966. In *The Documents of Vatican II*, edited by Walter M. Abbott, SJ, 199–316. New York: American Press.

Paul VI. *Ecclesiae Sanctae I.* 1966 (6 August). "Apostolic Letter, written Motu Proprio, on the Implementation of the Decrees Christus Dominus, Presbyterorum Ordinis and Perfectae Caritatis." Translated from the Latin text in AAS 58, 757–8. In *The Documents of Vatican II*, translated by Austin Flannery, 601. New York: Costello Publishing.

Pius XI. 1929. "On Christian Education (*Divini Illius Magistri*)." Libreria Editrice Vaticana. http://w2.vatican.va/content/pius-xi/en/encyclicals/documents/hf_p-xi_enc_31121929_divini-illius-magistri.html.

"Process Verbal of the Provincial Chapter of the Province of the Sacred Hearts of Jesus and Mary, Canada." 1969 (29 December). Sacred Heart College, Regina. All provinces 1964–9, section G, shelf 2, RNDM General Archives, Rome.

Provincial Chapter Canada. 1986 (February). *1984–1986, a Three Year Apostolic Plan.* [Copy provided to author by Provincial Superior of the Canadian Province, Sister Veronica Dunne, Winnipeg, Manitoba.]

Provincial Superior, Canada, Sister Jeanne Roche, to Very Reverend Mother (Superior General), 29 May 1966. Box 14, file 17, CPHSB. [The letter does not show the signature.]

Rohstock, Anne, and Daniel Tröhler. 2014. "From the Sacred Nation to the Unified Globe: Changing Leitmotifs in Teacher Training in the Western World, 1870–2010." In *Teacher Education in a Transnational World*, edited by Rosa Bruno-Jofré and James Scott Johnston, 111–31. Toronto: University of Toronto Press.

Sister Mary of the Holy Trinity, Sisters of Our Lady of the Missions in Canada, 1898–1923. n.d. Manuscript commemorating the Silver Jubilee of the RNDM. [Document provided to author by the Provincial Superior of the Canadian Province, Sister Veronica Dunne, Winnipeg, Manitoba.] Sisters of Our Lady of the Missions, Leadership Discussion.

Sisters of Our Lady of the Missions. 1964 (22 March). "Views with Regard to the Separate School Question as set down by the Sisters of Our Lady of the Missions." Box 54, file 7, CO7–14, CPSHSB.

– 2012 (August). Leadership Discussion. Group conversation organized by Provincial Superior of the Canadian Province, Sister Veronica Dunne, Winnipeg, Manitoba. [Document provided to the author by V. Dunne.]

Smeyers, Paul, and Marc Depaepe, eds. 2009. *Educational Research: The Educationalization of Social Problems.* (Educational Research 3). Dordrecht: Springer.

Smith, Christian. 1991. *The Emergence of Liberation Theology: Radical Religion and Social Movement Theory.* Chicago: University of Chicago Press.

Smith, Susan. RNDM. 2010. *Call to Mission: The Story of the Mission Sisters of Aotearoa New Zealand and Samoa.* Auckland: David Ling.

The Canadian Catechism: Come to the Father (English rev. ed.). 1972. Toronto: Paulist Press. [Copyright held by Office de Cathéchèse du Québec.]

The Convent on Victoria and Lorne, Brandon. n.d. manuscript. [There is a note saying that this is by Sr Cecile Jordang (name not clear), RNDM]. Box 54, file 17, Le Centre du Patrimoine, Societé historituqe de Saint-Boniface (hereafter CPSHSB).

Tröhler, Daniel. 2013. *Pestalozzi and the Educationalization of the World.* New York: Palgrave Macmillan. http://dx.doi.org/10.1057/9781137346858.

Vanderstraeten, Raf. 2014. "Religious Activism in a Secular World: The Rise and Fall of the Teaching Congregations of the Catholic Church." *Paedagogica Historica* 50(4): 494–513. http://dx.doi.org/10.1080/00309230.2014.904913.

Views with regard to the Separate School Question as set down by the Sisters of Our Lady of the Missions. 22 March 1964, box 54, file 7, CPSHSB, Winnipeg,

Witnessing to the Gospel: Beyond all Frontiers. 1984. Twenty-Second General Chapter of the Congregation of Our Lady of the Missions. Held at Casa Santa Rosa, Via Anagnina, Grottaferrata, Italy, 10 June–25 July 1984. Box 16, file 12, CPSHSB.

Wittberg, Patricia. 1994. *The Rise and Decline of Catholic Religious Orders: A Social Movement Perspective.* Albany: SUNY Press.

“Recibiendo la Luz / Argia Onartuz / Receiving the Light.” Sculpture by Joaquín Gogorza.

PART FOUR

Changes in Curriculum and the Catholic Classroom after Vatican II

10 The Conditions of Reception for the *Declaration on Christian Education*: Secularization and the Educational State of Ontario

JOE STAFFORD

Introduction

This chapter examines the conditions of reception for the Vatican II *Declaration on Christian Education* in the province of Ontario. Proclaimed by Pope Paul VI on 28 October 1965, the *Declaration on Christian Education* was one of the later Vatican II documents and was the product of many revisions and compromises. Its target audience was the larger Catholic community, in particular parents and educators, but the bishops were expected to provide the needed guidance and leadership. This chapter focuses on two central questions: What were the conditions of reception for the Declaration? And why did the conditions of reception make it extremely difficult for the Ontario bishops to defend and promote the principles articulated in the Declaration?[1]

To understand these conditions, it is essential to analyse the Declaration itself. For this analysis, Quentin Skinner's theoretical framework will be relied upon. Thus, the Declaration, the "text," must be examined in its proper societal context and not considered as the sole source for understanding. One cannot "insist on the autonomy of the text" (Skinner 1969, 39). However, this societal context alone – the social, political, economic, and cultural realities (or as Skinner expresses it, the "context of other happenings") – does not explain the essential meaning of the text (39). What must also be examined is the complex nature of intentionality, the "illocutionary force" of the Declaration. What was intended to be understood may differ from what was actually understood. It is argued here that the illocutionary force – that is, the purpose – of the Declaration is not entirely clear, and therefore its reception could take many forms depending on the particular philosophy or political perspective of the recipient. This is especially true in terms of the Church's new "openness" to the modern world, which was a major theme of Vatican II and therefore of the Declaration itself. Thus, the essential meaning (or meanings) of the Declaration with regard to the modern world was open to question and led to the possibility of varying understandings. Intentionality is much clearer when dealing with traditional Catholic principles of education and with the changed understanding of the concept of tradition itself.

The Declaration represented a major challenge to the bishops in terms of their own understanding of the intended objectives. They were further challenged, as this chapter asserts, by the complex configuration of various factors that led to the dramatic cultural changes of the late 1950s and 1960s. One of the key conditions of reception emerged from this configuration: an increasingly secular society. The complex process of secularization led to the international "religious crisis" of the 1960s as traditional religious practices and traditions were increasingly challenged and widely abandoned throughout the Western world. This posed a difficult challenge for the bishops since Catholics were not immune from this process, and by the 1960s lay Catholics had assumed a prominent role in the Catholic school system.

The other condition of reception involved the nature of the educational state of Ontario. The Church was opposed not so much to the concept of an educational state, as to its limited power within it. This chapter argues that in this educational state, the Catholic separate school system was tolerated as a "political necessity" and that Catholic leadership, especially the bishops, had limited power to defend and promote Catholic education in a province noted for its virulent anti-Catholicism.[2] It is argued here that even though the Catholic school system enjoyed a certain degree of independence, its subservient position within the educational state hindered the bishops' ability to defend and promote Catholic education, particularly in the late 1950s and 1960s – a period of dramatic cultural change. It is further contended that the Ministry's 1965 decision to grant more power to the school boards did not result in any significant improvement in the bishops' position. The bishops' relationship with the boards had always been a complex one and varied according to each diocese. Power was shared. Yet by the 1960s the boards' control of the schools was undisputed. Moreover, board administrators were preoccupied with many other priorities aside from defending and promoting Catholic principles of education. It will therefore be argued that it was extremely difficult for the bishops to defend and promote these principles articulated in the Declaration because of the dramatic cultural changes of the late 1950s and 1960s and their own limited power within the educational state of Ontario.

Analysis of the *Declaration on Christian Education*

In his overview of the Declaration, Bishop Johannes Pohlschneider emphasized that it represented continuity and progress with regard to earlier Church teachings, particularly Pius XI's 1929 encyclical, *Divini Illius Magistri* (Briel 2008, 384). This encyclical was quoted ten times in the notes of the Declaration (Pohlschneider 1969, 13). It is argued here that most of the principles articulated in the Declaration reiterated long-held positions of the Church and therefore intentionality is clear: fundamental Catholic educational principles were to be defended and promoted. In several articles, the question of the proper balance between the rights of the individual and the common good of the community was addressed. In the very first article, the relationship between the individual and his community was highlighted: "True education is directed towards the formation of the human person in view of his final end and the good of that society to which he [*sic*] belongs and in the duties, as an adult, he will have a share" (Flannery 1998, 727).[3] Furthermore, the skills learned by a child should be employed in pursuit of the common good (727). This overall purpose of a Catholic education – the "formation of individuals who will be good citizens" – had not changed since the time of Augustine (Arthur 2009, 233). The role of educator was also a shared one, including the parents, the state, and the Church (Flannery 1998, 731). The Declaration, in other words, defended the traditional concept of the "Catholic social order" wherein the Church determined the nature of the common good.

Much of the Declaration was also opposed to the "current tendencies" in education that made social progress "the sole yard-stick of the educational system" (Pohlschneider 1969, 15). The Church took a stand against the tendency in which "learning, fact-finding and instruction are all too easily confused with the whole human education" (15).[4] Nine of the twelve articles of the Declaration discuss these tendencies (15). The Declaration also understood education to be focused on the need to "build up religious and moral social structures" as the Church understood them (15–16). The Church's "redemptive mission in the world of education" was highlighted throughout the Declaration as its "dominant leimotif" (18).

Other traditional principles were articulated in the different articles. In the first article, "The Meaning of the Universal Right to an Education," the Church emphasized the need to educate all children no matter their intellectual ability (19), and exhorted those who were "in control of education to make it their care to ensure that young people are never deprived of this sacred right" (Flannery 1998, 727). A student's self-esteem and sense of self-worth was based on being a child of God, not academic achievement. Therefore, the Declaration also stressed academic excellence, that it was possible to educate all students and maintain academically rigorous programs (Pohlschneider 1969, 19). The importance of ensuring the "cultural legacy bequeathed to them by former generations" was highlighted (Flannery 1998, 730). The pursuit of knowledge was also a consistent theme. Indeed the Declaration concludes with an exhortation for educators to "strive so to excel in inspiring their pupils with the spirit of Christ, in their mastery of the art of teaching, and in their zeal for learning that they may not only promote the internal renewal of the Church but also maintain and augment its beneficial presence in the world today and especially in the intellectual sphere" (737).

Another traditional principle of Catholic education was also emphasized: the Church was opposed to any form of state monopoly on education, although in practice it was willing to partner with the state to gain control of the public system, as in the case of Spain under Franco. The danger of too much state control was a major concern at least from the time of Pius VII (1800–23) (Briel 2008, 385). In Article 6, the issue of public funding was addressed. The right of parents to send their children to Catholic schools was asserted, but it also declared that official recognition of this right was insufficient. Sufficient public funding must be provided – otherwise, the Church could not fulfil its mandate to educate all Catholics, including those without the financial means to send their children to private schools. There also should be no "practical administrative measures which makes this right ineffective" (Pohlschneider 1969, 26). The state must not impose a "monopoly of schools" wherein the Catholic schools lacked the freedom to defend and promote Catholic education (Flannery 1998, 731). In his analysis of the Declaration, Johannes Pohlschneider (1969) expresses in no uncertain terms the position of the Church: "There is an uncompromising rejection of any kind of State monopoly of schools. The school legislation of every State must be tested against this principle. This would show that in many States, which boast of democracy, there is in fact a school monopoly, not always extending to the entire system, but covering very large areas" (26–7). If the independence of Catholic schools was hindered by any form of state monopoly, the principles of Catholic education would be very difficult to uphold.

Thus, the Declaration is clear in its articulation of traditional Catholic principles of education. However, according to D. Braithwaite (2012), at the same time it reflected a new understanding of tradition itself that resulted from the Church's grappling with the challenges of modernity (916). With Vatican II, the Church no longer interpreted tradition as changeless and seemed to move beyond what Skinner referred to as the "mythology of doctrines" (Skinner 1969, 10). Tradition was now examined in terms of historical context. In the nineteenth century, Catholic scholars such as Johann Adam Mohler and John Henry Newman had developed the concept of "living tradition" (Braithwaite 2012, 927) that Yves Congar (1964) described as a tradition that "allows a progress that is not simply a repetition of the past" (2). Tradition was understood in terms of the complex relationship between the historical context of dogmatic development and the "continuity intrinsic to tradition" (Braithwaite 2012, 917). Tradition was not simply a "matrix of traditions as teachings and practices to be passed on" (918). The concept of tradition was also connected to a renewed understanding of God's relationship with the world and a "recovery of the personal reality of tradition for the believer" (916). This understanding of tradition is reflected throughout the Vatican II documents, in particular *Dei Verbum.* In contrast to Vatican I, *Dei Verbum* articulates a more "dynamic and interpersonal account of revelation" (918). Vatican II understood revelation as God speaking to human beings as "friends" invited to a relationship with God – a relationship that called for a commitment of one's "whole self" (918).[5] The relationship between scripture and tradition was also viewed differently, not as two separate sources of revelation, but as "intrinsically bound up with each other" (Flannery 1998, 751).

This new understanding of tradition is reflected in the *Declaration on Christian Education.* The Declaration emphasized that this transmission of a living tradition must lead to an "ever-growing understanding of sacred revelation" so that "questions arising from the development of thought be duly solved" (736). Although the fundamental principles articulated in the Declaration represented continuity, the focus was more on the transmission of a living tradition and not on specific content to be learned (Braithwaite 2012, 922). As Braithwaite states, "this statement could be made only in the wake of the dynamic theology of tradition drawn by *Dei Verbum* with which it sits in harmony" (922). Thus, Catholic education was understood as rooted in tradition, but a living tradition, open to the possibility of change in the future.

If the intentionality of the Declaration was clear in terms of traditional Catholic principles in the context of a new understanding of tradition, the same could not be said for the Church's overall approach to modernity even though some critical first steps were taken. One of these steps involved adopting a more positive attitude towards humanity itself as reflected in the constitutions of Vatican II. The Declaration must be read in the context of these constitutions. *Lumen Gentium*, the dogmatic constitution, emphasizes the dignity of the laity and its "exalted duty of working for the ever greater spread of the divine plan of salvation to all men" (Flannery 1998, 391). In Article 14 of *Sacrosanctum Concilium*, the constitution on sacred liturgy, the laity is encouraged to participate more in the liturgy, to assume a more active role worthy of "a chosen race, a royal priesthood, a holy nation, a redeemed people (1 Peter 2:9, 4–5)" (7–8). In *Gaudium Et Spes*, the pastoral constitution, an entire chapter is titled "The Dignity of the Human Person." This positive attitude is in direct contrast to the attitude evident in Pope Pius XI's 1929 encyclical on Christian education, *Divini Illius Magistri*, with its emphasis on sin. For example, Pope Pius XI emphasizes the importance of the traditional and influential Renaissance educator, Cardinal Silvio Antoniano, who stressed humanity's "misery and inclination to sin" (Pius XI 1936, 26). *Gaudium Et Spes* refers to sin but emphasizes redemption, hope, and how the world has "been freed from the slavery of sin by Christ, who was crucified and rose again in order to break the strangle hold of the evil one, so that it might be fashioned anew according to God's design and brought to its fulfilment" (Flannery 1998, 904). In Article 3, this positive attitude is again clear: Christ entered this world to "bear witness to the truth, to save and not to judge, to serve and not to be served." The influence of the Vatican II constitutions, in particular *Gaudium Et Spes*, on the 1965 *Declaration on Christian Education* is evident in its overall positive attitude and its lack of emphasis on the sinful nature of humanity. Indeed in the introduction of the Declaration, an increasing awareness of the "dignity and position" of the human person is emphasized.

Another critical first step was Vatican II's "new attitude of openness to the world," an attitude evident in the Declaration (Pohlschneider 1969, 13). This new attitude was clear from the tone of the Declaration compared with that of Pope Pius XI's 1929 encyclical, which was defensive with a strong emphasis on Church authority.[6] Also noticeable in the Declaration was a more open approach towards modern educational methods compared to the earlier encyclical.[7] This openness was reflected as well in a new concern for Catholics in non-Catholic schools (Pohlschneider 1969, 13). Article 8 on Catholic schools, the "heart" of the Declaration, (29) stated that the Catholic school must be "open ... to the situation of the contemporary world." However, what was meant by openness remained vague. This was due to the tensions between the conservative and progressive forces within the Church, and perhaps an overall uncertainty as to how to adapt to a rapidly changing modern world. Indeed, the term "declaration" was reserved for topics that proved too controversial to be formal decrees (Alberigo 2006, 103). Even one of the principle authors of the Declaration, Father Dezza, stated that it was marked by a "generality" caused by the complexity of the issues (Velati 1995, 230).

The Declaration itself underwent several drafts; in the end, this resulted in a lack of clarity, of intentionality, in terms of openness to the modern world. This is evident from Joseph Ratzinger's comment in 1966 that the Declaration was a weak document. He further commented that "the text wasn't treated by the council fathers with any special affection" (Briel 2008, 389). The bishops were in a difficult predicament. The illocutionary force of the Declaration in terms of modernity was unclear, and this created major difficulties "for the development of a coherent approach to education in the period immediately following the council" (Briel 2008, 384). The bishops were therefore in the position of defending and promoting traditional Catholic principles of education, but without any clear direction as to how to be "open" to the modern world. This fundamental weakness of the Declaration almost resulted in its rejection by the bishops – a fate avoided for two reasons: the obvious need to address the problems of education, and the decision to address these problems in the future (Velati 1995, 229–30). Thus it is stated in the introduction of the Declaration: "Accordingly the sacred Synod hereby promulgates some fundamental principles of Christian education, especially in regard to schools. These principles should be more fully developed by a special postconciliar commission and should be adapted to different local circumstances by episcopal conferences" (Flannery 1998, 726). The Declaration was a call for action, urging the universal Church to defend and promote these fundamental traditional principles, and later to clarify and develop them further in the context of an increasingly secular world (Briel 2008, 392).[8]

The Process of Secularization

It was this secularized, modern world that formed one of the difficult conditions of reception for the Declaration.[9] A complex configuration of various factors led to the dramatic cultural changes of the late 1950s and 1960s. Two major developments shaped the postwar period: unprecedented prosperity and a dramatic rise in the fertility rate,[10] both of which were connected to the eventual cultural changes. Both industrialization and urbanization accelerated after the Second World War because of the continued prosperity (Gidney 1999, 25–6).[11] Also central to this configuration was the consequent dramatic increase in the number of children. Their parents, who had suffered much during the Depression and the war, made them the centre of their lives in their search for a normal and stable life. Society itself became child-centred "to an unparalleled degree." These children grew up convinced that "society was designed" for them (Owram 1997, 135).

Young people were also conditioned to be wary of authoritarianism in all its forms. When the Civil Rights Movement gathered steam in the mid-1950s, youth were more inclined to be critical of their own society and government, especially after the assassination of John F. Kennedy in 1963. Taught to be critical of authority (Owram 1997, 126–7), they also viewed international crises differently from their parents, who tended to be loyal to the state against the communist threat posed by the Cold War. A "crisis of authority" marked the 1960s. Young people questioned the "received wisdom" of the adult world, of the "Establishment" (Owram 1997, 184), and the result was youth radicalism, the sexual revolution, and a proliferation of protest movements as the dominant social conservative mores and the institution of marriage itself were challenged as never before.

The bishops were well aware that Catholics were becoming more secular in their behaviour. For Catholics in the 1960s, the cultural changes had generated considerable confusion and indecision in terms of moral values. Within the Church itself a vigorous debate ensued between conservative and progressive forces over the degree to which the Church should adapt to secularization and over the essential nature of the Vatican Council reforms. Considerable confusion existed regarding what the reforms actually meant (Cuplinskas 2011, 18–19). The Church was one of the "established" institutions experiencing a "crisis of authority." Young people were challenging the "received wisdom" of the Church. Indeed, the Church was experiencing a crisis that was universal in scope as organized religion came under siege throughout the world.[12] Many religious began to question their vocation, resulting in a large exodus of priests and nuns from a fundamentally conservative Church (Cuplinskas 2011, 36). Such was the societal context of the *Declaration on Christian Education* – a challenging and difficult condition of reception for the defence and promotion of fundamentally traditional Catholic principles of education.

The Educational State of Ontario

The other major condition of reception was the nature of the educational state of Ontario. Catholics had been granted their own separate school system, but it fell under the direct supervision of the provincial Department of Education. Catholic schools were not entirely "separate." Catholic schools were to be tolerated at best, and Catholics were forced to fight for their educational rights. This was in direct contrast to the school system established for the Protestant minority in Quebec, where there was a parallel system that granted them "carte blanche" to organize and operate their own schools. Quebec Protestants were provided with "considerable resources," which they were permitted to use as they so desired. Indeed, it has been argued that the educational system in Quebec was "a model of freedom from political interference and of respect for the rights of parents and minorities" (Henchey 1972, 100). The Catholics of Ontario were denied such a model.

An excellent illustration of how Ontario Catholics lacked the freedom and resources they needed to maintain a vibrant school system accessible to all Catholics involved public funding for Catholic schools. Catholic schools were denied the same level of funding that the public school system received, even though both school systems were publicly funded (Brennan 2011, 22).[13] No funding was granted for separate senior high schools, and funding for grades nine and ten was much lower than for public high schools (Gidney 1999, 16). In 1960, when the federal government passed the Technical and Vocational Training Assistant Act in order to assist the provincial governments financially to build more vocational facilities, the Catholic schools did not receive any of these funds (Gidney 1999, 44). Nor did the Catholic schools receive any share of corporate taxes – a situation the government refused to change for fear of a public outcry (Gidney 1999, 18). In the 1960s, even after the government increased the grants they received, Catholic schools remained underfunded, viewed as a "second class" school system. Many Catholic families could not afford the tuition for senior high school, or they wanted their children to benefit from the better facilities in the public schools, so they did not send their children to Catholic schools. Furthermore, it was difficult to hire the best teachers, since the public school system was able to offer higher wages.[14] This type of "state monopoly," which the Declaration denounced, was a major condition of reception as the bishops attempted to defend and promote the principles of Catholic education.

The bishops' inability to influence the Ministry of Education is plain to see in the government's response to their October 1962 brief on Catholic education, presented to the government two weeks after the launch of Vatican II. In this brief, the bishops broached the major concerns that would later be articulated in the *Declaration on Christian Education*. Referring to the existing legislation governing Catholic schools as a "legislative strait-jacket" (Catholic Bishops of Ontario 1962, 31), the bishops asked for more control over curriculum development for Catholic schools: "We respectfully submit to the authorities of the Government that we feel that we require greater freedom of action in framing of the curriculum which is used in the separate public schools and greater possibilities of consultation and contribution in this matter" (34). The bishops also called for more control over teacher training, and criticized the teachers' colleges: "We cannot be satisfied with the training of Catholic teachers as presently attempted ... We are not interested, as such, in a simple course in Theology in the Teachers" Colleges. This is essential but it does not even constitute a necessary minimum' (35). The bishops also raised the possibility of establishing a "number of Catholic Teachers' Colleges," although they do not take a definite position on the issue, preferring to wait to "discuss the whole issue with the educational authorities of the Province" (35). The bishops did, however, insist that Catholic teachers were not being prepared properly "to teach according to Catholic principles," and they did not "feel that teachers should go into our Catholic classrooms without some knowledge of the philosophy of Catholic education" (35).

An entire section of the brief addressed the lack of sufficient funding for Catholic schools. The bishops were requesting not only an improvement in the existing funding for grades one to ten but also an extension of that funding to include senior high school (37–8). To allay any fears that an emphasis on religious education would somehow jeopardize the traditional academic excellence of Catholic schools,[15] the bishops were adamant that this would not be allowed to happen and that high standards would upheld in the context of a Catholic educational philosophy: "We seek for our children the highest possible intellectual development, but in an atmosphere in which that intellectual development is properly understood in the framework of their total destiny" (33). Later in the brief, they were even more emphatic: "No academic inferiority is tolerable in our schools" (37). According to the bishops, the greatest threat to academic excellence was not an emphasis on religious education, but the lack of funding that made it difficult to hire teachers and to provide modern facilities such as science labs. Here the bishops were adamant: "We maintain that we have achieved a high degree of excellence ... but we have serious and legitimate concern for the future. If any such weakening should take place it must be laid at the door of those responsible and certainly not be attributed to any acceptance of academic inferiority on our part" (37).[16]

Despite their efforts, the bishops failed to persuade the government. No Catholic teachers' colleges were established. Existing teachers' colleges would not offer any form of intensive training for Catholic teacher candidates in terms of Catholic educational philosophy and principles beyond a single course – not even the bare minimum requested by the bishops. Some funding improvements were introduced, but public funding was not extended to senior high school.[17] Nor did the bishops gain more control over curriculum development. The educational state of Ontario remained largely unresponsive. This would change in some dramatic ways in the 1960s, but without any meaningful input from the bishops, who remained quite powerless in the face of the emerging cultural changes and the resulting educational reforms. This was one of the most important conditions of reception for the *Declaration on Christian Education* – an educational state unprepared to allow the bishops any meaningful control over Catholic schools.[18]

This condition of reception did not fundamentally change when the Ministry of Education altered the power structure of the educational system by granting more powers to the school boards. The first step in this process was to consolidate the boards, many of which were so small that they did not have the tax base they needed to support the new powers they were to receive (Gidney 1999, 49). Overall, the number of Catholic school boards decreased from 500 in 1967 to 40 by 1970 (Dufferin–Peel Catholic District School Board 2009, 2). At the same time, the government transferred its supervisory powers to the boards, dismantling the system of province-wide school inspectors in 1968 (50). From now on, the boards would supervise schools' operations and evaluate teacher performance. For the first time since the mid-nineteenth century, the ministry no longer had direct contact with local schools. Board officials were now responsible for explaining and implementing ministry rules and regulations. Also, leadership in curriculum development was now vested in the boards, which were to supervise the development of courses of study. Even so, the ministry remained powerful. For example, it retained the power to establish the overall curriculum guidelines, to hire superintendents and directors, to determine funding policy, and to pass any education laws it believed necessary, including changing the powers of the boards themselves (Gidney 1999, 51). The educational state had changed considerably with the devolution of power to the school boards. Thus the bishops now had to operate within a more complex power structure. This meant dealing not only with a still powerful Ministry of Education, but also with forty separate school boards responsible for curriculum development and for maintaining the Catholic culture of their schools.

Perhaps this devolution of power should have improved the conditions of reception for the Declaration; after all, Catholics now controlled these boards and could protect Catholic education and the Catholic character of the schools. But this was not the case: there had been a significant power shift. Historically, the bishops and the boards had shared power, and even though the bishop had no legal right to intervene in board decisions, his influence was often substantial since school boards depended on religious teaching orders and parish funds to run their schools (Walker 1986, 137–8). This situation changed with the laicization of the teaching profession and with larger boards (132). The boards were now the undisputed leaders of Catholic schools. For example, in 1968 the former chair of the Toronto Metropolitan Separate School Board reiterated the commonly held view that the pastor "has the official status of visitor to the school. Actual authority is vested in the Principal and in the Separate School Board" (Walker 1986, 132). Many individuals within the Church hierarchy supported this power shift because of Vatican II's new emphasis on the important role of the laity. For example, Cardinal James C. McGuigan demonstrated his support, advising a priest to "stay away from their problems" and to "create good relations whereby you can enter the school to teach catechism and nothing else" (Walker 1986, 132–3).

The boards were also overwhelmed by many demands, such as to expand their services and build new schools. For example, student enrolment in the Metropolitan Separate School Board (Toronto) increased

431 per cent between 1951 and 1971 (Brown 1993, 276). In 1968, new and larger Catholic school boards were created such as the Dufferin–Peel Separate School Board, an amalgamation of eight smaller boards (Dufferin-Peel Catholic District School Board 2009, 2). One word aptly describes this period of expansion: scrambling (Gidney 1999, 37). School boards were scrambling to organize themselves, to build new schools, to hire more teachers, and to implement new curriculum. The promotion of the traditional principles of Catholic education was only one of many priorities.

Moreover, the increasing secularization of society, including the religious crisis of the 1960s, could not but affect Catholic school boards, their administrators, and the Catholic public they represented. The boards became more secular as the society became more secular.[19] In a fascinating study, "Comparing Religious Education in Canadian and Australian Catholic High Schools: Identifying Some Key Structural Issues," Richard Rymarz draws attention to the difficult predicament facing bishops, not only in Ontario but across Canada, with regard to the power of school boards. He argues that where the bishops play a more direct role in the schools, religious education is more of a priority. School boards, by contrast, with their secular administrators, are less likely to focus on the quality of religious education. In Ontario, for example, if a local bishop wants to implement a certain initiative, he must contact a superintendent, who may or may not agree to its implementation. In Australia, a central organization exists – the Catholic Education Office (the CEO), in which the bishops yield considerable influence. Unlike in Ontario, where public money is given directly to the school boards, in Australia the CEO controls these funds. This central organization also oversees the schools, developing curriculum, providing resources, monitoring religious education, and maintaining academic standards (Rymarz 2011, 183). In the educational state of Ontario, the bishops have never enjoyed this sort of independence and influence.

Further evidence of the bishops' difficult predicament involves the major curriculum reforms of the 1960s, particularly with regard to secondary education, as well as the need to address the new Vatican II understanding of tradition. It is important here to note that the Catholic educational community supported many of these reforms that led to a more "child-centred" educational system. Most Catholic educators agreed with the progressive educational philosophy reflected in the 1968 Hall–Dennis Report, which was highly critical of the existing system and condemned the "outdated curriculum," the "regimental organization," and the "mistaken aims of education" (Hall and Dennis 1968, 9). Many Catholic educators advocated for a pedagogy that relied less on rote memory, that emphasized inquiry, and that recognized the different academic needs of students. For example, as early as 1957, Professor Lawrence Lynch – president of the English Catholic Education Association of Ontario – was criticizing Catholic schools for their "moralistic interpretation of the truth" and appealing to teachers to arouse "a restless ... intellectual curiosity" (Walker 1986, 205).

Such thinking also reflected Vatican II's new understanding of the tradition and the need to ensure the transmission of this tradition to the next generation. Tradition no longer meant simply the transmission of changeless doctrinal precepts. Catholic educators recognized the need to modernize both the pedagogy and the resources used in schools. For instance, the textbook *Bible History*, first published in 1881, was still being used in some Ontario grade nine classes in the late 1950s. It covered the entire history of the Bible, and memory recall questions were provided on every page. *Our Quest for Happiness*, a series of textbooks used throughout North America, also reflected the pre–Vatican II approach, especially with its unquestioning approach to doctrine and to the historical accuracy of the New Testament. In those books, the Gospels were understood as "biographies" of Jesus whose authors were secretaries of the Apostles: "St Mark was St Peter's secretary and simply wrote down what St Peter preached. This is Peter's Gospel" (Elwell 1951, 492). For post–Vatican II high school classrooms, textbooks like these were no longer suitable.

But unlike at the elementary level, where the Canadian Conference of Bishops sponsored a new catechetical series, "Come to the Father," which incorporated both the "major insights of curriculum theorists" (Hurley 1997, 4) and the new Vatican II understanding of tradition and revelation, no such series was developed for the secondary level. According to Brother Domenic Viggiani, president of the Toronto private Catholic school, De La Salle, individual religion departments in each school often developed their own curriculum using whatever resources they were able to find.[20] In some cases the religious order responsible for the private school determined the curriculum and selected the textbooks.[21] In Ontario and elsewhere, religious education entered a period of experimentation with efforts to make religion more relevant to young people, resulting in a considerable amount of confusion for teachers (Rossiter 1988, 264). The situation was further complicated by the "religious crisis" of the 1960s, during which the religious teaching orders grew more preoccupied with their own declining numbers and declining morale than with defending the principles of Catholic education articulated in the Declaration and implementing a post-Vatican II curriculum.[22]

Conclusion

This chapter has focused on two questions: What were the conditions of reception for the *Declaration on Christian Education* in province of Ontario? And why did these conditions make it extremely difficult for the bishops to defend and promote the fundamental principles articulated in the Declaration? Relying on Quentin Skinner's theoretical framework, the Declaration itself was analysed. Its illocutionary force was clear in terms of the articulated fundamental principles of education, but the Declaration also reflected a new understanding of tradition as a "living tradition." Tradition was no longer understood as changeless; rather, it was a dynamic process involving both continuity and change. In terms of a new openness to the modern world, however, the illocutionary force of the Declaration was unclear, and this made its reception all the more problematic, especially given the conditions of reception that existed.

A key condition of reception was the dramatic cultural changes of the late 1950s and 1960s. A "crisis of authority" existed. Institutional authority, including that of the Church, found itself under challenge. Society was becoming more secular – a process that also affected the Church and its schools. All the while, the bishops had to contend with the reforms of Vatican II, which were a source of division and confusion within the Church.

The other key condition of reception was the educational state of Ontario, in which the bishops possessed little political power. When the ministry granted more powers to school boards, this rendered the bishops' position even more difficult since they now had to deal with both a powerful ministry and powerful Catholic school boards that were responsible for curriculum development and school organization. Confusion also existed in Catholic schools in terms of religious education, especially at the secondary level, where no clear curriculum policy was adopted after pre-Vatican II pedagogy and texts were abandoned. It was very difficult for the bishops to defend and promote the fundamental principles of education articulated in the Declaration in a school system over which they had limited influence. The authors of the *Declaration on Christian Education* were aware of the difficult conditions of reception that existed, not only in Ontario but worldwide, and thus the Declaration itself became a rallying cry for a concerted effort not only to defend and promote Catholic educational principles, but also to clarify them and adapt them to a changing, secular world.

NOTES

I would like to thank my PhD supervisor, Dr Rosa Bruno-Jofré, for her constant support and guidance in the completion of this chapter.

1 For a detailed analysis of reception theory, see Martyn P. Thompson, "Reception Theory and Interpretation of Historical Meaning," *History and Theory* 32(4) (1993): 248–72.
2 Egerton Ryerson, the first chief superintendent of education in Upper Canada, who held this position from 1846 to 1876, was adamant that the curriculum indoctrinate the youth with Protestant values, leading them away from the "evils of Catholicism" (Brennan 2011, 22).
3 Pope Paul VI, *The Declaration on Christian Education (Gravissimum Educationis)*, Article 1. Hereafter, this document will be referred to as the Declaration.
4 It is beyond the scope of this chapter to discuss in detail the educational philosophy of what is meant by the "whole child," except to note that the Church naturally considered the spiritual development of the child as of the utmost importance and that the principles discussed here reflect this philosophy.
5 Pope Paul VI, *Dogmatic Constitution on Divine Revelation (Dei Verbum)*, Article 5.
6 Pius XI, *Divini Illius Magistri*, 1929, Articles 16 to 20.
7 *Divini Illius Magistri*, Articles 5, 6, and 60–5. The "dangers" of naturalism in education are emphasized.
8 This call for action was not only for the bishops but also for the Sacred Congregation for Catholic Education and the laity. The congregation responded to this call by elaborating further on these principles in three documents: "The Catholic School" (1977), "Lay Catholics in Schools: Witnesses to Faith" (1982), and "The Religious Dimensions of Education in a Catholic School" (1988).
9 The term "secular" is contentious. According to James Arthur, it is "wisely contested because it is a socially and historically constructed word." In this chapter, secularization is defined as a process that "has weakened traditional religious faith, affiliations and practices along with insisting upon a stronger distinction/separation between religion and education" (Arthur 2013, 89).
10 The fertility rate in 1936 was 2.2 children. By 1961, there were nearly 4 children for each woman of childbearing years (Gidney 1999, 26–7).

11 Young families moved to the suburbs that were developing around the major cities. By 1961, almost 80 per cent of the population lived in urbanized areas – a massive increase over the postwar period.

12 For an in-depth examination of this religious crisis, see Hugh McLeod, *The Religious Crisis of the 1960s* (Oxford: Oxford University Press, 2008).

13 Some improvements in public funding were achieved over the years. In 1863, the Scott Act confirmed that Catholic school trustees had the right to an official share of governmental subsidies through the Common School Fund. In 1867, these rights were enshrined in Section 93 of the British North America Act.

14 This became a major problem in the 1950s and 1960s when the number of schools increased dramatically beyond the capacity of religious orders to provide teachers. Lay teachers, always present in Catholic schools, had become the norm by the late 1950s.

15 In 1946 the Grey Sisters of the Immaculate Conception proudly announced that the inspectors "consistently commended the high standards of teaching and the splendid school spirit maintained by the staff and pupils" (*Pamphlet* 23). More research is needed here to verify this statement. However, it does seem that Catholic schools were considered to have high academic standards.

16 Pre-Vatican II Catholic schools emphasized technical excellence, the mastery of specific skills and content measured by standardized tests, and "socializing students into forms of language and thought in relation to practices and standards" of a particular intellectual or scholarly discipline (Bruno-Jofré and Hills 2011, 338).

17 The government increased the amount of funding that Catholic schools received from grants, but fearing an outcry from the public schools, and therefore the public, did not change the corporate taxes.

18 Regarding the conditions of reception, also revealing is the reaction to the bishops' brief from the secular press. J. Bascom St John, a prominent journalist with *The Globe and Mail*, wrote a popular and influential daily column, "The World of Learning." On 1 January 1963 he published a detailed report on the bishops' brief in which he opposed the bishops' requests (St John 1963, 28).

19 J. Arthur refers to this process as "internal secularisation," whereby Catholic schools conform to "secular models of curriculum" devoid of Catholic values. The overwhelming influence of secular culture has also led to the "secularisation of consciousness," resulting in the unconscious adoption of secular values (Arthur 2009, 238; 2013, 95). This internal secularization has also occurred in American Catholic schools (Smith 2005, 214–16).

20 Interview with Brother Viggiani, 12 February 2015.
21 Ibid. According to Brother Viggiani, the period from 1968 to 1980 was one of confusion.
22 See ch. 9 in this volume by Rosa Bruno-Jofré, "The Sisters of Our Lady of the Missions (RNDM) in Canada."

REFERENCES

Alberigo, Giuseppe. 2006. *A Brief History of Vatican II.* Maryknoll: Orbis.

Arthur, James. 2009. "Secularisation, Secularism, and Catholic Education: Understanding The Challenges." *International Studies in Catholic Education* 1(2): 228–39. http://dx.doi.org/10.1080/19422530903138226.

– 2013. "The De-Catholicising of the Curriculum in English Catholic Schools." *International Studies in Catholic Education* 5(1): 83–98. http://dx.doi.org/10.1080/19422539.2012.754590.

Braithwaite, David SJ. 2012. "Vatican II on Tradition." *Heythrop Journal* 53(6): 915–28. http://dx.doi.org/10.1111/j.1468-2265.2012.00747.x.

Brennan, Terri-Lynn Kay. 2011. "Roman Catholic Schooling in Ontario: Past Struggles, Present Challenges, Future Direction?" *Canadian Journal of Education* 34(4): 22–33.

Briel, Don J. 2008. "The *Declaration on Christian Education, Gravissimum Educationis.*" In *Vatican II: Renewal within Tradition,* edited by Matthew L. Lamb and Matthew Leverin. Oxford: Oxford University Press. 383–97.

Brown, James. 1993. "The Formation of the Metropolitan Separate School Board (Toronto), 1953–1978." In *Catholics at the Gathering Place,* edited by Mark McGowan and Brian P. Clarke, 275–97. Toronto: Canadian Catholic Historical Association.

Bruno-Jofré, Rosa, and George Skip Hills. 2011. "Changing Visions of Excellence in Ontario School Policy: The Cases of *Living and Learning* and *For the Love of Learning.*" *Educational Theory* 61(3): 335–49. http://dx.doi.org/10.1111/j.1741-5446.2011.00407.x.

Catholic Bishops of Ontario. 1962. *Brief on Education.*

Congar, Yves. 1964. *The Meaning of Tradition.* New York: Hawthorn.

Cuplinskas, Indre. 2011. "Reporting the Revolution: The Western Catholic Reporter and Post-Vatican II Reform." In *Vatican II: Canadian Experiences,* edited by Michael Attridge, Catherine E. Clifford, and Gilles Routhier, 18–39. Ottawa: University of Ottawa.

Dufferin–Peel Catholic District School Board. 2009. *A Handbook for Catholic School Councils.* Revised.

Elwell, Clarence. 1951. *Our Quest for Happiness, Book One, Our Goal and Our Guides.* Chicago: Mentzer, Bush, and Company.

Flannery, Austin. 1998. *Vatican Council II: The Conciliar and Post Conciliar Documents.* New York: Costello Publishing.

Gidney, R.D. 1999. *From Hope to Harris: The Reshaping of Ontario Schools.* Toronto: University of Toronto Press.

Hall, Emmett M., and L.A. Dennis. 1968. *Living and Learning: The Report of the Provincial Committee on Aims and Objectives of Education in the Schools of Ontario.* Toronto: Province of Ontario.

Henchey, Norman. 1972. "Quebec Education: The Unfinished Revolution." *McGill Journal of Education* 7(2): 95–118. http://mje.mcgill.ca/article/view/6874.

Hurley, Robert J. 1997. *Hermeneutics and Catechesis: Biblical Interpretation in the Come to the Father Catechetical Series.* Lanham: University Press of America.

Owram, Doug. 1997. *Born at the Right Time: A History of the Baby Boom Generation.* Toronto: University of Toronto Press.

Pius, XI. 1936. *Divini Illius Magistri.* Washington DC: National Catholic Welfare Conference.

Pohlschneider, Johannes. 1969. "Declaration on Christian Education." In *Commentary on the Documents of Vatican II,* edited by Herbert Vorgrimler, 1–48. Montreal: Palm Publishers.

Rossiter, Graham M. 1988. "Perspectives on Change in Catholic Religious Education since the Second Vatican Council." *Religious Education* 83(2): 264–76. http://dx.doi.org/10.1080/0034408880830211.

Rymarz, Richard. 2011 (9 November). "Comparing Religious Education in Canadian and Australian Catholic High Schools: Identifying Some Key Structural Issues." *British Journal of Religious Education* 35(2): 175–87. http://dx.doi.org/10.1080/01416200.2011.628203.

Skinner, Quentin. 1969. "Meaning and Understanding in the History of Ideas." *History and Theory* 8(1): 3–53. http://dx.doi.org/10.2307/2504188.

Smith, Christian. 2005. *Soul Searching: The Religious and Spiritual Lives of American Teenagers.* New York: Oxford University Press. http://dx.doi.org/10.1093/019518095X.001.0001.

St John, Bascom J. 1963. "Separate Schools in Ontario." *Globe and Mail,* 1 January. <page?>

Velati, Mauro. 1995. "Completing the Conciliar Agenda." In *History of Vatican II,* vol. V, edited by Giuseppe Alberigo, 185–273. Maryknoll: Orbis.

Walker, Franklin A. 1986. *Catholic Education and Politics in Ontario,* vol. 3. Toronto: Catholic Education Foundation of Ontario.

11 Catholic Elite Education in Chile: Worlds Apart

CRISTIÁN COX AND PATRICIA IMBARACK

Introduction

Latin America is a region with some of the greatest economic and social inequality in the world. At the same time, its cultural identity is inseparable from the Catholicism that has permeated its culture since the Conquest. This historical and cultural conjunction brings deep questions about the Church and its educational institutions, as well as efforts to understand them, which can be said to have started with Max Weber's classic *The Protestant Ethic and the Spirit of Capitalism*. There is great tension between, on one hand, the doctrinal bases of a faith founded on values of fraternity and communion among brothers, and on the other hand, socio-economic structures that the Catholic Church, since Vatican II, and especially through documents of the Latin American Episcopate – from Medellín (1968) to Aparecida (2007) – condemns as a social sin. Vatican II heightened this tension, in particular for the religious orders running elite educational institutions throughout Latin America and also in other parts of the developing world (Smith 1982), affecting their educational mission in ways this chapter will analyse, using as an example the experience of Chile.

With regard to this socio-cultural backdrop, we intend to examine how different schools – that have historically served the Chilean elites[1] – address in their mission statements the socio-economic inequalities and marked patterns of social segmentation present in Chilean society; how they thematize dialogue between faith and culture; and how they conceive of, or do not refer to, preparation for political life. We will compare the mission statements with regard to these three dimensions of social formation, examining how the various educational projects relate to the teachings of Vatican II and Conferences of the Latin American Episcopate.

First, the chapter provides a very broad description of the distinctive characteristics of the congregations from which the educational projects will be compared. This is followed by a stylized description (selection of key quotations from official documents) of key features of Second Vatican Council and Latin American Episcopate Conference orientations, in relation to three selected analytical dimensions: social inequality, politics, and faith and culture. A third section compares definitions of the current educational projects of these congregations in Chile, identifying their distinctive features and their relation to the Church magisterium documents. A very brief concluding section questions the silences revealed in the mission statements of the examined institutions.

Catholic Religious Orders and the Impact of Vatican II on Elite Education in Chile

In Chile, as well as in the rest of Latin America, the first schools were linked to the religious orders that arrived on the continent in the wake of the Conquest. Mercedarians, Dominicans, Franciscans, and Jesuits arrived and established schools at the end of the sixteenth century. The first Jesuits arrived in 1593 and immediately started a dual-purpose educational mission, one that also characterized the work of other congregations: the education of Spanish and Creole elites, and that of the indigenous population. The Jesuits were expelled by the Spanish Crown in 1767, but restarted their activities in Chile in 1856, at a time of significant influx of new religious orders coming from Europe to set up schools for the education of the new nation's elites (Chile ended its wars of independence from the Spanish Crown in 1818). These new religious orders included the Sacred Heart Nuns (1830s), the Sacred Heart Fathers (1850s), the Sisters of the Divine Providence (1853), the Don Bosco Salesians (1880s), and the Divine Word Missionaries (1900), among others. Thus, Spanish, French, German, and Italian religious orders competed to educate the country's elites, many of whom were immigrants from these same countries. As we will see, North American influence in Chilean Catholic education began in the 1940s (Aedo-Richmond 2000; Martínez and Silva 1971; Serrano, 2000).

From the perspective of this chapter and its questions about the current educational work of religious congregations with contrasting missions, the key historical event, loaded with implications for the relationships of the

Catholic Church with the country's elites, consists of the post-Vatican II and especially post-Medellín changes made by the religious orders that sustained the traditional schools with the greatest influence among the elites at the time:[2] Colegio San Ignacio (Jesuits), St George's (Holy Cross Fathers), and Sagrados Corazones (Sacred Heart Fathers).[3] The changes involved two directions, and both were traumatic to the groups that were traditionally educated at such institutions. The first was the democratization of enrolment, which had been explicitly requested by the Conference of Bishops at Medellín,[4] through various strategies that sought to improve the diversity of the student body. This was accomplished, for example, by the North American Holy Cross Fathers giving scholarships to working-class students at their St George's School, as well as by the Jesuits offering differentiated fees and also scholarships for students at their San Ignacio schools.[5] The second change, in which several female religious orders also played a role, involved congregations deciding in favour of focusing on pastoral activities in poor and marginalized areas, which also meant subordinating or abandoning their educational mission with the elites.[6] The combination of these new orientations – which each congregation carried out in ways inspired by their interpretation of Vatican II and Medellín[7] – along with the political and socio-cultural turmoil of the "Chilean way to socialism" launched under President Allende, reached a climax with the initiative to hand some schools over to the government, as was attempted by the Society of Jesus and the Sacred Heart congregations in 1971. According to Princeton University's historian and political scientist Brian Smith,

> The Sacred Heart Fathers and the Jesuits announced in early 1971 that they planned to turn over some of their private schools to the government so as to reorient them more toward service to the poor. The U.S.-based Congregation of the Holy Cross kept its one school (St George's in Santiago) but raised tuition for rich students so as to give more scholarships to those from working class areas. (Smith 1982, 187)[8]

The initiative did not prosper,[9] and after the military coup of 1973 the Jesuits continued and later expanded their activities in the field of education; the Fathers of the Sacred Heart (Sagrados Corazones) Congregation, for their part, did not return to run the schools they had sustained for more than a century, instead transferring them to the Diocesan Church of Santiago.

The initial response to these events by part of the Catholic elite was to move their sons and daughters to newly set up schools operated by Opus

Dei. A decade later, in another socio-political setting (not threatened by a socialist revolution, but corresponding instead to the triumph of Pinochet's neoliberal revolution in economics and authoritarian rule in politics and culture), they moved their children to schools founded by the newly arrived (during the 1980s) Legionnaires of Christ, a religious movement of recent Mexican origin.

It has been more than four decades since these events, but the processes had such a profound impact on how the elites of the country pursued Catholic education that the division continues to the present day. To examine these processes, we ask: What are the principles and formative criteria declared in the educational mission statements of key congregations, two on each side of the divide established in the 1970s? On the one hand, there are the educational projects of two religious congregations with century-old origins, the Society of Jesus and the Order of the Holy Cross, and on the other hand, two contemporary religious movements, Opus Dei and the Legionnaires of Christ. As mentioned, we are interested in the relationship between declared educational purposes and the magisterium of the Church regarding poverty, injustice, inter-cultural dialogue, and politics.

To begin, we will briefly refer to the origins of the four congregations,[10] as well as to some basic features of their presence in Chilean education today, to provide some context to the interpretation of their educational projects and how they relate to the Church's magisterium.

Society of Jesus

The Society of Jesus was founded in 1540 by Saint Ignatius of Loyola and a group of students at the University of Paris. Its origins are viewed as one of the Catholic Church's answers to the schism of Protestant Reform. God, the human person, and creation are the three fundamental pillars of Ignatian experience. Ignatius defined a need for strong and prolonged preparation for an embracing of creation by "contemplatives in action," and the missionary zeal of the Society soon became central to its preference for work at the frontiers, both material and symbolic. The Jesuits became the leading order in the education of European Catholic elites for almost three centuries, with their curriculum, the *Ratio Studiorum*, becoming notorious for its conjunction between classical culture and Catholic doctrines (Durkheim 1977). Characterized by the intellectual weight of their preparation, Jesuits give much importance to constant socio-cultural analysis in order to have the necessary tools to enlighten and substantiate their work, with great relevance given to interdisciplinary and inter-cultural dialogue.

At present, the Jesuits in Chile, together with the two traditional San Ignacio schools in the capital, directly run eight schools from the north to the south of the country, as well as a network of associated Ignatian Schools (Red Educacional Ignaciana). Their mission is to "offer comprehensive quality education for boys, girls, youth, and adults, through educational communities that experience the society based on fairness and solidarity that we aspire to build, that contribute to improving national education, and collaborate with the evangelizing mission of the Church."[11]

Holy Cross

The Congregation of the Holy Cross was founded by Blessed Basilio Moreau on 1 March 1837 in Sainte-Croix, on the outskirts of Le Mans, France. Early on, the congregation focused on primary, secondary, and university education, becoming a missionary congregation of educators. The Congregation of the Holy Cross celebrates diversity as wealth, viewing differences as a gift for service.

Its history began with a group of missionary priests sent to the United States; they settled in Indiana, where they founded what was to become the largest Catholic university in that country, Notre Dame. The priests who came to Chile in 1943 to take charge of St George's College[12] came from the congregation's group in New Orleans, Louisiana (St George's College 2017). The spirit of service and the pluralist and pragmatic disposition of the Holy Cross priests quickly had an impact, and by the 1950s the school had 1,100 students.

In the 1970s the school became co-educational and the community acutely experienced the socio-political conflicts of the time. According to their own records: "The St. George's educational community sought to respond to the sign of the times and the teachings of the document on education by the Latin American Episcopal Conference held in Medellín" (St George's College 2003). "Some families," however, "did not share the educational plan of the school and withdrew their children. In 1973, several educational institutions were intervened by the Military Government, among these, Saint George's College" (ibid.).

After three years of military intervention, during which the school no longer belonged to the Church, the government handed it back to the Archbishopric of Santiago, which ran it for six years. The Congregation of the Holy Cross recovered the institution in 1987.

Opus Dei

Opus Dei was founded in 1928 by Spanish priest (now Saint) Jose María Escrivá de Balaguer, while he was carrying out spiritual work in Madrid. On 16 June 1950, Pope Pius XII granted definitive approval of Opus Dei, which allows married people to join the organization and secular clergy to be admitted to the Priestly Society of the Holy Cross.

Since its initial decade, Opus Dei's focus has been on encountering Christ through work, family life, and in all other day-to-day activities. Its evangelizing mission promotes and encourages a life coherent with the faith in all circumstances, and above all through the sanctification of work: "work well done conducts to God" (Colegio Tabancura 2017).

In Chile, the first Opus Dei priest, Adolfo Rodríguez, arrived in 1950, and the first schools were opened in 1969 and 1970.[13] They received immediate support and expanded quickly and substantially in terms of enrolment and influence. This was a direct result of the above-mentioned 1970s crisis in elite group relationships with traditional Catholic schools, which at the time were moving towards the democratization and pro-equity orientations promoted by Vatican II, and especially by the Medellín Conference of Latin American Bishops in 1968.

In the 1980s, Opus Dei founded the Universidad de Los Andes; then in the 1990s, it established the Nocedal and Almendral technical/vocational schools in disadvantaged areas of Santiago. It is through these initiatives that they began to offer education at both ends of the income, power, and status spectrum of Chilean society.

Legionnaires of Christ

The Legionnaires movement began in January 1941 when Mexican priest Marcial Maciel founded the Legion of Christ in Mexico City.[14] His main interest was in developing Catholic leaders. In Chile, the congregation arrived in 1981, when the then Archbishop of Santiago, Cardinal Raúl Silva, asked the Legionnaires of Christ to direct the Instituto Zambrano, a traditional Catholic school serving working-class groups in the central area of the city. A few years later, on 10 March 1986, the Legionnaires founded a school for the elite, Colegio Cumbres, under the leadership of two consecrated Regnum Christi devotees (the lay branch of the Legionnaires).

The Legionnaires acquired the Finis Terrae University in 1988 and expanded their educational work in the school system, founding the

Table 11.1 Four congregations and their schools in Chile, 2014

Congregation	Year of arrival in Chile	Total # of schools	Lower- & middle-income schools	Elite schools	Total enrolment
Society of Jesus	1593	10	5	5	10,465
Holy Cross	1943	2	1	1	3,694
Opus Dei	1950	9	2	7	6,853
Legionnaires	1981	5		5	7, 299

Source: authors, based on Ministry of Education, http://www.mime.mineduc.cl/mvc/mime/portada, as well as data collected directly from the congregations.

elite-serving Cumbres, Everest, and Highlands schools in Santiago, as well as the schools San Isidro and La Cruz outside the capital.[15]

As shown in Table 11.1, in terms of the number of schools and the enrolment of the four congregations, Legionnaires of Christ is the only one that does not have schools serving lower- or middle-income groups.

Mission: Magisterium Definitions

It is a task far beyond the scope of this chapter to account for the magisterium of the Church with regard to the three dimensions through which we wish to compare the four congregations' educational projects. Instead, we attempt in this section to show the broad features of the normative horizon established therein with regard to social inequality and injustice, politics, and the dialogue between faith and culture, which supposedly informs the educational projects in the Chilean case.

Vatican II

Vatican II, in the 1965 *Pastoral Constitution on the Church in the Modern World* (*Gaudium et Spes*), made explicit the Church's shift towards the world and its embracing of humanity and its history, denouncing as a grave error the separation of religious life from a commitment to "the earthly city." Its commitment underpins the shift towards valuing cultures, the role of lay people in the Church, the importance of politics, and preference for the poor:

> This council exhorts Christians, as citizens of two cities, to strive to discharge their earthly duties conscientiously and in response to the Gospel

> spirit. They are mistaken who, knowing that we have here no abiding city but seek one which is to come … think that they may therefore shirk their earthly responsibilities. For they are forgetting that by the faith itself they are more obliged than ever to measure up to these duties, each according to his proper vocation … This split between the faith which many profess and their daily lives deserves to be counted among the more serious errors of our age. (Pope Paul VI 1965, Article 43)

Regarding faith and culture, the shift established by Vatican II is declared in terms that value the richness of human cultures and calls for a "living exchange between the Church and the diverse cultures of people." Thus,

> from the beginning of her history [the Church] has learned to express the message of Christ with the help of the ideas and terminology of various philosophers, and has tried to clarify it with their wisdom, too … Indeed this accommodated preaching of the revealed word ought to remain the law of all evangelization. For thus the ability to express Christ's message in its own way is developed in each nation, and at the same time there is fostered a living exchange between the Church and the diverse cultures of people. (ibid., Article 44)

Gaudium et Spes (*Joys and Hopes*), written a half-century ago, is explicit about the value of politics and its definition as inseparable from the pursuit of the common good, wherein lies its "full justification":

> The political community exists, consequently, for the sake of the common good, in which it finds its full justification and significance, and the source of its inherent legitimacy. Indeed, the common good embraces the sum of those conditions of the social life whereby men, families and associations more adequately and readily may attain their own perfection. (ibid., Article 74)
>
> The Church praises and esteems the work of those who for the good of men devote themselves to the service of the state and take on the burdens of this office. (ibid., Article 75)

The document's climax lies in its discussion of politics, in which it calls for appropriate formation for all, especially youth, and those dedicated to this art, proposing the moral basis for citizens' practice as well as the clear-cut general purpose of "action against any form of injustice and tyranny":

> Great care must be taken about civic and political formation, which is of the utmost necessity today for the population as a whole, and especially for youth, so that all citizens can play their part in the life of the political community. Those who are suited or can become suited should prepare themselves for the difficult, but at the same time, the very noble art of politics, and should seek to practice this art without regard for their own interests or for material advantages. With integrity and wisdom, they must take action against any form of injustice and tyranny, against arbitrary domination by an individual or a political party and any intolerance. They should dedicate themselves to the service of all with sincerity and fairness, indeed, with the charity and fortitude demanded by political life. (ibid., Article 75).

Latin American and Caribbean Conferences of Bishops

The successive Conferences of Bishops of Latin America and the Caribbean since Vatican II[16] cover more than four decades of the history of the Church and the continent. As it is not possible in this space to explain the reach and multidimensionality of this double-edged historicity, we restrict our intent to identifying the direction of the Latin American magisterium, regarding the same three dimensions foregrounded in the Council's documents.

Social Inequality, Injustice, and Preference for the Poor

The denunciation of poverty and social injustice by the region's bishops is biblical in tone – "devastating and humiliating flagellum" (Third General Conference 1979, Article 29), which "cry to heaven" (Fifth General Conference 2007, Article 395, quoting Pope John Paul II). There is consistency among the four Conferences with regard to their sources in economic, social, and political structures:[17]

> The luxury of the few becomes an insult. This is contrary to the plan of the Creator and the honour due to him. In this anguish and pain, the Church discerns a situation of social sin, of greater gravity as it takes place in countries that called themselves Catholic and which have the capacity to change. (Third General Conference 1979, Article 52)

> This reality demands … personal conversion and profound changes in the structures that answer to the legitimate aspirations of the people for social justice, changes that in the experience of Latin America have not come, or have been too slow. (ibid., Article 30)

In Aparecida, almost three decades later – in quite different external as well as internal Church contexts – the tone and framing has changed. However, the direction of the earlier definitions of Medellín, Puebla, and Santo Domingo have remained the same:

> If we pretend to close our eyes against these realities [of poverty, exclusion and abandonment of many] we are not defenders of the life of the Kingdom and we situate ourselves on the path of death … It is necessary to underline "the inseparable relation between love of God and love of neighbour," which "invites everyone to suppress the grave social inequalities and the enormous differences in the access to goods" ... Both the concern for developing more just social structures and the transmission of the social values of the Gospel, are situated in this context of fraternal service to a life of dignity. (Fifth General Conference 2007, Article 358).

Faith and Culture

Two dimensions of the Conferences' successive addressing of "faith–culture" relationships need to be foregrounded for our analysis: how the Council's concept of the "enriching dialogue" between faith and culture is thematized, and how the cultural realities of indigenous and popular cultures and their religiosity are signified and valued. Both dimensions signal an "other" that brings important implications for the Latin American Church in its own "modern world" (Larrain 2000).

The questioning nature of popular religiosity for pre-Vatican II doctrinal and liturgical traditions was bluntly stated by Puebla in 1979:

> We are in an urgent situation. Transition from a rural agrarian society to an urban-industrial society submits the religion of the people to a decisive crisis … It shall be necessary to review spirituality, attitudes, and tactics of the elites in the Church with regard to popular religiosity. As Medellín well pointed out, "this religiosity places the Church before the dilemma of continuing to be the Universal Church or becoming a sect, by not thereby vitally incorporating such men who express that type of religiosity." (Third General Conference 1979, Chapter 3.4)

In Aparecida, the call to dialogue with the many manifestations of modern culture is widely encompassing and at the same time specific, distinguishing ambits and topics that the evangelizing mission should reach. Pope Benedict XVI, in his inaugural address at

Aparecida, repeated the principles and criteria established from Medellín onwards:

> Authentic cultures are not closed in upon themselves, nor are they set in stone at a particular point in history, but they are open, or better still, they are seeking an encounter with other cultures, hoping to reach universality through encounter and dialogue with other ways of life and with elements that can lead to a new synthesis, in which the diversity of expressions is always respected as well as the diversity of their particular cultural embodiment. (Fifth General Conference 2007, 3)

The final document of the Bishops at Aparecida is specific regarding the new fields and topics within which the dialogue between faith and culture needs to develop: "the world of communications, peace building, the development and liberation of peoples, especially of minorities, the promotion of women and children, ecology and protection of nature, and the 'immense "Areopagus" of culture, scientific research, and international relations.'" It explicitly declares that this priority should not be seen as "abandoning the preferential option to the poor." Thus, "evangelizing culture, far from abandoning the preferential option for the poor and the commitment to reality, arises out of passionate love for Christ who accompanies the People of God in the mission of inculturating the gospel in history, ardent and tireless in its Samaritan charity" (Fifth General Conference, 2007, ibid., Article 491).

Democratic Politics

Two quotations on the democratic politics of the Fifth General Conference of Bishops, and the special responsibility of the "constructors of society" for this area of development, eloquently express the Latin American Church's magisterium regarding the domain that Vatican II defined as both difficult and "very noble." Further, the bishops' last Conference explicitly connected the structures that provoke poverty with a "lack of fidelity to … evangelical principles" among those Christians who participate in leadership in the fields of politics, economics, and culture. Thus,

> we bishops gathered in the Fifth Conference want to be present to those who build society, for it is the Church's fundamental vocation in this sector to shape consciences, and to be an advocate of justice and truth and to educate in the individual and political virtues. (ibid., Article 508)

> The disciples and missionaries of Christ must illuminate with the light of the Gospel all realms of social life. The preferential option for [the] poor, rooted in the Gospel, requires pastoral attention devoted to the builders of society. If many contemporary structures produce poverty, it is partly due to the lack of fidelity to their gospel commitments on the part of many Christians with special political, economic and cultural responsibilities. (ibid., Article 501)

We turn now to the Chilean Catholic schools that serve the elite, to examine the ways this magisterium informs, or does not inform, their present educational definitions.

Four Educational Projects: Principles and Criteria

We started our project with the hypothesis that educational institutions belonging to the two sides of the key divide outlined above – a divide drawn at the end of the 1960s and still prevalent in the Catholic education of Chile's Catholic elite – would relate to the magisterium, both universal and Latin American, and in forms coherent with the origins, religious charisma, and value positions, as well as the history of each congregation's relationship with the elite. We thought the different projects would have a "re-contextualizing relationship" with the magisterium – that is, that their differences, and particularly those related to the two sides of the 1970s divide, would entail selecting and framing based on the Church's documents in consistently different ways that could be described through a comparative analysis

To conduct this analysis, we selected the educational projects of the four congregations, as they appear on the respective institutional websites, and then compared how they referred to our key selected topics: poverty and social injustice, faith and culture, and politics. As discussed above, these three dimensions express the fundamental shift towards embracing "the modern world" accomplished by Vatican II in *Gaudium et Spes.* They also condense fundamental dimensions of commitment to the "other" that the documents of the Latin American Bishops – despite the changing times, contexts, powers, and ideas – have consistently declared and specified in their practical consequences throughout more than four decades.

The first finding of our comparative analysis – to our surprise, and resulting in the breakdown of our hypothesis – is that the two new congregations, Opus Dei and the Legionnaires, do not carry out any "selection and framing" of the Church's documents, as they do not refer to the magisterium. Opus Dei's educational mission document for its schools never quotes or refers to Vatican II, or to any of the four post-1960 Conferences of the Latin American Episcopate. The Legionnaires' educational project does mention Vatican II once, but not with regard to any of the three dimensions of our analysis, and it does not quote any document.[18]

Conversely, the centuries-old congregations do refer to and quote the magisterium: both Vatican II and the Latin American Episcopate's Conference documents. In the case of the Jesuits' educational project (formulated in 2010), the Aparecida document (2007) is quoted four times.[19] In the case of the Holy Cross's educational project, which was formulated in 2003, the Second Conference (Medellín 1968) and Santo Domingo (1992) documents are both quoted twice, and a text of John Paul II to the Bishops of Latin America in 1999 is also quoted.[20]

While St George's College and the Jesuits explicitly anchor some of their fundamentals in the magisterium, it is worth noting that this takes the form of recognizing some principles, more than any specific translation into the action of their respective projects. For example, there is no reference in either of the educational projects to the specific duties of the "constructors of society" (the elite) regarding unjust economic, social, and political structures – duties that the magisterium makes abundantly clear. Even so, the general principle is consistently declared: the work of each school is to educate to transform society.

What follows is our comparative analysis of the four educational projects. We discern a pattern of differences between visions on the two sides of the divide in the 1960s and 1970s, which translates into the "worlds apart" nature of their respective educational missions today.

Table 11.2 presents the results of our comparative analysis. To provide the most valid illustration, we have selected *all* quotes from the educational projects of each of the four congregations that refer to the three dimensions, that thus comprehensively express the social dimension of their formative purposes.

Poverty, Social Inequality, Injustice

To examine what we have called the 1970s divide, we will now label the two sides. First, the magisterium-affirming (MA) label will refer to the educational projects of Jesuits and Holy Cross; magisterium-ignoring (MI) will denote the Legionnaires and Opus Dei on the other side of the divide. As expressed in our analytical dimension referring to poverty, inequality, and social injustice, Jesuits and Holy Cross declare that their educational goal is to prepare their students to transform society and

Table 11.2 Four educational projects in the Chilean Catholic elite: Key principles and orientations regarding social structures, culture, and politics

POVERTY, SOCIAL INEQUALITY, and INJUSTICE	
Ignatian Schools Society of Jesus	St George's College Holy Cross
The new society we dream of is just, fraternal, and most respectful of the dignity of all people, with structures that enable solutions to overcome inequity, poverty, discrimination, and exclusion. (EP, Article 37) Our education is at the service of the transformation of our society. We wish to promote in people and in communities a way of thinking able to propose alternatives to trends and ideologies that dehumanize and marginalize the majorities in poverty, encourage radical secularism, and exacerbate the logic of the market and consumerism. (EP, Article 46)	We seek to promote among students, teachers, and parents, an attitude that from the viewpoint of "faith in action" allows transforming the society in which they live, thus making visible the values of the Kingdom of God. (EP, Section 2.2.) On finishing secondary school, boys and girls shall be able to: Take part in committed action for change towards a more fraternal society, through profound social conscience and active solidarity in the context of a community of faith. (EP, Section 4.2)
Legionnaires of Christ Schools	Opus Dei Schools
Whenever a new school starts there is a clear purpose in mind, with regard to student participation in social action: conscience about Christian solidarity; that is, "firm and persevering determination to commit oneself to the common good." (John Paul II. Soll. Rei Soc. 38) (EP, Article 19) For the Legionnaires of Christ there are no rich or poor: only "man" exists. Men, with solidarity in sin and in the need for salvation. Just as Jesus Christ, they destine their supernatural mission equally to all men. Christian redemption excludes not one or the others. (EP)	It shall be attempted that students acquire the spirit of solidarity, gratitude, commitment, and service to others. With this purpose, each school shall promote concrete and specific actions that teach how to discover and resolve spiritual and material needs of the most disadvantaged. (EP, Article 12) [The schools of SEDUC], adapting to local realities, attend varied socio-economic groups, both in Santiago and Regions. (Mission)

(Continued)

Table 11.2 Four educational projects in the Chilean Catholic elite: Key principles and orientations regarding social structures, culture, and politics (Continued)

FAITH & CULTURE	
Ignatian Schools Society of Jesus	St George's College Holy Cross
In the multicultural context that we live in, we wish to learn, understand, and love those who are different to us, by means of dialogue based on truth, justice, and love. We believe educational institutions are privileged places for inculturating the Gospel and for the evangelisation of cultures. Hence we practice faith-culture dialogue, faith-science dialogue, faith-reason dialogue, and ecumenical and interreligious dialogue. We strive to form ourselves for these major challenges. (EP, par. 52) We need also to value popular culture, urban-marginal and rural, often times because we are inserted in those contexts, but also because from these we recognize a call to the whole of society, and particularly to our school curriculum. (EP, par. 63). We practice and educate for dialogue among the Catholic faith and cultures, ecumenical dialogue, inter-religious and inter-cultural, non-discrimination, unconditional respect for human rights, essential equality between man and woman, and care for creation and trans-generational responsibility. (EP, par. 133)	Work for the integration of faith, culture, and life, providing an intimate relation between religious knowledge and the various disciplines of human knowledge; animate and liturgically celebrate the gift of life, the mysteries of faith, and community events. (EP, section 3.3) We promote the formation of people who critically value national and Latin American culture as their own, seeking to favour a sense of belonging and identity. We are interested in people who may speak proudly of their own cultural roots as well as learn of the traditions of other peoples. (EP, section 4.1)
Legionnaires of Christ Schools	Opus Dei Schools
We wish to make of our School a place for comprehensive formation through the systematic and critical assimilation of culture. The School is therefore a living and vital encounter with the cultural heritage of our country and the world. It is our purpose to enable students to interpret the voice of the universe revealed by the creator and through the conquest of science, learn more of God and man. (EP, 14)	Comprehensive education: "Comprehensive education pursues a harmonious development of the personality. Therefore, it encompasses and includes the person's spiritual, intellectual, artistic, athletic, social and civic capacities, all of them integrated into a solid unit of life, at the service of God and other men." (EP, Article 6) SEDUC promotes the development and supports the operation of schools whose essential goal is the education of free and responsible persons, with a Christian vision of the world and culture. (Mission)

POLITICS

Ignatian Schools Society of Jesus	St George's College Holy Cross
From our institutions, from our local experience, we feel called upon to contribute to the national system, public policy, national debate, or specific requirements we may receive. (EP, Article 50) With humility and determination we strive to carry out joint actions to be present at decision-making instances, offering our experience and potential to contribute to the formulation of public policies, taking-on in these the corresponding responsibility. We also promote participation, above all by those who direct the institutions, [of the network], in associations, social movements, and other fora of effective political relevance. (EP, Article 199)	Those of us who belong to the Saint George's College educational community, aspire to a comprehensive education of the individual, preparing committed Christians and competent citizens. (EP, Section 2.1.) We educate for a lifestyle that values democracy, promotes peace and non-violence; values tolerance, peaceful and respectful coexistence, welcomes diversity, is concerned about the environment, in a collaborative effort integrated by all the smembers of our community. (EP, Section 2.2) Within the legacy of the Congregation of Holy Cross, the basic responsibility of teachers is to create and maintain an environment leading students to become committed Christians, and responsible and competent citizens. (EP, section 2.4)

Legionnaires of Christ Schools	Opus Dei Schools
This means the person should prepare for collaborative relations in political life, in social life, and in the world of labour, and especially in family relations, relations of friendship, and the relations that constitute religious life. (EP) For the appropriate formation of conscience it is indispensable to imprint on students a great appreciation for virtues, as for example justice, veracity, cordiality, responsibility, life coherence, nobility, respect for the person; all virtues that sustain civil coexistence. (EP, 6)	Freedom in matters of opinion: 'Respect for the legitimate opinions of all who are part of each school, and the atmosphere of harmony that is proper to them, require that SEDUC be foreign to all expression of ideas and opinions of political parties or groups. Each one practices their Civic rights and duties outside the school environment.' (EP, Article 11) We hope that our students become persons that stand-out in every ambit and are a reference in Chilean society. (Mission)

Source: Authors' selection of quotes from each congregation's educational project: (a) Red Educacional Ignaciana (2010), Proyecto Educativo de la Red Educacional Ignaciana, www.rededucacionalignaciana.cl; (b) Congregación de Santa Cruz (2003), Proyecto Educativo St George's College, www.saintgeorge.cl; (c) Colegios Legionarios de Cristo/Regnum Cristi (2010) Proyecto Educativo, www.regnumchristi.org; (d) SEDUC (Opus Dei) (n.d) Principios y Fundamentos de los Colegios SEDUC; SEDUC (Opus Dei) (n.d) "Visión y Misión" www.seduc.cl.

its unjust structures; by contrast, in the educational projects of both the Legionnaires and Opus Dei, there is no reference to structures but only to persons in poverty or affliction. Thus, in one case, the meaning of solidarity is faith in action to build a new society, and in the other, it is charity for disadvantaged and afflicted persons.

The word "poor" appears eleven times in the Jesuit case, four in the case of the Holy Cross project, three in the Legionnaires, and not at all in the case of Opus Dei. "Poverty" is mentioned eighteen times in the educational project of the Jesuits but is not mentioned in any of the other three texts. With regard to "justice," the count is Jesuits, thirteen; Holy Cross, nine; Legionnaires, seven; Opus Dei, none.

When we compare the two MA projects, which share a social (as opposed to individual or personalized) view of life in society and of the pursuance of the values of the Kingdom, we find that the Jesuit project is much more specific than the St George's project in its diagnosis of poverty, discrimination, and inequality, and of the structures that therefore need to be acted upon.

Likewise, there is a difference between the two MI projects: in the Legionnaires' project there is a concept of explicit connection between social action and the "common good," which clearly expands the notion of solidarity; this is not the case with the Opus Dei definition, which avoids the term "social" and consistently restricts solidarity to personal relationships.

The MA projects express and try to answer to a moral purpose, which is as much about the person and his or her will as it is about the person in relation to society and its inequities (the dimension we have foregrounded). The MI projects focus only on the first term, "being," as shown above, and are silent on the social dimension of their otherwise comprehensive and demanding *Bildung*. We have found quite interesting evidence about commonalities in the Catholic education of economic elites in Chile regarding this "personal dimension," or formation of the will ("character formation"). This contrasts starkly with the opposite nature of the visions and efforts of the different projects regarding the social and political dimensions of the person. According to a recent study based on interviews with members of the economic elite, there exist no differences in the answers of top executives coming from the Jesuit and Opus Dei schools regarding notions of self-control, perseverance, discipline, and duty; the idea that top executives should work hard, be honest, and have a decorous if not exemplary family life cuts across the economic elite (Thumala 2010).

Faith and culture

The two MA projects coincide regarding the centrality of their formative projects and the dialogue between their faith and different manifestations of culture: science, other faiths, other cultures. In both congregations' educational projects, inter-cultural dialogue and the evangelization of culture are conceived of in terms defined by *Gaudium et Spes*, as we have seen, and then developed and enriched by the Latin American Episcopate's successive Conferences. By contrast, both MI projects frame the problem in terms that dissolve the issue: by defining "comprehensive education" and the different dimensions of the person it needs to address. There is no such thing as faith and an "other" of any kind, nor is there a basis for any "inter"-cultural dialogue.

The two MA projects converge in their definitions of inter-cultural dialogue with regard to the faith/reason or faith/science dimensions, but have dissimilar approaches to cultural differences rooted in class or nation. Whereas the Jesuit project selects popular culture (urban and rural) as crucial when dealing with inter-cultural dialogue, the Holy Cross project refers to national and Latin American identities and their cultural basis as an important value for learning.

Similarly, the two MI projects also differ in this dimension. The Legionnaires' project refers to a "systematic and critical assimilation of culture" and mentions science and its connections to understanding the cosmos from a religious standpoint. The Opus Dei project mentions instead "a solid unit of life" and a "Christian vision of the world and culture," which does not recognize that these are two separate terms and that, since Vatican II, the relationship between them has been conceived in terms of dialogue and mutual ferment.

According to Vatican II historian John O'Malley (2010), a new language cuts across all its documents, conveying a spirit that means a change from closeness to openness, from condemnation to appreciation, and from universals to contextuality. These oppositions, we find, apply similarly to our MI and MA educational projects.

Politics

The political domain and preparation for democratic citizenship should stand as very important in everyone's education, and particularly so in societies – like the Chilean – with memories of tragic conflict and breakdown of democratic order. Moreover, it is not possible to think about changing structures without involving the political domain. So, how is this crucial aspect of preparation for adult life approached by the four projects?

The Jesuits' educational project adopts a special standpoint regarding the political and policy domains: it does not define goals and criteria to be communicated to students, but instead says it is in the interest of schools and their leaders and teachers to participate in the policy-making and decision-making with regard to education.

The St George's educational project is the only one of the four that explicitly refers to democracy and the importance of preparing competent and responsible citizens.

Crossing the MA/MI divide, the Legionnaires' project refers to the virtues and values required for adult life, and distinguishes between "political life" and "civil life," implying the value and importance of both, but not manifesting any normative view with regard to democracy or citizenship and its rights and responsibilities. The Opus Dei document mentions the political or civic domain, but only to underline that it is not a matter to be dealt with at school, making it something that is off limits.

Conclusion

In closing, we will now summarize the findings of our comparative analysis and put them against a broader canvas. Our main finding is that the orientations of both Vatican II and the bishops' documents regarding the three "other-oriented" dimensions chosen for analysis have been ignored by the two orders (and their schools) that began serving Chilean elites after the crisis of the 1970s, in explicit opposition to the path taken by the orders that had traditionally served these groups. The Jesuits and St George's, in following the social orientations of both Vatican II and the Medellín Conference of Latin American Bishops, actually broke their historically profound ties to Chile's traditional economic elite. Hence, we see the positions of Opus Dei and the Legionnaires in education as strong cases of *context ruling mission*, whereas *mission disrupting context* could be said to be the position of the MA projects.

From a sociological viewpoint, the examined contrasting projects relate to different elites within the Chilean upper socio-economic strata. The MI projects, issuing from religious congregations whose charisma celebrates the inner-worldly asceticism intrinsic to the sanctification of work (Weber 2003), in addition to their hierarchical view of the social order, appeal consistently to the economic elite (Madrid 2013; Thumala 2010). By contrast, the MA projects, issuing from orders whose charisma celebrates social and cultural diversity and a communitarian view of society, appeal more to the country's cultural and political elites. Thus, the doctrinal divide revealed by the mission statements, which so clearly relates to the "traditionalists" and "progressives" who were confronted at the Council half a century ago, can also be interpreted in terms of differences between the elites of the country and their value preferences. This concept of difference also coheres with the ideas, interests, and *habitus* that correspond to their belonging to the economic, political, or cultural fields (Bourdieu 1984, 1998; Joignant and Güell 2011; PNUD 2015).

Finally, the silence uncovered in three of the examined educational projects with regard to politics and citizenship as critical dimensions of the learning opportunities to be offered – a silence that cuts across the key ideological divide that affects them – needs to be noted. As mentioned earlier, only the St George's project is explicit about formation for democratic politics and its importance. This contrasts dramatically with the meaning granted to this domain by Vatican II and, consistently thereafter, by the Latin American Bishops' Conferences. Thus, silence on citizenship and democratic politics, in a world of radical socio-cultural pluralization and increased complexity of issues to be worked out in the public sphere, raises questions about the relevance of the formative experiences of these elites, and makes one wonder about the probable long-term effects of this most evident educational deficit on the future of Chilean democratic politics.

NOTES

We would like to thank the participants in the symposium *Catholicism and Education: Fifty Years after Vatican II (1962–1965) – A Transnational Interdisciplinary Encounter*, held at Donostia (Basque Country) in June 2015, and José Joaquín Brunner for helpful criticism and insights.

1 For a new sociology of these under-studied groups in Chile, see Joignant and Güell (2011).
2 Second General Conference of the Latin American and Caribbean Episcopate (Medellín), 24 August–5 September 1968.
3 Only one elite Catholic school for boys, of the four major institutions at the time, can be said to have eluded the process: Colegio Verbo Divino, a school belonging to the Divine Missionaries or Fathers of Steyl Congregation.
4 "Strive to apply the Council recommendation with regard to an effective democratisation of the Catholic school, so that all social sectors, without any

discrimination, may have access to it and there acquire an authentic social conscience to inform their life"' (Second General Conference 1968, Article 58).

5 The process was interrupted at St George's School by the military coup and thematized in the most seen film in the history of Chilean filmmaking, *Machuca*. However, this did not occur at the Jesuit schools, which managed to maintain a measure of social integration in their enrolments.

6 This also was explicitly requested in the Medellín Conference's conclusions: "The specific mandate of the Lord to 'evangelise the poor' should lead us to a distribution of efforts and of the apostolic staff to give effective preference to the poorest sectors in greater need and those segregated due to any cause, encouraging and enhancing the initiatives and studies already underway for this purpose" (Second General Conference 1968, Article 118). Other factors also contributed, including the aging of religious communities and the decline in new vocations, as well as the ideology of the time, as a result of which education in general – and especially paid education – was seen as responsible for maintaining an unfair social structure.

7 The hermeneutics of both the Council and Medellín by the referred Congregations in Chile correspond to what Cardinal Ratzinger, in a 1985 analysis, categorized as the "euphoric" phase in the reception of Vatican II. See Ratzinger and Maltier (1985).

8 For the discussion that the initiative triggered in the Church, see the following articles, cited in Smith (1982): "Congregación de los SS.CC adopta posiciones ante futuro de sus colegios," *Iglesia de Santiago* 8 (August 1971): 22–4; "¿Democratización de colegios clasistas?" *Mensaje* 20 (November 1971): 554–8; "Análisis de un camino para la Integración Escolar," *Iglesia de Santiago* 10 (August, 1972): 13–18.

9 The Chilean Bishops did not endorse the attempt, although they publicly declared their intentions of making diocesan schools "open to all Chileans without social or economic discrimination." Quoted in Smith (1982), 187: "Declaración del Comité Permanente del Episcopado sobre la entrega de colegios católicos al estado," in *Documentos del Episcopado,* edited by Carlos Oviedo Cavada, 24 August 1871, 110–11.

10 The four are, of course, comparable neither in their historical weight nor in their canonical status. For the distinctions between the terms congregations, orders, movements, and prelatures, see Vatican, *Congregation for Institutes of Consecrated Life and Societies of Apostolic Life,* http://www.vatican.va/roman_curia/congregations/ccscrlife/documents/rc_con_ccscrlife_profile_en.html. We will use the term "congregation" in an approximate, non-specialized form.

11 Educational Project of the Ignatian Educational Network – REI 39.

12 Invited by the Archbishop of Santiago, José María Caro, who in the midst of the Second World War found himself needing to replace the school's headmaster, the Irishman Charles Hamilton, after his son – a diocesan priest – preached at St George's Sunday mass against the Nazi genocide, unleashing a crisis with influential pro-axis groups among the local Catholic elite.

13 The Colegio Tabancura (for boys) opened in March 1970, and the Liceo Los Andes (for girls) opened one year earlier, in March 1969. "The times in that period," Colegio Tabancura now explains on its webpage, "were of uncertainty. The country's crisis … plagued by ideology … affected in a most direct way the religious formation of sons. To create a sane, safe school, was a necessity." See Colegio Tabancura, 2017.

14 In 2006, Pope Benedict XVI removed Maciel from active ministry based on the results of an investigation concerning sexual abuse with seminarians and children, as well as a double-life that included a wife and several children. The Legionnaire movement as a whole was then subject to a Vatican investigation. The movement condemned its founder in 2010.

15 See http://www.regnumchristi.org/es/?se=361&ca=956.

16 Second Conference (Medellín, Colombia), 24 August–5 September 1968; Third Conference (Puebla, Mexico), 27 January–17 February 1979; Fourth Conference (Santo Domingo, Dominican Republic), 12–28 October 1992; Fifth Conference (Aparecida, Brazil), 13–31 May 2007.

17 See Second General Conference (1968), Articles 4–11, 14; Third General Conference (1979), Articles 29, 30, 52, 53, 1134, 1165; Fourth General Conference (1992), Articles 178–181; Fifth General Conference (2007), Articles 358, 391, 395.

18 Vatican II is mentioned with no specific reference to any document, in the context of a paragraph on "manifestations of human maturity: stability of the spirit, capacity for prudent decisions, and rightfulness in judgment" (Legionarios de Cristo, *Proyecto Educativo*, 2010, 4–5). The document also quotes a text of Pope John Paul once (see first quote of Legionnaires in column 1, Table 11.2).

19 Fifth General Conference 2007, Articles 328, 257, 397, 398.

20 Pope John Paul II (1999), *Post-Synodal Apostolic Exhortation (Ecclesia in America)*, http://w2.vatican.va/content/john-paul-ii/en/apost_exhortations/documents/hf_jp-ii_exh_22011999_ecclesia-in-america.html.

REFERENCES

Aedo-Richmond, Ruth. 2000. *La Educación privada en Chile: Un estudio histórico-analítico desde el período colonial hasta 1990*. Santiago: RIL Editores.

Bourdieu, Pierre. 1984. *Distinction: A Social Critique of the Judgment of Taste.* Cambridge, MA: Harvard University Press.

– 1998. *The State Nobility: Elite Schools in the Field of Power.* Cambridge: Polity Press.

Colegios Legionarios de Cristo/Regnum Cristi. 2010. Proyecto Educativo. www.regnumchristi.org

Colegio Tabancura. 2017. Quiénes Somos. http://www.tabancura.cl/quienes-somos

Congregación de Santa Cruz. 2003. Proyecto Educativo St George's College. www.saintgeorge.cl

Durkheim, Emile. 1977. *The Evolution of Educational Thought.* London: RKP.

Fifth General Conference of the Bishops of the Latin America and the Caribbean (Aparecida). 2007. *Concluding Document – Disciples and missionaries of Jesus Christ, so that our People may have life in Him.* http://www.aecrc.org/documents/Aparecida-Concluding%20Document.pdf.

Joignant, Alfredo, and Pedro Güell, eds. 2011. *Notables, tecnócratas y mandarines: Elementos de sociología de las elites en Chile (1990–2010).* Santiago: Ediciones Universidad Diego Portales.

Larrain, Jorge. 2000. *Identity and Modernity in Latin America.* Cambridge: Polity Press.

Madrid, Sebastián. 2013. "The Formation of Ruling Class Men: Private Schooling, Class, and Gender Relations in Contemporary Chile." PhD diss., University of Sydney, Australia.

Martínez, Jaime, and Juan José Silva. 1971. "Antecedentes históricos." In *Educación particular en Chile: antecedentes y dilemas,* edited by Luis Brahm, Patricio Cariola, and Juan José Silva, 16–34. Santiago, Chile: CIDE.

O'Malley, John W. 2010. *What Happened at Vatican II.* Cambridge, MA: Harvard University Press.

PNUD. 2015. *Informe sobre Desarrollo Humano en Chile 2015. Los tiempos de la politización.* Santiago: Programa de las Naciones Unidas para el Desarrollo.

Pope Paul VI. 1965 (7 December). *Pastoral Constitution on the Church in the Modern World (Gaudium et Spes).* http://www.vatican.va/archive/hist_councils/ii_vatican_council/documents/vat-ii_const_19651207_gaudium-et-spes_en.html.

Ratzinger, Joseph, and J. Maltier. 1985. *Les principes de la theologie Catolique: esquisse et materiaux.* Paris: Tequi Editors.

Red Educacional Ignaciana. 2010. Proyecto Educativo. www.rededucacionalignaciana.cl

Second General Conference of the Bishops of the Latin America and the Caribbean (Medellín). 1968. *Final Document of Medellín.* http://w2.vatican.va/

content/benedictxvi/en/speeches/2007/may/documents/hf_ben-xvi_spe_20070513_conference-aparecida.html.
SEDUC (Opus Dei). n.d. Principios y Fundamentos de los Colegios SEDUC.
– "Visión y Misión." www.seduc.cl
Serrano, Sol, ed. 2000. *Vírgenes viajeras. Diarios de religiosas francesas en su ruta a Chile, 1837–1874.* Santiago: Ediciones Universidad Católica de Chile.
Smith, Brian H. 1982. *The Church and Politics in Chile: Challenges to Modern Catholicism.* Princeton: Princeton University Press. http://dx.doi.org/10.1515/9781400856978.
St.George's College. (2017). Congregación de la Santa Cruz: Historia. http://www.saintgeorge.cl/nuestro-colegio/historia/
Third General Conference of the Bishops of the Latin America and the Caribbean (Puebla). 1979. *Final Document of Puebla.* http://libguides.marquette.edu/c.php?g=36663&p=232900#s-lg-box-2409897.
Thumala, Maria Angélica. 2010. *Riqueza y piedad: El catolicismo de la elite chilena.* Santiago: Antártica.
Weber, Max. 2003. *The Protestant Ethic and the Spirit of Capitalism.* New York: Dover Edition.

"MAGNIFICAT (Lucas/Luke 1:46–55) no. 12." Ceramic tilework by María Cruz Bascones.

PART FIVE

Catholicism and Aboriginal Education in Canada

12 Balancing the Spirit in Aboriginal Catholic Education in Ontario

LINDSAY A. MORCOM

Introduction

Following Vatican II, the Catholic Church changed its attitude towards Indigenous peoples around the world in significant and meaningful ways. In sharp contrast to its past assimilative stance, the Catholic Church now recognizes the value of inculturation and encourages work for the survival of Aboriginal cultures and languages. At the same time, school boards across Ontario, following the efforts of the Ministry of Education, have recognized the need to provide Aboriginal students with culturally appropriate learning environments. Many boards have hired Aboriginal education experts (AEEs), whose job it is to foster a welcoming and engaging environment for Aboriginal young people, staff, and community members; to educate non-Aboriginal staff and students about Aboriginal peoples; and to enact spiritual inculturation in meaningful and appropriate ways. This chapter explores the perspectives on inculturation exhibited by AEEs in five Catholic school boards in Ontario and describes the forms that inculturation takes in Ontario Catholic schools. It also examines how AEEs encounter the history of the Catholic Church and use the school environment to help move towards reconciliation between Aboriginal peoples, the Catholic Church, and Canadian society as a whole.

Catholicism, Education, and Canada's Indigenous People

For many Aboriginal Canadians, spirituality is a central part of life. Given the tremendous diversity of First Nations, Métis, and Inuit peoples in Canada, the epistemologies and practices relating to spirituality take many forms. Today, many Aboriginal people self-identify as Christians, with the majority of those identifying as Catholic. In fact, in Ontario today, 62 per cent of people of Aboriginal identity also identify as Christian; of these, 56 per cent (i.e., 35 per cent of the overall Aboriginal population) are Catholic. That is similar to the wider population, where 65 per cent of Ontarians identify as Christian and 48 per cent of these, or 31 per cent of the overall population, identify as Catholic (Statistics Canada 2013).

It must be noted that only 5 per cent of the Aboriginal population identifies traditional spirituality as their religion (Statistics Canada 2013). However, this does not represent the reality of the situation; in many Aboriginal communities, traditional spirituality continues to inform individuals' world views, and Indigenous spiritual practices are still a part of everyday life. However, there is reticence in many communities to refer to traditional spirituality as a religion because it is non-dogmatic and goes beyond the realm of religion in a Western context to encompass other areas such as literature, science, medicine, and fine arts, to name a few. Also, because traditional spiritual practices were outlawed until the 1950s, there is some reluctance to talk openly about them today. Still, many Aboriginal people who identify as Christians also embrace elements of traditional spirituality. Combined spirituality may take the form of *syncretism* – the mixing of belief systems, or *inculturation* – the incorporation of practices from one culture or belief system into another while leaving the core beliefs and dogma intact (Langevin 2014). Still others may embrace *dimorphism*, which is the simultaneous acceptance of both traditional spirituality and Catholicism in their own rights (Murphy and Perin 1996).

Aboriginal people in Canada have been exposed to Christianity for a millennium, first through contact with Vikings and later with Basque whalers and traders, although neither of these groups seem to have made concerted efforts towards evangelization (Fitzhugh et al. 2011; Langevin 2014; Malakoff 2007; Murphy and Perin 1996). The era of colonization and evangelization commenced in earnest after Pope Alexander VI's 1493 *Inter Caetera* bull, which states that "among other works well pleasing to the Divine Majesty and cherished of our heart, this assuredly ranks highest, that in our times especially the Catholic faith and the Christian religion be exalted and everywhere increased and spread, that the health of souls be cared for and that barbarous nations be overthrown and brought to the faith itself" (quoted in Deloria 1973, 274). Further papal bulls justified the colonization of non-Christian territories, including

North America. These were expanded to become international law under the Doctrine of Discovery and through the concept of *terra nullius*. This concept at first meant that European heads of state could lay claim to land that was literally empty, but was later expanded to mean lands occupied by non-Christians; this in turn allowed European heads of state to justify the conquest of lands already inhabited by Indigenous people in the New World (Deloria 1973; Royal Commission on Aboriginal Peoples [RCAP] 1996).

In what is now Canada, the Catholic evangelization of Indigenous people commenced with French settlement. Catholic missionaries were sent out to work among First Nations, to provide them with religious instruction and eventual baptism (Dickason 2006; Murphy and Perin 1996). Intermarriage between French and Indigenous people (upon their baptism) was encouraged, and several religious orders established schools for both Indigenous and French children to provide further religious instruction (Dickason 2006). At first, evangelization was carried out reasonably respectfully and had the dual goal of forging alliances and trading partnerships, but as European settlement increased, Aboriginal people were no longer valued as trading partners; rather, they were seen as obstacles to resource extraction and economic development.

This led to a new era in which assimilation, rather than evangelization, was the goal, and out of this political and social milieu, the residential school system was born. The Bagot Commission of 1842–4 encouraged the development of the residential school system, and by the time Canada was created in 1867 several schools were already in operation (Dickason 2006; Murphy and Perin 1996; Nguyen 2011; Royal Commission on Aboriginal Peoples [RCAP] 1996; Truth and Reconciliation Commission [TRC] 2015a). In 1892, the government forged partnerships with Canadian churches, including the Catholic Church, the Anglican Church, the Presbyterian Church, and later the United Church, to run the government-funded schools, which they did until 1969. In total, 139 residential schools operated in Canada, and at least 150,000 children attended them (TRC 2015a). The last residential school closed in 1996. The schools provided religious instruction and basic academic and industrial skills; they also focused on assimilation, removing children from their home communities for many months at a time and punishing them for speaking their own languages or practising their own customs. Up to one quarter of these pupils died from disease, particularly tuberculosis. Many children experienced physical abuse, and some also experienced sexual abuse. All of them experienced cultural and emotional abuse at the hands of a system that was designed to "kill the Indian in the child" (RCAP 1996; TRC 2015a). It cannot be denied that the Catholic Church willingly participated in this system by running residential schools.

However, changes in Church doctrine following Vatican II, in tandem with an upsurge in cultural pride in Aboriginal communities, have led to meaningful changes in how the Catholic Church regards and respects its Aboriginal adherents. It must be noted that inculturation has been carried out since the birth of the Church, and it was done particularly successfully in a European context (Panganiban 2004). However, the concept as it is currently envisioned in a Catholic context has its roots in Vatican II, and inculturation has been truly solidified as Church doctrine through its inclusion in several key documents of Vatican II. Two of the four Vatican II constitutions, *Lumen Gentium* and *Gaudium et Spes,* include the notion of inculturation. *Lumen Gentium* describes the universal Church as made up of local churches that may maintain their own traditions but that are bound by the Holy Spirit (Panganiban 2004; Shorter 1999). *Gaudium et Spes* emphasizes again that the Church is universal and not bound by any one culture. It gains from the assets of the diverse cultures of its membership in the belief that people derive "true and full humanity only by means of culture" (*Gaudium et Spes,* in Panganiban 2004). In addition, the decree *Ad Gentes Divinitus* discusses the need for missions that celebrate the richness of diverse cultures through their pastoral care. This includes an understanding of local culture and how it connects to Christianity, and participation by laity who witness, understand, and guard their own cultures. In 1985, the concept of inculturation was revisited and defined in the report of the Extraordinary General Assembly celebrating the twentieth anniversary of Vatican II as "the intimate transformation of authentic cultural values through their integration in Christianity in the various human cultures" (Vatican 1985).

In 1987, Pope John Paul II discussed inculturation in a context specific to Native North America during addresses to Native American Catholics in Arizona and Aboriginal Canadian Catholics in Fort Simpson, Northwest Territories. He acknowledged the wrongs perpetrated by the Catholic Church in the colonial history of the Americas, and he encouraged people to move forward together towards reconciliation. In both speeches, he encouraged pride in Aboriginal cultures, languages, and values, and encouraged Catholics to work towards cultural and language revitalization: "I encourage you, as native people belonging to the different tribes and nations in the East, South, West, and North, *to preserve and keep alive your cultures, your languages, the values and customs* which have served you well in the past and which provide a solid foundation for the future" (1987a, emphasis in the original). Finally, he pointed out that from a Catholic perspective, "not only is Christianity relevant to the Indian peoples, but Christ, in the members of his Body, is himself Indian" (1987b). He reiterated the need for inculturation in the encyclical *Redemptoris Missio* (1990). In a Canadian context, in 1991 the Canadian Council of Catholic Bishops (CCCB) apologized for the role the Church played in residential schools, as did the Missionary Oblates of Mary Immaculate (Canadian Conference of Catholic Bishops [CCCB] 2015). Following an audience with Assembly of First Nations (AFN) Chief Phil Fontaine and CCCB President Most Reverend James Weisgerber in 2009, Pope Benedict apologized privately on behalf of the Catholic Church as a whole (Vatican 2009), although a public apology has not been issued as of this writing. This remains a gap in the Catholic Church's move toward reconciliation with Indigenous people; while various bodies including the CCCB and the Missionary Oblates of Mary Immaculate have issued apologies, there is no single body that is able to apologize on behalf of all religious orders and dioceses in Canada, and this task has been left to each of these individually. Unfortunately, "the result has been a patchwork of apologies or statements of regret that few Survivors or church members may even know exist. Roman Catholics in Canada and across the globe look to the Pope as their spiritual and moral leaders. Therefore, it has been disappointing to Survivors and others that the Pope has not yet made a clear and emphatic public apology in Canada for the abuses perpetrated in Catholic-run residential schools throughout the country" (TRC 2015a, 221).

It is vital to note that the Catholic Church had not been alone in its assimilative attitudes towards Aboriginal people; this attitude was shared by governments, school systems, and the non-Aboriginal public at large throughout Canada's history. Residential schools were only a part of Canada's assimilative policy. The conditions in the schools and the aggressive assimilation of Indigenous people were debated in Parliament and discussed in myriad government reports, and Canadian society was aware of these issues (Dickason 2006; Hawthorn 1967; RCAP 1996). However, government policy and public awareness have changed as well. Most notably, 2015 saw the culmination of the Truth and Reconciliation Commission of Canada (TRC). Over six years, the TRC documented the stories of residential school survivors and formulated a list of ninety-four calls to action to help Canada redress its past and help all people move forward in reconciliation (TRC 2015a, b). The current federal government has promised to fully implement the calls to action of the TRC (Trudeau 2015), including those pertaining to education.

In an educational context in Ontario, in recent years as part of widespread cultural change, school boards have launched efforts to better engage Aboriginal students and to share Aboriginal ways of knowing, understanding, doing, and honouring, with a view to closing the achievement gap between Aboriginal and non-Aboriginal students and offering a richer educational experience for all students. The provincial government launched its current program of Aboriginal education in 2003.

In 2007, following consultation with Aboriginal communities and different levels of government, the Ontario provincial government released its Aboriginal Education Strategy. This strategy is summed up in two documents. The first document – *Ontario First Nation, Métis, and Inuit Education Policy Framework* (Ontario Ministry of Education [OME] 2007b) – examines culturally appropriate education and discusses how to close the achievement gap between Aboriginal and non-Aboriginal students. The second document – *Building Bridges to Success for First Nations, Métis, and Inuit Students: Developing Policies for Voluntary, Confidential Aboriginal Student Self-Identification: Successful Practices for Ontario School Boards* (OME 2007a) – outlines how teachers and schools can encourage Indigenous students to self-identify to ensure that they receive cultural supports that will help them succeed. Steps for implementation have been developed over time since the release of these documents, with the newest Implementation Plan released in 2014. Since the majority of Aboriginal children attend provincial schools, it is vital that schools be able to ensure families who select a Catholic education that their child's intellectual, physical, personal, cultural, and spiritual growth will be supported within the faith community they choose to be a part of (Anuik and Bellehumeur-Kearns 2012; McGregor 2009). While policy goes a long way to supporting this, it is also important to grasp the need for human relationships in helping to ensure that all children will receive all the support they need in order to flourish. Because of this, an increasing number of school boards, both Catholic and public, have taken the step of hiring AEEs.

Methodology

To gain insight into the roles of AEEs in Catholic school boards and to better understand what challenges and supports they have in their work, I carried out semi-structured interviews with experts from five Catholic school boards in Ontario. In most cases, these were individuals whose work involved multiple tasks including oversight of First Nations, Métis, and Inuit (FNMI) programming, although some were dedicated solely to FNMI education. In one case, I interviewed an FNMI education expert alongside the school board's Catholic education expert to gain additional insight into issues surrounding spirituality in a Catholic school setting. For the purposes of privacy, all data have been anonymized here, but I have used direct quotes, including a quote from a participant at the beginning of each section, to help convey their authentic voices.

Interviews were carried out either in person or by telephone and were either audio recorded or recorded manually (in which case the transcripts were reviewed by the participant for accuracy). With respect to spirituality, all participants were asked the following questions:

1. Where do you see Catholic and Aboriginal education balancing well?
   a. In particular, how, if at all, do you see Catholic and Aboriginal beliefs, values and approaches to spirituality overlapping in your work?
2. What challenges do you see in balancing Catholic and Aboriginal education?
   a. In particular, what challenges, if any, do you see in balancing Catholic and Aboriginal beliefs, values, and approaches to spirituality?
   b. How do you overcome these challenges?
3. Based on your experience, what recommendations would you make to other Catholic school boards wishing to balance Catholic and Aboriginal approaches to education?

After the interviews were completed, the resulting data were transcribed and coded for patterns to identify trends in the experiences and advice of the participants.

The participating school boards are from around the province, and cover southern, northern, and far northern geographic areas, as well as primarily urban, primarily rural, and mixed regions. As shown in Table 12.1, they vary across regions with regard to the percentage of First Nations, Métis, and Inuit (FNMI) students present.

Most of the Aboriginal students in these school boards are from local traditional territories or are Métis,[2] but there are also students from other territories, including some Inuit students. This generates its own challenges; as one participant said, "It's a challenge for us to ensure that

Table 12.1 FNMI student presence in five regions of Ontario

Region	Dedicated Aboriginal education expert?	FNMI student presence[1]	Region and composition
1	No – AEE has multiple tasks	> 1%	Southern, primarily urban
2	No – AEE has multiple tasks	~13–14%	Northern, primarily urban
3	No – AEE has multiple tasks	~6%	Southern, primarily rural
4	Yes – and dedicated Catholic/ family life educator	~5–25%	Southern, mixed
5	Yes	Unknown	Northern, mixed

teachers realize there's no pan-Indian solution or answer, and you have to be aware that there are different Nations, and different people that are in our classrooms."

Of the participants themselves, three self-identified as Aboriginal people, and three self-identified as "settler allies" – that is, as non-Aboriginal people dedicated to working as partners with Aboriginal people. The AEEs all have formal or informal training in education or a related discipline, such as social work. Most have done graduate work in areas such as education, counselling, social work, Aboriginal studies, and religion. All have undergone continuous learning with Aboriginal communities; for some, that learning began in childhood, whereas for others, it developed out of their teaching careers, and for most it has involved both formal courses and informal work with elders and community members. The roles and responsibilities of AEEs are far-reaching; they must engage with and bridge a variety of groups and factors, including government, school board employees, curriculum and content, school environments, students, and the community. Although all get support from their school boards, especially their immediate superintendents, most work alone much of the time. A full description of their work is out of the scope of this chapter, but it is vital to recognize that in spite of the tremendous scope of their work in a spiritual context, the roles of AEEs extend even beyond that to touch on diverse aspects of school and community life.

Discussion: Balancing Aboriginal and Catholic Spiritualities in a Catholic School Context

"The balance between Aboriginal culture and spirituality and Catholic religion can be tricky, but if you take a step back and embrace both of them, it's not as tricky as it seems, because the message is exactly the same. Be a good person. Be nice to your neighbours. Follow your heart."

There has been a great deal of research on the incorporation of Aboriginal content and pedagogies into the mainstream school system in Canada, especially since the closing of the last residential school in 1996 and the general realization that the school system must be adapted to suit the learning needs of Aboriginal young people, rather than expecting the young people themselves to adapt. The importance of this research cannot be understated, and it is of great value to all school systems, both First Nations and provincial, because both must strive to meet the needs of all learners and help Canadian society move past its oppressive past. However, little of this research has focused on the adaptation of a specifically Catholic way of learning and teaching to suit Aboriginal learners. Because spirituality is central to both traditional Aboriginal and Catholic ways of understanding the world, this chapter focuses specifically on how AEEs bring these two perspectives together within Catholic school boards.

Shared Theology and Values

"The Second Vatican Council. So in 1965, the changing of the single word, right? So the Catholic Church is not *the* means of salvation, it's *a* means of salvation. And so the idea that there are other paths to God. That opens up the door to a different context of theology in terms of our shared understanding of God and what God is, and the way we find God in our schools."

Taking a non-exclusivist stance, as is in keeping with Vatican II and with traditional Indigenous spirituality,[3] the AEEs have succeeded in finding diverse overlaps between Aboriginal and Catholic approaches to spirituality. First and foremost, the Indigenous spiritualities of the First Peoples of Ontario are essentially monotheistic, as is Catholicism. Although other supernatural beings such as Sky Woman, Nanabush, and one's ancestors, as well as spirits within nature, figure prominently in Indigenous spirituality, there is recognition of a supreme Creator deity. The nature of the Creator varies across belief systems, and even across individuals; for some, the Creator is a knowable, anthropomorphic deity similar to the Christian God, whereas for others the Creator is panentheistic, permeating and transcending creation; for still others, the understanding of the divine may encapsulate elements of both of these belief systems. This core similarity opens the door to finding common ground. Given that Indigenous spirituality is generally either inclusivistic or pluralistic, it is possible to adapt Indigenous practices and prayers that are panentheistic in nature to a non-panentheistic world view.

Table 12.2 Core values of Aboriginal and Catholic belief systems

Seven Grandfather Teachings	Beatitudes (Matthew 5:3–11, New Jerusalem Bible)	Ten Commandments (Catholic Church 2012, Section 2)
1. Honesty 2. Humility 3. Respect 4. Bravery 5. Wisdom 6. Truth 7. Love	1. Blessed are the poor in spirit: the Kingdom of Heaven is theirs. 2. Blessed are the gentle: they shall have the earth as inheritance. 3. Blessed are those who mourn: they shall be comforted. 4. Blessed are those who hunger and thirst for uprightness: they shall have their fill. 5. Blessed are the merciful: they shall have mercy shown them. 6. Blessed are the pure in heart: they shall see God. 7. Blessed are the peacemakers: they shall be recognized as children of God. 8. Blessed are those who are persecuted in the cause of uprightness: the Kingdom of Heaven is theirs.	1. I am the LORD your God: you shall not have strange Gods before me. 2. You shall not take the name of the LORD your God in vain. 3. Remember to keep holy the LORD's day. 4. Honour your father and your mother. 5. You shall not kill. 6. You shall not commit adultery. 7. You shall not steal. 8. You shall not bear false witness against your neighbour. 9. You shall not covet your neighbour's wife. 10. You shall not covet your neighbour's goods.

Beyond monotheism, there are other core values and teachings that are similar between both belief systems to which practitioners adhere (see Table 12.2). From an Anishinaabe tradition, these values are expressed through the Seven Grandfather Teachings; in a Catholic world view, they are expressed through the Ten Commandments and the Beatitudes:

While these teachings do not map onto one another directly, they have clear similarities. The Seven Grandfather Teachings list a set of characteristics that one must strive towards in order to live a good life, or *mino-bimaadiziwin* (Benton-Benai 1988; Bouchard 2009). The Beatitudes do the same, although the characteristics differ. The Ten Commandments, by contrast, give behavioural instructions for being a good person. The essence of all of these teachings is the same: to live a good life, one must be humble, treat others well, act with wisdom, and be strong in the pursuit of that which is right. As depicted in Figure 12.1, the Seven Grandfather Teachings, along with many other sacred teachings, can be mapped onto the Medicine Wheel as part of a three-dimensional model

Figure 12.1 The Seven Grandfather Teachings

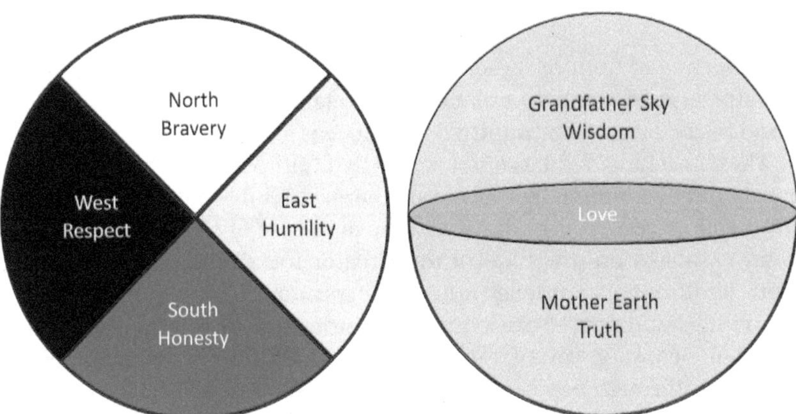

of spirituality as a part of the world around us; in this model, love is at the core of all Creation (Benton-Benai 1988; Bouchard 2009). It is also the core of Christian values as embodied in John 13:34, "love one another; you must love one another just as I have loved you."

In a Haudenosaunee tradition, rather than the Seven Grandfather Teachings and the Medicine Wheel, the means for living a good life come from the core values of Peace, a Good Mind, and Strength. For those AEEs working in areas with high Haudenosaunee populations, the concept of a Good Mind emerged as a core value:

> [A Good Mind means] a good way (righteous) of thinking. [It] means that people using their purest and most unselfish minds will achieve great thoughts, words and actions. It occurs when people put their minds and emotions in harmony with the flow of the universe and the intentions of the Creator (Six Nations Polytechnic [SNP] 2009).

These AEEs pointed out that a Good Mind is analogous to Holiness:

> All Christians in any state or walk of life are called to the fullness of Christian life and to the perfection of charity (Romans 8:28–30). All are called to holiness: "be perfect, as your heavenly Father is perfect" (*Lumen Gentium,* Section 2). In order to reach this perfection the faithful should use the strength dealt out to them by Christ's gift, so that ... doing the will of the Father in everything, they may wholeheartedly devote themselves to the

glory of God and to the service of their neighbor. (Catholic Church 2012, 2012–13)

The essence of both of these teachings is to find a relationship with the Creator and to strive to embody that relationship by working for the good of the larger community. Again, love is at the heart of both.

These teachings lead to other values that Catholic and Aboriginal traditions hold in common. For example, there is an inherent belief in respect for creation, respect for others, and the dignity of one's neighbour. There is an emphasis on gratitude to the Creator for all the gifts of creation. Both traditions acknowledge a need for spiritual cleansing; in Aboriginal tradition, smudging, sweat lodges, and other practices help one achieve spiritual cleansing, whereas in a Catholic tradition this is accomplished ultimately through baptism but also through the Eucharist and the use of holy water within the Mass and at other times. Both acknowledge the value of prayer and, as one AEE described, "creating a place for God within [oneself]." Both also emphasize respect for the wisdom of spiritual leaders, such as priests or elders, and both acknowledge a belief in an afterlife, although the exact nature of the afterlife varies across traditions.

All of the AEEs indicated that in many ways, having a common basis in these values simplifies inculturation. Although many of the AEEs still encounter fundamentalism within their work environments, for most the environment created by Vatican II and the similarity of these basic tenets allows for the incorporation of diverse ways of "becoming intimate with God," including both traditional Christian practices and practices from other cultures, such as meditation or connection with nature. Several of the AEEs noted that the faith basis of the school simplifies, rather than complicates, the process of inculturation. Rather than having to "talk around God for fear of offence," in a Catholic school environment, the AEEs, religious leaders, and elders are able to speak honestly about their epistemologies and world views. As one AEE stated, "I think in some ways that may be an easier connection for us than for a school board that doesn't have a faith or value base because they are embracing so many faiths and values that it's harder to make those connections."

Inculturating practices

"The sacraments are very parallel with traditional ceremonies. You know, things such as prayer, it happens in both, they're both held very high ... It may not be going to a church, it may be going to a ceremony, but ultimately you're getting the same out of both, just in a different way. You may speak to the Creator, but you're still in tune with that faith and that spirituality."

Based on these shared values, all of the AEEs found unique ways of respectfully inculturating Catholic practice with Aboriginal spirituality. For many, these were small but consistent gestures, such as the inclusion of Aboriginal spiritual artwork, especially Aboriginal Christian artwork, into the school environment. In some schools, the presence of these works may be subtle; in others, particularly those with higher Aboriginal student populations, efforts have been made to include Aboriginal spiritual items, such as sweetgrass braids or Medicine Wheels, throughout the school. As one AEE pointed out, these items may go unnoticed or spark curiosity in non-Aboriginal people, whereas for Aboriginal people they are very meaningful and create a welcoming and inclusive environment. Other small but meaningful gestures cited by AEEs include the use of Aboriginal languages where possible, such as in a morning greeting or even a prayer in the local language, or the use of that language to greet students in class or the hallway. This requires significant peer education so that teachers and other students have an understanding of what they are seeing and hearing and are able to participate. It also requires significant community consultation with priests, church employees, elders, community members, and families to ensure that inculturation is done in an appropriate, respectful, and authentic way.

This is even more the case for some of the larger examples of inculturation. These include the practice of Aboriginal ceremonies or the incorporation of Aboriginal ceremonies into classrooms and religious celebrations within the school. Sacred medicines, and in particular, the practice of smudging, were used to some degree by all of the participating school boards, according to local sensibilities. Some smudged regularly with students and performed smudges in classrooms; others chose not to smudge without an elder present. This again required education of students and teachers to ensure that the practice was treated with due respect and that participants understood what they were doing in terms of both Aboriginal tradition and their Catholic faith. Other larger examples of inculturation included incorporating Aboriginal practices into the Mass; for example, one school board held an Aboriginal-centred Mass, which was celebrated by an Aboriginal priest. In this case, the four directions and corresponding colours, smudging, sacred medicines, traditional dance and regalia, and drumming were incorporated into a large public Mass that was attended by staff, students, parents, and community members from across the school board.

At times, to ensure that the Catholic nature of the schools remains intact, Aboriginal practices have been adapted. An example several participants gave was the Haudenosaunee Thanksgiving Address. The Thanksgiving Address, which is traditionally recited at all ceremonies and meetings of more than two people, acknowledges all the elements of creation by type and thanks them for the roles they carry out as given by the Creator. When these non-human entities are greeted, there is an indication that they have their own spirits, which is not in keeping with Catholic doctrine. In employing the Thanksgiving Address in a Catholic context, the AEEs may change the words to thank God for creating the elements around us. This is not without controversy, and AEEs have the difficult job of ensuring that such adaptation is done in a way that does not suggest cultural appropriation. However, it is at this point that the agency of the parents must be underscored; the Aboriginal students in these school boards have been placed there by their parents, who have chosen a Catholic education for them. As one AEE stated, "the Aboriginal students that are in our schools, that are in our classrooms, are there because it's a Catholic community. And so they're not there as traditional people rejecting the Christian or Judeo-Christian approach. They're there because they're traditional people who are also Christians."

In terms of spiritual development, the AEEs are aware that many students from all ethnic backgrounds are from "culturally Christian" homes but do not necessarily practise Christianity regularly; for these students, the goal is not necessarily to develop them as Catholics but rather to develop them as spiritual people. As one participant said, "What we hope for all of our students is that whether they become practising members of the Catholic Church or not, that they have a relationship with God. And so we can do that with our Aboriginal students as well. They may or may not in the future be able to embrace both. They may make a choice where they feel that to remain traditional they cannot incorporate Christianity into their faith, but they have built a relationship with God. And that for us is important."

Challenges to Inculturation

"Sometimes the more you know, the more challenging it gets because then you are very conscious of things. I'm thinking it will become more challenging before it is not a challenge anymore, because more people are going to understand and know, and then be responsible and have those conversations."

Although all of the AEEs emphasized that they were generally meeting with success, their roles are not without their challenges. An analysis of participant responses indicates that challenges to inculturation come from within the school board and from families and the wider community. All of the AEEs have developed philosophies and practices to mitigate these challenges.

One of the most commonly cited challenges is teacher and staff attitude. The doctrine of the Catholic Church has changed to support inculturation, and most teachers are supportive of this, but some are not. There is pushback at times against incorporating beliefs and practices into Catholic spaces that are not specifically or traditionally Catholic. Overcoming this may involve adapting practices, as discussed previously. It may also involve working with staff to explain Aboriginal beliefs and practices, pointing out how they are in keeping with Catholic doctrine. That may be accomplished by coordinating formal professional development opportunities, but it is more often dealt with through face-to-face dialogue. It is vital to make time for that dialogue and to create a safe space for it. Teachers who challenge inculturation, who are shy to ask questions, or who ignore Aboriginal content often do so out of ignorance; the only solution to that is education, with an acknowledgment of the Catholic Church's past teachings and an emphasis on current doctrine on inculturation.

Another challenge is posed by teachers who are overzealous about incorporating Aboriginal practices without fully understanding the cultures in which they are rooted. AEEs spend time with these teachers explaining concepts such as cultural appropriation, talking about the diversity of Aboriginal cultures and the significance of beliefs and practices and ensuring that they inculturate their classrooms and practices with appropriate respect for each community and Nation. That involves challenging the status quo in schools and encouraging teachers to change how they approach the classroom.

In addition, Aboriginal community members and families may present challenges to inculturation. Some young people are disconnected from their Aboriginal heritage and may be reluctant to engage with it in a school context. For family members who had negative experiences in the school system, particularly those who experienced residential school, schools may be threatening places. This can lead to a lack of engagement in their children's education or to a misinterpretation of school activities or events. In such cases, AEEs often step in as moderators, educating school staff on Aboriginal perspectives, explaining why family members may react negatively to certain situations, and creating a welcoming environment for family members. This opens the door for family members to tell their own stories, leading to even better education for staff and students. However, this storytelling must be done with care. Due to the injustices of the past, some of the AEEs – especially those who are non-Aboriginal, as well as the staff members with whom they work – have encountered aggression from Aboriginal people towards non-Aboriginal society and towards the school system. Although understandable, in their experience this can detract from bridge-building efforts and intimidate staff members who otherwise would have been open to inculturation.

In some Aboriginal communities, the current political climate places pressure on students to choose between Christianity and traditional spirituality and places blame on current Christian communities for past injustices and their after-effects. While AEEs understand these attitudes, several of them expressed frustration because they can be counterproductive. However, they can also be beneficial, in that they can open the door to dialogue about the Church's past perspectives and how those perspectives have changed. That said, these are still Catholic schools, and the AEEs are faced with the challenge of finding elders and knowledge keepers whose views are in keeping with the ethos that the schools follow. As one AEE said, "just because you're a community member or an elder, doesn't necessarily mean that what you say is going to be within the proper context of our Catholic schools, or is going to help the students within our Catholic schools."

Finally, AEEs face ongoing budgetary constraints. As mentioned previously, many have duties other than Aboriginal education, and all work within fixed budgets since Aboriginal education is only one of many concerns for their school boards. That, combined with risk and logistical considerations, places limits on scope and means that certain things cannot be accomplished in a school context.

Truth, Reconciliation, and History

"Hidden histories of oppression still oppress people."

AEEs have the additional challenge of interfacing with the history of education in Canada and of the past doctrine of the Catholic Church.

This challenge is clearest when dealing with the Catholic Church's involvement in Canada's residential school system. As several of the AEEs emphasize, the Catholic Church was one of several churches involved in the residential school system, and the schools were overseen by the federal government. All of that aside, it is impossible to move forward in truth and reconciliation as a Catholic community without dealing with that aspect of history. As one AEE put it, "in public schools they can distance themselves but Catholic teachers have to hear about it and identify with it." That can be painful for teachers, for young people, and for their family members, who may be survivors of residential schools.

AEEs pointed to several key elements that are important when engaging with this past. First, it is important to begin by looking at what unites Catholic and Aboriginal communities. Also, it is vital to clarify the actual role the Catholic Church played in residential schools. All of the AEEs acknowledged that the Church was involved in running residential schools and is culpable in terms of that. However, they also emphasized that culpability ultimately rests with Canada as a whole, given that the schools were run by the federal government with full knowledge of the Canadian public; therefore, it is unfair to place blame solely on the Church. Still, they recognize that given the Church's emphasis on reconciliation, it is incumbent upon Catholics to take a leadership role in truth and reconciliation efforts.

In addressing the issue of residential schools with staff, and particularly with teachers, different AEEs take different approaches. Some choose to acknowledge residential schools and talk about them openly, while others approach the subject less frankly. This usually has to do with the proportion of Aboriginal staff members in the schools and the existing knowledge thresholds of the staff in general. Given the sensitivity of the subject, some AEEs working in regions where teachers have little knowledge of residential schools approach it very carefully to avoid making teachers feel guilty or uncomfortable, which would discourage them from learning and teaching about the subject. Regardless, all acknowledge the importance of talking about residential schools with teachers. Some do so through formal professional development events and conferences, while others prefer individual dialogue and providing resources to individual teachers. The goal is always to not just educate teachers but to provide them with the tools to in turn educate their students. Residential schools are one of the darkest chapters in Canadian history. It is vital for students to know what occurred and to think critically about how to prevent similar atrocities in the future. As one AEE stated, "just because [it] happened and the government says it, doesn't mean it's right. You're trying to bring up kids, and they're going to be contributing members of society. They need to know right from wrong and what's good and bad, and not everything is great. They have to think critically."

Conclusion

"We celebrate. We have a wonderful time. We get outside. We put our feet upon the land. We gather to celebrate our faith. We have a terrific time. But along with having that fun we're left with the responsibility to ensure that this time we set the story straight and do it right."

AEEs in Catholic school boards today have a challenging but fulfilling role. The doctrine of the Catholic Church has not always been open to inculturation and acceptance of Aboriginal values and practices; neither has the Ontario school system. However, following Vatican II and in keeping with changes in attitudes across society, inculturation is becoming increasingly normalized in Ontario Catholic schools. AEEs have the formidable task of supporting schools, churches, and entire communities in acknowledging past wrongs and building bridges for better education for the future. As Pope John Paul II said: "It is time to think of the present and of the future. Today, people are realizing more and more clearly that we all belong to the one human family, and are meant to walk and work together in mutual respect, understanding, trust, and love" (1987a). Both Aboriginal and Catholic spirituality call the faithful to act with love above all. There is no better way to plant the seeds of that love than by building safe, respectful, and inclusive school environments for all children, and teaching them there to honour the beauty of diversity.

NOTES

My thanks to Dr Kylee-Anne Hingston, Dr Chris Beeman, and Elizabeth Amirault, M.Div., for their guidance on this chapter. I would also like to express my heartfelt thanks to the participants in this study. You are all passionate people whose accomplishments inspire others to see the potential and beauty of Aboriginal education. Your school boards are blessed to have you doing the important work you do. Thank you for sharing your gifts with me. Miigwech, ni:áwen.

1 All AEEs note that the presence of FNMI students in their school boards is certainly much higher than the number who are formally self-identified. They also note a significant difference between the number of students who formally self-identified as Aboriginal according to Ministry of Education policy, and the number of students who in informal settings or non-government surveys self-identified as being of Aboriginal heritage.

2 Aboriginal Ontario is very diverse. The land that is now Ontario is home to the traditional territories of the Cree, Oji-Cree, Lenape, and Anishinaabeg (Ojibwe, Odawa, Pottawatomi, Chippewa, Saulteaux, Nipissing, Mississauga, and Algonquin) peoples, as well as the Nations of the Six Nations Confederacy (Seneca, Cayuga, Onondaga, Oneida, Mohawk, and Tuscarora). There are territories traditional to the Neutral and Huron peoples. There is also a significant Métis population (people of mixed usually French and Aboriginal heritage, generally dating from the time of the fur trade, who have their own unique cultural identity).

3 Exclusivism is defined here as the belief that there is only one true religion or one true path to God. While the Catholic Church still professes to be the "sole Church of Christ" (Catholic Church 2012, 811), it used to be much more exclusivist. The shift seen in Vatican II has changed this; now, it has an inclusivist stance, in that it "recognizes in other religions that search, among shadows and images, for the God who is unknown yet near since he gives life and breath and all things and wants all men to be saved" (843).

REFERENCES

Anuik, Jonathan, and Laura-Lee Bellehumeur-Kearns. 2012. *Report on Métis Education in Ontario's K-12 Schools.* Métis Nation of Ontario. http://www.metisnation.org/media/246898/anuik%20kearns%20m%C3%A9tis%20education%20in%20ontario%20report%20final%20draft%202012%20%5B3%5D.pdf.

Benton-Banai, Edward. 1988. *The Mishomis Book: The Voice of the Ojibway.* Hayward: Indian Country Communications.

Bouchard, David. 2009. *Seven Sacred Teachings: Niizhwaaswi Gagiikwewin.* North Vancouver: More Than Words Publishers.

Canadian Conference of Catholic Bishops [CCCB]. 2015. *Apology on Residential Schools by the Catholic Church.* http://www.cccb.ca/site/eng/media-room/files/2630-apology-on-residential-schools-by-the-catholic-church.

Catholic Church. 2012. *Catechism of the Catholic Church.* Vatican City: Libreria Editrice Vaticana.

Deloria, Vine, Jr. 1973. *God Is Red.* New York: Grosset and Dunlap.
Dickason, Olive Patricia. 2006. *A Concise History of Canada's First Nations.* Toronto: Oxford University Press.
Fitzhugh, William W., Anja Herzog, Sophia Perdikaris, and Brenna McLeod. 2011. "Ship to Shore: Inuit, Early Europeans, and Maritime Landscapes in the Northern Gulf of St Lawrence." *Archeology of Maritime Landscapes: When the Land Meets the Sea* 2: 99–128. http://dx.doi.org/10.1007/978-1-4419-8210-0_6.
Hawthorn, H.B., ed. 1967. *A Survey of the Contemporary Indians of Canada: Economic Political, Educational Needs and Policies.* Ottawa: Indian and Northern Affairs Canada. https://www.aadnc-aandc.gc.ca/eng/1291832488245/1291832647702.
Langevin, Breena. 2014. *Hybrid Churches of Canada: A Space for Religious "Inculturation"?* MEd Thesis, University of Guelph.
Malakoff, David. 2007. "Uncovering Basques in Canada." *American Archeology* 11(2): 12–17.
McGregor, Linda. 2009. *Community Members Speak: First Nation, Métis, and Inuit Education Kindergarten to Grade 12.* Report prepared for the Simcoe Muskoka Catholic District School Board in response to the Ontario First Nation, Métis, and Inuit Education Policy Framework. Barrie: Simcoe Muskoka Catholic District School Board. http://www.smcdsb.on.ca/UserFiles/Servers/Server_29970/File/Programs/Aboriginal%20Education%20Project/Final%20Report%20-%20Community%20Members%20Speak/Report%20Nov%2010.pdf.
Murphy, Terrence, and Roberto Perin. 1996. *A Concise History of Christianity in Canada.* Toronto: Oxford University Press.
Nguyen, Mai. 2011. "Closing the Education Gap: A Case for Aboriginal Early Childhood Education in Canada: A Look at the Aboriginal Head Start Program." In *Approaches to Aboriginal Education in Canada: Searching For Solutions,* edited by Frances Widdowson and Albert Howard, 38–56. Edmonton: Brush Education.
Ontario Ministry of Education [OME]. 2007a. *Building Bridges to Success for First Nations, Métis, and Inuit Students.* http://www.edu.gov.on.ca/eng/aboriginal/buildbridges.pdf.
– 2007b. *Ontario First Nation, Métis, and Inuit Education Policy Framework.* http://www.edu.gov.on.ca/eng/aboriginal/OFNImplementationPlan.pdf.
– 2014. *Implementation Plan: Ontario First Nations, Métis, and Inuit Education Policy Framework.* http://www.edu.gov.on.ca/eng/aboriginal/OFNImplementationPlan.pdf.
Panganiban, Patricia. 2004. "Inculturation and the Second Vatican Council." *Landas* 18(1): 59–93.

Pope John Paul II. 1987a. *Apostolic Mission to the United States of America and Canada: Meeting with the Native Peoples of the Americas.* http://w2.vatican.va/content/john-paul-ii/en/speeches/1987/september/documents/hf_jp-ii_spe_19870914_amerindi-phoenix.html.

– 1987b. *Apostolic Mission to the United States of America and Canada: Meeting with the Native Peoples of Canada.* http://w2.vatican.va/content/john-paul-ii/en/speeches/1987/september/documents/hf_jp-ii_spe_19870920_indigeni-fort-simpson.html

– 1990. *Redemptoris Missio.* http://w2.vatican.va/content/john-paul-ii/en/encyclicals/documents/hf_jp-ii_enc_07121990_redemptoris-missio.html.

Royal Commission on Aboriginal Peoples. 1996. *Report of the Royal Commission on Aboriginal Peoples.* http://www.collectionscanada.gc.ca/webarchives/20071115053257/http://www.ainc-inac.gc.ca/ch/rcap/sg/sgmm_e.html.

Shorter, Aylward. 1999. *Toward a Theory of Inculturation.* Eugene: Wipf and Stock.

Six Nations Polytechnic [SNP]. 2009. *Five Branches of Hodinohso:ni/Rotinoshyonni Philosophy: Cultural Underpinnings of the Indigenous Knowledge Centre.* http://www.snpolytechnic.com/templates/protostar/pdf/WEBSITE-IKC%20document%20Five%20Branches%20of%20Haudenosaunee%20Philosophy.pdf?lbisphpreq=1.

Statistics Canada. 2013. Ontario (Code 35) (table). National Household Survey (NHS) Aboriginal Population Profile. 2011 *National Household Survey* Statistics Canada Cat. no. 99-011-X2011007). Ottawa. http://www12.statcan.gc.ca/nhs-enm/2011/dp-pd/aprof/index.cfm?Lang=E.

Trudeau, Justin. 2015. Statement by Prime Minister on Release of the Final Report of the Truth and Reconciliation Commission. http://www.pm.gc.ca/eng/news/2015/12/15/statement-prime-minister-release-final-report-truth-and-reconciliation-commission.

Truth and Reconciliation Commission of Canada [TRC]. 2015a. *Honouring the Truth, Reconciling for the Future: Summary of the Final Report of the Truth and Reconciliation Commission of Canada.* http://nctr.ca/assets/reports/Final%20Reports/Executive_Summary_English_Web.pdf.

– 2015b. *Truth and Reconciliation Commission of Canada: Calls to Action.* http://nctr.ca/assets/reports/Calls_to_Action_English2.pdf.

Vatican. 1985. *The Final Report of the 1985 Extraordinary Synod.* https://www.catholicculture.org/culture/library/view.cfm?recnum=5132.

– 2009. "Communiqué of the Holy See Press Office." 29 April. http://www.vatican.va/resources/resources_canada-first-nations-apr2009_en.html.

13 Indigenous Education as Failed Ontological Reconfiguration

CHRISTOPHER BEEMAN

Introduction

Might there be reasons, best described as ontological, why changes to education that could be reasonably supposed to occur as a result of the Second Vatican Council were unlikely to meet the needs of Aboriginal students? That is the central question posed in this chapter. The direction I take is a philosophical one, based in history but not reliant on historical documents alone. I take this approach largely because I think that the kinds of answers that can be found through a philosophical investigation may offer insights unavailable through other means. In this chapter I use the term *ontological*, for reasons I will later examine, because no other simple term exists in English. But this work began with the idea that there are different ways of being in the world that extend beyond the usual discussions about diversity (an idea that is today acquiring more resonance in academe).[1] And while I do make connections to historical documents, this work focuses on another way of understanding the destructive effects of colonial schools on their residents. I begin by looking into the central question and related terms. I proceed with some background on Vatican II. Then I look to some stories of elders and places that may shed light on just how great a difference may exist between the ontologies I refer to.

To give away the punchline – by which I mean, a possible conclusion – one explanation for the continued inability of educational systems in general to meet the needs of Aboriginal[2] students is the failure, on the part of the modern, global West, to recognize, understand, and accommodate diversity, more deeply understood. In other words, despite the generally progressive direction and effects of Vatican II, noted below, the way of being in the world of certain Aboriginal (and other) students might have been so different in the era of residential schools, and might in certain cases be so different today as to be unrecognizable as a kind of difference, one that needs to be honoured by appropriate educational modes, by those who teach. If such a difference in ways of being in the world really did (and does) exist, it may be the case that this inhibits, except in rare cases, any meaningful dialogue across ontologies, thus preventing the emergence of educational practices capable of bridging these (assuming this to be possible). Hence my suggestion that the education of First Nations, Métis, and Inuit students, as practised in missionary schools and elsewhere, may, in some circumstances noted in this chapter (i.e., where Indigeneity/Authochthony and Aboriginality coincide and overlap),[3] be described as a failed attempt at ontological reconfiguration. The sometimes intended and sometimes unintended effects of educational attempts, at the level of the individual actor (in addition to the intentional attempts to assimilate, at the level of government policy, for example) to change Aboriginal students had to fail because underlying ontological roots of difference were never addressed.

Methodology

Most of the chapters in this book are historical examinations of educational issues related to the theological and policy changes that arose from Vatican II. This chapter takes a different tack: it notes certain historical moments relating to Vatican II, but it mainly considers the words of elders, in conjunction with my own experiences in wild places. It extrapolates from these, rather than from historical clues, to make its case.

In research, information usually comes to me in the form of conversations or experiences. I record spoken words in writing or in audio or video files. I keep coming back to some of the seminal conversations I have had with elders, and over repeated visits, these have gained some historical aspects. But the process I use – which is partly informed by Aboriginal history, identity, and various shaping political influences – tends to be one of building relationships; talking with, interpreting, writing, checking back with elders; parsing my own experience; and talking and writing again. I employ narrative and discursive interpretive tools. The work I do tends to be rooted in hermeneutics, and this is the case in this chapter. And because I am coming at this from a philosophical perspective, I am less interested in moments in history, although these can be important, and more interested in the relationship between ideas.

So when I speak with elders, the purpose of conversations – besides our common interest in sustaining valued relationships – is not to gather quantifiable data, for this would be to misconstrue both the valuable ideas and relationships. Rather, the purpose is to gain an understanding of the ideas that walk beside me as I try to make sense of my own experience of differing states of being.

Ontologies

In this chapter I look at the ontological difference between those living Autochthonously[4] ("Indigenously") and those not – a difference encapsulated in earlier work through the use of the term *attentive receptivity*[5] – and how this would ultimately limit the capacity of any religiously conceived educational system to bridge the divide. (A later section examines this in detail, but by "ontological" I mean approximately the more awkward term "ways of being in the world.") It follows that Vatican II would have had little effect on educative practices relating to Aboriginal peoples – at the pointy end of the pencil, as it were – for the changes it called for did not address the way of being that was at the heart of the difference between those living Indigenously and those not.

This is the broad overview. To make this case, I will also look at some criticisms of how I make use of an ontological argument – in particular, the tendency for this argument to seemingly oversimplify and delineate differences between ontologies, to limit the possibility of accident and crossover between ontological positions and, in short, to find impediments to the possibility of communication between ontologies.

These aspects are a part of this argument, to which I naturally feel attached, now that I have made it. However, in the course of my research, experience really did precede theory in reporting ontological difference, just as being precedes a description of being. I know that what is written here may seem uncomfortably un-postmodern for many readers. It may appear too reified or certain. But in the spirit of intellectual honesty, the barriers to communication between ontologies appear to me to be very real. Perhaps it is possible, in ways I have not yet experienced, that they can be overcome. But what would ontological difference consist in, if not in deeply incompatible states of being? I will also later argue (doubtless unpopularly again) that state of being, while influenced by the words and stories around it and thus never wholly independent of these, ultimately does in practice – and ought to, in interpretation – take precedence over descriptions and analysis.

Attentive receptivity is a way of being in the world that sustains the life of the human participant and the health of the ecosystem, and that expresses, in moment-by-moment awareness, the ecocentric interdependence of all being (Beeman, 2006). This is a distinctly different state of being from that of *Homo mobilis*, which is the term I assign to the way of being in the world of participants in the modern, global West and North. It is one that some of the elders with whom I meet experience in part of their lives, and one which I have experienced in long solo travels in wilder places. One lives this mode of being rather than thinks it, although one also has an awareness of it.[6] That this systemic, being-related difference between those living Indigenously and those not has been neither understood nor taken into account is, I believe, at the root of the failure of religiously based (and most other) educative practices to meet the needs and to accommodate the difference of Aboriginal peoples in Canada. And because this difference has not been understood, even the sometimes progressive changes embodied in Vatican II have failed to bridge the ontological gap.

This work derives from earlier research suggesting that there is an incommensurable difference between the ways of being enacted in Autochthony or Indigeneity and the ways of being encompassed in existence as a member of *Homo mobilis*. In earlier work, I also tried to distinguish between the ethnic circumstance of Aboriginality and what I posit to be an ontological condition of Autochthony/Indigeneity. And while in practice a relatively large number of Aboriginal people enact a mode of being of attentive receptivity, so do some non-Aboriginal people.[7] Moreover, there are many Aboriginal people – for example, youth living in cities with little interest in the more than human world – who do not enact an ontology of attentive receptivity. Thus attentive receptivity, understood as an ontological condition, bridges ethnic divides, making possible ways-of-being alliances that may accommodate Aboriginal *and* non-Aboriginal people. In this way the existence of attentive receptivity challenges the dominance of the modern global West on grounds other than those on which it is normally challenged. These grounds are not simply the historical colonization in ethnic terms of non-white (in the case of Canada, predominantly Aboriginal) peoples: they are a further colonization of ways of being in the world. In this characterization, both Aboriginal and non-Aboriginal peoples may participate as ontological colonizers, although in practice it is non-Aboriginal people who tend to enact the state of being that makes possible the colonization of those who enact the state of being of attentive receptivity. I consider this state of being to be both universal in (human) possibility and rare in occurrence. More remains to be said about ontologies in this chapter, but for the time being, some details of Vatican II need to be brought to this discussion.

The Second Vatican Council, *Dignitatis Humanae*, and the *Declaration on Religious Education*

A brief history of the Second Vatican Council is required here. Let us shift gears for a moment to consider some of the changes wrought by Vatican II, the implications they had for education, and why, from a philosophical position, those changes failed to improve the education experience of Aboriginal students. In particular, I will examine the *Dignitatis Humanae*, the *Declaration on Christian Education*, and the *Populorum Progressio*.

The Second Vatican Council, Pope John XXIII's famous effort to open the windows of the Church to let in some fresh air, took place over four periods spanning two papacies, beginning in 1962 and ending in 1965. Vatican II represented, in Baum's words, "a paradigm shift in the Catholic tradition" (2011, 377). The declarations emerging from it were not simply an apparent departure from convention. They represented a significant shift in views among the majority of the magisterium – the body governing Catholic policies – and they have shaped policy ever since.

The main purpose of Vatican II was to examine the Catholic Church's relationship with a changing world. After the death of Pope John XXIII, in the second period, beginning in September 1963, more specific purposes – articulated by Pope Paul VI – included restoring unity among all Christians and opening a dialogue with the contemporary world. A major product of the final, fourth period was the *Dignitatis Humanae,* a document pertaining to religious freedom, which had strong relevance for education. *Dignitatis Humanae* outlined several important changes in the direction of the Catholic Church. For example, it recognized a person's fundamental right to religious liberty, it delineated the state's responsibility, and it accepted that religious freedom is a necessary aspect of Christianity. While any document must be examined in the context of the myriad forces influencing its drafting and interpretation, and while this document has been at the heart of existing differences in the Church, its overall intent is consistent – it is to open the Church and its people to other faiths and other world views.

The Declaration's stance on the fundamental right to religious liberty rests on the essential dignity of every individual – a dignity that is granted by God. This is, in effect, a Christian argument for why religious freedom must extend to all people: the inherent dignity of individuals demands that each be allowed to choose his or her own path. The document also asserts that such dignity extends, in particular, to the choice of religious education: "This freedom from coercion in religious affairs must also be recognized as a right when persons act in community. As such a community, and in fact a society in its own original right has the right to live its own domestic religious life in freedom, in particular the freedom to choose religious education" (Pope Paul VI 1965b).

The Declaration does not address what constitutes religious education, nor does it consider the rights of people too young to make informed decisions. But it does hold that the principles of Christianity are transgressed if religious freedom is not upheld. In the section on religious freedom and Christianity, the case extends further to the freedom of all people to choose their own religious path, whether Christian or not. The document would seem to strongly support educational practices suited to people of widely varying backgrounds.

Thus there would have been a strong impetus, for those following the Church's teachings, to educate in ways consistent with this new paradigm. My argument goes as follows: Vatican II led to a paradigm shift towards openness to new possibilities in connectivity between world views, including a respect for other routes to God, as many of the commentators in Attridge, Clifford, and Routhier's *Vatican II* (2011) point out. This had significant implications for how educative practices on reservations and in convent schools and other locations ought to have played out. Yet the colonial project of educating Aboriginal people in North America has never succeeded. In particular, Eber Hampton's early articulation, in "Towards a Redefinition of Indian/Alaskan Native Education" (1993, 261), of both the failure of Aboriginal education in North America, and his ideas about how Aboriginal education might work, suggests that only a self-generated education will ultimately succeed. Leaving aside – for now – linguistic, cultural, historical, political, and cosmological differences, it is likely that religious education from a Catholic perspective simply presupposed a way of being of all people that may not have applied equally to First Nations, Inuit, and Métis peoples in Canada. In other words, while cultural and religious difference could be accommodated by Vatican II, ontological difference could not.

The *Declaration on Christian Education* was more directly related to education, yet it perhaps said less. Joe Stafford provides an excellent and detailed analysis of it in this volume. In brief, it seems that the Declaration does not fully agree with *Dignitatis Humanae*; indeed, it admits to needing further work (Pope Paul VI 1965b). Particularly important is the "illocutionary force" of the document – that is, the words themselves may not provide a full understanding of its import, and social context, history, and intents may all play a part in how it is understood and how its meaning is interpreted within an existing Church.[8] Among other things, Stafford points out that it quotes on ten occasions the 1929 *Encyclical*, a document reflecting much earlier and less tolerant views. Clearly, then, this document was to be a continuation of relatively conservative Catholic teaching. Thus, even if the earlier *Dignitatis Humanae* were without problems, there may have been hidden conservative elements within the magisterium of the Catholic Church that were unwilling to permit the relative freedom proposed by *Dignitatis Humanae*. In Section 2, for example, the document reads: "A Christian education does not merely strive for the maturing of a human person as just now described, but has as its principal purpose this goal: that the baptized, while they are gradually introduced to the knowledge of the mystery of salvation, become ever more aware of the gift of Faith they have received, and that they learn in addition how to worship God the Father in spirit and truth (cf. John 4:23)" (Pope Paul VI 1965a).

The above quotation is suggesting that the purpose of a Catholic school education is to progressively bring students into the faith. But it is also clear that the faith itself is at odds with attentive receptivity, which is the ontological condition of living in an Indigenous way. The term I use to describe the process of bringing students to the faith is *ontological reconfiguration*. Whatever the intention of the particular teacher, the effect of such an education is to move the ontology of the learner from the more-than-human world, to the human- and God-centred world of the global modern West. The parameters of this chapter do not permit a more in-depth analysis of the text of the Declaration, but passages similar to the one I have just quoted are frequent.

A later encyclical, *Populorum Progressio*, circulated in 1967, reflects even more conservative views. This is perhaps the more revealing document, because it seems to be *trying* to speak in a liberalizing way. But witness this excerpt from Section 7 on the effects of colonialism. It begins with a familiar lament: "It is true that colonizing nations were sometimes concerned with nothing save their own interests, their own power and their own prestige; their departure left the economy of these countries in precarious imbalance ... Certain types of colonialism surely caused harm and paved the way for future troubles."

But then: "On the other hand, we must also reserve a word of praise for those colonizers whose skills and technical know-how brought benefits to many untamed lands, and whose work survives to this day. The structural machinery they introduced was not fully developed or perfected, but it did help to reduce ignorance and disease, to promote communication, and to improve living conditions (Pope Paul VI 1967)."

It is beyond the scope of this chapter to critique missionary practices in general. Of relevance in this passage, though, is the sense that only contact that *tamed* non-European peoples could be construed as "successful," and that the untamed was roughly what was found on Turtle Island and resisted the colonizing process. Perhaps the "untamed" can also be equated with a way of being that was not recognized as having intrinsic worth.

Rosa Bruno-Jofré's work on the Missionary Oblate Sisters offers a detailed understanding of some earlier residential schools, from the very human perspective of some of the Sisters working in them. Of particular interest are the Sisters' own responses to the male-generated, centre-oriented magisterial *dicta* – responses that often emphasized the human local work that needed to be done. Writes Bruno-Jofré: "the ethnocentric character of the missionary work with the Native people and the prison[-]like character of the residential schools contrasted with the Sisters' counterhegemonic stand in the Franco-Manitoban communities" (2005, 138). It is possible that despite their counter-hegemonic stance, those well-intentioned and honourable Sisters could not conceive of a world view and way of being that – to be fully honoured in accordance with Vatican II – required a system of education completely different from what Catholicism could offer.

But the point of this chapter is not to unearth historical evidence of changed educational practice. Rather, it is to posit why, whatever the practitioners' inclinations, and whatever the struggles between members of the Church, no meaningful change in educational practice – that is, no change that resulted in education that could readily work for them – actually reached Indigenous students. Possibly, the ontological difference was so great that it could not be bridged or even recognized as difference. This would not have been the case for all Aboriginal students, but as mentioned earlier, if this different way of being in the world was an based on ontology, then it would have been students living a particular way of life, and enacting a particular state of being, who were most affected. Add to this the other factors affecting many Aboriginal students during the residential school era as articulated in *Shingwauk's Vision* (Miller 1996), and we find a recipe for academic, social, and political trauma.

Ontologies and *ontos*

The term *ontology* and the limitations of its use need explanation. Ontology, the study of being, was of great significance from the time of the pre-Socratics and throughout Hellenic philosophy. Heidegger's *Being and Time* (1962, first published in 1927) resurrected the idea, but at least in the Anglo-American analytic tradition, ontology and metaphysics were always suspected of being just a little too European, a little too *Continental* a branch of investigation. In very recent years, ontology has emerged as a significant and suddenly hip new area through the work of the object-oriented ontologists.[9] Generally, however, ontology has lurked in the background of Western philosophy, for being defies ready explanation. After all, at the heart of Heidegger's early project was the question of *why* there is something rather than nothing. Husserl's criticism that as soon as *Dasein* – the being for whom Being is a question (i.e., humans) – was introduced, Heidegger's project (1993) changed from an ontological one to an anthropological one, exposes some of the difficulties in even approaching Being: there is never an easy way to know what the parameters of the discussion are. And even in philosophical circles, this is not the kind of problem one generally sorts out before breakfast – even, as it were, a Continental one.

The term derives from the Greek *onto-* – the word-forming element, from the root *on* (the genitive case of which is *ontos*) – *being*. So we are dealing with the study of being. And herein lies the first problem. The English language has only one term, *ontology*, to distinguish two quite distinct ideas: the condition of being, and a study of being. Add to this that *ontology* has come to be used so broadly as to become meaningless. Until recently, I have used the term *ontology* to refer to a condition of being because that was its common use. I have begun to think this ought to change. In recent work, I have proposed that we begin to simply use the Greek *ontos* to refer to the condition of being. *Ontology* would continue to refer to its study. I propose to employ *ontological* in its usual way, as the adjective relating to being or its study. I make these suggestions to permit easy access to words that bring particular attention to *being*, apart from the usual, everyday use of "being." So I will do that from this point in this chapter.

In the move I propose, some have lamented the separation of *ontos* from *logos*, and hence, the separation of being from the words that relate to it.[10] I acknowledge that the being described in this chapter is one shaped in some part by the words of both the elders I have worked with and their stories and ideas. Thus, words are shaping influences in understanding the being state to which I refer. There is no doubt that *logos* has influenced *ontos* in the research I have done: the words of elders, for example, have permitted a different kind of examination of my own lived way of being, thus showing the possibility of accident and movement influencing *ontos*.[11]

Add to this that *ontos* is not static. It interacts with the world and with, I would argue, the only other predominant state of being – which I enact in writing chapters like this one and in engaging in most of what I do in everyday life. This is the being-state of *Homo mobilis*. The two are capable of being aware of each other, at least for some elders with whom I work. That said, a narrow post-structural stance, in which the description or words around the being state would predominate, is problematic in at least two ways. First, it represents the situation unfairly: the mode of communication about the ontological state is given dominance over the thing in itself. And while the mode of communication that uses words works for the state of being of *Homo mobilis*, the natural form of communication for attentive receptivity is otherwise. And leaving aside for the moment the obvious critique of this from a post-structural stance, I can only argue phenomenologically here: there appears to be such a thing as another way of being in the world as reported by elders,[12] and while it may be influenced in some small part by words around it, it can exist independently of these, no matter how attractive may appear the (word-based) contrary.

Second, words, like the words on this page, are the predominant representation of *Homo mobilis*'s reason. But when we give primacy to them, the being state of attentive receptivity is overshadowed and diminished in importance. This is not surprising, for it is the tactic of *Homo mobilis* to only fight ontological arguments on its own grounds. By virtue of its global dominance, *Homo mobilis* can afford to ignore those *ontos* that are not encountered there – in the world of words. Again, if this view is accurate, it has unexpected support in recent neuroscience.[13] Said another way – in words, of course – it is very difficult, using words, to access even the slightest nuance of attentive receptivity.

In short, I am trying to give voice – and (a version of) identity – to a way of being in the world that, as soon as it can identify itself, is likely to be misunderstood, overshadowed, ridiculed, or ignored. In practice, I can think of no better terms to describe the ways in which First Nations, Inuit, and Métis people in Canada have historically been regarded. If this insight is accurate, then this is probably more than a coincidence.

But the proposed removal of *logos*, when discussing ways of being, does another thing: it permits a focus on the being-state, which is the primary phenomenological event that emerges in my work with elders. It also points to the primacy of the being-state, and perhaps permits reconsideration of the thinking or *wording* or study about it. I know that this perspective is unpopular now. I can only say that I am attempting to accurately describe a phenomenon *qua* phenomenon, which somewhat inconveniently may not accommodate or conform to current popular ways of describing it.

The relevance of this background information to the current collection is this: a wish for intellectual accuracy has compelled me, in research during the past decade, to describe what I had initially thought were simply very different ideas expressed by the elders with whom I worked, as being ontologically different rather than simply, say, culturally, spiritually, or cosmologically different. By this, I mean that they could not be consistently explained as simply deriving from another perspective, point of view, cultural stance, or linguistic situation, or any of the standard ideas around difference (such as gender, race, sexual orientation, cultural, religious, or spiritual positions) normally recognized in Western discourses as related to diversity. They could only be understood, I came to believe, as deriving from a very different way of being in the world – one so different as to be utterly foreign to the way of being lived by all of us, in the now globally dominant, modern West – indeed, as to be unrecognizable as existing at all.

Of course, I am not referring to some universalizable condition for an idealized and reified notion of the noble savage. A few – a very few – elders expressed these ideas and understandings of another way of being, and they did not do so intending to "teach" me. It was simply that I was in a position to hear their words because I had lived, in ways relevant to this understanding, a certain kind of life. It might be said that I at times enacted a certain *ontos* that permitted an understanding of the *ontos* to which they referred. Later, I realized that some non-Aboriginal people were expressing some similar ideas. Thus, I posited that a state of being, rather than ethnicity per se, was at the heart of this idea, and that Indigeneity could be considered separately from Aboriginality (Beeman 2006).

For a very long time, I tried to accommodate rationally what the elders were saying to me, within a paradigm I had grown up with. To do this, I interpreted their words as metaphor. But they kept on speaking in ways that continued to niggle at my understanding – they were very literally being in the world in a different way than was comprehended as possible by the global, modern West. The *ontos* they were describing was different from my own – or at least from the ontological position I normally occupy. And if this was the case, then it, more than any other factor, would limit the capacity of an otherwise-enacted *ontos* to teach it.

Elders Speak

Let me give you an example of this: Alex Mathias, when I asked him about finding food on the land, said:

> well, I was led to it
> the partridge is presented to me ...
> if I wasn't meant to get a partridge
> I wouldn't even have seen it. (Mathias in Beeman, 2006)

The use of metaphor is common. And generally, when we hear metaphor, we tend to do a little subconscious, or perhaps just high-speed, interpreting. When I hear Alex's words, my natural inclination is to process them something like this: *Alex is saying he was "led" to the animal ... But there was no one there to lead him. So, presumably, Alex is using these words as metaphor to indicate that he "felt as though" he were being led. And then Alex found the animal. So, it is natural that Alex thinks that what felt like it was leading him actually did result in his finding the animal. It was "presented." In other words,* "if I wasn't meant to get a partridge I wouldn't even have seen it."

It is also possible to interpret Alex's statement in such a way as to very easily place, as religious teachers might have done, God, or perhaps a spiritual being, as the force doing the leading. Using this model, a translation and understanding of Alex's words becomes quite easy: God led, and God meant Alex to find.

At the heart of this particular issue is that I now believe myself to have been completely incorrect in my interpretation – a very well-intentioned interpretation – that Alex was speaking metaphorically. I now believe that Alex spoke, very literally, that he was meant to find food. And the meaning-making was not by an externally operating God with Alex's interests at heart, but by (and with) something like the ecosystem as a whole, at this particular instant. Alex's part in this ecosystem, at this time, was to find food. Another being's part was to be found *as* food. Alex is an active participant in this ecosystem but does not "direct" it. He does not have, nor was he ever given, "dominion" over it. From previous conversations, I understood that to sense the apt unfolding of this moment, in this ecosystem, Alex had to be in a particular state of being. And only by being in a particular state was he able to find the food that he and his family needed.

This is a much less convenient interpretation than my initial one. What, after all, does it mean to occupy a particular or different state of being? In the modern global West, the individualized and disconnected subject holds prime importance. One reasons; one researches; one prepares. One comes to know everything one can about a certain subject, both with the mind and perhaps with the feelings. Then one acts in ways that are consistent with the gathered knowledge. And one "finds food" or "does not find food" in the endeavour. Or so, at least, goes the story. But Alex's statement suggests that he was conceiving and enacting of a way of being within an ecosystem such that his very being, his *ontos,* was linked to state of being, the *ontos* of the whole. In this system, the individualized self-interest of a globally Western, rational operant played very little part and the "self" as it is construed in the modern West, disappears.

Let us turn to another philosopher – Baruch Spinoza – for some insight into Alex's position. Spinoza's family came from Portugal to Amsterdam at the time of the Thirty Years' War. They were Jews, who were generally despised and poorly treated at the time, living precariously close to Inquisition Spain. As Jews, they sought the relative tolerance of Amsterdam during the trying Christian disputes of that era. So we find Baruch being born about one-third of the way through the 1600s to a prosperous Jewish family, in Amsterdam, just as Descartes's radical theorizing was coming into vogue, with, given the context of his precarious life and ideas, an almost unimaginably well-developed sense of how to speak subtly about controversial issues. Despite this ability, Spinoza was exiled – "anathematized" – from his synagogue through the utterly terminal ceremony of the Herem, which exiled him not just from his place of worship but from all of his family and friends – and God – forever. He was being punished for his radical views, and we can suppose that those views included his understanding of God.

Spinoza's reimagining of God solved a major block in Descartes's system of philosophy. In Descartes's *Meditations,* God comprises all substance, but in a move that still perplexes philosophers, mind and matter are necessarily completely separate. Yet God must also be able to move between the worlds of mind and matter. So God is either breaking his own rules, or he is constantly *ex machina.* But for Spinoza, God was *equivalent* to Nature. And by Nature, Spinoza meant the *Natura naturans* – the *being* force in all nature. God was all the "stuff" (and non-stuff) in all-that-is. This resolved the mind/matter problem, because God, being the stuff itself (Substance) had also all the Attributes of the mind–matter continuum. (Mind and matter are the only two Attributes, among the infinitely possible ones, that humans are able to comprehend or conceive of.) Thus, the problem of division between mind and matter was resolved by Spinoza's positing of a pantheistic universe (Spinoza, 2006).

Perhaps more significant is that Spinoza felt he had resolved a residual conflict, which then permitted "the intellectual love of God." In other words, Spinoza's proposed new framework permitted an accurate knowledge of the parts in conjunction with an understanding of the whole. Or, in Spinoza's own phrasing, it is knowledge gained "from an adequate idea of the formal essence of certain attributes of God to an adequate knowledge of the essence of things" (Spinoza 2002, 267). Through Spinoza's *intuition,* or *intuitive* way of knowing, the particular is understood in the context of knowing the whole. Similarly, the episteme (in a Foucauldian sense, the conditions of possibility of their occurrence) of Alex's knowledge of what food is "presented" to him rests on a particular way of his being in the world. And for Alex, as for Spinoza, this way of being is predicated on a moment-by-moment awareness of the all-that-is as container and constituent of all knowledge and being, in conjunction with one's own position *within* that system. So one is both observer and part of what is being observed, as it were.

When we return, again, to Alex's statement, with Spinoza's cosmological modifications in mind, we may come to hear it as not simply metaphorical. Perhaps the entire world is singing, at each moment, the intents and desires of each being. Perhaps the outcome of such a symphony is an overall intent (not a priori, but collaboratively, as it unfolds) for the world to progress in a certain way. What distinguishes this stance from a God-centred one is that God does not "direct"; what takes the place of God is the direction itself. Or, one might say, God could be the moving force behind the all-that-is – the *naturans* in *Natura naturans,* returning to Spinoza.

And what might an educational system suited to such a different way of being look like? The point is, of course, that any educational system – no matter how progressive – that has been in existence on Turtle Island since the coming of Europeans, has been in almost absolute opposition, in terms of its underlying orientation, to this view. This has informed my initial scepticism about the possibility for overlap between the world views and ontologies of Catholicism, and those of Indigenous peoples.

Shingwauk and We

In *Shingwauk's Vision,* J.R. Miller gives an excellent account not only of the tragedy of residential schools, but also of what education might have looked like before contact with European settlers. In his account, education was rarely if ever a separate practice, segregated from the rest of life. Learning was done in the context of other activities and was overseen by caring people who knew the child. Direct punishment was avoided; favoured instead was coaxing, as well as occasional embarrassment in contexts in which the child could reflect creatively on his or her own actions (Miller 1996, 15–38). Each child was treated as a whole person with talents or inclinations that, if fostered, could benefit the group. Interference with anyone's path – a child's included – was discouraged. In relatively small communities, each person's skills or abilities were seen as potentially beneficial to all, and they needed to be encouraged, in their unimaginable variation.

Education, as Mark Twain has reminded us, is different from schooling. Every culture must educate its young if the culture is to thrive. But in Aboriginal cultures, traditionally, education was based on fostering and caring for the spirit of the young person, rather than requiring each young person to know a certain body of material. For example, in the "walking out" ceremony, boys and girls, at very young ages – at about six years – were encouraged to take a little expedition on their own, in which they mimicked the actions of a grown-up person by walking out of their dwelling, "hunting" or "gathering" foods left for them to find, and then returning to the dwelling. In other words, they were encouraged to begin behaving in a way that an adult in their group would behave (ibid.). There was no pressure to do so; there was only praise for their playing the part. Imitation and playing the part of right action have long been recognized ways of teaching "right action."

And here is the problem: it would be a mistake to think that by simply "gentling down" educational practices in response to the dictates of Vatican II, the education of Aboriginal youth, in any Catholic school, no matter how enlightened, could be made to suit the students who had only known and enacted the way of being of another *ontos.* Another way of regarding and interpreting the scenarios above is to approach them from the perspective that every practice, linguistic choice, cultural pattern, set of relationships, and certainly educational system not only reflects an underlying world view – this much is already known – but also is the expression of a certain way of being in the world. So to simply enact educational practices that more closely resemble those of Aboriginal peoples would be to miss the point: the underlying purpose of education differs between these cultures because each wants to create a different kind of person. Recall the statement quoted above, from the *Populorium Progressio.* Some of the qualities that were valued in members of the community would overlap, but their relationship to the world, as expressed in the actions taken to live in it, would be, by definition, different. So from a philosophical position, the capacity for integration between the worlds would be illusory.

Conclusion

The changes in teaching practice consistent with Vatican II still have not met the needs of Aboriginal students. It is reasonable to ask why not. A case can be made that crosses historical reasons and moments: Catholic educational practices since Vatican II continue to fail Indigenous students because there is simply no comprehension of the depth of difference between ways of being in the world, quite apart from ways of describing this difference. And lack of capacity in teachers to access such a difference has been firmly rooted in a theology, world view, and enacted *ontos* that is not only unconscious but also ultimately incapable of comprehending the *ontos* still reported by living elders.

NOTES

I would like to offer recognition to the elders with whom I have worked now for many years, including, in this chapter, Alex Mathias, a person of the Teme Augami Anishinaabe. I would also like to acknowledge the valuable critiques of earlier versions of this chapter by participants of the San Sebastián symposium, who are members of the Theory and History of Education International Research Group. And while the following will seem strange to ears of the modern global North and West, I would also like to acknowledge some of the significant places that have contributed to the shaping of the ideas included here, including Cheeskon-Abikong and surrounding areas, in Temagami; my family's ancestral land at Carruther's Point, Kingston; and wild areas near Sandefjord, Norway, and Stromstad, Sweden. All of these persons or places helped to shape the orientation and ideas of this chapter; without them, the chapter would not have taken the form it has.

1 My 2006 doctoral dissertation is titled "Another Way of Knowing and Being." The term "ways of being" is nowadays used frequently in presentations relating to environmental learning – for example, at the 2015 World Environmental Educators Conference in Gothenburg, Sweden. It is used to refer to what amounts to ontological difference. For parallels in neuroscience, see also Iain McGilchrist, *The Master and His Emissary: The Divided Brain and the Making of the Western World* (New Haven: Yale University Press, 2009).

2 Between the time of initially presenting this paper and its publication, the terms *Aboriginal* and *Indigenous* have undergone change when used in a Canadian context. Until recently, in academic contexts, the term *Aboriginal* was used to refer to First Nations, Métis, and Inuit peoples in contexts involving broad reference to all groups. Such is frequently the case when referring to general effects of colonization. The term *Indigenous* was used to refer to First Peoples in other places. Currently, the term *Indigenous* is more frequently used to refer to First Nations, Métis, and Inuit peoples in Canada

as well, although it is preferable to refer to particular nations or persons, where appropriate. The context of this paper is broad because it refers to overall effects of colonization. In this context it is desirable to use a term that can refer (although imperfectly) to all groups. To avoid confusion with other meanings of *Indigenous* that I introduce in this paper, I use the term *Aboriginal* to refer to First Nations, Métis, and Inuit peoples.

3 Hence the choice of *Indigenous*, rather than *Aboriginal*, in the title. The two often overlap, but – as in the description I give later, which is designed to make room for the being state – are not always identical.

4 While I find the term "living Indigenously" useful, I am concerned about the possible colonization of yet another thing relating to Aboriginal peoples. I have begun to introduce Authochthonously, which is rarely used in this context in English, as a possible alternative. It, *Indigenous* and *attentive receptivity*, and "ways of being," are all used roughly interchangeably.

5 See Beeman, from 2006 onwards.

6 Thus described, it is clear that while attentive receptivity may, in practice, be enacted much more commonly in some groups of people than in others, it is emphatically not an ethnic condition. In philosophical terms, this allows much more work to be done by the idea. It permits also a bridging across identity, as commonly construed, and provides other means for critiquing modern Western culture.

7 "Aboriginal people" refers to First Nations, Métis, and Inuit (FNMI) peoples. The formal and legal term "Indian" as specified in the Indian Act of 1876 has been historically used to control, assimilate, and limit.

8 In chapter 10 of this volume, Joe Stafford quotes the work of Quentin Skinner in "The Conditions for the Reception for the *Declaration on Christian Education*."

9 For example, see Graham Harman, *Tool-Being: Heidegger and the Metaphysics of Objects* (Peru: Open Court Publishers, 2002).

10 I am indebted to William Pinar for this observation.

11 McGilchrist (2009) provides a nuanced analysis of recent brain-based research suggesting why this phenomenological perception may have reasons well-rooted in neuroscience.

12 See Beeman (2006).

13 McGilchrist's work (2009) suggests that conveniently, although not too accurately named, classic "left-hemispheric" functions such as analysis and rationality, by virtue of their utility, have come to trump other thinking modes. I need hardly mention that for the current work to be reduced only to cognitive or neural function would be to irrevocably distort it.

REFERENCES

Attridge, Michael, Catherine E. Clifford, and Gilles Routhier, eds. 2011. *Vatican II: Canadian Experiences.* Ottawa: University of Ottawa Press.

Baum, Gregory. 2011. "Vatican Council II: A Turning Point in the Church's History." In *Vatican II: Canadian Experiences*, edited by Michael Attridge, Catherine E. Clifford, and Gilles Routhier, 360–78. Ottawa, ON: University of Ottawa Press.

Beeman, Chris. 2006. "Another Way of Knowing and Being." PhD diss., Queen's University, Kingston, Ontario.

Bruno-Jofré, Rosa. 2005. *The Missionary Oblate Sisters: Vision and Mission.* Kingston and Montreal: McGill-Queen's University Press.

Hampton, Eber. 1993. "Toward a Redefinition of American Indian/Alaskan Native Education." *Canadian Journal of Native Education* 20(2): 261–310.

Heidegger, Martin. 1962. *Being and Time.* Translated by J. Macquarrie and E. Robinson. New York: Harper and Row.

– 1993. "Building Dwelling Thinking." In *Basic Writings*, 2nd ed., edited by David Farrell Krell, 343–64. New York: HarperCollins.

McGilchrist, Iain. 2009. *The Master and His Emissary: The Divided Brain and the Making of the Western World.* New Haven: Yale University Press.

Miller, John. 1996. *Shingwauk's Vision.* Toronto: University of Toronto Press.

Pope Paul VI. 1965a (28 October). *Declaration on Christian Education (Gravissium educationis).* www.vatican.va/archive/hist_councils/ii_vatican_council/documents/vat-ii_decl_19651028_gravissimum-educationis_en.html

– 1965b (7 December). *Declaration on Religious Freedom (Dignitas humanae).* http://www.vatican.va/archive/hist_councils/ii_vatican_council/documents/vat-ii_decl_19651207_dignitatis-humanae_en.html.

– 1967 (26 March). *Encyclical of Pope Paul VI on the Development of Peoples (Populorum Progressio).* w2.vatican.va/content/paul-vi/en/encyclicals/documents/hf_p-vi_enc_26031967_populorum.html.

Spinoza, Baruch. 2002. *Spinoza: Complete Works*, translated by Samuel Shirley, edited by Michael L. Morgan. Indianapolis: Hackett Publishing Company.

– 2006. *The Essential Spinoza: Ethics and Related Writings*, translated by Samuel Shirley, edited by Michael L. Morgan. Indianapolis: Hackett Publishing Company.

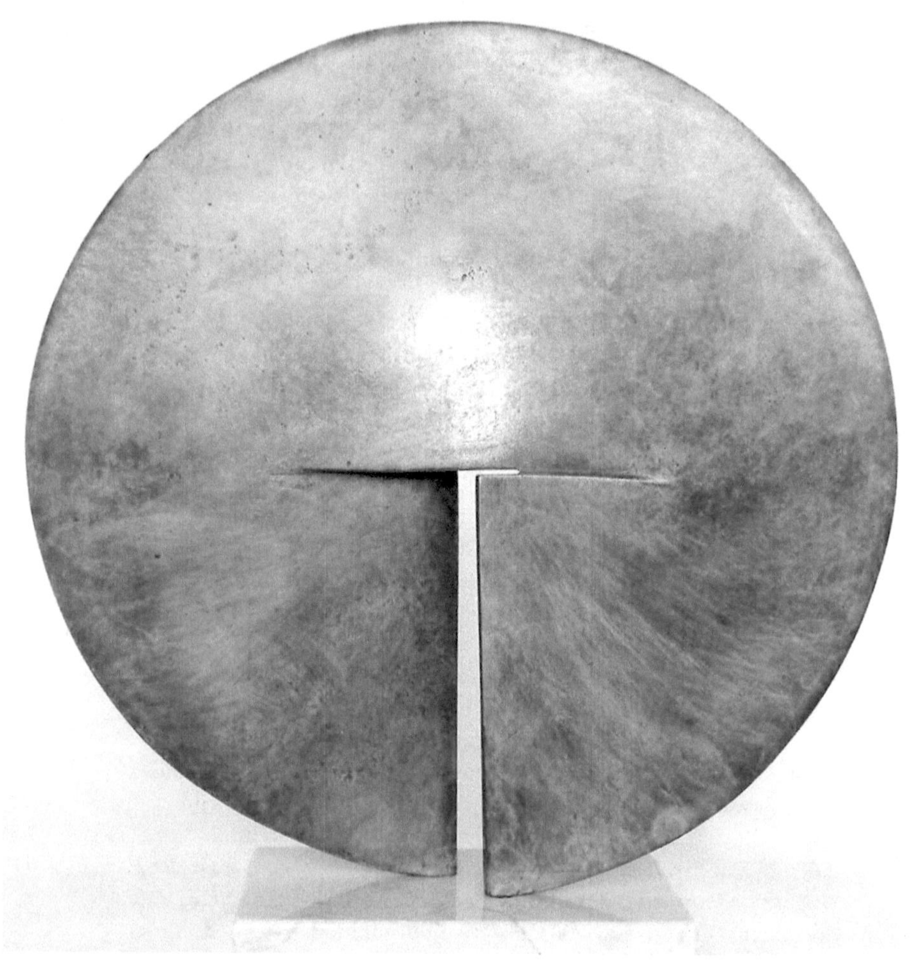

"Puerta Abierta / Ate Irekia / Open Door." Sculpture by Joaquín Gogorza.

PART SIX

Religious Renewal and Public Pedagogy

14 "The Scandalous Revolutionary Force of the Past": On Pasolini's *The Gospel According to Saint Matthew*

WILLIAM F. PINAR

What would a cosmopolitan[1] curriculum convey? Prominent among Catholic replies was what Brad Petitfils (2015, 22) characterizes as the "innovative curriculum" that (the later Saint) Ignatius Loyola developed, one that "combined" Renaissance culture with medieval Catholic mysticism, inspiring the Jesuits to create "the first global network of education." Such a curricular juxtaposition[2] of the temporal, pedagogical, and spiritual also structures a 1964 film dedicated to the memory of Pope John XXIII.[3]

That film – *The Gospel According to Saint Matthew* – was made by the Italian poet, novelist, and public pedagogue Pier Paolo Pasolini (1922–75) who, it must be acknowledged, is not often associated with Catholic education or even with Catholicism itself. As early as 1943, Pasolini, a former schoolteacher,[4] was keeping a notebook of "religious meditations" that would form the basis of *The Nightingale of the Catholic Church*, the title he gave to the collection of Italian[5] poetry he composed between 1943 to 1949 and published in 1958 (Sartarelli 2014, 13). Pasolini was, Castelli concludes, "an anti-clerical Catholic" (2014, xxii), a characterization that conservative Catholics might have also composed for Pope John XXIII, whose Second Vatican Council emphasized that "the Church is in the world and not over and against the world."[6]

The worldliness of Pier Paolo Pasolini is, I suggest, associated with his cosmopolitanism, a mix of politics, sexuality, and savvy that took several aesthetic forms in addition to film.[7] Despite having been expelled[8] from the Communist Party, Pasolini retained his commitment to communism well into the 1960s, when he would finally lose that form of faith and return to religion (Testa 1994, 183). "In me," Pasolini reflected, "[ideological uncertainty] took the form of this regression to certain religious themes which nonetheless had been constant in all my work" (quoted in Testa 1994, 183). Indeed, they were intertwined: "[my] adoption of Marxist philosophy is due, at its origin, to an emotional and moral impetus, and is therefore continually permeable to the insurgence of the religious and, naturally, Catholic spirit [this position] presupposes" (Pasolini, quoted in Sartarelli 2014, 33). For Pasolini, the Catholic Church consecrated – and desecrated[9] – a "lost sense of the sacred" (Maggi 2009, 23).

What constituted "the sacred" for Pasolini? "Grace, the gift of the sublime," he wrote, "is ... initially ... only a moral behavior ... the transmutation of the self in an idealistic sense ... Later, sanctity can become rejection of the world, asceticism ... a quest for an unreachable self-understanding" (quoted in ibid., 24). The "self" that Pasolini sought was also crafted to "intervene in the culture of his moment" (Castelli 2014, xxii). The "sacred" manifested itself "not only incarnationally but also carnally, disrupting bourgeois conformity and ushering in something like a crisis of the sublime" (ibid., xxxii). "Every blasphemy," Pasolini declared, "is a sacred word."[10]

Pasolini "detects the sacred" among peasants living in Italy's rural south (Maggi 2009, 23). In one poem he laments: "The church I loved in adolescence / had died over the centuries, living / only in the old and sorrowful scents / of the fields" (quoted in Sartarelli 2014, 38). Pasolini felt sure that the bourgeoisie lacked this sacred sense.[11] What many of his contemporaries calculated to be progress – industrialization, urbanization, socialization – Pasolini considered a cultural catastrophe.[12] "The great enemy of Christianity," he chided, "is not Communist ... but bourgeois materialism" (quoted in Testa 1994, 183).[13]

In any effort to contest bourgeois materialism and the capitalism that encouraged it, art, Pasolini thought, would play a pivotal role. Pasolini was hardly the first to think so; Walter Benjamin – working in very different political circumstances and religious traditions – also imagined a crucial role for art in the restoration of experience through remembrance.[14] Benjamin had wondered if the appearance of a new "image space" could enable the historical emergence of a new "body space," a "transformation in the experience of space and time," and with that experience, a "new form of human collectivity" (Eiland and Jennings 2014, 10). "I want my images," Pasolini proclaimed, "to cause a surge in vitality" (quoted in Viano 1993, 345n7).[15] Given the complicity of his compatriots with capitalism – their often-eager conversion from supplicants and citizens to consumers – Pasolini grew less sanguine about "collectivity," but he remained resolved to teach, even if the public sphere had dissolved into "the marketplace."

Pasolini hoped that the imagery of his poetry, fiction, and cinema might startle his "students" – the public of Italy, of the world – into reimagining who they were. Pasolini hoped his "spectators" would not "consume passively what they are being shown" (Baranski 1999, 313). He wanted to "encourage [them] to think about the epistemological status of what they are seeing." Specifically, in *The Gospel According to St Matthew*, Pasolini was determined to teach that viewers' impressions of Christ had been "constructed out of many different perspectives, and that each of these perspectives is governed by its own conventions" (313). In the juxtaposition of these perspectives and conventions – "between a fixed past and the present," a "space ... is opened," structured "by the plenitude of history: the specificity of the film's reading of the Gospel and its subjective impact are located with the filling" (Gordon 1996, 222). Through such a cinematic expression of "indirect subjectivity,"[16] he might startle his viewers into self-study, a consciousness of their complicity with the world that had degraded them.

Pasolini's personification of this "indirect subjectivity" was his portrait of Christ who was "both hard and soft ... perplexed and perplexing," adjectives that could describe the filmmaker as well (Schwartz 1992, 444). Indeed, Pasolini asserted that "Christ, in his time, was an intellectual, thus his friends were intellectuals, as mine are now" (423). "As mine are now": in that phrase, it becomes clear that "Pasolini took the stuff of his life to make his art. But he also transformed autobiography into myth and found in myth the stuff to render his autobiography cogent" (444). This movement from autobiography to allegory[17] becomes audible in those "long periods of silence," when "the camera focuses on character and location" (Baranski 1999, 297).

Pasolini's Jesus is "an angry Christ," "a revolutionary" (Viano 1993, 141), a characterization at odds with the biblical text, as one interviewer noted: "many" consider Matthew "the most counterrevolutionary of the Evangelists," in fact "a moderate" (quoted in Schwartz 1992, 451). Pasolini sidestepped the issue: "I was not interested in reconstructing the whole situation exactly. It is the feeling of the Gospel as a whole when you first read it that is revolutionary. Christ going around Palestine is really a revolutionary whirlwind: someone who walks up to a couple of people and says, 'Drop your nets and follow me' is a total revolutionary. Subsequently, of course, you may go into it more thoroughly, historically and textually, but the first reading is profoundly revolutionary" (451).

While admitting here that he is no biblical scholar, nonetheless Pasolini pledges allegiance to the text, "at ease," however, with "temporal" and "topographical transpositions" (Castelli 2014, xxxiii). His determination to "persevere a pure and universal theological message (one aligned with his political commitments)" creates a "stark contrast to the corruptions of the institutional Church" (xxxiii).

This issue over fidelity to the Gospel underscores the importance of "cultural translation," the project that Castelli (2014, xviii) associates with the overall "theoretical importance" of Pasolini's oeuvre, "its deeply analogical" (xxvi; see also endnote 3) character, as he recast the classics, indeed canonicity itself, as a kind of critical "commentary" (xxvi) on the historical moment (xxviii).[18] That moment is new *and* the same as it was in ancient time: for Pasolini, temporal difference was in the end illusory.[19]

Pasolini portrayed Jesus's life and death in black-and-white to mimic newsreel reality, enabling *The Gospel* to emerge "from centuries of incense-beclouded church rituals with striking immediacy" (Sartarelli 2014, 47).[20] Sartarelli characterizes this sense of immediacy as a "clairvoyant realism" (45),[21] which Pasolini accomplished in part through a "subjectively 'poetic' handheld camera" (47). Immediacy was also achieved by employing non-professional actors, including one of the young men he had discovered while scouring the slums for sex. As Schwartz (1992) notes, fifteen-year-old Ninetto Davoli[22] was given "the tiny part of a shepherd boy," providing him with what Pasolini afterwards admitted was "a kind of screen test" (446). Pasolini's desire for Davoli also conveyed his "love" for the poor and oppressed, a love that for him dissolved "class division" (Siti 1994, 66).

Pasolini's desire for young men was matched (if not symmetrically) by his "emotional and aesthetic affinity" for "young mothers" (Ryan-Scheutz 2007, 8). That affinity is apparent in the film's opening scene, a long shot of the young and pregnant Mary. Neither sexualized nor sublimated, the "imminent greatness" of this young Mary – played by Margherita Caruso – "is conveyed through numerous close shots of her face, which, in conjunction with her silence, imbue her with an aura of mystery" (140). Mary becomes a "symbol of spiritual plenitude and social difference" (142). To play the aging Mary – whose grief at her son's crucifixion fills her face – Pasolini chose his mother, Susanna Colussi Pasolini, whose presence exposes "the film's autobiographical dimension" (Gordon 1996, 199; Viano 1993, 145).[23]

In the mid-1960s, Pasolini theorized a "double mode of filmmaking that reflects the particularly non-verbal approach to female subjectivity we see in the young Mary and other saints" (Ryan-Scheutz 2007, 143). There, she continues, Pasolini theorized that underneath the film is "free indirect subjectivity," wherein an artist can "mesh his own point of view with that of his characters" (143).[24] Such subjectivity allows one to convey "ideological messages" and acknowledge "autobiographical subtexts" – interwoven with what Pasolini termed the "dominant psychological state of mind in the film." There was, he was suggesting, "another film or text underneath this surface-level film," one without (Pasolini's phrase) any "pretext of mimesis" at all (143).

There is, Viano (1993, 143) agrees, a "powerful subtext in the film," for him created by Pasolini's "own homosexuality" and his resolve to respect Matthew's original text. Ryan-Scheutz (2007) detects this "subterranean" text "in the filming of the young Virgin and her silence" (143). Pasolini recodes this palimpsest technically, using "repeated close shots of the young woman's face," done in adagio, "thereby granting her freedom of expression beyond any mimetic responsibilities or linguistic codes" (144).

Yet the matter of mimesis remains, due to Pasolini's pledge of allegiance to the biblical text. There have been many such "Jesus films," but "none" – save Pasolini's – "go directly to scripture for the text" (Testa 1994, 182). Indeed, "not one word in the film is Pasolini's invention": "The whole being a long faithful quotation from the original. True, there is a lot of Matthew that is omitted and the film does not rigidly follow the order of the written text, but it is nonetheless evident that, for the first time, Christianity is being treated like a text" (Viano 1993, 140).

Despite this textual fidelity – contested, you recall, by one interviewer – Pasolini was acutely conscious of the context in which the movie would be viewed, conceiving of his movie as "the life of Christ plus two thousand years of story-telling about the life of Christ" (quoted in Gordon 1996, 222).

"I have an idea of Christ that is almost inexpressible," Pasolini remembered. "He could be almost anyone, and in fact I looked for him everywhere" (quoted in Schwartz 1992, 446). He considered Jack Kerouac, but "then I discovered that the photograph of Kerouac [I had] was ten or fifteen years out of date" (447). Nico Naldini reports that Pasolini also considered Allen Ginsberg and the Spanish poet Luis Goytisolo. He also wrote to Yevgeny Yevtushenko in Moscow.[25] Accident, not design, produced the saviour.

An economics student named Enrique Irazoqui had read *Ragazzi di Vita*[26] and had resolved to meet its author. "I came back to the house and found this young Spaniard waiting to see me," Pasolini recalled, "and as soon as I saw him, even before we had started talking, I said, 'Excuse me, but would you act in one of my films' – even before I knew who he was or anything. He was a serious person, and so he said no. But then I gradually won him round" (quoted in Schwartz 1992, 447–8). Irazoqui had no acting experience. His voice was "dubbed by Enrico Maria Salerno, a famous actor with an easily recognizable voice" (Viano 1993, 138). "The practice of dubbing with voices heavily marked by regional dialects in order to induce analogical associations in the viewer is not without its ideological and artistic validity," Viano adds (1993, 138).

For Schwartz (1992), Irazoqui was "thin, stoop-shouldered, heavy-browed," not exactly "the muscular Christ of Michelangelo" (448). Pasolini's Christ looked like a "preoccupied thinker," as if capable of honouring (quoting Pasolini) "a violent summons to the bourgeoisie that has stupidly thrown itself toward the destruction of man" (448). In that line is registered both Pasolini's Communism and his Catholicism, the latter perhaps prerequisite (he came to think: see Sartarelli 2014, 33) to the reanimation of the former. For Pasolini, "a 'regressive' surrender to religious impulses will restore ideological certainty – or least a radical contradiction with modernity" (Testa 1994, 184–5). His contempt for the bourgeoisie, Rohdie (1995) reminds us, was political and historical but also self-referential, indeed self-confrontational, as "by birth and education … and in practice, he was a bourgeois writer" (48).

Baranski (1999) notes that the Pharisees represent the bourgeoisie, the "enemies" of "progress" and "emancipation" (302). Pasolini's Jesus was an advocate for the poor of Galilee; for him they were the ancestors of the poor of Friuli. "Misery is always, in its most intimate characteristic, epic," Pasolini told students at the Centro Sperimentale di Cinematografia. "This, my way of seeing the world of the poor, of the subproletariat, has consequences, I believe ... in the very style of my films" (quoted in Schwartz 1992, 448). "Misery" is what images of the denuded hills of Calabria would communicate to viewers, he felt, accented by a sound track almost absent original compositions.[27] While everything said on screen came from the Gospel, there were also "long stretches completely without dialogue" (449). Pasolini cautioned that the film was to be viewed as "by analogy ... I was not interested in exactitude, I was interested in everything but that" (443). In my terms, *The Gospel* is an allegory-of-the-present.

For Baranski (1999) such "secularization of the Gospel in political terms is not the film's main preoccupation, but only part of a more complex operation" (300). He points out that Pasolini does not focus exclusively on Christ but on several characters as well as the crowds, using techniques associated with *cinéma vérité*, thereby fragmenting the film's narrative focus (301). Jesus's "words" and "actions" galvanize his listeners, who "do not abandon him, even on the road to Calvary"; this testifies to the "socio-political significance of Jesus" (301). These scenes "echo newsreels of modern demonstrations," and their juxtaposition with Russian revolutionary songs and Prokofiev's music to Eisenstein's *Alexander Nevsky* intensify the sense of historical momentousness (301).

Testa (1994, 191) suggests, apparently contradicting Baranski, that while we are shown Jesus speaking "close-up," "his talks do not seem to 'resonate' with his listeners. While giving the Sermon on the Mount, Jesus has almost no listeners at all. The Last Supper is 'all close-ups'" (194). Maggi (2009) also notes Pasolini's use of "unmoving single images" accented by silence; the "close-up," he adds, "must be described as all but a trademark of his cinematographic gaze" (54). It conveys "a sense of an atemporal revelation" (54). Despite Jesus's didacticism and even dissociation from those surrounding him, he does enlist several, a fact resolving the contrary accounts Baranski and Maggi appear to provide.

There are moments – during the trial, the march to Calvary, and the Crucifixion – when, Testa (1994) notes, "Matthew narrates swiftly and laconically, [and] Pasolini's camera withdraws into long-shot distance from Jesus, redolent of television-news shooting" (194). The film is, finally, a "mixed style," one Pasolini termed "epic," in which "compression, ellipsis, and distension alternate in accord with a principle that Pasolini sometimes terms 'absolute' representation, distinguishing it from naturalistic verisimilitude" (195). Testa references Sergei Eisenstein as the "great master of this epic style in cinema," associated with "eliminating the intervals between, and distensions of, significant moments" (195). Dilating the moment can underline its significance.[28]

Pasolini "repeatedly remarked on the violence of Jesus," and "this violence is revolutionary" (Testa 1994, 196). More than Luke and John, Matthew invokes tropes of "condemnation" and "threat," according Jesus's preaching a violent and confrontational quality (197). This quality is enacted not only through Enrique Irazoqui's "severe performance," but also through Pasolini's "framing" and "cutting," one effect of which is that Jesus never seems "conversational" (197). As Testa emphasizes, his preaching – what before I summarized as "didacticism" – is presented as an "incommensurable confrontation," not democratic dialogue, a fact that "Pasolini's use of frontal close-ups makes emphatic" (197).

For location, Pasolini considered Israel or Palestine, but, he said later, "I realized it was no use – that was after a few hours driving" (quoted in Schwartz 1992, 426). While monuments of the biblical past remained, Pasolini felt that "the past itself was gone" (Rohdie 1995, 161). The people of Palestine and Israel seemed modern. But, Pasolini thought, "a Southern Italian peasant ... is still living in a magical culture where miracles are real like the culture in which Matthew wrote" (quoted in Schwartz 1992, 426). It was southern Italy – specifically the town of Matera[29] – that, Pasolini decided, "belongs completely to a past which resembles the Palestine of the Bible" (Rohdie 1995, 161). Pasolini's Christ would be a "social reformer within a magical, sacred world, the world that produced the Gospels" (161).

For Pasolini the sacred is not, then, otherworldly. "Pasolini goes out of his way to question Jesus' divinity," Baranski (1999, 310) argues. "Because I'm not a believer," Pasolini explained, "I had to narrate the Gospel through the eyes of someone else who isn't me, namely a believer: I fashioned 'a free indirect discourse'" (311). "Indirect vision," Baranski explains, "presupposed a contamination between the believer and the non-believer" (311–12). That "contamination" has its stylistic consequences. In his introduction to the script, Pasolini tells us: "By literally following Matthew's 'stylistic accelerations' – the barbaric-practical workings of his narration, the abolition of chronological time, the elliptical jumps within the story which inscribe the 'disproportions' of the didactic, static moments such as the stupendous, interminable, discourse on the mountain – the figure of Christ should finally assume the violence inhering in any rebellion which radically contradicts the appearance and shape that life assumes for modern man: a grey orgy of cynicism, irony, brutality, compromise and conformism" (quoted in Testa 1994, 184).

Testa concludes that Pasolini sought to duplicate in his film the quality of Matthew's text that was, in a Gramscian sense, a "national-popular epic" (184).That required not only fidelity to Matthew's text but "contamination" of it. "The style in the Gospel," Pasolini reflected later, "combines ... an almost classic severity with moments that are almost Godardian ... The stylistic unity is only my own unconscious religiousness, which came out and gave the film its unity" (quoted in Schwartz 1992, 450). While a "national-popular epic," then, *The Gospel* is also an expression of indirect subjectivity.

Both meld in the "zeal" and "anger" animating Jesus, who expresses "indignation with the present. Christ, like Pasolini, was an anti-modern" (Rohdie 1995, 161). In modernity the past had dissolved; being anti-modern meant appreciating the present *as* empty. The barren landscape would convey that emptiness: "These are the deserts of Pasolini, which make prehistory the abstract poetic element, the 'essence' co-present with our history, the archaean base which reveals an interminable history beneath our own" (Deleuze 1989, 244).[30] Such imagery encodes the alterity of history.

It wasn't obvious the film would be made. Alfredo Bini, who had financed Pasolini's first feature film, struggled to find underwriters. "The heads of five banks turned him down," Schwartz (1992, 430) reports; it seemed "no one in Italy wanted to pay for a film about Christ by the notorious Pasolini." Promoting Pasolini, Bini admitted, "was like going to bed with a leper" (430). When the state-controlled Banca Nazionale del Lavoro finally agreed to a partial underwriting, it was on the condition that the script pass the censorship board. Full financing remained elusive, and the uncertainty plagued Pasolini, who told his *Vie Nuove* readers: "I have been passing terrible days, days of anxiety ... If we do not succeed in making *Il Vangelo*, for external reasons, I do not know what to do with my life at this point" (437).

Financing was finally secured, and as promised, Pasolini submitted the script for approval to the priests at Cittadella. Timing was favourable, as Pasolini acknowledged: "Everything was made easier by the advent of Pope John XXIII who objectively revolutionized the situation. If Pius XII had lived another three or four years I'd never have been able to make *The Gospel*" (quoted in Schwartz 1992, 444). While Pasolini personalized the shift, he could easily have ascribed it to Vatican II.

The movie was first screened at the 25th Venice Film Festival[31] on the evening of 4 September 1964, "only hours" after Pasolini had finished editing it (Baranski 1999, 281).[32] At the festival's Palace of Cinema, Pasolini was greeted by whistles, then tomatoes and raw eggs, followed, inside the theatre, by more eggs and spitballs thrown at both the screen and the audience (Schwartz 1992, 451). The ruckus made the premiere "good news copy," as "intellectuals" and "the rich in tuxedos and evening gowns" were photographed finding their way through the police – there to protect Pasolini from those intent on assaulting him – to see the film (Schwartz 1992, 542). Once the festival ended, Pasolini left for a vacation with Ninetto Davoli, who, much to Pasolini's pleasure, shouted while swimming "how beautiful life is!" (452).[33]

In April of the next year the *Nastro d'Argento* (Silver Ribbon) – Italy's version of the Oscars, awarded by the film critics' association – went to Pasolini for best picture, to Delli Colli for best director of photography, and to Danilo Donati for best costumes (Schwartz 1992, 545). Earlier, the jury of the *Ufficio Cattolico Internazionale del Cinema* (OCIC) had awarded a prize to the film. The citation acknowledged the film as public pedagogy: "The author, without giving up his own ideology, has faithfully translated, with simplicity and piety, often very movingly, the social message of the Gospel, in particular love for the poor and the oppressed ... It shows the real grandeur of his teaching stripped of any artificial and sentimental effect (quoted in Rohdie 1995, 162). Such a scale – "grandeur" – requires the teacher to take the world as his or her classroom.

The whistles at Venice, film critic Tullio Kezich reported, had been drowned out by the "ovation which the public gave the poet of *Le ceneri di Gramsci*" (quoted in Schwartz 1992, 452). *The Gospel*'s success – it would be "the most famous" and "popularly successful" of all Pasolini's films (Testa 1994, 180) – infuriated Pasolini's enemies: it was inconceivable that the pariah Pasolini had made a film characterized by *Catholic* critics as "a fine film, a Christian film that produces a profound impression" (quoted in Schwartz 1992, 454). "Endless confrontations" followed that "forced nearly everyone, from Right to Left, to take a stand" (Viano 1993, 134). *Il Tempo* alleged that Pasolini had made a devil out of the Son of God. A Roman paper was sure that the OCIC prize would be "to the immense profit of Communism" (quoted in Schwartz 1992, 454). "To have given this work a prize," the magazine *Folla* asserted, "and even in the presence of Fathers [of the Church], was a humiliating concession to error ... to confusion" (454–5). When Goffredo Fofi reviewed it negatively in the leftist *Quaderni Piacentini*, Pasolini replied in kind (452). Two years later, he attacked that magazine again, this time dismissing it as a "refuge" of the "worst Marxist critics," perpetrators of a "*beatnik* Stalinism" (453).

Having awarded *The Gospel* its Grand Prize, the Catholic Film Office arranged for the film to be screened in Paris, within the walls of Notre Dame, with Pasolini present. After a Mass in the filled cathedral, the film was shown, followed by a round-table discussion. Later, Maria Antonietta Macciocchi would characterize Pasolini's encounter with the French intellectual left as "tempestuous." For them, she wrote, "the film was a slap right in the face. They are laical, rationalist, like Voltaire" (quoted in Schwartz 1992, 457). Indignation was evident in the review that Michel Cournet wrote: "It is ... religious propaganda beneath the façade of a faithful transcription of the Gospel made by a Marxist ... I do not know if M. Pasolini is a prodigy of unawareness or a little champion of publicity." Claude Mauriac wrote: "No, it is not sacred art, nor art. It is only a fantasy. It is nothing" (457). Pasolini replied: "The French intellectuals are deaf, out of touch with the historical reality of the whole world ... Sartre is the only one who has understood" (457–8).

Jean-Paul Sartre had agreed to meet Pasolini the day after the Notre Dame showing. Pasolini and Macciocchi set out for the Le Pont Royal – Sartre's customary café – but got lost; they arrived, Schwartz (1992, 458) reports, only after reaching Simone de Beauvoir by phone. "We arrived two hours late," Macciocchi remembered, reporting that "Sartre was ensconced on a red velvet sofa, smoking his hundredth Gitane. 'Did you really think I wouldn't wait for you? Now, about Saint Matthew'" (458).

Sartre told Pasolini that Marxism, at least in France, had yet to confront Christianity, quipping that "Stalin rehabilitated Ivan the Terrible; Christ is not yet rehabilitated by the Marxists" (quoted in Schwartz 1992, 458). The only way to placate French critics was to show the movie in Italian, not the version that had been dubbed (evidently done "badly by a French priest"), juxtaposed with *La Ricotta*,[34] to demonstrate that Pasolini was no Catholic apologist. That, Sartre thought, would silence his country's anticlerical thought police.

"I have been faithful to myself," Pasolini told Sartre, "and I have created a national-popular work in the Gramscian sense" (Testa 1994, 184). "Had I been French," Pasolini told Sartre, "I would have set the Gospel in Algeria, and that would have shaken them, just as the Italians are shaken because I set my Gospel in Lucania.[35] Maybe that way they would have then understood" (quoted in Schwartz 1992, 458). Sartre asked Pasolini to return to Paris the following January – after *The Gospel* had been shown in both Budapest and Prague – to open a discussion about his film between the lay left and Catholics, especially those priests who had been engaged in the fight to free Algeria.[36]

"Religion," Castelli (2014, xxxii) remarks, "retains for Pasolini the revolutionary power of human solidarity, a bulwark against the materialist noise of bourgeois culture." Such solidarity is an expression of a "revolutionary and profoundly unsentimental authenticity (as a counterweight to bourgeois conformism)"; it provoked Pasolini to "address the question of temporality through recourse to myth," a genre that accents what is universal within contingency (xxix). No fusion of the two, Pasolini's recourse to religion had enabled him to "stage a confrontation between two incommensurate systems of value" in which he mounted a "vigorous defense of the religious and the sublime – what Pasolini called his 'nostalgia for the sacred,' set against the dominant forms of power and cultural value" (xxix). For Pasolini, then, pining for the past was political.

The "Christian reference," Alain Badiou (2014) acknowledged, "played a role of primary importance in the formation of Pasolini's thought" (vii). As *The Gospel According to Saint Matthew* testifies, Christianity – Catholicism specifically – is more than a reference for Pasolini; it is an animating influence in his art, pedagogy, and politics. These Sartarelli (2014) characterizes as "Marxist, anarchist, and Catholic" (34). There is "spiritualism" and "sensualism," as well. Sartarelli imagines these as "twin poles" (46), but they seem to me intertwined, contaminated (Pasolini might say) in an embrace. It is through "spiritualism" and "sensualism" that Pasolini takes – as Sartarelli suggests – "his pedagogical vocation to the metaphysical level" (46). Metaphysical and worldly too, I emphasize, as the metaphysical becomes incarnate and not only in the body of Christ. It is made flesh in the suffering of the subaltern – in the beauty of youth and the devotion of the aged, the latter gendered in the person of his mother Susanna, the former sexualized in his lover Ninetto Davoli. "Perhaps the homosexual," Pasolini pondered, "has the sense of the sacred origin of life more than those who are narrowly heterosexual. Respect for the sanctity of the mother predisposes him to a particular identification with her ... [against] the terrible power of the father, of the profaner. I would say that the homosexual tends to preserve life, not contributing to the cycle of procreation-destruction, but rather substituting the coherence of culture, the continuity of consciousness, for the survival of the species" (quoted in Rohdie 1995, 70).

Pasolini overstates his case – a characteristic move – but he has a point.[37] Even so, perhaps it is in sin, not virtue, that the key elements of Pasolini's intertext intersect. "In the portrayal of the untenable dilemma of a body that cannot but live in sin," Viano (1993) suggests, "it is possible to detect the point at which the Marxist and Catholic discourses intersect with the homosexual one" (190–1). Might study of that intersection serve as one site of a cosmopolitan curriculum?

Submerged within a "universal profanation," Pasolini pledged allegiance to the "memory of sacred" (Sartarelli 2014, 49) by rendering vivid and immediate the ancient and invisible. Despite his fidelity to the Gospel as textual source, Pasolini was engaged, Castelli (2014)[38] emphasizes, in "translation," specifically its "capacity" for (as Pasolini put it) "regeneration," and of "the necessity of elective affinities, of mysterious historical correspondences" such that, he knew, "translation is primarily, explicitly or implicitly, a historiographical act" (xx–xxi). Such translation is a form of public pedagogy, reactivating the past so that the present becomes clarified, and in so doing, reconstructed. A curriculum cosmopolitan in its Catholicity, for Pasolini, would be curriculum that was temporally encoded and pedagogically enacted. Through such a "contaminated" curriculum one might possibly prevent what Pasolini worried was the "final spasm," when "this last / consecration is also exhausted / there is no place [...] where the Lord *might be*" (quoted in Sartarelli 2014, 50). For Pasolini, then, "to yearn for the sacred" within modernity, as Maggi (2009, 21) emphasizes, was "to yearn for something that does not exist," a pedagogy for a public that could – would in fact – crucify him. To experience the sacred means to excavate "the void lying within the present reality" (21–2). It is that void that Vatican II addressed, that the anti-cleric but passionately Catholic Pasolini pledged to contest, and in so doing renew a faith deconsecrated by capitalism.

NOTES

This chapter's title comes from a phrase by Pasolini (quoted in Castelli 2014, xxviii) from the closing lines of his documentary *Le mura di Sana'a* (The Walls of Sana'a), which he made as a plea to UNESCO to preserve the cultural legacies he encountered in Yemen while filming *The Arabian Nights*: "In the name of simple men whom poverty has kept pure. / In the name of the grace of obscure centuries. / In the name of the scandalous revolutionary force of the past." As recent events (early 2015) indicate, "grace" is now absent from Yemen.

1 Definitions differ, but I suggest that a "curriculum for cosmopolitanism cultivates comprehension of alterity" (Pinar 2009, vii). Efforts towards such "comprehension" may be ongoing and may support subjective social reconstruction, as life lived passionately can become a public service, as my portrait of Pasolini in *The Worldliness of a Cosmopolitan Education* makes clear.
2 Or, as Pasolini would prefer, "contamination." As Welle notes, Pasolini himself claimed to work "under the sign of contamination" (Pasolini, quoted in Welle 1999, 95), the "collision of two sometimes very different minds" (Pasolini, quoted in Wagstaff 1999, 196). For a discussion of the concept, see Pinar (2009), 185n32. Related is the concept of "analogy," a "basic concept of Pasolini's poetics," Maggi (2009, 21) notes, "a postcolonial rhetorical device that includes both similarity and opposition."
3 "The new Pope," Pasolini wrote in praise of John, "in his sweet and mysterious turtle smile, seemed to have understood that he must be the pastor to the most miserable" (quoted in Schwartz 1992, 434).
4 For details see Pinar (2009), 105–6.

5 He first wrote in the Fruilian dialect, in Jewell's (1992) view, poiesis as resistance to that state authority.
6 See http://www.vatican2voice.org/2need/need.htm. Accessed May 2, 2015.
7 See Pinar (2009), 142.
8 The story is well-known; for a summary, see Pinar (2009), 106–7.
9 "This Christian faith is bourgeois,' Pasolini complained, "the Church is the merciless heart of the State" (quoted in Schwartz 1992, 445). See also Castelli (2014), xxxix.
10 Quoted in Castelli (2014), xv.
11 See Maggi (2009), 23. Accordingly, "the film was a gallery of unfamiliar, wrinkled faces, whose southern traits could not escape the Italian spectator's notice" Viano (1993, 138). Casting so, Pasolini conveyed, Viano continues, "a second meaning apart from the fictional one," namely, Italy's "social reality," from which "subproletarian faces" are absent (138).
12 See, for instance, Sartarelli (2014), 38.
13 As Pasolini told an English journalist: "To conclude I would like to say however that the 'opposite' of religion is not communism (which, despite having taken the secular an positivist spirit form the bourgeois tradition, in the end is very religious); but the 'opposite' of religion is capitalism (ruthless, cruel, cynical, purely materialistic, the cause of human beings' exploitation of human beings, cradle of the worship of power, horrendous den of racism)" (quoted in Castelli 2014, xxxii).
14 See Eiland and Jennings (2014), 10.
15 "The English word vitality," Viano cautions, "may fail to reproduce all the connotations (energy, zest, desire) of its Italian counterpart, which was, indeed, one of Pasolini's favorite words. Be that as it may, Pasolini's argument is yet another proof that for him the viewer's body is the ultimate recipient and gauge of the image" (1993, 345n7).
16 For Pasolini such subjectivity seemed an eruption of the unconscious; see Pinar (2009), 14.
17 Cf. Pinar 2012, 43ff.
18 Referencing biblical scholar George Aichele, Castelli (2014, xix) suggests that the technical translation – converting biblical text into film – "interrupts the 'biblical' nature of the Gospel, and foregrounds the instability of authority claims about scriptural meanings." Translation, she adds, "is also an act of violence and an act of betrayal" (2014, xx).
19 See Castelli (2014), xxxiv. Castelli (2014, xxxv) reminds us that Pasolini's sense of the "tactile and experiential presence of the past" is evident in a poem – "Tarsus, from a Distance" – he composed in 1969 while shooting the

film *Medea* in Turkey: "Of course, if a thing changes / it still remains what it was first ... Of course, the egg-shaped form of time connects everything."

20 In the colourized version this sense of immediacy is, it seems to me, largely lost.

21 Sartarelli's characterization is redolent of Pasolini's relationship to neorealism; see Pinar (2009), 185n33.

22 Davoli would prove to be no "trick" but a lasting relationship. For Pasolini, Siti (1994, 64) suggests, he represented nothing less than the "paradoxical" unification of "*eros*" and "*agape*," of "desire" and "affection."

23 Gordon (1996, 199) points out that "self-representation is also found Pasolini's films in less direct forms of autobiographical self-portraiture, often based on 'oblique allusion,' an instance of which would include the casting of his mother as the older Virgin Mary in *Vangelo*."

24 This identification of Pasolini with the saints was not only an expression of "free indirect subjectivity," but one made by others as well. "In an unpublished interview," Castelli (2014, xxiii) tells us, "the famed Italian film director Bernardo Bertolucci called Pasolini a saint."

25 See Schwartz (1992), 447.

26 Literally the "boys of life," the novel was a "graphic description of life in Roman underclass, not simply sex and street talk" but a testimony that many "were being left out of Italy's 'new prosperity,' living as precariously under democracy as they had under Fascism" (Schwartz 1992, 277). The novel took fourth place among the five finalists for the 1955 Strega Prize, but Ragazzi did win the Colombi–Guidotti Prize at Parma and came in second place for the Viareggio Prize (Schwartz 1992, 276).

27 The soundtrack, with which Elsa Morante helped, was mostly Bach, supplemented with Webern, Russian revolutionary songs, original music by Luis E. Bacalov, and the recently released *Missa Luba* from the Congo. For the Massacre of the Innocents, Pasolini used the same Prokofiev that Eisenstein had used in 1938 in *Alexander Nevsky*. For the Baptism of Christ, Pasolini chose the American black spiritual "Sometimes I Feel Like a Motherless Child" and Mozart (see Schwartz 1992, 450–1).

28 Agathocleous (2011, 173–4) notes that both Virginia Woolf and Joseph Conrad before her "use dilated moments of mutual recognition as ways of registering connections between individuals; in place of panorama both compose an overarching sense of evolutionary time that makes evident the finitude of human history. These temporalities, 'the moment and the end of time,' produce a new kind of cosmopolitan sublime."

29 The town's "hauntingly beautiful Sassi (the old section, virtually untouched), was a daring visual translation of Jerusalem," Viano (1993, 138) suggests.

30 "Not only would the desert appear in *Il Vangelo secondo Matteo, Medea,* and *Il fiore delle Mille e una notte,*" Viano (1993, 131) points out, "but it would also acquire a structural significance in *Edipo re, Teorema,* and *Porcile.*"

31 The Venice Festival awarded *Gospel* a Special Jury Prize, but the Golden Lion for first place went to Antonioni's *Red Desert.* About it, Pasolini wrote in *Vie nuove*: "It seemed to me an extremely beautiful film" (quoted in Schwartz 1992, 453).

32 Still, Baranski (1999, 281) insists it had "not been a hurried project." Pasolini had been working on the film for two years; see Schwartz (1992), 448.

33 Evidently Davoli's marriage to a woman did not end the intimacy. When Pasolini flew to Stockholm on Monday, 27 October 1975 (a week before his assassination) as the "sole Italian candidate for the Nobel Prize in Literature" (Schwartz 1992, 4), they shared a hotel room (Schwartz 1992, 5).

34 *La ricotta* enacted a "comic reversal" of the Gospels; it was "condemned and sequestered for being blasphemous" (Schwartz 1992, 426). Fellini knew that its condemnation was "incredible, unacceptable, a source of anguish … It seems the best spirits are always blocked by the obtuse … Those people are putting him [Pasolini] in a condition to express in his coming film on the *Gospel* exactly what is the sadness of not being understood" (quoted in Schwartz 1992, 419).

35 Lucania is an ancient territorial division of southern Italy corresponding to most of the modern region of Basilicata, with much of the province of Salerno and part of that of Cosenza.

36 See Schwartz (1992), 458.

37 Against "resistance" – ensuring "reproduction" – the straight son's rage against the father was more adroitly expressed as "seduction." So I argued in 1983 (Pinar 1998, 227). Regarding the generalization, Pasolini himself disclaimed identity politics; see Pinar (2009), 131–5.

38 See also Pinar (2009), 15.

REFERENCES

Agathocleous, Tanya. 2011. *Urban Realism and the Cosmopolitan Imagination in the Nineteenth Century.* Cambridge: Cambridge University Press.

Badiou, Alain. 2014. Foreword to *St Paul: A Screenplay,* by Pier Paolo Pasolini, vii–xi. London: Verso.

Baranski, Zygmunt C. 1999. "The Texts of *Il Vangelo secondo Matteo.*" In *Pasolini Old and New,* edited by Zygmunt G. Baranski, 281–320. Dublin: Four Courts Press.

Castelli, Elizabeth A. 2014. Introduction to *St Paul: A Screenplay,* by Pier Paolo Pasolini, xv–xlii. London: Verso.

Deleuze, Gilles. 1989. *Cinema 2*, translated by Hugh Tomlinson and Robert Galeta. Minneapolis: University of Minnesota Press.

Eiland, Howard, and Michael W. Jennings. 2014. *Walter Benjamin: A Critical Life.* Cambridge, MA: Belknap Press of Harvard University Press.

Gordon, Robert S.C. 1996. *Pasolini: Forms of Subjectivity*. Oxford: Clarendon Press.

Jewell, Keala. 1992. *The Poiesis of History*. Ithaca: Cornell University Press.

Maggi, Armando. 2009. *The Resurrection of the Body: Pier Paolo Pasolini from Saint Paul to Sade.* Chicago: University of Chicago Press. http://dx.doi.org/10.7208/chicago/9780226501369.001.0001.

Petitfils, Brad. 2015. *Parallels and Responses to Curricular Innovation.* New York: Routledge.

Pinar, William F. 2009. *The Worldliness of a Cosmopolitan Education.* New York: Routledge.

– 2012. *What Is Curriculum Theory?*, 2nd ed. New York: Routledge.

Pinar, William F., ed. 1998. *Queer Theory in Education.* Mahwah: Lawrence Erlbaum.

Rohdie, Sam. 1995. *The Passion of Pier Paolo Pasolini.* Bloomington: Indiana University Press.

Ryan-Scheutz, Colleen. 2007. *Sex, the Self, and the Sacred: Women in the Cinema of Pier Paolo Pasolini.* Toronto: University of Toronto Press.

Sartarelli, Stephen. 2014. "Pier Paolo Pasolini: A Life in Poetry." In *The Selected Poetry of Pier Paolo Pasolini*, edited and translated by Stephen Sartarelli, 1–58. Chicago: University of Chicago Press.

Schwartz, Barth David. 1992. *Pasolini Requiem.* New York: Pantheon.

Siti, Walter. 1994. "Pasolini's 'Second Victory.'" In *Pier Paolo Pasolini: Contemporary Perspectives*, edited by Patrick Rumble and Bart Testa, 56–77. Toronto: University of Toronto Press.

Testa, Bart. 1994. "To Film a Gospel ... and Advent of the Theoretical Stranger." In *Pier Paolo Pasolini*, edited by Patrick Rumble and Bart Testa, 180–209. Toronto: University of Toronto Press. http://dx.doi.org/10.3138/9781442678484-015.

Viano, Maurizio. 1993. *A Certain Realism.* Berkeley: University of California Press.

Wagstaff, Christopher. 1999. "Reality into Poetry: Pasolini's Film Theory." In *Pasolini Old and New*, edited by Zygmunt G. Baranski, 185–227. Dublin: Four Courts Press.

Welle, John P. 1999. "Pasolini *Traduttore*: Translation, Tradition and Rewriting." In *Pasolini Old and New*, edited by Zygmunt G. Baranski, 90–129. Dublin: Four Courts Press.

“MAGNIFICAT (Lucas/Luke 1: 46–55) no. 8.” Ceramic tilework by María Cruz Bascones.

Conclusion
Catholicism and Education: Points of Intersection, Opposition, and Configuration

CARLOS MARTÍNEZ VALLE AND GEMMA SERRANO

"Vejo agora a nova Igreja se libertando dessa burguesia. Vejo a nova Igreja empenhada na mais corajosa das revoluções para superar a Igreja do passado, intransigente, paternalista e cujo destino do altar se confundia com o destino dos tronos."

"I see now the new Church freeing itself from the bourgeoisie. I see the new Church working for the most brave revolution, to get over the past Church which is intransigent, paternalistic and which destiny, the destiny of the altar, got confused with that of the thrones."

Ligya Fagundes Telles, *A disciplina do amor: Memoria e ficção* (1980).

The chapters in this book provide ground-breaking research into what the Second Vatican Council has meant for different educational stages in different settings, in Chile, France, Spain, and within Canada as well as in Canadian missions in Latin America, and in the Church as a global institution. The profound consequences of Vatican II for education are revealed through descriptions of how various actors (male and female religious congregations, bishops, teachers, professors) have interacted in diverse political and social contexts. This book has also examined the thought of some intellectuals – such as Illich and Pasolini – who welcomed the Council as a hand extended to the poor or who rejected it as a move towards Protestantism, modernization, and the loss of the essence of Catholicism. These varying responses to the Council have been made in the face of the Church's need to work out answers to the modern world. Most of the chapters have centred on the preparatory elaboration period of the Council and the first phase of its reception, from the 1950s to the mid-1980s.

While this book has presented a panorama of Catholic education, it had focused largely on Canada and Canadian-related female orders. The reason for this is not simply the relevance that the study of female orders has achieved in recent times – for instance, in the works of Rebecca Rogers and Carmen Mangion. This book's Canadian and female foundation is also due to the pioneering work of its editor, Rosa Bruno-Jofré.

In this conclusion we will not refer to all of the chapters in the book. That said, its four sections illustrate myriad facets of Vatican II's impact: the progressive detachment of Church from state, the dialogue and openness to plurality and interculturalism, the light of the Gospel for social and spiritual action, and new pastoral ways. This transnational study has done more than describe the processes of change at work within the Church; it has reviewed other factors as well, such as the very different social, religious, and cultural changes we call secularization. The latter is explicitly addressed in some chapters; in others it is implicit in the argument.

The effects of different forms of secularization have determined related academic debates and the general state of relations between religion and society, including between Vatican II and education in different countries. In Canada, religious and social pluralism has allowed more neutral scientific approaches that do not entail apology and denunciation; in Spain, the secularization process has been highly controversial and polarized (Montero and de la Cueva 2007). The religious cleavage in countries other than Canada makes it much more difficult to maintain an analytical distance and develop academic debate. For example, in France, where official secularism has diminished the social and academic relevance of religion, research on religion tends to be marginalized.

The socio-political religious cleavages in the European and South American countries analysed in this book, and the focus on gender issues and women in Canada, explain the relative lack of contributions examining the role of laypeople. Carlos Martínez's study of active forms of catechesis, in which laypeople hold a paramount (although insufficiently explored) role, points clearly to the need to include this topic in analysis. However, to accomplish this, it would be necessary to adopt strong multidisciplinary approaches as well as new sources and historiological instruments and approaches.

Vatican II has generated plenty of interpretative difficulties. The Council was an attempt to lay open the Church's values and objectives, to ask for changes, and to publicly demand that Catholic people and institutions rethink their language, institutions, and ways of life. Its purpose, that is, was to clarify, for itself and the world, the Church's identity and mission.

However, a too cursory interpretation of the Vatican II resolutions, the Latin American conciliar reception at Medellín (1968) and Puebla (1979), and the first reflections by the congregations on the sense of their mission can foster a naive reading of conciliar and post-conciliar texts and events. Such interpretations would focus on the fractures between pre-modern, pre-secular, and pre-conciliar education and those of post-conciliar education. They would underline the distances between the following: traditionalists and progressives; teaching that is idealized and teaching that has been liberated by plurality; teaching exclusively for the wealthy, and teaching specifically for the poor; and priests and laypeople. From within these dualities, a space might grow for perspectives of liberation and renovation, or for perspectives of lived nostalgia or failure. But a hermeneutics of rupture and opposition, of loss or gain, would fail to analyse, in an impartial way, Vatican II and its reception in Catholic teaching. To reduce complexity to duality does not account for the contradictions or the metamorphoses of the Church during this first phase of reception.

Furthermore, theological research cannot be satisfied with a unilateral reading.[1] In the Church, an ambivalence towards modernity seems to remain. On one hand, it harbours a kind of "resentment" because of the loss of its privileged social and political position; on the other, it trusts modern projects such as science, tolerance, and human rights. This double-sentiment is visible in the history of the neo-Scholastics and its relation to freedom – in the experience of the subject, in the understanding of conscience, and so on. Chapter 1, "From Objectivity to Subjectivity," echoes these contradictions and changes.

But this is not the only interpretative problem faced by analyses of Vatican II and its impact. As with other major socio-political and constitutional texts and moments, another challenge arises in the temporalization of the phenomenon. Clearly, any vision of the Council will vary with the period being studied. In other words, the perception will change depending on whether the researcher views Vatican II as a departure from the modernist crisis or as contrary to the foundation of Cardijn's Jeunesse Ouvrière Chrétienne (Young Christian Workers) in 1924 – moments, respectively, of radical rejection of the modern world, and of embracing it. Defining the end of the period under study, for example, at the end of the papacies of Giovanni Montini, Karol Wojtyła, or Joseph Ratzinger, or the first year of Jorge Bergoglio (as conventional dates), will also affect our understanding of the Council and its achievements. For instance, most of the chapters in this book stop on the eve of the reaction to it under Wojtyła, and thus the chapters are permeated with a moment of hope and realization. These different assessments do not relate so much to the doctrinal teachings of the Church; an intertextual analysis of Vatican II documents and other conciliar documents, such as the 1987 encyclical *Sollicitudo Rei Socialis* or the 1999 *Post-Synodal Apostolic Exhortation (Ecclesia in America)* (Pope John Paul II 1987, 1999)[2] points to their doctrinal and social continuities, which consistently condemn liberal capitalism and communism. Rather, such evaluations are related to the processes of reception of the documents all over the globe, and to the ethos and practices that mediated or were mediated by those receptions. In particular, they are connected to the nuanced stances relating to the charismata of the popes who have applied the norm: their position towards communist regimes and parties, their attitude towards condemning and suppressing liberation theology, their promotion of different kinds of prelates, and the breadth of their condemnation of liberalism (inequality and exploitation) beyond liberal sexual morals.

These differences highlight the importance of the charismata of the popes (and of the different orders of the Church); they also bring to light the malleability of *all* constitutional texts and the relevance of ethos and practices for the life of the Church. All of this points to large problems in intellectual history: the independence of discourses and praxis, the different rhythms in the transformation of ideas and practices, and the relevance of practices *vis–à-vis* doctrinal principles.

Constitutional texts that are intended to rule such large, culturally, socially, and politically diversified, even contradictory, social organisms as the Church must be sufficiently vague that implementation agreements are possible. Because of the need to deploy a broad range of meanings for different subsystems, such texts require hermeneutic work. This hermeneutic tension is evident in the texts themselves: on the one hand they are legal documents, with a constitutional law on one side, and a message and rhetoric of the texts – a language that O'Malley has called epideictic, the rhetoric of celebrations and of virtue (Curnow 2010) – on the other. Another difficulty lies in the spirit of the Council and the promises that liberation theology encountered in Vatican II, Medellín, and Puebla.

So it is interesting to study these texts for what they tell us about the theology and the history of ideas, but this should be accompanied by an analysis of related practices so as to contribute to the wider social history.

The 1965 *Decree on the Adaptation and Renewal of Religious Life* (*Perfectae Caritatis*) demands that all Church organizations rethink their principles and renew themselves in light of the historical objectives for which they were created. Linked to this, it asks the Church's congregations and institutions to examine their experiences and open themselves up to the world and culture around them. Renewal and a return to the roots thus becomes a means to address contemporaneous problems – a means to communicate with the world.

This book has offered plenty of examples of conciliar principles of renewal that allow for new, more "democratic and participative practices," in which laypeople and the religious have come together and created spaces of common debate and reflection. Communion with the lives of the flock and their problems – which Elizabeth Smyth has examined elsewhere, regarding the Sisters of St Joseph in Guatemala – is one practice that allows the Church to communicate with individuals and cultures around the world, giving them voice, activating them, and transforming the principles of religious people. With regard to the Sisters of St Joseph, this communion changed their conception of mission. They went from occupying a compound of the United Fruit Company to sharing the lot – even to the point of martyrdom – of poor indigenous peasants. This practice, more than any doctrinal incitation, led to their transformation as they took up positions against the injustice, violence, and political repression experienced by the people. Indeed, they were missionalized by those who were supposed to have been missionalized. They changed their own minds; instead of doing charity work, they aroused the socio-political awareness of their flock to enable them to stand up for their own rights.

Another important example of renewal is the abandonment by the Sisters of the Infant Jesus of their elite school in Madrid to missionalize the poor in Bembibre. Like the St Joseph nuns, they were missionalized by their flock, and they created an open community around the school, a *learning community*. Also in Spain, the adoption of the Life Review conscientized and turned many Catholics to the left; this was instrumental in the *Transición* (transition) to democracy, as Martínez Valle discusses in chapter 3. As these examples show, in order to fully understand Vatican II – both its summoning and its effects – it is helpful to research the related practices as well.

The review of the original charismata and objectives requested by the *Decree on the Adaptation and Renewal of Religious Life* and the widespread idea of deinstitutionalization of the faith and its missionalization had a strong impact on educational conceptions and practices. This impact is documented in the questioning of the traditional educational system, in particular in the case of Illich, and in the approach of Catholic intellectuals and artists to the new "mass media" as *the* new educational and missionalization instruments par excellence. Passolini's work acquires in this context an extreme analytical potential, and not only as a religious discourse that, in the spirit of the Council, changes the values of the Church, placing charitas – in particular for the socially marginalized as young poor homosexuals – at the centre. Passolini's work is also relevant as a form of "mass media" popular religious education in the secularizing Italy (Europe) of the time. Furthermore, it is a central object of analysis for understanding the complex relations between the new educational means of the popular pedagogy and the old and new messages.

Some readings of the Council, especially in Latin America, construed it as an irenic or conciliatory attempt to open the Church to the contemporary world after the culture wars of the nineteenth and early twentieth centuries. As after other moments of great inner and outer confrontation – for instance, the wars against Protestantism and such internecine struggles as *De Auxiliis* debates and the fights to suppress mysticism (the process against Molinos, the condemnation of quietism) in the sixteenth and seventeenth centuries – some readings of the Vatican focus on practical piety and charity. This is visible in the transformations of the studied communities of women religious, which now involve themselves not only in charitable works but also in the creation of communities.

But we cannot give all of the credit for such transformations to Vatican II. It is difficult to analyse the practices of religious orders without considering secularization and the lay world and its ideas, such as communism, communitarism, radical democracy, and colonial and gender studies. For example, were the Sisters completely ignorant about the literature that examined the missions as colonization agents? What were their reactions to being housed in the compound of the United Fruit Company in Guatemala? Furthermore, other organizational factors and experiences, such as moving to other communities and countries, also allowed for innovation, as well as closer and less hierarchical, confessional, and proselytizing relationships with the locals.

Vatican II distinguished the doctrinal substance from the means of presenting it. But there are questions, echoing Marshall McLuhan's work, regarding the media and the forms through which the message was transmitted. Did new forms of liturgy or new catechetical methods work to convey new and sometimes secularizing meanings, such as new understandings of hierarchy, and therefore of ecclesiology, or of experience and subjectivity? Indeed, implicit or explicit forms of secularization are an omnipresent issue in this book, and certainly also in the decision to organize Vatican II. However, the concept of secularization gathers such a wealth of meanings and different culturally and spatially determined processes that the term makes for a very unsatisfactory analytical instrument. Indeed, a vast array of literature discusses the meaning of "secularization." This book provides new examples for reconsidering the concept, and – especially in the chapters devoted to Illich and Pasolini – some profound insights into it.

The functional differentiation of the educational system – one of the main characteristics of secularization – opposes traditional Catholic conceptions of education as a casuistic doctrine, and tends to concede a progressive autonomy to the discipline. Teaching requires a large amount of technical "immanent" knowledge that is not directed by any transcendental moral or religious principles whatsoever. Again, the transformation from exogenous to inherent, from objective to subjective, appears as constitutive of the process. The principal document of Vatican II devoted to education, the *Declaration on Catholic Education* (*Gravissimum Educationis*), is remarkable because of its very unspecific, general stance on education. It acknowledges the universal right to education "with the aid of the latest advances in psychology and the arts and science of teaching."[3] However, this could mean that it concedes to psychology and educational science its traditional subsidiary or ancillary helping role in the transmission of educational knowledge – and perhaps not only because of the difficulties of specifying Catholic positions on myriad educational situations. The document refers to a later development of the principles by "a special post-conciliar commission [to be] applied by episcopal conferences."

The Declaration on Catholic Education thus devotes itself to elucidating the Church's role in education. In light of rising pluralism and social secularization, and rather than maintaining the magisterial power of the Church, it prefers to focus on the "sacred right" of all individuals to a religious education, and it reminds parents of the duty to educate their children in the faith in conditions equal to those of other subjects. Nonetheless, the short document expediently states the Church's will to "penetrate and ennoble with her own spirit" all schools; it feels "the weighty responsibility of diligently caring for the moral and religious education of all her children" through "the ministry of priests and laymen who give them the doctrine of salvation [in the school] in a way suited to their age and circumstances and provide spiritual aid in every way the times and conditions allow."

Even more than this Declaration, other documents of Vatican II and the councils of Medellín and Puebla distil some principles for moulding Catholic education, as shown in some of this book's chapters. In light of the myriad cultural and political contexts examined in this book and of the conditions in which transformations have taken place, some qualitative elements of education can be underscored, for example:

Addressing the needs of students and the local community by creating a context of life and an educational climate. This careful response can go as far as the process of *euskaldunization* (becoming Basque-speaking and acquainted with Basque culture), through which the De La Salle Brothers became *euskaldunes* (Basque-speaking), in particular during the 1970s, with obvious political consequences for the historical situation of the Basque Country.[4] The same principle arises in the notion of a "school without doors," where building large educational communities becomes the priority.[5] Local rootedness is an early sign of witness through the Word that has become flesh.

A focus on educating the poorest, the most fragile, the most underprivileged, and placing them at the centre of the school's efforts. The radical option for the poor is present in most of the cases in this book; in particular, it was clearly adopted by the Sisters examined by Rosa Bruno-Jofré and Elizabeth Smyth. However, the practices are varied. We would point out, in particular, the chapter by Cox and Imbarack, "Catholic Elite Education in Chile." This analysis of various congregations (Opus Dei, Legionnaires of Christ, Jesuits, Holy Cross) and of their relationships with culture, politics, and the poor, as requested by Medellín and Puebla, highlights the complexity of the stakes and of decision-making. The preferential option for the poor should not be one alternative among others for the Church, but a leading principle:

> In sticking with the non-equivocal words of the Gospel, in the person of the poor there is a special presence of Christ that imposes on the Church a preferential option for them. By such an option we witness to the way God loves, to his providence, his mercy and in a certain manner we sow once more in history the seeds of the Kingdom of God that Christ himself has sown during his life on earth by going to meet those who turned to him for all their spiritual and material needs. (Pope John Paul II 2001, Article 49)

The capacity to measure oneself when faced with the educational challenges of gratitude, respect, and enhancement of diversity. Psychological, social, cultural, and religious diversities do not have to be denied; indeed, they ought to be welcomed so as not to transform them into inequalities. The two chapters in Part V of this book, "Catholicism and Aboriginal Education in Canada," offer examples of how this diversity can be faced in practice. Lindsay Morcom, in "Balancing the Spirit in Aboriginal Catholic Education in Ontario," describes how putting theoretical and practical tools in place throughout schools allows for greater knowledge of others and self, as well as greater awareness of one's own cultural values and those of others. Open exchanges help us understand differences, but this requires a rereading of Aboriginal history and conflicts. Acculturation, which is not to be confused with syncretism or eclecticism, challenges the link between faith and other cultures. It is therefore related to enriching intercultural dialogue, a principle supported by the Church for its schools (Congregation for Catholic Education 2013, Article 28).

Openness towards the pluralistic contexts of secularization. There can be no simple description of openness between the Church and the world. The passion for the world that the Church declares in the various texts of Vatican II flows out of the scandal of the Cross: the proclamation of the death and resurrection of Jesus Christ. In chapter 9 by Bruno-Jofré on Our Lady of the Missions (RNDM), we learn how, by opening itself to the world's plurality, this congregation found ways to radically live the Gospel's message: "The Sisters opened to the plurality of the world, not as an enemy, not limited by rules and regulations, but in a way that started a cognitive process that led to a new understanding of their mission. Their constitutions broadened the notion of education representing a reality – the movement away from schools – while Sisters discovered the self and cultivated new apostolate recreated through inherent difficulties over many years – a new collective identity."

Another type of dialogue is described by Joe Stafford in chapter 10, "The Conditions of Reception for the *Declaration on Christian Education.*" He writes about how the succession of crises – of faith, authority, transmission, identity – brought about by secularization have placed in a difficult position the great traditional principles of education proposed by the Declaration. While the goal is to maintain its objectives, the principles upheld by the bishops of the diocese of Ontario and their interpretation of that text have complicated dialogue with the state.

Bearing witness to faith in the face of all situations of domination, whether political, ecclesiastic, or cultural, and maintaining attachment to tradition. The new roles and missions of female congregations and their audacity when faced with external powers are clearly demonstrated in chapter 7 by Elizabeth Smyth, "From Serving in the Missions at Home to Serving in Latin

America"; and in chapter 8 by Heidi MacDonald, "Women Religious, Vatican II, Education, and the State in Atlantic Canada."

With regard to these principles, the first question that arises is whether Catholic schools follow them. Here, regional and cultural differences are relevant – in particular, the traditional position of the Church in the educational and political system. Schools in countries where the Church historically has played a key role in education (which often has impeded the creation of the state school system) are more likely to ignore the above-mentioned principles.

Chapter 11, "Catholic Elite Education in Chile" by Cristián Cox and Patricia Imbarack, highlights the differences in charismata, principles, objectives, and educational methods encountered *within* the Church, among various congregations; it also, as suggested by the title, highlights an emphasis on the elites over the poor. In particular, Opus Dei and the Legionnaires of Christ focused on the dictatorship's elites as a missionalization and power-maintaining strategy, rather than on the poor and destitute in marginalized neighbourhoods, who were paid only some pastoral attention. Furthermore, Catholic schools did much to drive the dictatorship's liberalization policies, which questioned universally equal access to education. And Chile is not an isolated case.

Religious schools in Spain have been the driving force behind the creation of segregated systems; the middle classes have abandoned public education, leaving it to the lower classes, including immigrants. In France, Catholic schools have raced to compete with state schools for the best students. But the challenges are even greater than the possible hypocrisy of some religious agents or their rejection of the values discussed above. In challenging the supposedly unstoppable advance of secularism, Catholic schools have gained educational terrain even in secularist France. But the expansion of "Catholic" schools in both countries does necessarily mark an advance in *Catholic* education.

The chapters described above ask, is there actually one thing that can be called *Catholic education* beyond a confessional religious teaching that includes a set of moral prescriptions? Are not these principles better served by good state school system (which in many southern European and Latin American countries were traditionally hindered by the Church)? The same question unfolds in other chapters with regard to whether denominational religious teaching in schools is effective for the community of believers and for society in general, and whether it is democratic and just to support confessional schools and subjects in contexts of increasing plurality and economic differentiation – keeping in mind that the state does not provide similar support for other religions and does not foster, in similar measure, social and school equity.

To answer these questions, we consider three issues, whose weight varies with the specific countries we discuss. First, pedagogically there is no specific Catholic education. The recent adoption by some Jesuit provinces of the project method is a clear indication of the absence of differentiation from the lay world. In a narrow understanding of curriculum, the specifically Catholic content would be taught in a confessional proselytizing class. But as analysed below, such classes in schools are not free from criticism, even within the Church. Another notable aspect of this question relates to the world of values and faith transmitted in the broader curriculum – for instance, in specifically Catholic approaches to intercultural education. Perhaps these could be embraced and implemented by other religions, societal groups, or institutions.

Second, if Catholic education involves the vicarious learning received from believers who daily express their faith or who model virtues related to their beliefs, the problem arises that – as shown by the case of the women's order universities in eastern Canada analysed by MacDonald – the orders and the clergy are not recruiting enough priests, nuns, and monks to cover vacancies. The result is that Catholic schools are becoming label-only institutions with staff similar to those of any other non-confessional school. But secularization does not show itself only in a shortage of vocations and staff.

Third, as Serrano and Hugonnier point out, in many European countries, social secularization has rendered political secularization obsolete: for parents who choose a Catholic school for their children, "the denominational criterion is no longer the priority"; rather, the criteria are "quality," "specific educational projects," "commitment with the students," "seriousness," "attention, supervision, individual follow-up, discipline, sense of effort, tolerance and rigor" – which can be read also as "distinction" and "segregation" (Prost 2014). Serrano and Hugonnier write that parents who choose Catholic schools recognize a tradition ultimately concerned with the person. But how can the resulting quality be explained? By financial stability, by how staff and pupils are recruited, by how well teachers have been trained? Hence, a critical question: Do Catholic schools fulfil their social role? At present, the main reproach aimed at these schools is that they cull their students from the privileged classes, who are the easiest to educate. Thus the education they offer is not accessible to all – most notably, not to disadvantaged students. As Serrano and Hugonnier write, "the origin and the specific nature of Catholic education would need to be made explicit."

The education wars are not over. The myriad processes of secularization mean that Catholic religious education has carved political and educational cleavages in southern Europe and Latin America, as the chapters in this book have shown. In Spain, one of the sharpest cleavages relates to the compulsory offering of school catechesis in all public schools, and the emphasis placed on it, overlooking the historical evidence of its failure. This issue has polarized debates about education, thus paralyzing legislative efforts at reform. Grassroots catechists have questioned the existence of the school catechesis, viewing it as a holdover from the dictatorship (from which the Church benefited) and as an inadequate, even counterproductive, instrument. As early as the 1960s, young people were rejecting the confessional contents of the school catechesis, as the authors of the *Jornadas de Catequesis Educativa* attest. The social secularization of Spanish society provides evidence of this. Many authors argue that a catechesis can create new believers and strengthen the faith of the old ones only if it is offered outside schools, in the community, through social pastoral activities. Spain's Catholic hierarchy might do well to consider deinstitutionalizing Catholic institutes and subscribing to the position of one classic catechist, Joseph Colomb, who defended laicism (Bonato 2013).

With regard to France, where no proselytizing is allowed in schools, Hugonnier and Serrano write in chapter 2 that French Catholic schools faces two main challenges. The first is to overcome the "holy ignorance" within schools when it comes to religions. This can be addressed through classes on religious culture and by fostering intercultural and interreligious dialogue. The second challenge is that "while ancient school inequalities depended on large social and cultural categories as well as on unequal access to secondary education, new school inequalities are due to small initial inequalities that mount up and multiply to create great inequalities at the end of the pathway" (Dubet 2014). As Hugonnier and Serrano note, structural inequality can be countered by a preferential option for the poor. To that end, they tell us, Catholic schools should establish themselves where poor students live, away from the city centres, in poor neighbourhoods. This is one of the main challenges Catholic education now faces.

New Issues for (Catholic) Religious Education

As mentioned earlier, referring to social secularization, the present situation – what we call post-conciliar, post-atheistic, post-modern, or even trans-modern – is not the same as that of the three decades described in this book. It suffices to compare the ways of being Catholic in the 1950s with those in the second decade of the twenty-first century, or simply to compare the ways of teaching. The reception of Vatican II has entered a new phase that deserves to be studied in a critical way. The elements singled out in this book remain actual, but the future is open and brings new questions, not just for Catholic schools but for religious teaching in general. Confession and proselytism belong in parishes, not schools. So we pose two questions that have only been touched on in this book but that should play a major role in the debate going forward: Should schools also offer a cultural history of education? And if yes, how is it to be connected with the sociohistoric comparative approach to religion, which is widespread in religious teaching throughout most of the Western world?

The Teaching of the Cultural History of Religion and the Cultivation of Spirituality

It is clear that in our twenty-first-century society, historic religions are no longer linked with the real-life experiences of people, and religious culture is, for many reasons, no longer part of a general culture.

Should schools play a role in cultivating the (generic) spirituality of young people? And if they should, then how? These questions are fuelling a strong debate. It is true that new forms of religion and spirituality are surging and that some of them are strongly fundamentalist and sectarian. At the same time, Church authors have adopted an old apologetic tradition that maintains that the Church's teachings (or, for our purposes, the general religious cultivation of spirituality and knowledge of the cultural history of religion) help to control superstition, fanaticism, and fundamentalism. However, when we think through the responsibility for providing critical knowledge about *all* religions in our society, we bump against the question of how confessing, celebrating, living, and knowing all relate to one another. The two authors of this conclusion differ with regard to the relationship between faith and the public sphere. For Carlos Martínez Valle, a separation is needed for the sake of democracy and freedom, and the Church should focus on pastoral work outside the classrooms. For Gemma Serrano, it is not desirable to consign beliefs to the private sphere, because such beliefs cannot subsist outside of daily life, which is social, political, public, and so on. Serrano maintains that beliefs are still a deeply human need and are not resolved by conflating them with educational courses on responsible citizenship, or by viewing them through comparative syntheses that omit the differences and richness proper to each religious cultural tradition.[6] What is required is a critical and transnational study of the situation of Catholic teaching from the 1980s to the present day.

The Concern to Educate the Poorest, the Most Fragile, the Most Underprivileged, and Place Them at the Centre of the School's Attention

New forms of poverty have emerged since the end of the 1980s, and they have worsened inequality and injustice and prevented many people from attending school.[7] The questions around this issue are global and transnational. For example, how do religious congregations dedicated to teaching meet this reality today? How has their mission evolved?

Religion and Intercultural Education

The above-mentioned issue is linked to the fact that in the future, intercultural education will have to take diversity into account and teach students to respect different spiritual practices. Intercultural education is based in a

> dynamic conception of culture that avoids the consideration of cultures as closed, and of differences as mere stereotypes or folklore. Intercultural strategies are efficacious if, avoiding separating people in autonomous and hermetic cultural worlds, they foster dialogue and mutual knowledge and transformation for easing conflict solving and coexistence. It aims at constructing a new intercultural attitude oriented towards the integration of cultures in mutual acceptance. (Congregation for Catholic Education 2013, Article 28)

Directions for Future Research

We finish by moving from more philosophical and socio-political general reflection and questions to the historical research agenda. We have already mentioned questions that are still being debated or that remain unattended by the literature – broadly, what is and what should be Catholic education? Apart from this overarching avenue of inquiry, new research should examine local specificities in the reception–adoption process and focus on the role of lay believers by deepening investigations of intersectional issues. This implies the study of grassroots movements and a focus on all kinds of practices, from reading practices and the reception of the conciliar texts to liturgical practices. Correspondingly, this agenda will need to apply ethnographic, iconographic, and new historic as well as comparative approaches. Rosa Bruno-Jofré, for instance, has used in-depth interviews and focus groups in researching the Bembibre nuns. Oral history and ethnographic and iconographic approaches could be used to study the relationship between active practices in the liturgy and those in the classroom. Relations between the Church and the social environment could be studied through iconographic sources.

For instance, comparative studies would help shed light on the different reception processes and results of Vatican II in different countries and cultural contexts. It could be very interesting to consider the Council's reception in countries undergoing different forms of secularization. A comparison within the same order or congregation between those members who changed the place in which they lived, and those who remained in old settings, would help clarify the importance of changing spaces for the renewal process and members' sensitivity to different contexts. For instance, it would be interesting to compare the nuns who moved to Bembibre with those of the same order who remained in their old schools. The study of these practices together with prosopographic studies could help us understand the relations between Vatican renewal proposals and progressive education.

Comparative studies could also shed light on possible gender differences in the processes of renewal of female orders, and especially within branches of the same order. In this sense, intersectional studies could bring attention not only to different questions of power, domination, and resistance, avoiding hagiography, but also to the diversity in the reception and implementation of Vatican II.

The study of practices using iconographic sources could also shed light on possible related transformations in liturgy, catechesis, and didactics. One focus in this regard could involve how democratization and participation (and the consequent dignifying of lay members) affected liturgy and catechesis so that the two influenced each other. Another valuable research strand would examine the relationship between educational levels (primary, secondary, and tertiary) and the application of Vatican II resolutions as they intersect with different orders and religious groups, social strata, and increasingly elitist institutions.

It would also be interesting to analyse, across countries with different secularization patterns, the possible role of Catholic education after

Vatican II in fostering democratic participation. This line of inquiry would advance many different studies. First, it would address the political conflicts around Catholic education and its socio-political and structural fit with different educational systems. What role does Catholic education play in different countries, considering the existence of concordats or not? These questions have been formulated and answered in different ways depending on the secularization context. Second, beyond the study of the relations between two value systems (secular and religious), one could analyse educational practices and cultures – that is, the factual training provided by Catholic schools and universities both in general, and specifically with regard to democratic participation. Such studies could focus on education for peace, justice, environmental issues, human rights, and a wide definition of defence of life. These potential avenues of inquiry will be important to Catholic education as we move further into the twenty-first century. Does education, be it Catholic or non-Catholic, create just and caring citizens? Have Catholic schools opted for isolating themselves from the rest of the world or, on the contrary, have they opened themselves up to the world? All of these questions are dealt with explicitly in the 1965 *Pastoral Constitution on the Church in the Modern World* (*Gaudium et Spes*) (Pope Paul VI 1965) and in other texts of Vatican II aimed at Catholic educational institutions.

There are many issues related to the mutual influence of education and Vatican II, and they will continue to be of interest now that the spirit of the Council seems – fifty years later – to have been reawakened with Pope Francis.

NOTES

1 A sketch of the contrary positions about the novelty of the Second Vatican Council can be found in John O'Malley, "Vatican II: Did Anything Happen?," *Theological Studies* 67 (2006): 3–33.

2 See http://w2.vatican.va/content/john-paul-ii/en/apost_exhortations/documents/hf_jp-ii_exh_22011999_ecclesia-in-america.html.

3 See http://www.vatican.va/archive/hist_councils/ii_vatican_council/documents/vat-ii_decl_19651028_gravissimum-educationis_en.html.

4 See ch. 4 in this volume, by Dávila and Naya: "Turning Need into a Virtue."

5 As described by Rosa Bruno-Jofré in ch. 5 of this volume, "The Sisters of the Infant Jesus in Bembibre": "There was something unique in Bembibre, in line with the congregation's renewal efforts. The mission took shape

along the way: the school, day care, boarding for girls, integration with the parish, pastoral work with those on the margin, building relationships with the people, and perhaps, most importantly, taking the school to the street (*Sacamos la escuela a la calle*), hence making the school a public space for the community."

6 We cite only a few texts that, notwithstanding their diverse methodological but also interpretative options, coincide in the diagnostic: Charles Taylor, *L'Âge séculier*, (Paris: Seuil, 2011); Marcel Gauchet, "Le désenchantement désenchanté," in *Charles Taylor: Religion et sécularisation*, ed. Sylvie Taussig (Paris: CNRS, 2014), 73–83; Olivier Roy, *La sainte ignorance* (Paris: Seuil, 2012); Luigi Berzano, *Una spiritualità senza Dio* (Milan: Mimesis, 2014); and Peter Berger and Thomas Luckmann, "Secularization and Pluralism," *Internationales Jahrbuch für Religionssoziologie* 2 (1966): 73–86.

7 "Today millions of people – children, women and men of all ages – are deprived of freedom and are forced to live in conditions akin to slavery. I think of the many *men and women labourers, including minors, subjugated* in many sectors ... I think also of the living conditions of *many migrants* who, in their dramatic odyssey, experience hunger, are deprived of freedom, robbed of their possessions, or undergo physical or sexual abuse" (emphasis in original). "Message of his Holiness Pope Francis for the Celebration of the World Day of Peace. 1 January 2015. No Longer Slaves but Brothers and Sisters." https://w2.vatican.va/content/francesco/en/messages/peace/documents/papa-francesco_20141208_messaggio-xlviii-giornata-mondiale-pace-2015.html.

REFERENCES

Bonato, Graziella. 2013. *Elogio alla laicità*. Mantua: Cittadella.

Congregation for Catholic Education (for Institutes of Study). 2013. "Educating to Intercultural Dialogue in Catholic Schools: Living in Harmony for a Civilization of Love." http://www.vatican.va/roman_curia/congregations/ccatheduc/documents/rc_con_ccatheduc_doc_20131028_dialogo-interculturale_en.html.

Curnow, Rohan M. 2010. "John O'Malley on Vatican II and Bernard Lonergan's Realms of Meaning." *Irish Theological Quarterly* 75(2): 188–203. http://dx.doi.org/10.1177/0021140009344454.

Dubet, François. 2014. *La préférence pour l'inégalité. Comprendre la crise des solidarités*. Paris: Editions Seuil.

Montero, Feliciano, and Julio de la Cueva. 2007. *La secularización conflictiva*. Madrid: Biblioteca Nueva.

Pope John Paul II. 1987. *Sollicitudo Rei Socialis.* http://w2.vatican.va/content/john-paul-ii/en/encyclicals/documents/hf_jp-ii_enc_30121987_sollicitudo-rei-socialis.html.

– 1999. *Post-Synodal Apostolic Exhortation (Ecclesia in America).* http://w2.vatican.va/content/john-paul-ii/en/apost_exhortations/documents/hf_jp-ii_exh_22011999_ecclesia-in-america.html.

– 2011. *Novo Millennio Ineunte.* http://w2.vatican.va/content/john-paul-ii/en/apost_letters/2001/documents/hf_jp-ii_apl_20010106_novo-millennio-ineunte.html.

Pope Paul VI. 1965. *Pastoral Constitution on the Church in the Modern World (Gaudium et Spes).* http://www.vatican.va/archive/hist_councils/ii_vatican_council/documents/vat-ii_const_19651207_gaudium-et-spes. retriev

Prost, Antoine. 2014. “L’enseignement privé prisonnier de son héritage.” *Revue Projet* 2(333): 33–41.

Contributors

Michael Attridge is Associate Professor in the Faculty of Theology, University of St Michael's College, Toronto. He teaches courses in ecclesiology, Christology, the Second Vatican Council, and nineteenth- and twentieth-century theologians and movements that shaped modern Catholicism. His areas of research are the reception and interpretation of Vatican II, especially as it relates to the Canadian ecclesial context and contemporary society. Among his scholarly articles, book chapters, and other contributions is a co-edited volume titled *Vatican II: Experiences Canadiénnes / Canadian Experiences* (University of Ottawa Press, 2011). In 2012 he founded the Institute for Research on the Second Vatican Council in Canada at the University of St Michael's College.

Christopher Beeman, through his research, attends the more-than-human, enacts a progressively more Autochthonous life, learns from elders, and mentors students. He explores film, print, and paint to express findings. He is Assistant Professor teaching in the area of Indigenous Studies in both undergraduate and graduate programs at Brandon University's Faculty of Education.

Rosa Bruno-Jofré is Professor at and former Dean (2000–10) of the Faculty of Education, cross-appointed to the Department of History, Faculty of Art and Sciences, at Queen's University, Canada. Her areas of expertise are history of women religious, history of education, and educational theory from a historical perspective. Her current research is funded by the Social Sciences and Humanities Research Council of Canada. Over the past few years, she has worked with Jon Igelmo Zaldívar to analyse the life and work of Ivan Illich. Her recent authored and co-authored articles have appeared in *Educational Theory, Hispania Sacra, Paedagogica Historica, Journal of Ecclesiastical History* (Cambridge), *American Catholic Review, Historical Studies* (Canadian Catholic Historical Association), *Bordón, Bildungsgeschichte,* and *International Journal for the Historiography of Education,* among others. She has authored and edited books, independently and with colleagues, published by McGill-Queen's University Press, University of Toronto Press, Routledge, and Wilfrid Laurier University Press.

Cristián Cox (sociologist, PhD University of London) is head of the Centre of Comparative Policies in Education (CPCE) and Professor at the Faculty of Education, Universidad Diego Portales, in Santiago de Chile. Previously he was dean of the Faculty of Education at the Catholic University of Chile and head of the Curriculum and Evaluation Unit of Chile's Ministry of Education (1998–2006), where he led the design and implementation of the curriculum reform of his country's school system in the late 1990s. Since 2010, he has led the technical secretariat of UNESCO-OREALC's Teachers Regional Strategy for Latin America and the Caribbean. He has worked as a consultant on educational policies for OECD, The World Bank, and the Inter-American Development Bank and is currently a member of IEA's Project Advisory Committee for its International Civic and Citizenship Study (ICCS-2016). He has been Visiting Professor at Stanford and Leiden universities and has published extensively on educational policies, curriculum, teacher education, and citizenship education.

Paulí Dávila is Professor of History of Education at the Universidad del País Vasco / Euskal Herriko Unibertsitatea. His research work has centred on the History of Education in the Basque Country, with special emphasis on topics such as educational policy, literacy, teacher training, national curriculum, textbooks, vocational training, school attendance, abandoned children, and religious orders. He is the main researcher of the Group for Historical and Comparative Studies in Education, recognized by the Basque government, as well as a member of the Unity of Education and Research group, "Education, Culture and Society."

Bernard Hugonnier is currently Professor of Education at the Catholic University of Paris, Research Director at the Collège des Bernardins, and an international consultant in education and in economics. From 2002 until 2012, he was Deputy Director for education at the Organisation for Economic Development and Cooperation (OECD) where he previously held positions as head of the Territorial Development Service, Deputy Director for Public Affairs and Communication, Director of the Publications Service, and Senior Analyst for liberalization of capital movements and multinational enterprises. He received a PhD in Economics from the University Paris IX and a MA in Economics from the University of Pittsburgh.

Jon Igelmo Zaldívar is a postdoctoral fellow at the University of Deusto, with a Juan de la Cierva scholarship from the Spanish Ministry of Economy and Competitiveness. He defended his PhD thesis in 2011 at the Universidad Complutense de Madrid (Spain). He is a member of the eDucaR research team (Universidad de Deusto) and an external member of the research group Cultura Cívica y Politicas Educativas (Universidad Complutense de Madrid). Since 2013, he has been the assistant to the coordinators of the Theory and History of Education International Research Group based at Queen's University, Canada. His recent authored and co-authored articles have appeared in *Educational Theory*, *Bordón*, *Hispania Sacra*, *Journal of Ecclesiastical History*, and *Educación XX1*. He has been invited to write two texts for the *Encyclopedia of Educational Theory and Philosophy* (Sage, 2014) and the *Encyclopedia of Educational Philosophy and Theory* (Springer, 2016). He has also authored a book edited by Enclave de Libros (2016). In the past few years, he has worked with Rosa Bruno-Jofré to research the life and work of Ivan Illich.

Patricia Imbarack completed a PhD in Education and is Associate Professor at the Faculties of Education and Theology at Pontifical Catholic University of Chile, where she also obtained a degree in clinical psychology. Between 2011 and 2014 she was a researcher at the Centre for Studies of the Ministry of Education of Chile. Her present research is on teachers' professional development, youth, and Catholic education. Since 2016 she has been head of the Interdisciplinary Centre for the Study of Religion (CIERUC) at her university.

Heidi MacDonald is a historian of twentieth-century Canada with specializations in Atlantic Canada, the Great Depression, women religious, and youth. Her recent publications include articles in *Historia de la Educación* and *Canadian Journal of Sociology*, and chapters in *The Difference Kids Make*, edited by Gleason and Myers (Oxford, 2017); *Writing Feminist History: Productive Pasts and New Directions*, edited by Janovicek and Carstairs (UBC Press, 2013); and *Vatican II: Experiences Canadiénnes / Canadian Experiences*, edited by Attridge and colleagues (University of Ottawa Press,

2011). Her current SSHRC-funded project is on women religious in Atlantic Canada since 1960.

Carlos Martínez Valle, Professor at the Faculty of Education, Universidad Complutense, Madrid, holds a PhD in Political Science and Sociology. His doctoral thesis focused on the relations between religious and political conceptions of freedom in sixteenth- and seventeenth-century Europe and was published as *Anatomía de la Libertad* (Editorial Universidad Complutense, 2008). He worked as a research fellow and Assistant Professor at the Center for Comparative Education, Humboldt University, Berlin, and as a postdoctoral fellow at the Faculty of Education of Queen's University, Canada. His work combines the history of ideas, comparative education, and history of education. His research on the relation of religion, education, and politics has been published as "Jesuit Psychagogies" (*Paedagogica Historica*, 2013), "Conciencia libre y ley natural en el Calvinismo y Molinismo" (*Res Publica*, 2008), and "Early Modern Probabilism as a Secularizing Doctrine" (*Religion and Its Other*, 2008).

Lindsay Morcom (Algonquin Métis, Bear Clan) is an interdisciplinary researcher with experience in education, Aboriginal languages, language revitalization, and linguistics. She earned her Master's degree in Linguistics at First Nations University through the University of Regina in 2006. She then completed her doctorate in General Linguistics and Comparative Philology as a Rhodes Scholar at Oxford University in 2010. She is currently Assistant Professor and coordinator of the Aboriginal Teacher Education Program at Queen's University, Canada.

Luis M. Naya teaches in the area of Comparative Education at the Universidad del País Vasco / Euskal Herriko Unibertsitatea. His main lines of research have revolved around the use of information and communication technologies, minority languages in education systems, religious orders and education, and children's rights. He is a member of the Group for Historical and Comparative Studies in Education, as well as main researcher of the Unity of Education and Research group, "Education, Culture and Society."

William F. Pinar teaches at the University of British Columbia, where he holds a Canada Research Chair in Curriculum Studies. He is the author, most recently, of *Educational Experience as Lived: Knowledge, History, Alterity* (Routledge, 2015).

Gemma Serrano is Professor of Theology at the Faculty Notre-Dame de Paris. She is co-Director of Research (Department of Human Societies and Educational Responsibility) at Collège des Bernardins. In this department, since 2012, she has directed seminars including "Developing Souls and Bodies," "School and Republic," and "Journalism and Common Good in the Time of Algorithms." Her areas of research include fundamental theology and phenomenological theology.

Joe Stafford is a retired history teacher from the Algonquin and Lakeshore Catholic District School Board in Ontario, Canada. He has twenty-nine years of classroom experience and was a department head for seventeen years. In 2008, he received the Governor General's Award for Excellence in Teaching Canadian History. He is currently a History of Education PhD candidate at Queen's University, Canada.

Elizabeth M. Smyth is Vice-Dean (Programs) at the School of Graduate Studies, University of Toronto, and Professor of Curriculum Teaching and Learning at the Ontario Institute for Studies in Education. She is a member of the University of Toronto Governing Council and a Senior Fellow of Massey College and the University of St Michael's College. In 2010 she received the George Edward Clerk Award for outstanding contribution to Canadian religious history. Her most recent edited collections are with Deirdre Raftery, *Education, Identity and Women Religious: Convents, Classrooms, and Colleges* (Routledge, 2015), and with Tanya Fitzgerald, *Women Educators, Leaders, and Activists* (Palgrave Macmillan, 2014).

Index

www.ingramcontent.com/pod-product-compliance
Lightning Source LLC
LaVergne TN
LVHW090148080826
844660LV00013B/722/J

* 9 7 8 1 4 8 7 5 0 2 0 6 5 *